WORLD WAR III

NUCLEAR WAR

BY

GARY L. WILSON

PUBLISH
AMERICA

PublishAmerica
Baltimore

© 2005 by Gary L. Wilson.

First printing

ISBN: 1-4137-3434-0
PUBLISHED BY PUBLISHAMERICA, LLLP
www.publishamerica.com
Baltimore

Printed in the United States of America

TABLE OF CONTENTS

WORLD WAR III

NUCLEAR WAR

BY
GARY L. WILSON

CHAPTER I

Revelation

The book of Revelation was dedicated to Jesus Christ by St. John in Revelation 1:5,6. It is the revelation of Jesus Christ himself, and this is written in Revelation 1:1. It is a book of prophecy, and there can be no other classification for this book, except that it is the conclusion of the mystery of God, and that it is prophecy. This is written in:

Revelation 1:3	Revelation 10:7	Revelation 19:10
Revelation 22:6	Revelation 22:7	Revelation 22:9
Revelation 22:10	Revelation 22:18	Revelation 22:19

The angel in Revelation 1:1 was sent from God to St. John. The phrase, "signified it by his angel," means that it was shown by signs or by symbolic means. The book of Revelation is written in symbolic language. To understand it, you must translate the symbols into your own native language. I will point out here that the majority of people who read the book of Revelation get confused or frustrated because of the symbolism. I know this because the same thing happened to me when I was younger. I will use an example to explain the procedure, which I use now. When you find a prophecy such as Revelation 13, you must:

1. Read the prophecy
2. Write down the symbols
3. Translate the symbols into your language
4. Substitute the translated symbols into the prophecy
5. Read the new prophecy

This is not an easy task in the case of Revelation 13 because there are 22 symbols used in it. However, you will not be so confused because you will translate the symbols before you try to decipher the prophecy. This is the key to understanding the book of Revelation, and this is written in Revelation 1:20.

The seven stars are the angels of the seven churches. The seven candlesticks are the seven churches. Therefore Revelation 1:20 shows us how to solve the mysteries of the book of Revelation by translating the symbols into English. I will proceed to write about the parts of this book which I understand.

Revelation 1:10: "I was in the Spirit on the Lord's Day, and heard behind me a great voice, as of a trumpet."

The voice that St. John heard was from Christ. This is written in Revelation 1:10,11 and in Revelation 4:1. Therefore Christ is the trumpet of God in I Thessalonians 4:16, which describes the rapture of the church.

In Revelation 1:11-16 Christ stands in his glory, and is wearing the armor of God described in Ephesians 6:11-18. The elements of this are:

1. Loins covered with the truth
2. Breastplate of righteousness
3. Feet shod with the preparation of the gospel
4. Shield of faith
5. Helmet of salvation
6. Sword of the Spirit
7. Praying always, and watching

In chapters 2 and 3 are the messages from Christ to the seven churches. There is some prophecy in these chapters because here Christ tells the churches how he wants them to be. The AIDS prophecy is in Revelation 2:20-23.

The prophecy of Revelation 3:17-19 is a warning to the church about the works of faith. The church, which says it doesn't need the works of Christ, is severely reprimanded by him. The gold tried in the fire in Revelation 3:18 is actually the Little Book from Revelation 10:2. I can clarify this somewhat here:

The demons have been causing the death by suicide of people in the church and the people in the world for 1900 years, and no one knew it. Christ said the church was wretched, and miserable, and poor, and blind: because it didn't even see its own people being killed.

In Revelation 4:1 John saw a door opened in heaven, and Christ said: "Come up hither, and I will shew thee things which must be hereafter."

The following chapters have scenes, which took place in heaven because of the open door in Revelation 4:1. Some of these chapters are prophecy, and some are accounts of things, which happened in heaven, or on earth.

Chapter 4 describes the throne of God, and the angels and elders who worship him in heaven. In Chapter 5 is the book sealed with seven seals, and the Lamb who was found worthy to open it. In Chapter 12 is the account of Mary and Joseph, who traveled to Bethlehem, where Christ was born. After his birth, they went to Egypt to avoid the soldiers who were sent by King Herod. This chapter is written in symbolic language, and I've written my interpretation of it, which is later in this same chapter.

All of the remaining chapters are prophecy. This includes Chapters 6-11, and Chapters 13-22. This means that there are 19 chapters of prophecy when you include Chapters 1-3. There are 19 chapters of prophecy in the book of Revelation.

In Chapter 6 are the events of the seals, the first four, which include the Four Horsemen of the Apocalypse. These horsemen are riding:

Revelation 6:2: The white horse   Revelation 6:4: The red horse
Revelation 6:5: The black horse   Revelation 6:8: The pale horse

The man riding the white horse in Revelation 6:2 is the Antichrist who will conquer or take control of Europe and Germany. This will occur peacefully at first because he had a bow, and a crown was given to him. The Four Horsemen of the Apocalypse are the same man. He is the Antichrist. The four horses are used to show a progression of his power, while showing a progression of the coming World War III.

This prophecy is a window into the future, or a time machine in four steps. In Revelation 6:2 the Antichrist will take control of Europe in a peaceful manner because the crown was given to him. In Revelation 6:4 he is riding a red horse. He has a great sword, and power was given to him to take peace from the earth. In Revelation 6:5,6 he is riding a black horse. He has a pair of balances in his hand and a voice said, "A measure of wheat for a penny, and three measures of barley for a penny."

This phrase along with the symbol of the balances is used to predict a man-made famine. This is also verified by Revelation 13:17. In Revelation 6:8 the man is riding a pale horse. His name that sat on him was Death, and Hell followed with him. And power was given to them (the army of the Antichrist), over the fourth part of the earth. This means that the Antichrist will rule over one fourth of the land area of the earth. His army will have power to kill with sword, and with hunger, and with death, and with the beasts of the earth.

Revelation 6:8 also verifies the famine predicted in Revelation 6:5,6, and it states that the famine will be man-made. The reason for the famine is written in Revelation 13:17, to cause more people to accept the swastika. All four of the horsemen were included in the first four seals in Revelation 6:1-8.

The fifth seal gives us a picture of the saints, which stand under the altar before God in heaven, and is written in Revelation 6:9-11. The sixth seal from Revelation 6:12 gives us a picture of the day of the wrath of the Lamb. The men on the earth hid themselves in the dens and in the rocks of the mountains.

Revelation 7:1-17 is not included in the seven seals. It is written between the sixth seal in Revelation 6:12, and the seventh seal in Revelation 8:1. The entire chapter of Revelation 7 is devoted to the sealing of the servants of God in their foreheads. This is important later because the Antichrist will cause all of the people in Europe to receive a mark in their right hand or in their forehead. The servants of God must have a seal on their foreheads to set them apart from the army of the Antichrist.

In Revelation 14:14-16 Christ harvested the people from the earth who were faithful to him. In Revelation 14:17-20 the angel with the sickle harvested the non-Christians, and cast them into the great winepress of the wrath of God. The process of harvesting the earth will be made simpler because the servants of God will be sealed on their foreheads. This is the reason for Chapter 7.

In Revelation 8:1 the seventh seal was opened, and there was silence in heaven for half an hour. This brings our attention to this fact: These events are still happening in heaven. St. John went through the door into heaven in Revelation 4:1. Also, the seven trumpets are included in the seventh seal because they occur precisely when the seventh seal is opened, in Revelation 8:1.

In Revelation 8:7 the first angel sounded his trumpet. There was hail and fire mingled with blood. A third part of the trees were burnt up. The references to the third part of the trees, a third part of the sea, and everything else that happens in third parts in these verses means that the wrath of God is coming for the third part of the angels that followed Satan. This is written in Revelation 12:9, and in Revelation 12:4.

Revelation 12:9: "And the great dragon was cast out, that old serpent, called the Devil, and Satan, which deceiveth the whole world: he was cast out into the earth, and his angels were cast out with him."

The wrath of God is coming upon Satan too. The events in the seven trumpets are a warning to the people on the earth about the judgment, and the wrath of God.

In Revelation 8:8 the second angel sounded his trumpet. A great mountain burning with fire was cast into the sea. The third part of the sea became blood. This is a volcano exploding.

In Revelation 8:10 the third angel sounded his trumpet. A star falls from heaven. It fell upon the third part of the water on earth, and men died. This is a nuclear missile, and the fallout kills people.

In Revelation 8:12 the fourth angel sounded his trumpet. The third part of the sun was smitten. This is nuclear winter.

In Revelation 9:1 the fifth angel sounded his trumpet, and hell was opened. Locusts like scorpions came out of it. In Revelation 9:4 the scorpions were commanded to hurt only the men who did not have the seal of God in their foreheads. This is another reason why the servants of God were sealed in their foreheads in Revelation 7.

In Revelation 9:13 the sixth angel sounded his trumpet. A voice came from the altar, which is before God, telling the sixth angel to loose the four angels, which are bound in the great river Euphrates. These angels are the Cherubims which have the flaming swords, and which protect the Garden of Eden in Genesis 3:24.

These angels will cause the soldiers to kill each other with their own tanks and weapons. This is written in Revelation 9:15-20. Therefore 66.6 million soldiers in the army of the Antichrist will be killed by their fellow soldiers. This is verified in Ezekiel 38:21.

The seventh angel sounds his trumpet in Revelation 11:15. The phrase, "The kingdoms of this world are become the kingdoms of our Lord, and of his Christ; and he shall reign forever and ever," indicates the rapture of the church.

These events are written after the Little Book in Revelation 10:2, and after the two prophets appear in Jerusalem in Revelation 11:3-9. If you put the events in chronological order, they would look like this:

1.	The Little Book	Revelation 10:1-11
2.	The Berlin Wall	Revelation 13:3
3.	The Antichrist in Germany	Revelation 13:11
4.	The famine in Europe	Revelation 13:16,17
5.	The Antichrist in Israel	Revelation 11:2
6.	The two prophets fight	Revelation 11:3-9
7.	The first Armageddon	Revelation 19:19-21
8.	Satan bound 1000 years	Revelation 20:1-3
9.	The first resurrection	Revelation 20:4-6
10.	The Rapture of the church	I Thessalonians 4:16-18
11.	The Millennium and Mount Zion	Revelation 20:4-6

In 1990 the Little Book was written, the Berlin Wall was taken down, and the Jews left Russia and returned to Israel. This fulfills the parable in Matthew 24:32,33. The fig tree in the parable represents Israel. The Berlin Wall and the dividing line in Germany is the wound in Revelation 13:3.

Here is my interpretation of Revelation 12. The woman clothed with the sun is the Virgin Mary. The sun is the symbol for judgment. The moon is under her feet, and upon her head is a crown of 12 stars. These represent the 12 Apostles, who will be 12 angels judging the twelve tribes of Israel in heaven. This is written in Revelation 21:12. In Revelation 1:20 the symbol for the angel is the star, and this is why there is a crown of twelve stars on Mary's head. These symbols are used because the entire universe is subject to the Virgin Mary. Her son is the Word of God, who became man by means of the Immaculate Conception. He is Christ, the Saviour of the world.

When Mary was with child, travailing in birth, the dragon sought her to kill her son. The dragon is Satan. This is written in Revelation 20:2. The dragon's tail drew a third part of the stars because one third of the angels followed Satan when he was cast out of heaven. This is written in Revelation 12:9. In Revelation 12:3, the seven heads represent the seven mountains of Rome. This is written in Revelation 17:9, and in Revelation 17:18. The ten horns represent the ten Common Market Nations, and their leaders. These symbols will come into play later.

The dragon stood before the woman, and was ready to kill or devour her son as soon as he was born. In verse 5, her son was caught up to God, which means that Christ ascended up to heaven after his resurrection. In verse 6, the woman fled into the wilderness, and lived there 1260 days. This is the same number of days in verse 14, which is three and one half years. Therefore these verses tell us that the phrase, a time, times, and half a time actually means: a year, two years, and one half a year. When you add this together, you get three and one half years, which is the same length of time as 1260 days in verse 6.

The wings of the eagle given to the woman have two possible interpretations. It could represent the taxation, which Joseph and Mary went to pay in Bethlehem. It could also represent the angel that warned them in a dream to flee into Egypt. They did go to Egypt, and stayed there until they received notice that King Herod was dead.

In verse 15 the dragon cast out of his mouth water as a flood that he might cause the woman to be carried away by the flood. This is symbolic language that represents the journey of the wise men that King Herod sent to find Christ in Bethlehem. They were supposed to advise him of the location of the birthplace of Christ. Herod also told them to return to Jerusalem with this information.

In verse 16 the earth helped the woman, and swallowed up the flood, which the dragon cast out of his mouth. This is symbolic language, which represents the warning that God gave to the wise men in the dream to depart another way, and not to return to Herod in Jerusalem. This is written in Matthew 2:7-15. Therefore the wise men were like a flood, which came from Satan and Herod in Jerusalem, and were swallowed up by the earth when they went to their own country another way.

In Revelation 12:12,13 the dragon persecuted the woman, which had the man child because Christ was born to Mary to be crucified, to rise from the dead, and to ascend into heaven. Christ did all of these things for us in order to establish the judgment, which will cause Satan to be cast into the Lake of Fire. This is written in Revelation 20:10. This is why the dragon went to make war with the seed of the woman, which keep the commandments of God, and the testimony of Jesus Christ. This is written in Revelation 12:17.

I've already written my interpretation of Revelation 13, and it is included on the next pages. I left out a few symbols, which are written in Revelation 13:2. The beast is the nation of Germany, and it was like unto a leopard. I think this means that it uses camouflage very well to deceive the people, as a leopard would do to its prey. Its feet were as the feet of a bear, which is the symbol for Russia. This means it will be a very big and a very strong nation, or group of nations. The beast also had the mouth of a lion, which means that it will devour much people, as a lion would devour its prey. This means that its army will conquer all of Europe.

The dragon gave him his power, and his seat, and great authority, in Revelation 13:2. This means that Satan gave power to the nation of Germany, and to the Antichrist who will sit as sovereign ruler over Germany and Europe. The seat in verse 2 means the position of the Antichrist as ruler. The great authority means that he will rule all of Europe.

REVELATION 13

The events in Germany in 1990 are being hailed by people everywhere. There is one problem with that outlook: The separation of Germany into two parts was done by Russia and the USA after World War II for this reason: Germany would no longer have the power to cause war in Europe, as long as it was divided into two separate nations. It seems like the world has forgotten this, perhaps because it looks like a great victory for democracy now that Germany is reunited. In a few years we will see that it isn't.

There are several unknown symbols in Revelation 13. I will define them here, in order to decipher the code, and translate the prophecy

1. Revelation 13:1: The beast: The nation of Germany
2. Revelation 13:1: The seven heads: The seven mountains of Rome
3. Revelation 13:1: The ten horns: The ten kings of Europe
4. Revelation 13:1: The Ten crowns: The ten nations in the Common Market
5. Revelation 13:2: The dragon: Satan
6. Revelation 13:3: The wound: The Berlin Wall, and the dividing line
7. Revelation 13:3: The wound was healed: The Berlin Wall was taken down
8. Revelation 13:11: The lamb with two horns: The Antichrist
9. Revelation 13:13: The fire of the Antichrist: Damnation of his people
10. Revelation 13:16: The mark of the beast: The swastika
11. Revelation 13:4: The sword: A symbol of war
12. Revelation 13:18: The 666: The number 666 means World War III

In Revelation 13:1 the beast is a nation because it rose up out of the sea. In Genesis 1:9 the land appeared out of the sea, which is the same principle. In Revelation 13:3 the beast was wounded. In Revelation 13:14 the wound was caused by a sword. The sword is a symbol of war, and therefore World War II caused the wound. When you look at East and West Germany on a pre-1989 map, you see a dividing line drawn through the middle of the nation. That dividing line is the wound in Revelation 13:3. It was caused by World War II because the USA and Russia divided Germany into two parts in 1945, at the end of the war. After September 1990 there is no longer a dividing line. Now the wound is healed, and Germany is reunited; now the Berlin Wall has been taken down.

Revelation 13:3: "and his deadly wound was healed: and all the world wondered after the beast."

Now go back to the first paragraph of this prophecy: The events in Germany are being hailed by people everywhere. This is what the phrase means, "and all the world wondered after the beast."

The people who worshipped Hitler in World War II committed a sin. In World War III it will happen again, and the sin will be an insult to the Lord God. The people who worship the Antichrist will be without excuse. This is written in Romans 1:20. The Lord God will send strong delusion to the people in Germany because of it. This is written in II Thessalonians 2:11. The Lord God will give the Antichrist the power to bring down fire from heaven, and the people will think the Antichrist is a god.

Revelation 13:13: "And he doeth great wonders, so that he maketh fire come down from heaven on the earth in the sight of men."

The people will lust after power and money in World War III, and they will even follow the Antichrist to get it. When they believe he is a god, they will accept the mark of the beast, and they will fulfill this prophecy from II Thessalonians 2:12.

II Thessalonians 2:12: "That they all might be damned who believed not the truth, but had pleasure in unrighteousness."

The Lord God will execute wrath upon the people in Germany, and when they accept the mark of the beast, they will be condemned at the judgment. This is written in Romans 1:18.

The most difficult part of this prophecy is in Revelation 13:18. When you know that the beast is Germany, then you know there will be a war coming. The number 666 is the number of the beast, and the number of a man. The number 6 in Bible terminology means death. The number 666 means death three times. The way the nations cause death is by war. Then you substitute war, and you get war, war, war. Then war three times equates to mean World War III. Therefore the number 666 means the number of a man who will cause World War III. This will be the Antichrist.

The phrase, "mark of the beast," means the track, which the beast left on the ground, indicating the direction in which it has traveled before. Germany caused World War I and World War II, and it will cause World War III. The mark of the beast is the swastika, and this is the track left behind in each of the world wars. The swastika will also be used to mark all of the people who belong to the Antichrist in World War III.

Revelation 13:17: "And that no man might buy or sell, save he that had the mark, or the name of the beast, or the number of his name."

The mark of the beast will be like a cattle brand, which will be used to mark the people in Europe during World War III. They will have to receive the mark of the beast to buy or sell food and the necessities of life. This is explained in another verse, which is Revelation 6:8.

Revelation 6:8: "And I looked, and behold a pale horse: and his name that sat on him was Death, and Hell followed with him. And power was given unto them over the fourth part of the earth, to kill with sword, and with hunger, and with death."

To kill with hunger means to kill with a famine. There will be a man-made famine in Germany and in Europe during the war. It could last four years, and the people will either accept the mark of the beast, or they will starve to death.

The son of perdition, or the Antichrist, will appear in Germany. He will be popular, but his intent will be to cause World War III. He will cause the people to worship Germany, written in Revelation 13:4. He will also cause the people to worship Satan, written in Revelation 13:4. The people in Europe will be forced to receive the mark of the beast in their right hand, or in their forehead. It will be the swastika, and anyone who receives it will belong to the Antichrist and to Satan.

Revelation 14:11: "And the smoke of their torment ascendeth up forever and ever: and they have no rest day nor night, who worship the beast and his image, and whosoever receiveth the mark of his name."

This means that the people who receive the mark of the beast will be cast into the Lake of Fire with the Antichrist, and they will burn forever. The Lake of Fire is the sun, and Satan will also go there after the 1,000 years. This is written in Revelation 20:2, and in Revelation 20:10.

This was the third translation of the Revelation 13 prophecy, and I rewrote it again in July 1993. I've found that there are really 22 symbols in the 18 verses of this prophecy. In the next translation I found that the Antichrist will use six or seven of the propaganda methods used by Hitler in World War II. It is really Satan who plans each world war, and you can see the improvements in his strategy each time. There is an increase of land area in each world war, as well as a better way for Satan to get human souls.

During World War II Hitler persecuted the Jews. This was not merely an accident. Satan gave Hitler the power to rule Europe by planning the war and by convincing political leaders to follow him; and Hitler gave Satan the six million Jews, which he killed during the war. This will also happen in World War III, but this time Satan has improved his methods. The mark of the beast is a method used by the Antichrist to get souls for Satan.

It will be a swastika, which is used like a cattle brand to mark the people who belong to the Antichrist and to Satan.

Therefore Satan will give the Antichrist the power to put millions of men into his armies by using the mark of the beast; and the Antichrist will give Satan millions of human souls by using the same method. The man-made famine will be imposed upon the entire continent of Europe, and the people will be forced to accept the mark of the beast, or they will starve to death. This time the concentration camp will cover all of Europe, and I recommend the people move.

In Revelation 14, the Lamb is Christ, and the 144,000 with the seal of God written in their foreheads are the same as those in Revelation 7. These are the 12,000 saints from each of the 12 tribes of Israel. The reference to Mt. Zion in Revelation 14:1 means the holy city of new Jerusalem in Revelation 21. It will be in Israel where the city of Jerusalem is located now. It is called Mt. Zion in Hebrews 12:22. It will be there for 1000 years. This is written in Revelation 20:4-6, and in Revelation 21:9-14.

The 144,000 saints will sing a new song in heaven. They will also follow Christ wheresoever he goes. They are the first fruits to God and to the Lamb. In there mouth is found no guile, and they are without fault before the throne of God. This is written in Revelation 14:1-5.

In Revelation 14:6 the angel flies in the midst of heaven, having the everlasting gospel to preach to the people on earth. This is one of the major signs of the end of the world, which is also written in Matthew 24:14, and is verified by Revelation 14:7.

In Revelation 14:9-12 is a description of the punishment, which is given to those people who receive the mark of the beast. They will drink of the wine of the wrath of God, and will be tormented with fire and brimstone in the presence of the holy angels, and in the presence of the Lamb. Revelation 14:11 describes their torment in the Lake of Fire, which is the sun. This is why their smoke ascends up forever and ever.

In Revelation 14:13-16 is the harvest of the souls by Christ at the end of the world. In Revelation 14:17-20 is the harvest of the wicked people at the end of the world. This is written in the explanation of the parable of the tares in Matthew 13:37-43, and in Matthew 25:34-46.

In Revelation 15:1 is a description of the seven angels, which have the seven vials full of the seven last plagues for the earth. The plagues of the seven vials are all directed at the kingdom of the Antichrist, and they are all meant to make them repent. The reason is written in Revelation 16:6. They killed saints and prophets during World War III.

The entire chapter of Revelation 15 shows a picture of the people who had gotten the victory over the beast, which is Germany. They all stand on the sea of glass in heaven, having the harps of God.

The plagues of the seven vials are all beneficial to mankind because they are all directed at the kingdom of the Antichrist. The seven angels were given the seven vials, and the temple in heaven was filled with smoke from the glory of God. No man could enter into the temple until the plagues were fulfilled.

In Revelation 16:2 the first angel poured out his vial on the earth. The people in Germany and in Europe are tortured with pain and with sores because they worship the Antichrist.

In Revelation 16:3 the second angel poured out his vial upon the sea, and it became blood.

In Revelation 16:4 the third angel poured out his vial upon the rivers and fountains of waters, and they became blood.

In Revelation 16:5-7 is an explanation of the judgment of God in the first three vials. The wrath of God comes upon those men who have killed the saints and the prophets. This is verified in Revelation 13:7, where they will make war with the saints, and overcome them. They have shed the blood of saints and prophets, and they were given blood to drink.

In Revelation 16:8 the fourth angel poured out his vial upon the sun, and power was given to him to scorch men with fire. The men spoke blasphemy because of the fire, and repented not to give glory to God. This verse tells us the reason for the plagues: repentance.

In Revelation 16:10 the fifth angel poured out his vial upon the seat of the beast, and they were filled with pain.

In Revelation 16:12 the sixth angel poured out his vial upon the river Euphrates. The water in the river was dried up to prepare the way for the tanks of the army of the Antichrist to cross. Then the army will go south to take the world oil supply, and to invade Israel.

In Revelation 16:17 the seventh angel poured out his vial into the air. There came a great voice out of the temple of heaven saying, "It is done." There was an earthquake and a great hailstorm.

The events in the seven seals, seven trumpets, and seven vials all happen concurrently, and they all happen before the rapture of the church. The reason is that the sixth seal and the seventh trumpet announce the rapture and the judgment. The first six vials are plagues against the kingdom of the Antichrist. Therefore all 21 plagues happen before the return of Christ. These plagues are meant to cause people to repent, and this is written in Revelation 9:21, Revelation 16:11, and in Revelation 16:21.

In Revelation 16:18,19 the earthquake divided the city into three parts. The city is Babylon, which is today called Rome. This is written in Revelation 17:9, and Revelation 17:18.

There is a description of the great whore in Revelation 17, and an explanation of her sins. In verse 2 the kings of the earth committed fornication with her. The woman sits upon a beast, which has seven heads and ten horns. The beast is Germany and Europe, which will be under the control of the Antichrist. The woman is the city of Rome, which will ride upon the beast. The kingdom of the Antichrist will be subject to Rome. In

Revelation 17:16,17 the ten Common Market nations of Europe will hate Rome because the Vatican will complain about the Antichrist and his army.

The woman is called Babylon, the mother of harlots, and abominations of the earth.[1] She was drunk with the blood of the saints, and with the blood of the martyrs of Jesus. There were 100,000 Christians killed or crucified in Rome from AD 95 to AD 305. In Revelation 17:12,13 the ten horns are ten kings, and will unify themselves with the beast, which is Germany. This is the meaning of the phrase, "These have one mind, and shall give their power and strength unto the beast." This is why they receive power as kings one hour with the beast. This is a description of the meeting where unification of the Common Market occurs.

In Revelation 17:14 the unified Europe and Germany will make war with the Lamb, and he shall overcome them, for he is King of Kings, and Lord of Lords. This verse verifies that Europe and Germany will cause World War III, and then Christ will win the war. This is written in Revelation 19:11-21.

The unified nations of Europe and Germany will take Rome. In Revelation 17:16 the ten kings will eat her flesh and burn her with fire. The phrase, "eat her flesh," is a description of a beast devouring its prey. Therefore the armies of the beast will overrun Rome, destroy it, and burn it to the ground. Some scholars say this happened during the reign of Nero, but it will happen again.

In Revelation 18 is another description of Rome, and its judgment and destruction. Babylon is fallen. All nations have drunk of the wine of the wrath of her fornication.

In Revelation 18:8: "Therefore shall her plagues come in one day, death, and mourning, and famine; and she shall be utterly burned with fire: for strong is the Lord God who judgeth her."

In Revelation 19:5-9 the reign of God is at hand, and the marriage supper of the Lamb is come. The Lamb is Christ and the wife of the Lamb is the church. She wears fine linen because the fine linen is the righteousness of saints. This is written in Revelation 19:7,8.

In Revelation 19:9 is the marriage supper of the Lamb, which will take place just after the rapture of the church.

Revelation 19:9: "And he saith unto me, Write, Blessed are they which are called unto the marriage supper of the Lamb. And he saith unto me, These are the true sayings of God."

This is also written in the parable of the marriage feast in the gospel of St. Matthew 22:1-14.

In Revelation 19:10 the testimony of Jesus is the spirit of prophecy. This is the testimony of suffering and death: just as Jesus suffered and died on the cross. This testimony is the spirit of prophecy because:

I Peter 4:13,14: "But rejoice, inasmuch as ye are partakers of Christ's sufferings; that, when his glory shall be revealed, ye may be glad also with exceeding joy.

If ye be reproached for the name of Christ, happy are ye; for the spirit of glory and of God resteth upon you: on their part he is evil spoken of, but on your part he is glorified."

The spirit of glory and of God in this verse is the spirit of prophecy from Revelation 19:10. In my case, I suffered because of the demons, which plagued me for 37 years. This is the meaning of the "fiery trial," from I Peter 4:12. Therefore the person who battles with the enemy, which is Satan, will receive more grace from Christ, in order to save him and his testimony. This person is also a partaker in Christ's suffering.

In Revelation 19:11-21 is the victory of Christ over the armies of the Antichrist. The supper of the fowls in Revelation 19:17,18 is the opposite of the marriage supper of the Lamb in Revelation 19:9. The kings and their armies would not repent and be invited to the marriage supper of the Lamb; therefore they will provide a very large supper for the fowls. In other words, they will be the main course in that supper.

In Revelation 20:1-3 Satan is put into hell for 1000 years, and is bound with chains. In Revelation 20:4 the saints that were beheaded for the witness of Jesus are given thrones and judgment. They will also live and reign with Christ for a thousand years. This is the millennium. The first resurrection will occur before the millennium. This is written in Revelation 20:4-6. Those people in the first resurrection will be in Zion during the thousand years.

Revelation 20:5,6: "But the rest of the dead lived not again until the thousand years were finished. This is the first resurrection.

Blessed and holy is he that hath part in the first resurrection: on such the second death hath no power, but they shall be priests of God and of Christ, and shall reign with him a thousand years."

These verses tell us that there is a first and a second resurrection. The most holy people will be included in the first resurrection. These people will be exempt from punishment in the Lake of Fire because they are holy. They will live and reign with Christ for a thousand years in the heavenly city, which is new Jerusalem. This city is called Mt. Zion.

Hebrews 12:22: "But ye are come unto Mount Sion, and unto the city of the living God, the heavenly Jerusalem, and to an innumerable company of angels."

Mt. Zion is also referred to several times in the Psalms. This city will come down from God out of heaven, and will be in Israel for a thousand years. The city of Zion is also described in Revelation 21, and 22. The people from the first resurrection will be in Zion, and will be priests of God and of

Christ. These people will be transformed into angels at the first resurrection, and will be in Israel for the millennium. This is written in Matthew 22:29,30. Also, there will be an innumerable company of angels there. This is written in Hebrews 12:22.

There are two resurrections, and this is written in Revelation 20:5, and in Revelation 20:12. The first is for the most holy people. This will take place at the rapture of the church. The second resurrection will be more general. It will include people who are sinners, as well as people who may go to heaven. This resurrection will occur just before the judgment. This is written in Revelation 20:12. Some of the people in the second resurrection will be cast into the Lake of Fire. Compare this to Revelation 20:6: "Blessed and holy is he that hath part in the first resurrection: on such the second death hath no power." The second death has power only in the second resurrection. Included in the chapter of Revelation 20 in chronological order are:

Satan is bound for 1000 years	Revelation 20:1-3
The first resurrection	Revelation 20:4-6
The millennium and Mt. Zion	Revelation 20:4-6
The second Armageddon	Revelation 20:7-9
The judgment of Satan	Revelation 20:10
The second resurrection	Revelation 20:12
The judgment of mankind	Revelation 20:11,12
The Second Death	Revelation 20:14
The book of life	Revelation 20:15

There are two Armageddons. The first is written in Revelation 16:16, and in Revelation 19:17-21. The beast and the armies of the Antichrist are described in Revelation 13:1-18. They will gather for battle at the pass of Armageddon, which is located ten miles southwest of Nazareth in Israel.

The second Armageddon will occur at Mt. Zion, around the holy city of new Jerusalem. Satan will be bound with chains and put into hell after the first Armageddon. He will be loosed from hell after the millennium, and he will gather the nations of Gog and Magog for the battle against the saints at Mt. Zion. This is written in Revelation 20:7-9.

Fire will come down from God out of heaven, and will devour the armies of Gog and Magog. This is written in Revelation 20:9. Then Satan will be cast into the Lake of Fire to burn forever.

Revelation 20:10: "And the devil that deceived them was cast into the lake of fire and brimstone, where the beast and the false prophet are, and shall be tormented day and night forever and ever."

Then the dead, small and great, will stand before God for judgment. This is written in Revelation 20:11,12. Then death and hell will be cast into the Lake of Fire. In Revelation 20:15, whosoever was not found written in the book of life will be cast into the Lake of Fire.

The Lake of Fire is the second death, which lasts forever. The souls of people will be put there, with the spirits of devils. These verses tell me that a person's soul will not be destroyed by the fire, but will suffer severe pain, which will last forever. In Psalm 19:4 the Lake of Fire is the sun:

Psalm: 19:4: "Their line is gone out through all the earth, and their words to the end of the world. In them hath he set a tabernacle for the sun."

The line though all the earth is blasphemy, which is caused by the demons. Their words go to the end of the world, for they cause people to speak profanity. Satan will burn forever on the sun.

The book of life in Revelation 20:15 is the written record of the people who ask for the salvation of Christ, and are saved. I think when a person accepts Christ, reads the Bible, and goes to church on Sunday, their name is added to the book of life in heaven. It is a mistake to feel excluded from the book of life because you can still receive Christ and be saved. The book of life is open for anyone who will be saved. It is not closed to anyone, except the son of perdition. It is most important to be saved by Christ, and not to be cast into the Lake of Fire. I'm writing this book, so that you may believe in the Lord Jesus Christ, and have your name added to the book of life.

In Revelation 21 and 22 is a description of the new heaven and the new earth.

Revelation 21:1,2: "And I saw a new heaven and a new earth: for the first heaven and the first earth were passed away; and there was no more sea.

And I John saw the holy city, new Jerusalem, coming down from God out of heaven, prepared as a bride adorned for her husband."

The entire chapters of 21 and 22 describe the holy city of Zion. It looks to me like the people who are saved can enter into the city of Zion, and see the angels, and Christ himself. This is written in Revelation 21:24-26.

God will dwell with his people. There will be no more tears, no more death, and no more pain in the new heaven. God will make all things new. There will be a fountain of the water of life. He that overcomes this present world will inherit all things in the new heaven.

The unbelievers and the abominable will be put into the Lake of Fire.

In Revelation 21:9-27 is a description of the holy city, which is also called the bride, the Lamb's wife. The verses in Revelation 21:9,10 tells us that the people who are taken up into heaven at the rapture of the church will be in the new Jerusalem, for a thousand years with Christ. The Lamb's wife is the church, which is written in verse 9. In verse 10 the Lamb's wife is also called the holy Jerusalem. Therefore the first resurrection is the rapture of the church, and the people who are taken into heaven at the rapture will be in the holy Jerusalem. This may also be the reason for the phrase, "according to the measure of a man, that is, of the angel," in Revelation 21:17. The people in the rapture of the church will be transformed into angels. This is written in several places in the Bible:

Matthew 22:30	Mark 12:24,25
I Corinthians 15:42-45	I Corinthians 15:51-53
Luke 20:34-36	

The holy Jerusalem will have 12 foundations in which are written the names of the 12 Apostles of the Lamb. In verse 18 the city is made of pure gold, like unto clear glass. In Revelation 21:19 the foundations were garnished with precious stones. In verse 12 there are 12 gates into the city, and every gate is made of one very large pearl. In verse 22 the Lord God Almighty and the Lamb are the temple of it.

I wrote that the new Jerusalem would be visited by normal or mortal human beings, while having immortal people or angels in the city. This seems to be the reason for the millennium, or the 1000 years, which is written in Revelation 20:4-6. However, only those which have their names written in the Lamb's book of life will be allowed into the city. This is written in Revelation 21:27.

In Revelation 22:1,2 is the river of life, proceeding out of the throne of God and of the Lamb. The tree of life is in verse 2 and 14. This is the tree of immortality, which was taken away from Adam and Eve in Genesis 3:22,23, when they were deceived by Satan. They could not have immortality after they knew good and evil, having eaten of the forbidden tree.

Therefore those people who accept Christ and are saved will have the right to eat of the tree of life, and become immortal.

Revelation 22:14: "Blessed are they that do his commandments, that they may have right to the tree of life, and may enter in through the gates into the city."

The leaves of the tree of life will be used for the healing of the nations. The throne of God and of the Lamb will be in the city, and there will be no more curse. There will be no need for the light from the sun, for the Lord God gives them light. This is written in Revelation 22:1-5. In verses 6-21 is the proof that the book of Revelation is prophecy. The Lord God of the holy prophets sent his angel to show to his servants the things which must shortly be done.

John fell down to worship the angel that showed him the revelations, and the angel said, "See thou do it not: for I am thy fellow servant, and of thy brethren the prophets, and of them which keep the sayings of this book: worship God."

The angel also gave instructions to John. Then the words of Christ are written in:

Revelation 22:12,13: "And behold, I come quickly; and my reward is with me, to give every man according as his work shall be.

I am Alpha and Omega, the beginning and the end, the first and the last."

There are two verses, which give warnings about the use of this book of prophecy. These verses are Revelation 22:18,19.

He who testifies the things written in this book is Christ Jesus. Amen, even so, come, Lord Jesus.

The grace of our Lord Jesus Christ will be with you all. Amen.

THE MEEK SHALL INHERIT THE EARTH

Right now the US Government operates from political principles. All of the analysts talk about politics. The senators and representatives work and talk about politics; and the President talks to them and to the political leaders from other nations. In the years of World War III the US Government has to change from politics to survival. A lot of projects, which were important before, may not be important at all when considered in the light of preparations for World War III. This means that the jobs of the people in the US Government may stay the same, but the money appropriations and expenditures will have to change for the people of America to survive the war.

The US Government will have to follow the instructions of Christ to prepare for World War III. Spending the $7.4 trillion dollars of the national debt wasn't very wise; and now the interest from the national debt must be postponed for 20 years, until World War III is over. Putting US troops into active military fighting anywhere in the world during World War III will invite attack on America by the Antichrist; but I could write this a hundred times, and the President could still put American troops into active fighting during World War III, since he does things for political reasons. This is where the American people must protest; and it is why I must have some leverage over what the President does by convincing the people to keep America neutral during World War III.

The safety of America must come first during World War III, in the eyes of the President, the Congress, the Pentagon, and the CIA. This means that

NATO, the United Nations, and all other political considerations must take second place. In fact all of these types of political activities should be discontinued after 2006. This will be our method used to switch from politics to survival in the US Government:

Isaiah 26:20,21: "Come, my people, enter thou into thy chambers, and shut thy doors about thee: hide thyself as it were for a little moment, until the indignation be overpast.

For, behold, the Lord cometh out of his place to punish the inhabitants of the earth for their iniquity: the earth also shall disclose her blood, and shall no more cover her slain."

These verses say to retreat back into the USA, and to have very limited foreign relations during World War III. This is verified in Amos 5:13, Isaiah 2:10-12, and Zephaniah 2:3. The phrase, "seek meekness," in Zephaniah 2:3 refers to Matthew 5:5.

Matthew 5:5: "Blessed are the meek: for they shall inherit the earth."

Anyone who is not meek will not survive World War III. They will be destroyed by the Antichrist. Those people who are meek will inherit the earth when Christ destroys the Antichrist. Thus the President and the Congress must seek meekness because it is the only way to survive the war, and it is why the meek shall inherit the earth.

The President and the Congress normally work for the best interests of the people, but they don't know what will happen during World War III. I will also work for the people and I do know what is going to happen. To work together, I will tell the TV news and the press what the US Government should be doing; and then the people can put pressure on the government to get satisfactory results. This is why I must have some leverage over what the President does to make him conform to what I know is going to happen in World War III. Then we can work to help America survive the war.

The most important thing to do is to seek meekness, and to be neutral throughout World War III. This means that there should be no military fighting at all by American troops. The meek shall inherit the earth because the people who are not meek will be destroyed by the army of the Antichrist. Therefore Matthew 5:5 gives us the formula for survival. This is very important, and the American people should make the government follow this commandment.

This won't be easy to do because of the Pentagon. They have the most powerful Air Force, Army, Navy, and Marine Corps in the world. Therefore to make them become meek, you have to take away their offensive military power, and leave them with defensive military power only. This has to be done with all four branches of the military, and this is what I've done in the

27

Church Committee Plan. Therefore the American people must support this plan.

The President should give the Church Committee Group the power to launch all mainland US nuclear missiles. The Congress should give them the power to declare war; and then the Pentagon will give their offensive military power to the Church Committee Group. This means that all of these branches of the government will have to get permission from the Church Committee to start a war. Then the President, the Congress, and the US military will conform to Matthew 5:5. They will then become meek, and America will survive World War III.

The importance of this can be seen in Revelation 9:16, where the army of the Antichrist will have 200 million soldiers. This is two-thirds the entire population of the USA. Then in Revelation 13:4 is the phrase, "Who is like unto the beast? who is able to make war with him?" This verifies the huge army, which will be in Europe. The danger is that if the US Government will not give up their offensive military powers, then the President, Congress, and the Pentagon will retaliate if the Antichrist attacks Puerto Rico or Hawaii. It will be nearly impossible for them not to retaliate, and this is why they must give these powers to the Church Committee.

CHAPTER II

The Weapons of Satan

Blasphemy is a weapon that Satan uses against people. He does it by using 50 million devils to create thoughts in the minds of people while they are talking. This is written in Psalm 19:4, and the line through all the earth is blasphemy. This is why the third commandment says, "Thou shalt not take the name of the Lord thy God in vain."

This is why the people should not be angry with God about World War III. Blasphemy against the Holy Spirit is a sin, which will put you into the Lake of Fire. You can talk about Christ while referring to the Holy Trinity, and you will avoid speaking blasphemy. Then Satan will not be able to use this weapon as effectively as he could before. This is written in Matthew 12:32. Jesus protected us from blasphemy by forgiving a person who speaks a word against him. You must not deny Christ, however, and this is written in Matthew 10:33.

In the following pages is a list and a description of some of the other weapons that Satan uses against people.

The battle between Christ and Satan takes place in the minds of people. The Spirit of Christ gives us faith, while the spirits of devils cause doubt and unbelief in our minds. Satan uses the following weapons against people:

1. Condemnation
2. Lies
3. Murder and the fear of death
4. Commandments of men
5. Temptation of people
6. Temptation of the Spirit of God
7. The devouring lion

8. Pride
9. Nuclear war: Revelation 8:10-12
10. The Antichrist: II Thessalonians 2:2-12
11 Suicide: I Corinthians 3:16,17
12. Famine: Revelation 6:5-8
13. False religion: Exodus 20:1-6
14. Common Market: Revelation 17:12-17
15. World Oil Supply: Daniel 11:23-25
16. Evil: Genesis 3:1-7

CONDEMNATION: I TIMOTHY 3:6

Satan has convinced the people of the world that they have to fight at the battle of Armageddon, when they really don't. He has done this by using 50 million devils to create thoughts in the minds of people here on the earth to convince them that they are condemned, and he has done this through the generations of people for 1900 years, since the book of Revelation was written. Therefore the theologians and the people on earth thought they would be condemned at Armageddon. Satan also made the people believe that the prophecy of the Four Horsemen of the Apocalypse, Revelation 13:1-18, and the prophecies about the plagues in the book of Revelation were written to condemn the people when these prophecies were written to save us. He has actually made the people afraid of the entire book of Revelation and this has also made the prophecies in it almost impossible to understand.

Satan is able to convince the people that they are condemned by creating thoughts and doubts in their minds; and when they believe this, then they will not have enough faith to be saved. This is what Jesus meant in Matthew 8:25,26, when he upbraided his disciples because of their lack of faith.

In Matthew 21:19-22 Jesus said we should have faith and not doubt. In Luke 7:48-50 faith is what saves us. In Luke 8:25 Jesus asked his disciples, "Where is your faith?" This verse tells us that we must state our faith to Christ and to the world, in order to be saved. This is verified in Romans 10:8-13, and in Matthew 28:18-20.

In Revelation 21:8 the people who do not believe in Christ will be condemned to the Lake or Fire. These are the people who fell into unbelief because of Satan. It is the second half of this process that the people don't see; and it is by creating thoughts in their minds that Satan is able to deceive them.

LIES: JOHN 8:44

Satan has convinced the people that the book of Revelation condemns the entire human race; and for this reason the people think they have lost World War III before it even begins. This is the biggest lie that Satan has ever told, and the world believes it. The political leaders believe that their armies have to be at Armageddon to fight against the army of the Antichrist, but they don't. The most perfect lies that Satan uses are those that are the exact opposite of the truth. Satan is able to make people believe his lies because he uses world-famous politicians to propagate them. In Genesis 3:1-7 Satan convinced Eve to eat from the tree of knowledge of good and evil, instead of the tree of life in Genesis 2:9. Therefore Adam and Eve were condemned to die, instead of receiving immortality. This is why Jesus said that Satan is a liar, and the father of lies, written in John 8:44. Satan was the first to ever tell a lie on the earth, and this is why he is the father of lies.

The choice between the truth of Christ and the lies of Satan is really the point of the entire theology of salvation during World War III, and the choice itself is where the critical point of decision is. This will determine whether entire nations will be saved or destroyed during World War III. In Matthew 24:4,5, and in Matthew 24:23-27 Jesus told us that many false prophets will appear during the last days. He warned us about this so we would not be fooled by the lies of Satan.

MURDER: JOHN 8:44

In John 8:44 Satan was a murderer from the beginning of creation because he murdered the entire human race when he deceived Adam and Eve. You can see how serious these decisions are because of this example. If the people make a wrong decision during World War III, either their entire nation will be destroyed, or their souls will go to the Lake of Fire, or both. For these reasons, the politicians of the world must realize that Satan and his devils can and will create thoughts in their minds to make them use their military forces during the war, which would cause World War III to escalate. This could cause a nuclear war, and it is why the churches should have authority over what the politicians and the military forces plan to do. They should have the authority to review any action, which would lead their nation into the war; and they must have the authority to override decisions that would do this, in order to prevent nuclear war.

This is where the deception of Satan really is: in lies, war, and in murder. The people in the world do not realize how important these decisions are. They must learn from the example in the Garden of Eden, where the entire human race was murdered because of the wrong decision of two people. Again, this is why the churches should have authority over their governments and the military in their nations during World War III.

COMMANDMENTS OF MEN: MATTHEW 15:9

In Matthew 16:23 the phrase, "Get thee behind me Satan: thou art an offence unto me: for thou savourest not the things that be of God, but those that be of men," means that Satan is able to convince people that their way of looking at things is correct, and this is how they are deceived. This is written in Matthew 15:9, where the people of Israel followed the commandments of men, rather than the commandments of God. The people of Israel rejected the word of the Lord, and they went into war and captivity from 606 BC to 586 BC. This happened again in 70 AD, after they rejected Christ. This is written in Matthew 23:37-39, and in Luke 13:34,35. You must realize the importance of the decision to choose between Christ or Satan, before World War III starts, so your nation will be saved.

TEMPTATION OF PEOPLE: MATTHEW 22:17-19

In Matthew 4:1-11 Jesus went into the desert to be tempted by Satan. He did this so we would see his example, so that we would know what to do when it happens to us. I worked nine years in the desert from 1953 to 1962, and there was nothing to be tempted with while I was there. In other words, Satan may have offered things to Jesus, but there was nothing in the desert to be tempted with. This is also true about hell: The demons that plague me offer money, power, women, and publication of my book, while none of these things are in hell, where the demons came from.

TEMPTATION OF THE SPIRIT OF GOD: ACTS 5:9

In Hebrews 3:6-19 the Hebrew people saw the works of God in the desert, and they chose to murmur or complain against him. The verse that says this is Hebrews 3:9, and this is a weapon that Satan uses against people. By complaining, the people tempted the Spirit of God, which is blasphemy. This is written in Matthew 12:31,32. These people failed at the point of critical decision. If they had decided to obey the word of the Lord, then they would have been saved. In Hebrews 3:9,10 the Lord was grieved when these people disobeyed by complaining. In Hebrews 3:11-13 is the warning to us about the critical decision between the unbelief caused by Satan, and the faith given to us by the Spirit of Christ.

In Hebrews 4:11 the example of unbelief of the Hebrews is written to warn us about the importance of our decision. In Hebrews 4:12 is a warning of the power of the word of God, in its ability to create or destroy people or nations. This is also written in Genesis 1:1-31, John 1:1-5, Revelation 19:13-15, and in Revelation 19:21. The people in the world should know that complaining against God is to go to the Lake of Fire.

To complain is the opposite of giving thanks to God. This is why Satan causes complaining through people; you can see that the weapons, which Satan uses, are opposites of the truth, which is written in the Bible. This is written in Job 40:19. Satan knows what is written in the Bible, and he knows how to use his weapons to condemn people. In Luke 17:12-19 is the story of the ten lepers. When Jesus healed them of their leprosy, only one returned to thank him. Jesus said to him, "Were there not ten cleansed? But where are the nine?"

The people must not make this mistake during World War III because it could cause their nation to be destroyed. You must remember that you have to give thanks, glory, and honor to Christ in order to be saved. We must continually give thanks to the Lord God during the trying times of World War III, and we will keep our faith in him, and we will be saved. In Luke 9:56 Christ came to save men's lives, and not to destroy them. This is verified in Revelation 16:16; and in Revelation 19:19-21, where Christ has already won the battle of Armageddon for us.

THE DEVOURING LION: I PETER 5:8

If the people of the world condemn themselves before World War III even begins, and if they refuse to make a decision for Christ, this means they have rejected the word of the Lord, which came through me to save them. Then they will have 11 years of war instead of peace. The free nations of the world must make the decision for Christ because this is the decision that is required in order to obey the prophecies. In the case of the nations in Europe, the people there must move to avoid the famine of the Antichrist. The plan for this is written in The Souls of Europe chapter.

In the Old Testament of the Bible, prophecy works like this:

1. The Word of the Lord comes through the prophet and to the people.

2. The people obey and they are saved; or they refuse and are condemned. Because Satan is able to convince the people that their way of doing things is correct, he can cause them to reject the word of the Lord, which comes

through the prophets. In Romans 10:3 the people of Israel followed their own righteousness, instead of the righteousness of God. Satan does this by creating thoughts, and by other methods, but the important thing is that he devours the prophets, when the people refuse to obey the word of the Lord, which comes through them.

In the Old Testament the people of Israel killed the prophets.

This is written in:

Jeremiah 2:30: "Your own sword hath devoured your prophets, like a destroying lion."

This verse is proof that Satan causes the people to kill the prophets, and this is verified in I Peter 5:8. The words, "devoured," and, "as a roaring lion," are the words which connect these verses. The phrases are a little different, but they still connect these verses. The Apostle Paul was nearly killed many times. This is written in II Corinthians 11:23-27. In II Timothy 4:17 is the phrase, "And I was delivered out of the mouth of the lion." Therefore you can see that the Apostles and the prophets are the Christians that Satan comes after first. In II Timothy 4:18 Paul said that the Lord would deliver him from every evil work.

In Acts 7:52 the people of Israel persecuted and killed the prophets, which were sent by the Lord to save them. In I Peter 5:8 our adversary the devil, as a roaring lion, walks about, seeking whom he may devour. Again, the prophets are the ones that Satan comes after first. The terrible thing here is that the people are condemned when they reject the word of the Lord, and when they kill the prophets. In Jeremiah 1:17-19 he was the only person who was saved in all of Judah, and he received immortality in heaven. The rest of the people were condemned because they did not obey the word of the Lord.

It is not possible for a prophet to give his responsibility to any other person or to a government because it is a continuing duty. In II Corinthians 4:7 the prophet as well as the Christian has the treasure of Christ in his own body, that the excellency of the power may be of God, and not of men. In Galatians 4:16 Paul asked, "Am I therefore become your enemy because I tell you the truth?" Paul made a reference here to the Old Testament prophets, who were killed by the people.

The prophets also have the responsibility of protecting the gift, which is in them, so it will not be corrupted by the unclean spirits of devils, or by mankind. This is written in I Corinthians 10:21, which says, "Ye cannot drink the cup of the Lord, and the cup of devils: ye cannot be partakers of the Lord's table, and of the table of devils." This means that people and governments, as well as Christians, cannot work for Satan and Christ at the same time. If they do, they will fall into the trap of Satan. One of the weapons of Satan is to cause people to tempt the Spirit of the Lord God. And when they do this, they will be condemned. This is the meaning of I Corinthians 10:22.

Here is a verse from a poem written by Joseph Addison Alexander:

There is a line, by us unseen,
Which crosses every path,
Which marks the boundary between
God's mercy and his wrath.

This line is the point of critical decision where we must have the faith of Christ to be saved; and since we cannot see this line or boundary, we must be diligent to give all thanks, glory, and honor to the Lord Jesus Christ. We should also give thanks to the Lord God Almighty, and we will stay on the mercy side of the line. This means we will be in the saving grace of the Lord Jesus Christ, and this is the reason for giving thanks to him.

I'm telling you this now, in order to save the millions of people who would otherwise complain against God, or against Christ during World War III. This could cause nations to be condemned, if the people refuse to accept Christ before the war. This will also cause the people to go to the Lake of Fire.

PRIDE: I TIMOTHY 3:6

Satan uses pride to condemn people. This is written in I Timothy 3:6. In Job 41:15 his scales are his pride, which means he can hide the truth, which is written in the Bible. This is what Satan has done with the entire book of Revelation because he has made people afraid of the Four Horsemen of the Apocalypse, Revelation 13:1-18, and the plagues in Revelation 6:1-17, Revelation 8:7-13, Revelation 9:1-21, and in Revelation 16:1-21.

In Job 41:34 Satan beholds all high things, which means he watches the church and everything that is important to it. In the same verse, he is a king over all the children of pride. Since pride is the opposite of humility, we know it is another weapon that Satan uses against people. The reason for this is written in James 4:6, where God resists the proud, but he gives grace to the humble. In James 4:10 we should humble ourselves in the sight of the Lord. This means that we should go to church and worship the Lord God there.

Now if a person is proud, he will not humble himself before the Lord. In fact, he will not be able to humble himself because his pride will not allow him to do so. This is how Satan uses pride against people. The people who don't go to church will not humble themselves to worship Christ, and they are therefore condemned by Satan. The way he does this is by creating thoughts of pride in the minds of the people.

NUCLEAR WAR: REVELATION 8:10-12

In John 8:44 Jesus said that Satan was a murderer from the beginning of Creation because he murdered the entire human race when he deceived Adam and Eve. You can see how serious these decisions are because of what happened in the Garden of Eden. The entire human race suffered death because of the wrong decision of two people. If the people make a wrong decision during World War III, either their nation will be destroyed, or their souls will go to the Lake of Fire, or both.

For these reasons, the politicians of the world must realize that Satan and his devils can and will create thoughts in their minds to make them use their military forces during World War III. This will cause the war to escalate, which could cause a global nuclear war. For these reasons, the churches in every free nation should have authority over what their politicians and their military forces plan to do. They should have the authority to review any action that would lead their nation into the war; and the churches must have the authority to override any decisions which would do this, to prevent nuclear war.

To do this the churches can organize their own committees by electing ministers, archbishops, bishops, and pastors to form groups in each denomination of the church. An example of this would be: They could choose 50 ministers from each denomination for their Committees, from: Assembly of God, Baptist, Catholic, Church of Christ, Episcopal, Gospel Church, Methodist, Presbyterian, Quaker, and Seventh Day Adventist Churches.

The government in every nation, which is outside of Europe, will have to contact the National Headquarters of each church; and the President, the Congress, the Parliament, and other government offices will have to pass legislation to give wartime authority to the Church Committees.

The United Nations Organization can help to get this information to each nation; and they can also explain the importance of this plan. Satan murdered the entire human race in the Garden of Eden, and he did it by creating thoughts in the minds of Adam and Eve. Therefore death came upon all people because of their wrong decision. The nations can eliminate the possibility of this type of mistake during World War III by giving the churches wartime authority over their politicians and their military. The idea of doing this is to allow the faith of Christ to save us; and to give the authority for wartime decisions to more than one or two people in the governments.

The Church Committees can read I John 4:2 aloud before they vote on an issue to be sure that demons are not present. The politicians and military would not think to do this, and it is why they are so easily fooled by Satan. Therefore the governments in each nation would have to contact the Church Committees before they can take any military action during World War III. This plan would be nearly foolproof, especially when the Committees are in different places in each nation. This will make it more difficult for Satan to influence the people voting on an issue.

The United Nations could make this plan mandatory for every nation before World War III begins. The churches themselves will need fax machines in their headquarters so each minister could fax or call in his vote; and the headquarters could notify the ministers about an issue that requires their vote.

If 75% of the nations in the world agree to follow this plan during World War III, then they will not be involved in nuclear war. The United Nations Organization can help to get the nations to follow it; and they can use this formula:

AGGRESSION LEADS TO MORE AGGRESSION

The nations that do not fire nuclear missiles during World War III will not be involved in the nuclear war. There is 25% of the land area of the earth in Europe and in the Middle East, which the Antichrist will control during World War III. This is written in Revelation 6:8. The churches in the world can save 75% of the earth by having authority over their governments and their military forces during World War III. The nations themselves will have to give the churches wartime authority to do this, and it will save millions of lives. The politicians and leaders of the nations, which are not in Europe or the Middle East, should approve this plan.

I think that 10 or 20 nations in Europe, all of Russia and China, and Korea will be included in the nuclear war at the end of World War III. This is why the nuclear fallout and the nuclear winter in Revelation 8:10-12 will cover one third of the earth. This is verified in Matthew 24:22, and in Daniel 11:44.

If it is possible, the United Nations Organization can try to convince the political leaders in China and in Korea to move their people to South China before the nuclear war starts. This way they will sacrifice some of their land to the Antichrist, but they will save the lives of 1.7 billion people by avoiding the ground war against the army of the Antichrist, and the nuclear war resulting from it. The United Nations can try to get financial aid from member nations to give to China and Korea to help the people move south.

The idea for the Church Committee Plan came from the Old Testament. In Exodus 18:13-27 Moses was judge over six million people. His father-in-law told him that the task was too great for one man, and Moses then elected other judges. I realized that advising all nations in World War III would be too great a task for me. Therefore the Church Committee Plan would give the nations more advisors. In Proverbs 11:14 there is safety in the multitude of counselors. With 400 to 500 ministers in each nation, Satan can't influence them as well as one or two politicians.

Wisdom is described in Proverbs 8:1-12. In Proverbs 8:14 counsel, wisdom, and understanding come from the Lord. In Proverbs 8:17 wisdom loves them that love her. This wisdom comes to us through the churches of Christ.

There may be a problem with pride or mistrust on the part of some of the political leaders in the United Nations. In Proverbs 13:10 contention comes with pride because a person who is proud will not yield to the church. These people should know that a unanimous vote to approve this plan would save 75% of the earth from nuclear war. In Proverbs 13:14 the law of the wise advises us to depart from the snares of death.

The Antichrist will own 25% of the land on earth, and in Revelation 8:10-12 there will be nuclear fallout and nuclear winter over 33.3% of the earth. The nuclear attack will happen in 2022. However, the land, which is actually hit with nuclear missiles, could be only 15% of the land area on earth.

In Proverbs 4:24 we should avoid speaking with a froward mouth during World War III. The Antichrist will retaliate against anyone who speaks against him. He will have 200 million soldiers, so don't insult him in the TV news.

The political leaders in the United Nations may object to this plan because they would say that the 500 ministers on the Committees would never allow any military action by their nation. This is true of offensive action, but they could allow defensive military action to protect their nation. Therefore their nation would never be in danger of nuclear attack by the Antichrist because they would not provoke him. This plan actually takes away Satan's power to cause a global nuclear war because his power to do this works through offensive military action, which he causes by influencing one or two politicians in each nation.

The governments in each nation would have to pass legislation to give wartime power to the Church Committees; and the United Nations could help to do this by writing the legislative plan to make it standardized for all of the nations. In other words, the plan would be the same for all nations, with the help of the United Nations Organization.

In Revelation 12:7-9 Satan threw away immortality to get more power because he knew that one third of the angels would follow him. In Isaiah 14:12-14 it was pride that caused him to do this. Now he causes people to do the same thing on earth. Satan uses pride and nationalism to cause men to lust for power, and then they start wars. This is written in James 4:1,2. In Revelation 20:7-9 Satan has planned World War IV before World War III even starts. The way to defeat Satan is to take away his ability to use pride and nationalism against people; and this plan does it by giving wartime authority to the churches of Christ.

FALLOUT SHELTERS

There will be a need for fallout shelters to protect the people in all nations during World War III. There are several different types of underground structures in every large city, and this is where the governments in each nation should start looking. There are underground warehouses, subway tunnels, parking garages, and other structures; but the underground garages would be the best in my opinion. With the larger and more recently built skyscrapers, they are earthquake proof, which makes the underground garages almost indestructible. The only thing needed to convert an underground garage to a fallout shelter would be one or more garage doors to close at the entrances. This could be done now, so the shelters would be ready at any time in the future. This will work until the great earthquakes destroy the large cities. This is written in Revelation 16:19.

The government in each nation could make it a requirement for each state, province, or city to count all of the underground garages in their area or territory, and to hire engineers to build doors to put up at their entrances, at no cost to the owners of the garages. The doors can be a square or rectangular wall of steel, which moves on a track, with rollers at the top of the door. They will have to be designed so the doors will not fall off the tracks during bombing attacks. If there isn't enough room for the doors to roll open (on the inside or outside of the entrances), the engineers could design or make large garage doors, which open and roll upward with a remote control switch. These could be similar to home garage doors, only larger.

This project would have to be watched very closely by the governments in each nation, and the rights of all of the owners of the garages would have to be respected; but the need for these structures should be emphasized. In the event of an emergency, or an attack with bombing or nuclear weapons, the cars in the garages would not have to be moved. There would be a need for smaller doors, for each person to go in or out one by one. These normal type doors could be built into the garage walls, or into the larger steel doors. Then the large doors could remain shut during attacks.

In nations that are not likely to be attacked with bombing, the people at work in the city, or driving in traffic would go to the shelters, instead of going home. This means that all of the people would have to have a diagram of the city, with the locations of the shelters on it. This could be done by the newspapers, which could print the maps or diagrams several times a year. The people who are at home should stay there if the bombing attack isn't very serious. In the case of a nuclear attack, the best way to survive the fallout is to stay indoors for up to two weeks. With this in mind, the governments could build cement walls and rooms to store food (like chocolate candy, and other types of snack food) and water within each underground parking garage. If the food is old, it should be replaced; and if it is used up, it should be restocked. The water should be distilled and put into tanks in each garage, or in one-gallon containers.

In nations like England, Ireland, or Japan where the possibility of attack is greater, the people at home may have to go to the fallout shelters to survive heavy bombing in their city. In these nations the governments may wish to build shelters, which are made better, and have better walls and facilities. I know that London is always under heavy bombing attacks during world wars. Therefore England may wish to use this advice about underground garages, and to build better fallout shelters as well. The reason for the greater danger for England, Ireland, and Japan is that they are very close to Europe, and they are on islands. This will make it very easy for the Antichrist to blockade and starve the people there.

The governments in each nation should also make it a point to ask for an increase in production for the companies that make gas masks. They could check to make sure they are made well, with high quality; and then the government could purchase the gas masks and protective clothing. This should also be done now, in order to supply all of the needs of the people before World War III starts.

The nations that border Europe will need more preparation for World War III. These nations are: Turkey, Afghanistan, Pakistan, India, China, and Mongolia. The nations that will suffer the most damage are: Turkey, Syria, Lebanon, Israel, Jordan, Egypt, Iraq, Iran, Kuwait, Saudi Arabia, Yemen, and Oman. These nations will be invaded by the army of the Antichrist, and their armies will either fight or move. The Antichrist will move south to take the world oil supply. This is written in Daniel 11:25. These nations must store food for a seven-year famine and build bunkers and fallout shelters.

There is one additional note here about building fallout shelters under the large skyscrapers or tall buildings. In Revelation 16:19 the phrase: "And the cities of the nations fell," means that the very tall buildings will fall during the great earthquakes. This means that a lot of people will be killed if they are in these cities. This is yet another reason for the people to go to church throughout World War III. It is also a good reason to stop using the underground garages for fallout shelters.

THE ANTICHRIST: II THESSALONIANS 2:2-12

Hitler would have been forgiven for all of his murders, and all of his sins, if he would have repented, accepted Christ, and went to church. Adolf Hitler didn't devise a scheme to take human souls for Satan, although he tried experiments with death and atrocities. There are verses in the Bible which seem to oppose this idea, like I John 3:14,15; but when a person comes to Christ, he will be forgiven for his sins, and he will be a new creature. This is verified in Revelation 2:20,21, where Jezebel was given space to repent.

The Antichrist, or the son of perdition, is prevented from any chance of going into heaven. This is written in John 17:12. When he invented the mark of the beast, and the famine, he devised a way to take 800 million souls for Satan. By doing this, the Antichrist will commit blasphemy against the Holy Spirit of Christ. In John 3:16, and in John 12:50 the commandment of God is everlasting life. The Antichrist will prevent people from going into heaven by forcing them to receive the mark of the beast. Therefore he will magnify Satan, and he will go to the Lake of Fire with him, along with all of the people who work for him. This is written in Revelation 14:11.

In Revelation 13:1, and in Revelation 13:5,6 the Antichrist will speak blasphemy against God. In Revelation 13:2, Revelation 13:4, Revelation 13:8, Revelation 13:11,12, Revelation 13:15, and in Revelation 13:16-18 the Antichrist will cause all of the people in Europe to worship Satan, himself, and Germany. This is why he is the only person in the history of the world who will not have any chance of going into heaven.

I've written this to give the people in Europe a better idea of how evil the Antichrist will be. When he comes into power, he will make Hitler look like a boy scout. You must remember that Satan plans every world war, and he improves his tactics in each one of them. Therefore the Antichrist will be more evil than Hitler because his tactics will be more evil. Hitler didn't take human souls for Satan, but the Antichrist will. You should also know that the Antichrist will be a popular man in Europe. He will be well liked by the people, and this is how they will be deceived. The thing that will make him evil is what he will do for Satan. He will put the souls of 800 million people into the Lake of Fire, to burn there forever. This is why he is called a vile person in Daniel 11:21.

You should know that a human life is worth less than $1000 dollars, while one human soul is worth more than the earth and the entire universe. This is written in Matthew 24:35, James 1:18, and in John 3:16. In II Peter 3:10-13 the heavens and the earth will pass away, while the soul of a Christian will live forever. Christ is the Saviour of the world, and he has already won World War III for us.

The Antichrist will still rule over 24 nations in Europe, and the Christian people there will have to move, or they will lose their lives in the famine of the Antichrist; and if they cannot endure the suffering, they will lose their souls too. If the saints stay in Europe, they will have to die for their faith to be saved by Christ. This is written in Matthew 16:25. This means that if you accept the mark of the beast to save your life, you will lose your soul to Satan. When you save your life on earth, you will lose eternal life in heaven. In Matthew 16:25 the person who will lose his life for Christ, will receive everlasting life in heaven. This verse describes the theology of the first life on earth, and the second life in heaven, which lasts forever. Matthew 16:26 says that one human soul is more valuable than the whole world.

In Revelation 13:7 the Antichrist will make war against the saints, and he will overcome them. He will do this by means of the famine, and this is the meaning of the phrase, "and shall wear out the saints of the most High," in Daniel 7:25. In Revelation 13:8 all of the people in Europe who are not Christians will worship the Antichrist.

The Antichrist will take NE China just above North Korea because he will want to expand his kingdom to include Japan. This means he will take all of the land north of Beijing, China; and he will take all of Korea. The Antichrist will have so much economic power with control of 24 nations in Europe including the USSR, that other nations, like Africa, Afghanistan, China, England, Ireland, India, Mongolia, and Pakistan will have to make sure that their political leaders don't sell their souls to him. The people in these nations should make it clear that they will revolt if their political leaders make any kind of a deal with the Antichrist. And their armies should fight if they are invaded by his army.

The difficult part of this situation is that these nations will have to conduct trade with some of the nations controlled by the Antichrist in Europe. This means that their political leaders and business leaders will have to deal with the business leaders in the EEC. They will have some kind of relationship with the Antichrist, or with business leaders from his empire. Considering the fact that 800 million people in Europe will lose their souls to the Antichrist and to Satan because of their lust for power and money; it will be very difficult for the people in the nations surrounding Europe to restrain their leaders from doing the same thing.

For these reasons, the nations such as China can use the idea of Church Committees. These committees can review decisions by political and business leaders, before they can take action. The governments in these nations must agree to give their people a way to protect themselves from Satan; and the best way to do it is to give authority to them so their approval is needed before the political leaders can make any kind of an agreement with the Antichrist. The people should have the same power over the business leaders in their nation, and over the corporations. The greatest danger to these nations will be with the corporations and businesses, with the pressure they put on the political leaders to make deals with the Antichrist.

Then the Governments in China, Mongolia, Turkey, India, and other nations can give their people a voice during World War III; and they can do it by giving wartime authority to the Church Committees. The theology for this procedure is based on Proverbs 11:14, where there is safety in the multitude of Counsellors. This is true because Satan can influence one or two political leaders, but when the decision has to be approved by a committee of 500 people, then he can't work very well.

The devils can create thoughts in the minds of people; therefore they can cause greed and lust. This is why the 500 ministers on the committees can nullify Satan's power. They will be sure that the safety of their people is always top priority.

These nations have religions other than Christianity, and therefore the Church Committee can have representatives from each religion. I will ask for half of the committee to be from the national religion, and half to be Christians from the same nation, who speak the native language. This would mean that in India, 250 committee members would be Hindu; and the other 250 members would be Christians, who speak the Hindi language. There could be one committee of 500 people in charge of political decisions, and another committee of 300 ministers in charge of major business decisions, which involve corporations in the European Community of nations.

There will be a problem with bribery by corporations, or with the governments, and therefore the churches must be sure that their ministers are kept in solitude. It may be necessary for the churches to elect a new committee, if there is a bribery attempt, and this should be done within one day. The corporations will try to convince the political leaders of the nations to make deals with the Antichrist. This is how the greed and lust will manifest itself, and the committee of 300 ministers will know what to expect, and how to deal with it. They will vote to cancel any action or decision, which could endanger their people. These 300 ministers would be half national religion, and half Christians from their nation, who speak the national language.

This system will work for the good of the political and business leaders, and for the people. The reason is that revolt is the other choice, and watching two billion people come after you to kill you, can be very terrifying.

CHINA, KOREA AND THE CHURCH COMMITTEE PLAN

There have been thousands of people in China who have watched Billy Graham Crusades. It may be possible for him to work with the people and the governments in China and Korea to help prevent the deaths of millions of people in these countries in the big nuclear war at the end of World War III. This war is described in Daniel 11:44, and in Revelation 8:10-12. In Matthew 24:22 Christ will return to earth early to stop it. This will reduce the effectiveness of it, which will save the human race. Reverend Billy Graham could also reduce the effectiveness of this nuclear war by helping to convince the people and the governments in China and Korea to adopt the Church Committee Plan, which will help to prevent nuclear war. This could save the lives of about one billion people in Europe, Russia, and China.

The prophecy in Revelation 8:10-12 says that one third of the drinking water on the earth will be contaminated with nuclear fallout; but the duration of this war could be reduced, if the Church Committee can withhold the power to declare war by the Chinese and Korean governments. Then instead of starting in the sixth year of World War III, the ground war between China, Korea, and the Antichrist would start in the ninth year of World War III. This would delay the nuclear war until the last year of the war; and then the nuclear fallout in Revelation 8:11 would kill 500 million people in Europe, China, and Korea, instead of killing 1.7 billion people.

I also thought of moving millions of people from NE China and Korea south into China before the nuclear war takes place. This idea combined with the withholding of the power to declare war from the Chinese Army could possibly reduce the effectiveness of this war by 70%. To do this you must use the Church Committee Plan. This is why I thought of asking Reverend Billy Graham to do this because he is more famous than I am, and he also has great influence with the people in China and Korea.

When there is a greater demand for ministers and churches of Christ in China during World War III, the missionaries and evangelists can go there to preach the gospel of Christ to them. It would be a big job to preach to two billion people in China and Korea, and for 760 million people in India, but the ministers would be glad to do it.

When church attendance increases during World War III, the ministers could preach by having alphabetical groups of people attend church each day of the week, using last names. The plan would look like this:

ABCD	SUNDAY
EFGH	MONDAY
IJKL	TUESDAY
MNOP	WEDNESDAY
QRST	THURSDAY
UVWX	FRIDAY
YZ	SATURDAY

Then with four Church Services each day. The times would be:

10 AM   1 PM   4 PM   7 PM

By using this plan the churches could get from 14 to 28 times more people into church every week. Therefore millions of people would be saved for Christ. The rapture of the church will happen by 2025, and the people who want to be saved by Christ must go to church now. In Revelation 20:6 the people in the first resurrection must be holy; and then they will be in the holy city, new Jerusalem for 1000 years. This is written in Revelation 20:6, and in Revelation 21:10.

In Revelation 19:9 the people who are called to the Marriage Supper of the Lamb are those who are in the first resurrection; and they will receive immortality with Christ. If you would like to devote the next 20 years to Christ, and then receive immortality, you can study to become a minister or a pastor in the seminaries and churches. The women can work for the churches as secretaries, lectors, cup servers, or ushers. These are all honorable ways in which people can work for Christ. You should ask for more churches in China, India, Korea, Mongolia, and other nations in Asia and Africa, so more people can serve the Lord Jesus Christ.

You should always remember that the best way to defeat Satan is to bring more people to Christ. This is true for World War III, which Satan will cause. If you accept Christ and go to church, your soul will go into heaven if you are killed during the war. In Revelation 8:7-13 the plagues, and in Revelation 6:12, and Revelation 16:18 the earthquakes are designed to cause people to go to church, so their souls will be saved for Christ. This is verified in Acts 2:19-21. In Acts 2:21 whosoever shall call on the name of the Lord will be saved.

To avoid sin you must be married or celibate. In I Corinthians 6:18 St. Paul said to flee fornication. If you sin against your own body, you deny the resurrection. Therefore you must be married or celibate to be holy. One of Satan's weapons is suicide, and anyone who kills themselves will go to the Lake of Fire. The letter on the next page will help stop suicide. This will be a serious problem during World War III, and all nations and churches must work together to stop it. The people can let their friends read this letter.

SUICIDE: I CORINTHIANS 3:16,17
THIS LETTER WILL HELP TO PREVENT
SUICIDE THROUGHOUT THE WORLD

A person's soul is more valuable than the earth, and the entire universe. The universe will be destroyed after the judgment, but a person's soul will live forever, when they accept the salvation of Christ and go to church. This is written in II Peter 3:10-13.

I Corinthians 3:16,17: "Know ye not that ye are the temple of God, and that the Spirit of God dwelleth in you?

If any man defile the temple of God, him shall God destroy; for the temple of God is holy, which temple ye are."

The human body is the temple of the Holy Spirit, and if a man defiles or destroys his own body, then God will put that man's soul into the Lake of Fire in Revelation 20:14. In Psalm 19:4, Psalm 21:9, and in Matthew 25:41 the Lake of Fire is the sun. This is the meaning of the phrase, "everlasting fire," in Matthew 25:41. The fires on the sun will burn for 10 billion years according to scientists. When a man destroys his body as in suicide, he denies the resurrection; and then his soul will be put into the Lake of Fire after the judgment.

Life is a gift from the Lord, and each person should live for Christ. Then you will be equal to the angels at the resurrection. This is written in Matthew 22:30, and Luke 20:36. Christ said a person's soul is more valuable than the whole world in Matthew 16:26,27. The way to reduce suicides during World War III is to have the suicide hot lines refer people to comfort groups; and the churches can help the groups get started, and they can play a major role in the project.

When Christ returns to the earth in the glory of the Almighty Father, he will reward everyone according to their works. You can get this reward by helping the comfort groups, and by telling your friends about this letter because this is important work. The churches should inform all of their members everywhere about this letter.

FAMINE: REVELATION 6:5-8

The Antichrist will take the world oil supply. The nations that do not have their own fuel supply when this happens, will not be able to grow crops. They will run out of food, and cannibalism will spread like wildfire. Famine is a weapon, which Satan will use during World War III, and it will be a major problem in Europe, Japan, Africa, India, and possibly England.

In the 24 nations of Europe the Antichrist will declare his man-made famine. The people there will be imprisoned within their own cities, and they will either receive the mark of the beast, or they will starve to death. When the starvation begins, cannibalism will spread. It is not morally correct to eat another human being, and this is why I've recommended mercy killing as an alternative. If the people resort to cannibalism, Satan and his demons will cause mass suicides by causing guilt and shame in the minds of the people who did it.

In Japan there are 125 million people, and they don't have any fuel within their nation, therefore they will not have enough fuel to grow crops. Their farmland cannot be increased because of the mountains there. If the Antichrist blockades Japan, the people will starve, and they will resort to cannibalism. The people will commit suicide when the guilt sets in. The Japanese people believe in Hara Kari because they think it is more honorable to die this way, rather than to resort to cannibalism, or to other forms of death. Therefore Satan and his 50 million devils will concentrate their efforts on Japan, in order to cause millions of suicides. This is why I've explained the theology of suicide in this chapter. I may have been insensitive to Japan here, but I did it because of the danger that the Japanese people will face during World War III.

Africa and India will have trouble growing crops when their fuel supply is cut off. Besides the trouble with farming, there will be no way to transport the food to markets. This will happen in Asia, South America, the Philippines, and several other nations. This is why I've written a plan to convert the vehicles to natural gas, or to other types of fuel before World War III. This plan is written in The USA and World War III chapter. If the nations run out of fuel, they will run out of food, and then cannibalism will spread. Then Satan will cause suicides. He does this by causing guilt and shame in the minds of the victims, and then he uses this to cause suicides. Anyone who commits suicide will go to the Lake of Fire.

The mercy killing must be done to prevent cannibalism. It has to be done without any effort or intent on the part of the victims. Therefore the person who does the mercy killing must do it by himself. The victims can't participate. This could be done by having 50 people gather in an underground

47

tunnel, where they could be shot in the head. It must be done so the people who are waiting can't see or hear what is happening. Their souls will be preserved blameless for Christ in this manner, if they do not kill themselves. It will be very important for these people to accept Christ, and go to church at least three months before the mercy killing is done. This time period will ensure that the people receive the gift of faith from Christ, before they die. The people should really go to church as soon as the Antichrist declares the famine.

It will be one or two years after the blockade, when the people in England run out of food. They have their own fuel supply, and they can increase their farmland by 100%. I will recommend that Japan, England, Africa, India, and the Philippines should build thousands of vertical grain silos to store food for their people. These are round cement structures, which are 150 feet high. They can have roofs, which overlap the outside walls, so the rain doesn't get into the grain. These structures will take less space than buildings, and therefore you can build more of them to store food in.

All nations that do not want their people to resort to cannibalism during World War III will have to build hundreds of thousands of grain silos and food warehouses. They must do this now, and then they can spend the next four or five years storing food in them. I think cannibalism is a sin; and Satan caused sin and death to come into the world, when he deceived Adam and Eve in the Garden of Eden. This is written in Genesis 3:1-7. Evil, sin and death came through the tree of knowledge of good and evil in Genesis 2:16,17. Satan and his devils make people believe that sin is something to be desired because it is associated with pleasure. Therefore sin is a weapon, which Satan uses against people. This is written in Ephesians 2:2,3. The way to defeat sin is to accept Christ, devote your life to him, and go to church every week. This is written in Ephesians 2:4-8.

FALSE RELIGION: EXODUS 20:1-6

By far the greatest weapon that Satan has is false religion. Not only will the people in false religion go to the Lake of Fire if they don't convert to Christianity, but they will also try to kill me, when I try to save them. In Revelation 20:14, Psalm 19:4, Psalm 21:9, and Matthew 25:41 the Lake of Fire is the sun. The chief priests, scribes, and Pharisees crucified Christ because he told them they were in false religion. This is written in John 8:24-29. Therefore when the people in false religion today try to kill me, they will prove that Christianity is the only true religion because I will follow the example of the Lord Jesus Christ. This is written in:

John 14:6: "Jesus saith unto him, I am the way, the truth, and the life: no man cometh unto the Father, but by me."

The phrase, "no man cometh unto the Father, but by me," means that Christ is the only Saviour of mankind. No one will go to the Almighty Father in heaven, unless they believe in the Lord Jesus Christ. This means that while other religions seek to worship God, they are not doing it the correct way. This is written in John 4:23-26. Therefore the people in these religions must convert to Christianity now:

Animist	Islam	Taoism	
Buddhism	Communism	Hinduism	Judaism

If anyone in these religions is killed during World War III, their soul will burn forever in the Lake of Fire, which is the sun. I know that I will not be very well liked by these people, but I am telling you the truth, so you will convert to Christianity and be saved. All you have to do is to go to a church of Christ in your nation, and get baptized and then receive Communion in church every week. You may have to go to a class and study the sacraments first, but you will be saved because you believe in Christ. There are churches of Christ in almost every nation of the world, and you can find their addresses in the Yellow pages of the Telephone book. Then you should call them, and get the times of church services, and then choose the one which you like the best. Then your soul will go to heaven, and Christ will save you. On page 62, 68, and 69 of *Halley's Bible Handbook* there are stories, which are like the Creation story in Genesis.[2] On page 69 of *Halley's Bible Handbook*, the other stories of creation were found in Persia, Hindu, Greek, Chinese, Mongolians, and other nations. The original Creation Story was passed on to other people, and to other cultures.[3]

The Babylonian and Assyrian Creation stories are Polytheistic, but they seem to be copies from the Bible story. Polytheism is a belief in more than one God; and it goes directly to idolatry. Satan invented idolatry, and he has caused mankind a lot of grief because of it. This is why the first two Commandments in the Bible are written to stop idolatry. In Genesis 6:5 the wickedness of man was great in the earth, and every imagination of his heart was only evil continually. This happened because there were 50 million devils with Satan, and there were less than one million people. Therefore the devils created thoughts of evil in the minds of men continually. In Genesis 6:11-13 God saw that the earth was corrupt, and he told Noah to build the Ark. Therefore it was idolatry that caused the flood.

In Leviticus 19:4 the Lord told Israel not to serve idols. In Deuteronomy 7:1 the Lord delivered seven nations into the hand of Israel to be destroyed.

The reason for this was to destroy the idolatry, which the people in these nations practiced. This is written in Deuteronomy 7:2-5. In Deuteronomy 7:6 the people of Israel were saved to be a holy people unto the Lord. In Deuteronomy 7:8,9 the Lord loves the people who love him.

Satan eventually caused the people of Israel to fall into idolatry. In II Chronicles 33:6 the people of Israel sacrificed their children in the fire. This is also written in Jeremiah 7:31, and in Jeremiah 32:35. In this verse Molech was the god of fire, and he was a false god.

The people in the world will see one of Satan's patented moves, when the Antichrist causes 24 nations, and 800 million people in Europe to worship himself, Satan, and Germany. When this happens, there will be a shift of 22 Christian nations over to the false religion category, which belongs to Satan. Now you will see proof of Satan's rule over idolatry, when the Antichrist appears, and takes control of Europe. The 120 Christian nations in the world will be reduced to 98; and the 74 nations, which have false religions, will be increased to 96. After the Antichrist takes Europe, there will be 4.3 billion people in false religions in the world. There will be 1.7 billion people who are Christians.

This will be proof of Satan's corrupting influence on mankind, and proof of his ultimate goal of destroying all human life on the earth. He will do this to nullify the judgment of Christ, and this is why devils are called the spirits of antichrist in I John 4:3. The Bible has the only test which works against demons, and this is written in I John 4:2. In I John 2:18 when you see many antichrists in Europe, you will know that the end of the world is near.

In I John 3:8 Christ came into the world to destroy the works of the devil. This also means to stop false religion. In I John 5:13 everyone who believes in the name of the Son of God has eternal life. In I John 5:20 the Lord Jesus Christ is the Son of God, and he is the true God, and eternal life for mankind. In John 3:16, and in John 12:50 the Commandment of God is everlasting life.

The greatest weapon that Satan has is false religion. Jesus warned us about this in Matthew 24:4,5, Matthew 24:11, Matthew 24:23-26, and in Matthew 24:27. In John 14:6 Jesus said that no one could go into the kingdom of heaven unless they accept Christ first. The phrase, "I am the way, the truth, and the life," means the way to the Almighty Father in heaven, the truth about the creation of mankind and salvation, and the everlasting life that only Christ can give.

There will be a famine caused by the fuel crisis and the Antichrist. It will not be caused by a drought; therefore your nation can have plenty of rain and abundant crops all the way through it, if your people go to the churches of Christ. This is a blessing written in Leviticus 26:3-6, Deuteronomy 28:12, and Deuteronomy 28:8. Your nations must also store dry foods to prepare for the nuclear war.

In Leviticus 26:6 you can have peace in your nation during World War III, if your people worship Christ in church. This will be true except for Europe, the Middle East, NE China, Korea, and South Africa.

One of the worst weaknesses of the human race is to kill a man who came to save the lives and the souls of your people, just because he says his religion will lead you to the true God and eternal life in I John 5:20. These nations must convert to Christianity:

Islam Nations

Afghanistan	Comoros	Iraq	Morocco	Somalia
Albania	Djibouti	Jordan	Niger	USSR
Algeria	Egypt	Kuwait	Nigeria	Sudan
Bahrain	Gambia	Libya	Oman	Syria
Bangladesh	Guinea	Malaysia	Pakistan	Tanzania
Brunei	Guinea Bissau	Maldives	Qatar	Tunisia
Burkina Faso	India	Mali	Saudi Arabia	Turkey
Chad	Indonesia	Mauritania	Senegal	UAE Arab
Singapore	Yemen			

Buddhist Nations

Bhutan	China	Mongolia	Taiwan
Burma	Japan	South Korea	Thailand
Cambodia	Laos	Sri Lanka	Vietnam

Animist Nations

Benin	Congo	Mozambique	Togo	Zimbabwe
Botswana	Liberia	Sierra Leone	Zambia	

Communist Nations

USSR   Eastern Europe

Hindu Nations

Fiji	Guyana	India	Nepal
Mauritius			

GARY L. WILSON

Moslem Nations

Iran   USSR

Taoist Nations

China

In Matthew 24:14 the gospel of Christ will be preached to all nations, before the end of the world comes. This is also written in Revelation 14:6, and the angel flying through the midst of heaven has the gospel to preach to all nations, languages, and people. In Revelation 10:1,2 the Archangel Gabriel has the Little Book in his hand; and in Revelation 10:11 I am sent to prophesy before many people, nations, languages, and kings.

The book of Revelation was written to save the people in the world from Satan and World War III. The one key to unlock all of the prophecies is the Little Book in Revelation 10:1-11. The seven seals in Revelation 5:1 relate to the seven thunders in Revelation 10:4. This is verified in Revelation 6:1, where the noise of thunder was heard when the Lamb opened the first seal.

To write the Little Book, I suffered because of Satan and his demons for 20 years. This is the key because I followed the Lamb of God example of Jesus Christ. Jesus died to save mankind, and this is why he was the only one found worthy to open the seals in Revelation 5:5. In Revelation 5:9 Christ is the Lamb who was slain, or crucified, to redeem us to God, out of every people, nation, and language on the earth. This is verified in Revelation 14:6, Revelation 10:11, and in Revelation 5:9; where the angel, the prophet, and the Lord Jesus Christ all work to save all of the people in every nation of the world.

In Zechariah 14:16-19 the nations of the world will be required to go to Israel every year to worship the King, the Lord of hosts, and to keep the feast of tabernacles. In Zechariah 14:17 the nations which will not go to Jerusalem to worship the King, the Lord of hosts, will receive no rain for their crops. Then of the nations that have no rain, and still do not come to worship the Lord at Jerusalem, they will get the plague in Zechariah 14:12, and Zechariah 14:15. This is written in Zechariah 14:18,19. This plague is nuclear annihilation to everyone who will not obey the commandment in Zechariah 14:16-19.

What this means is that it will be a crime for the nations to refuse to worship Christ in Zion, after the rapture of the church. This crime will be punishable with starvation because of no rain; and then when this doesn't work, those nations will be destroyed in the nuclear plague described in

52

Zechariah 14:12. I wrote earlier that the United Nations Organization could make it an international crime for anyone to refuse to convert to Christianity, and Zechariah 14:16-19 explains why.

The people of all nations will come to worship Christ the King on the highway, the way of holiness, in Isaiah 35:8-10. In Zechariah 14:20 upon the bells of the horses will be:

HOLINESS UNTO THE LORD

The reward for worshipping the Lord Jesus Christ is everlasting life to all of the people of all nations, when they accept Christ and go to church every week. The people who refuse to convert to Christianity, and to worship Christ in church, will not only get the nuclear plague, and no rain for their crops; but they will also be condemned to the Lake of Fire at the judgment. In Revelation 20:14, Psalm 19:4, and Matthew 25:41 the Lake of Fire is the sun.

THE COMMON MARKET: REVELATION 17:12-17

The EEC or the Common Market is described in the Bible, and it is associated with the appearance of the Antichrist, and the beginning of World War III. The verses are Revelation 17:12,13, and in Revelation 17:16,17. In Daniel 7:7,8, Daniel 7:20, and in Daniel 7:24 the ten horns represent the ten kings of the Common Market in Europe. This is actually stated in Daniel 7:24, and in Revelation 17:12. The ten Common Market leaders in Europe will give their power and strength to the Antichrist in Revelation 17:13, and in Revelation 17:17.

The importance of the Common Market can be seen in the three verses in Daniel 7:7,8, Daniel 7:20, and in Daniel 7:24. In each verse the ten horns appear first, and the one horn comes next. This means that the ten Common Market leaders will appear just before the Antichrist comes into power in Germany. Their relationship to the Antichrist can be explained best by looking at Revelation 13:1.

In Revelation 13:1,2 the beast is the kingdom of the Antichrist, and it has seven heads. In Revelation 17:9 the seven heads are the seven mountains of Rome. In Revelation 17:18 the woman is the city of Rome. This means that Rome will be associated with the kingdom of the Antichrist, which is the beast in Revelation 13:1. Everything that will happen to the kingdom of the Antichrist is described with the symbols in Revelation 13:1,2, or it is written later in the same chapter. This is how the symbolism works in this prophecy. In Revelation 17:16 the ten Common Market kings will tell the Antichrist to destroy Rome, which is the whore in the same verse.

The ten horns in Revelation 13:1 represent the ten Common Market kings or leaders. The ten crowns in the same verse relate to Revelation 17:12,13, where the ten Common Market leaders will meet with the Antichrist, and will give their power and strength to him. This seems to be the meeting that unifies the Common Market, and it is also described in Revelation 17:16,17. It looks like the ten Common Market leaders will give their kingdoms to the Antichrist because they want him to use their armies to destroy Rome. This explains the 200 million soldiers in Revelation 9:16. The Antichrist can get 60 million from Russia, and 40 million from Eastern Europe, while 40 million soldiers will come from the Common Market nations of Western Europe. This is the meaning of the phrase:

Revelation 17:17: "For God hath put in their hearts to fulfill his will, and to agree, and give their kingdom unto the beast, until the words of God shall be fulfilled."

I think that the people in Europe will follow the Antichrist like they did with Hitler. They will lust after power and money like they did in World War II, and then the Lord God will cause the ten Common Market leaders to give their kingdoms to the Antichrist. He will do this to condemn them, when they accept the mark of the beast. This will happen because they lusted after the power and money.

The reason why the Common Market leaders will want to destroy Rome is that the Pope and the Vatican will object to the methods used by the Antichrist to take Europe with his famine. The Antichrist will make a deal with the ten Common Market leaders before he declares the famine; and this is why they will be angry at the Vatican, instead of the Antichrist. In Revelation 17:14 the ten Common Market leaders will be antichrists because they will make war with the Lamb of God, who is the Lord Jesus Christ. These ten kings will want to destroy Rome in Revelation 17:16, and in Revelation 17:17 they will give their kingdoms to the Antichrist. This also means they will be antichrists themselves. Therefore the Pope and the Vatican should not object to the Antichrist, but they should leave Italy. When they do object however, they must move during the time between their objection, and the Common Market meeting in Revelation 17:12,13. This is written in Revelation 18:4. The Christian people as a group should move away from Italy, France, Albania, and Greece before the Antichrist gains power.

The danger to Western Europe is that the ten Common Market leaders will be antichrists themselves. This means that no one will fight the 100 million soldiers from Russia and Eastern Europe. These soldiers will enforce the famine of the Antichrist in Western Europe, and they will take the entire continent within six months. This will be the first indication of World War III, and the Antichrist will do exactly what Hitler did in World War II. He will take Western Europe without even fighting. The armies of the nations there will not resist or fight against the army of the Antichrist because they will give their kingdoms to him.

There is a way to determine when these events will take place. I did some research on the EEC, which is the Common Market in Brussels, Belgium. In 1987 the Single European Act, an amendment to the Treaty of Rome, came into effect.[4] This act provided for the creation of a single European Market by 1992. In April 1989 a Committee headed by Jacques Delors, the President of the European Commission, proposed a three-stage plan to achieve monetary and economic union.

The three-stage plan by Jacques Delors in 1989, and the Maastricht Treaty in 1991 both indicate that the Common Market unification will happen soon. In Daniel 7:7,8, Daniel 7:20, and in Daniel 7:24 the Antichrist will appear after the ten kings, which are the leaders of the Common Market. When you see the ten kings arise in Daniel 7:24, this signifies the completion of the Common Market legislative plans which I've just described. In the same verse, the Antichrist will appear after this happens.

There is another factor, which will determine the time when the Antichrist will appear in Germany. It is the wound in Revelation 13:3, and in Revelation 13:14. In Revelation 13:14 the wound was caused by a sword, which is the symbol for war. The beast in Revelation 13:1 is Germany, and World War II caused the wound, which was the Berlin Wall and the dividing line between East and West Germany. Now the dividing line is gone, but East Germany is not fully recovered from its economic failure yet. I said earlier that the wound was healed, but I was a bit premature. The healing process written in Revelation 13:3 will tell us when the Antichrist will appear. When East Germany is completely recovered from its economic disaster of 1989 and 1990, the Antichrist will appear, and he will bring East Germany into the Common Market. This is one reason why he will be so popular with the people in Europe. This is written in Daniel 11:21, and in Revelation 13:4.

West Germany is already in the Common Market, and there could be ten nations in it, but the Antichrist will bring East Germany into it as well, and this will make Europe whole again. This could be why he will appear after the ten kings in Daniel 7:24. He is called a king like the ten Common Market leaders in this verse. This is why he will be the Renaissance man there. His popularity is described in Daniel 11:21 in the phrase, "but he shall come in peaceably, and obtain the kingdom by flatteries." In Revelation 13:8 the people will worship the Antichrist.

The World Oil Supply: Daniel 11:23-25

There are more verses about the Antichrist in the book of Daniel. In Daniel 11:22 the arms of a flood are the 80 million soldiers of Russia and Germany, which will take Western Europe and enforce the famine for the Antichrist. The Russian army will be perfect for this job, and they will sovietize Western Europe. This means to force into conformity with Soviet governmental policies. Since there is only one verse in Daniel 11:22 which describes the takeover of Western Europe, it will probably happen within six months.

In Daniel 11:23 the Antichrist will go to Saudi Arabia, and will make a deal with the oil nations under peaceful negotiations, like he will do in his first year in Europe. In Daniel 11:23 the Antichrist will then work deceitfully against Saudi Arabia and the oil nations. This verse was difficult to understand, until I reversed the two phrases. First the Antichrist will become strong with a small people, which is a description of the oil nations. They have billions of dollars, but very few people. Then the Antichrist will work deceitfully against them. In Daniel 11:24 is a description of the peaceful negotiations. The Antichrist will bring soldiers into the fattest places of the province, which are the cities in Kuwait, Saudi Arabia, UAE, Oman, and Yemen. The verse is phrased as if he will bring his army into the Middle East, and into the oil nations. This will happen just the same way as when Iraq invaded Kuwait in 1991. Their army came right into Kuwait, into the cities, and no one even fought against them at first.

Then next in Daniel 11:24 the Antichrist will do that which his fathers have not done; he will take the world oil supply. The phrase, "his fathers," and, "his fathers' fathers," means the predecessors of the Antichrist. This would be Adolf Hitler in World War II, and the German dictator in World War I. Hitler made negotiations with Saudi Arabia in World War II, but there wasn't enough oil there at that time to cause him to take control of it.

In Daniel 11:24 the Antichrist will scatter among his soldiers the prey, which will be the women of Saudi Arabia, UAE, Oman, Yemen, and Kuwait. The spoil will be the new cars and houses. The riches will be the gold, silver, jewelry, and money from the oil nations. The Antichrist will use devices or military strategy against the strongholds, which will be the people in bunkers, and fallout shelters who will not give up or surrender. In Daniel 11:25 the phrase, "for they shall forecast devices against him," could mean that the soldiers of the Antichrist will use chemical warfare against the oil nations. This is described in Matthew 24:12, where iniquity shall abound because of the famine in Europe, and the exploits of the army of the Antichrist in the Middle East. In Daniel 11:24 the phrase, "even for a time," means one year.

In Daniel 11:25 the king of the south would be the king of Saudi Arabia, or the United Arab Emirates. They will hire a very great and mighty army to fight against the Antichrist. The army of the king of the south will not stand, however. In Daniel 11:26 one of the king's friends, officers, or family will kill him. Then his army shall overflow against the army of the Antichrist, and many of them will be killed. This could mean three million soldiers, who advance on the army of the Antichrist because of bad military strategy.

In Daniel 11:28 the Antichrist will return to Germany with great riches from the oil nations. His heart shall be against the holy covenant because of Satan. In Daniel 11:29 he shall return, and come toward the south. In Daniel 11:30 the ships of Chittim shall come against him. These are the ships from Italy, and they will attack the army of the Antichrist in Israel because he destroyed Rome with nuclear missiles.

These ships will be battleships and aircraft carriers. The land of Chittim and the ships are described in Numbers 24:24, Isaiah 23:1, and Ezekiel 27:6. The Antichrist will be grieved in Daniel 11:30. This is what will cause him to have intelligence with the terrorist nations, which are the enemies of Israel, and then he will use chemical warfare against Jerusalem. This is why the people of Israel should flee in Matthew 24:16-21.

In Daniel 11:31 the army of the Antichrist will take the daily sacrifice, or they will occupy the churches and synagogues in Jerusalem. In Daniel 12:11 they will be in Jerusalem for 1290 days. Then they will use the chemical warfare in the holy city. In Revelation 11:2 the army of the Antichrist will be in Jerusalem for 42 months, and they will place the abomination of desolation in Daniel 11:31, which means to make the city desolate with chemical warfare. Then the two prophets in Revelation 11:3-6 will be translated from heaven to fight against them.

In Daniel 11:36 the Antichrist will do according to his will. In Daniel 11:36,37 the Antichrist will speak blasphemy against God. This is why the beast has the name of blasphemy on its heads in Revelation 13:1. This is also written in Revelation 13:5. In Daniel 11:38 the Antichrist will worship the god of forces, who is Satan. This is why the Antichrist is said to be a, "king of fierce countenance, and understanding dark sentences," in Daniel 8:23. In Revelation 6:8 the Antichrist is called Death, and Hell follows with him because he will take human souls for Satan. The phrase, "fierce countenance," in Daniel 8:23 refers to the terrifying look of the Antichrist in Revelation 6:8, where he is called Death with a capital D. In Revelation 13:4 he will cause the people in Europe to worship Satan.

In Daniel 8:24 the phrase, "and his power shall be mighty, but not by his own power," means that the Russian army will take Western Europe for the Antichrist. This is the meaning of the bear with three ribs in Daniel 7:5. In

Daniel 8:24 the Antichrist will destroy the mighty and the holy people. This is probably the people or the saints in Europe, written in Revelation 13:7. This will not take very long because of the size of his army, and because the ten Common Market leaders will give their kingdoms to him.

In Daniel 11:40 the Antichrist will fight against the king of the south. This is probably the new king of Saudi Arabia, who will be elected after the first one was killed in Daniel 11:26. The Antichrist will have many ships to use in this battle, which means he will probably build a navy base in South Africa. He will do this because the ships of Chittim fought against him in Daniel 11:30. These are the ships of Italy, and the Antichrist will be grieved because of them. Then in Daniel 11:40 the army of the Antichrist will invade Saudi Arabia, and the oil nations. In Daniel 11:41 he will invade Israel, and will overthrow many countries. In Daniel 11:42 he will invade Egypt, and in Daniel 11:43 he will have power over the gold and silver in Egypt.

World War III will start soon, and the time span of the war will be ten to eleven years. The first two years of the Antichrist will be with peace in Europe. This is written in Daniel 11:21, Daniel 8:25, and in Revelation 6:2. In his third year he will use the Russian army to enforce his famine in Europe. This is the meaning of the great sword in Revelation 6:4, and the pair of balances in Revelation 6:5,6. During the second year of World War III he will go south to Saudi Arabia, and he will make a deal with the oil nations. This is written in Daniel 11:23. Then he will take the world oil supply, and in Daniel 11:24,25 he will fight against the oil nations with his army. In Daniel 11:24 the phrase, "even for a time," means one year. All of these events will happen within three years after the Antichrist comes into power in Germany, and in the Common Market. Therefore he will have control of the world oil supply by the third year of World War III.

The Antichrist will do exploits against Israel from the third to the sixth year of World War III. His army will occupy the land of Israel for seven years. In the seventh year of World War III the two prophets in Revelation 11:3-5 will fight against his army in Jerusalem. The battle of Armageddon will happen in the last year of World War III, and in it Christ will destroy the army of the Antichrist with the two edged sword which proceeds out of his mouth in Revelation 19:19-21. This means that the Second Coming of Christ will happen at the end of World War III.

EVIL: GENESIS 3:1-7

Evil is one of Satan's weapons, and it is a curse, which he caused in the Garden of Eden. This is written in Genesis 3:1-7. It is the fundamental principle in all of his other weapons. This means that Satan's weapons are evil, and they are in most cases the opposite of the goodness and blessings of Christ. It is also true that Satan can convince people to follow good or righteous causes, and deceive them by doing it. He did this in 1990 when the Berlin Wall was taken down in Germany. The opposites of his weapons with respect to the blessings of Christ can be described as:

1. Condemnation — Opposite of — Salvation
2. Lies — Opposite of — Truth
3. Murder — Opposite of — Life
4. Commandments of Men — Opposite of — Commandments of God
5. Pride — Opposite of — Humility
6. Blasphemy — Opposite of — Praise and Holiness
7. False Religion — Opposite of — True Religion in Christ

It is very important to know this because Christ has overcome Satan. The Bible is the key to this victory in Christ because it tells us how to overcome Satan's weapons.

When you are confronted with evil, you know that you must survive it to live. This is what I did from 1979 to 1985. I knew that the hazing was evil, and that the profanity came with it; and I knew that I had to survive. I didn't retaliate against anyone, and I didn't kill anyone. The people in the nations, which are not in Europe, will have to adopt this same attitude during World War III. They cannot retaliate against the Antichrist, or it will cause a nuclear war. The principle for this is written in Matthew 5:39.

CHAPTER III

Nuclear War

The people in the USA believe that America is the defender of democracy and freedom in the world. Now because of this, the USA could cause a global nuclear war during World War III because the Pentagon wants to protect the nations in Western Europe. This type of thinking must be changed, and it must be changed very quickly. The offensive military power, and $320 billion dollars per year must be taken away from the Pentagon now, or they will use fear to start a nuclear war, when the Antichrist appears in Germany.

I was born on May 24, 1944, one year before the atomic bomb was used in 1945. I saw the vision in Genesis 28:12 in 1951, one year before the hydrogen bomb was developed in 1952. My purpose here is to stop nuclear war. The nuclear attack on Rome, Italy cannot be stopped because of the judgment in Revelation 17:1-6. There is another nuclear war described in Matthew 24:22, which will occur before Christ returns. This war can be avoided by changing the military system of the USA. This chapter should not be edited because it has my plan to do this.

Now before you read about the nuclear wars, which will happen in the next 20 years, you should understand why nuclear missiles are so difficult to remove from existence, once they are built. I will explain this here. In the next quote, Jerome B. Wiesner, President Emeritus of MIT, and Science Advisor to President Kennedy, gives a description of Robert S. McNamara's book, *Blundering Into Disaster*:

"This little volume could mark the turning point in man's crazy dash to oblivion."[5]

This book was published in 1986, and now the nuclear arsenals of the USA, Russia, and China are still very well stocked with nuclear missiles. All of the military, scientific, and political books in the world aren't going to prevent nuclear war, if you don't know the theology of how evil came into the world. This is illustrated in the following quote by George Kennan:

"I see this competitive buildup of armaments conceived initially as a means to an end, but soon becoming the end itself. I see it taking possession of men's imagination and behavior, becoming a force in its own right, detaching itself from the political differences that initially inspired it, and then leading both sides, invariably and inexorably to the nuclear war they no longer know how to avoid."[6]

Now the point of this is that evil came into the world through the tree of knowledge of good and evil in Genesis 2:9. This is why the words good and evil are included in the name of the tree; and the phrase, "knowledge of good and evil," means that once a person knows what evil is, it becomes a part of them. Therefore Adam and Eve came to know evil when they ate from the tree, and this is why they were not allowed to eat from the tree of life in Genesis 3:22. They could not be allowed to live forever because they were corrupted by evil. This is why people today must have their sins forgiven by Christ, before they can go into heaven. They must first remove the evil from themselves; and this principle is also the way to remove the threat of nuclear war. You must remove the evil by dismantling the nuclear missiles.

The reason for the Garden of Eden itself was to establish the judgment of Satan and his devils, when they were cast out of heaven. This is written in John 16:11, and in Revelation 12:7-9. You see, angels are a higher form of life than mankind, and Satan was given an opportunity to choose between good and evil in the Garden of Eden. Satan chose evil, he caused the mortality or the first death of mankind, and he inherited the second death in Revelation 20:14. It is called the Lake of Fire, and in Psalm 19:4, Psalm 21:9, and Matthew 25:41 the Lake of Fire is the sun. Therefore Satan and his devils will burn there forever because he chose evil in the Garden of Eden. This is written in Revelation 20:10.

With respect to nuclear arms the good and evil concept is apparent from this quote from the book, *The Nuclear Reader*, by Charles Kegley, and Eugene R. Wittkopf:

"On the one hand, nuclear weapons threaten the destruction of human civilization as we know it; on the other, they are the very instruments relied on to avert the threatened disaster."[7]

This sounds very much like an addiction to drugs, which is also evil; and it is a perfect description of the good and evil package, which comes together with nuclear missiles. One side won't dismantle its missiles because it feels threatened by the nuclear weapons of the other side. What is even more frightening than this is that some scientists and military generals actually believe that nuclear missiles will prevent nuclear war. Satan brought evil into the world through the tree of knowledge of good and evil, and the nuclear scientists improve the evil by their research. This is what knowledge is.

This is what is meant by the phrase, "the tree of knowledge of good and evil," described in Genesis 2:17, and in Genesis 3:22. What happens is that the people in the Pentagon and the nuclear weapons industry believe it is the evil in the nuclear missiles that will save them; and this is why they believe that nuclear weapons will deter or prevent nuclear war. The more evil a drug or a nuclear weapon is, the more difficult it is to overcome the addiction to it. This is why you must understand the theology of good and evil, before you can prevent nuclear war.

With deterrence the principle is: nuclear missiles give each side deterrence because they are evil. Since no one really wants this evil to happen, this is what causes the deterrence. Mankind has already proven to itself that nuclear war is unacceptable because no nation has used nuclear missiles against another nation since 1945. Therefore the correct way to save the human race is to rely on the concept of good instead of evil. The world has six years until the Antichrist will appear in Europe, and during this time it will be very important to dismantle as many nuclear weapons as possible in the USA, Russia, China, England, and other nations. The urgency of this can be seen in Revelation 18:1-19, where the Antichrist will destroy Rome with nuclear missiles in the first year of World War III.

The verses describe a city, which is desolate and uninhabitable; and in Revelation 18:8 the plague of nuclear war will happen to Rome in one day. In Revelation 18:10, and Revelation 18:19 Rome will be made desolate in one hour. This is possible only with nuclear missiles. In Revelation 17:12-18 the ten Common Market leaders and the Antichrist will destroy Rome, when the Vatican complains about the army of the Antichrist. The people in the USA and the world must focus their efforts to change the attitude of their military leaders. To do this, they can use the entire chapter about nuclear war in this book. The people in America must change the attitude of the Pentagon towards good and evil. This can be seen by the question: Will the Pentagon try to save America by using evil against the Antichrist? On the next pages I will describe the nuclear wars, and how to reduce their effectiveness to reduce the number of people that will be killed in them.

NUCLEAR DETERRENCE

If the nuclear scientists are improving the evil that comes into the world through the tree of knowledge of good and evil by improving the evil destructive power of the nuclear missiles that they make, then you can say that nuclear deterrence is a doctrine of devils. The aim of nuclear deterrence is to keep the world armed to the teeth with nuclear weapons, which Satan can then use to cause a global nuclear war during World War III. The war will start within six years, and I will describe how Satan will cause the nuclear war later.

For now I will make a comparison. It is true that Satan hopes to avoid the judgment by destroying the entire human race. Of course the best way to do it is by using a global nuclear war. Here is the comparison:

1. Satan thinks he can nullify the judgment by killing everyone on earth. If there is no one left alive on the earth, then Satan thinks that Christ will not return for the judgment. Therefore Satan believes that the more evil he is, the better chance he will have to survive.

2. The concept of nuclear deterrence says that the more nuclear weapons you have, and the more evil you appear to be, then the less chance your enemy will start a nuclear or a conventional war against you. Therefore nuclear deterrence says that the more evil your nuclear weapons are, the better chance you will have to survive.

You can see that these two ideas are almost alike; because they both say that evil is the best way to survive, rather than good. Satan caused evil to come into the world by convincing Adam and Eve to eat the fruit of the tree of knowledge of good and evil in Genesis 2:17, and Genesis 3:1-7. Since they disobeyed the Lord God, sin, death, and evil came into the world.

Then Satan and his angels acquired the name devils because the name breaks down this way: d + evil = devil. Therefore devils are the evil angels. In Revelation 12:9 Satan is called the old serpent and the Devil because he made evil come into the world in the Garden of Eden. In Revelation 12:17 Satan has continued to make war against mankind throughout his existence on the earth. When you know that he wants to destroy mankind, and you know that he will use a global nuclear war to do it, then you must realize how urgent it is to dismantle as many nuclear weapons as possible before the Antichrist appears in Europe.

The Antichrist is called the man of sin and the son of perdition in II Thessalonians 2:3. In John 17:12 Jesus called him the son of perdition. The Antichrist will be the most evil man to live on the earth since the beginning of time, and Satan will try to use him to cause a global nuclear war. This is one of the methods that Satan will use to destroy mankind, and another one will follow later.

The phrase, "doctrines of devils," is used in this verse:

I Timothy 4:1: "Now the Spirit speaketh expressly, that in the latter times some shall depart from the faith, giving heed to seducing spirits, and doctrines of devils;"

You can see that this refers to the last days because it says, "in the latter times." When you combine nuclear weapons with doctrines of devils you get perilous and evil times. This is described in II Timothy 3:1, Ecclesiastes 9:12, and in Amos 5:13. Now look at this verse:

Matthew 24:12: "And because iniquity shall abound, the love of many shall wax cold."

This means that wars and terrorism will occur during World War III. Then in Matthew 24:22 Christ will have to shorten the days of World War III in order to save mankind from being destroyed in a global nuclear war.

Now the second method which Satan will use to cause a global nuclear war is described on pages 78 and 79 of the book, *The Spread of Nuclear Weapons: A Debate*. All three of the following quotes demonstrate the ability of devils to cause people to use bad judgment and to make mistakes during wars or confrontations between nuclear nations. They can do this by creating thoughts in the human brain. In Matthew 27:29, Mark 15:17, and in John 19:2 Christ wore the crown of thorns at his crucifixion to show mankind that devils can create thoughts in the human brain. This is how they cause the infirmities described in Mark 9:18, and Mark 9:22. "He foameth," means excess salivation in the mouth. "And pineth away" means depression. "It hath cast him into the fire, and into the waters, to destroy him," means clumsiness, which was used to destroy the young man. You can read more about the infirmities in the 7 chapters about devils in my book, *Evil Spirits*.

The quotes from pages 78 and 79 are:

"At the start of the 1962 Cuban Missile Crisis, the Strategic Air Command secretly deployed nuclear warheads on 9 of the 10 test Intercontinental Ballistic Missiles in place at Vandenberg Air Force Base and then launched the tenth missile, on a prescheduled Intercontinental Ballistic Missile test, over the Pacific. No one within the responsible organizations thought through the risks that Soviet intelligence might learn of the nuclear weapons deployment and the alert at Vandenberg and then, in the tension of the crisis, might misinterpret a missile launch from that base."[8]

In this case devils could have caused stubbornness in the minds of the senior officers at Vandenberg Air Force Base, which caused them to launch the test Intercontinental Ballistic Missile in spite of the Cuban Missile Crisis. Here is the next quote from page 79:

"A second safety problem occurred at Malmstrom Air Force Base in Montana at the height of the Cuban Missile Crisis, when officers jerry-rigged their minuteman missiles to give themselves the independent ability to launch missiles immediately. This was a serious violation of the minuteman safety rules, but when an investigation took place after the crisis, the evidence was altered to prevent higher authorities from learning that officers had given themselves the ability to launch unauthorized missile attacks."[9]

In this case the devils caused either panic, fear, carelessness, or hatred toward the Soviet Union and Cuba during the crisis. Now you should realize that devils have a regular menu of human emotions to choose from during a nuclear crisis. They can cause stubbornness, hatred, fear, panic, and several other reactions at critical times. This is why the world has to dismantle the nuclear missiles now. Here is another quote from page 79:

"A third incident occurred on October 28, when the North American Air Defense Command (NORAD) was informed that a nuclear-armed missile had been launched from Cuba and was about to hit Tampa, Florida. Only after the expected detonation failed to occur was it discovered that a radar operator had inserted a test tape simulating an attack from Cuba into the system, confusing control room officers who thought the simulation was a real attack."[10]You can see here that devils can also cause people to make mistakes. In I John 4:6 they are called the spirits of error, since they can cause people to commit errors by creating thoughts in the human brain. Actually they can cause people to be incompetent, which is true in all three of these cases. The only time this will happen is during a nuclear missile crisis. It will happen during World War III because the entire 11 years of the war will actually be a nuclear crisis. I have found that the Pentagon will become involved in 9 nuclear wars against the Antichrist if they have the capability to launch nuclear missiles during World War III.

With the knowledge that nuclear deterrence is a doctrine of devils because it increases the number of nuclear missiles on the earth, thus giving Satan a better chance to destroy mankind in a global nuclear war; and with the knowledge that devils can cause the nuclear war by creating thoughts in the human brain, it is time for America and for all nations to dismantle 99% of the nuclear weapons on the earth before the Antichrist appears in Europe, and before World War III begins.

MILITARY STRATEGY IN EUROPE

The relationship of the President to the Pentagon will be more dangerous than his relationship to the Antichrist during World War III. If he gives the sword of war to the US military, which means to begin fighting, he will never be able to take it back, or to stop them. The Pentagon fights in wars to win them, and this is why they will escalate the war if they begin fighting. If they have to fight against 100 million soldiers, and if their fuel supply is cut off, then they will have to use nuclear missiles to win. All of the nuclear weapons in the USA were made to be used in World War III, and this is what the Pentagon will do in order to win.

The President should never commit American troops to fight in World War III, no matter what the reason. If he does, then he will not be able to recall them without losing favor; and once the Pentagon has the sword of war, their propaganda will prevent the President from stopping them. They will use the fear of the Antichrist, and the fear of Russia's nuclear missiles to instigate the war in the minds of the American people; and then they will escalate the war intentionally, so they can use nuclear weapons to win it. Thus the intentional escalation of the war is why the Pentagon will be more dangerous than the Antichrist.

Revelation 13:10: "he that killeth with the sword must be killed with the sword."

This means that anyone who fights against the army of the Antichrist will lose; and it also means that the army of the Antichrist will be killed by the sword which proceeds out of the mouth of Christ in Revelation 19:21. This is very profound, when you think about it, but it means that anyone who fights in World War III will be destroyed. In other words, this is a command to stay out of World War III.

Right now the Pentagon has a few hundred US military bases in Europe. Some of them are in Germany, Belgium, France, Greece, Italy, and England. In Revelation 9:16 the Antichrist will have 200 million soldiers in his army. In Daniel 11:22 this army will start out at 60 million Russian soldiers, and 40 million soldiers from the Eastern Bloc European nations. This is 100 million soldiers, and it is the meaning of the phrase, "And with the arms of a flood," in Daniel 11:22. In Daniel 7:5 the bear with the three ribs in its mouth represents the Russian army. The bear is also described in Revelation 13:2 where the phrase, "and his feet were as the feet of a bear," means that the army of the Antichrist will be the Russian army, which will walk on its feet. The bear is the symbol for Russia in these verses.

The Antichrist will use the pretense of a Unified European Army to recruit the soldiers, and this is why the army will be so big. In Revelation 13:1 the ten horns represent the ten Common Market leaders, and the ten crowns represent the kingdoms of these political leaders, which they will give to the Antichrist in Revelation 17:12,13. This explains why the army of the Antichrist will start out at 100 million soldiers.

Now the Pentagon believes that they have to stop the invading Russian tanks, before they take Western Europe. The US military has several neutron bombs positioned at the US military bases in Western Europe, which were made specifically for this purpose. This will cause two problems: First the US military bases will have to be defended against 100 million soldiers. Second the Pentagon will have to kill the 100 million soldiers to ensure a US military victory. This is not good news because a battle of this size will also kill at least 200 million civilians in Europe. This will cause the Antichrist to use total nuclear retaliation against the USA for certain. The neutron bombs are, "enhanced radiation" weapons, which were made to kill the men in the Russian tanks, without destroying the tanks themselves. The reason for this is that the neutron bombs will not cause the total destruction of a normal nuclear explosion, and for this reason the Pentagon believes they can use them in a limited nuclear war, in which the civilian casualties would be very few. It won't work that way with 100 million soldiers in the army, however. The Antichrist will have this many soldiers because the objective of the Common Market is to unify the currency, the economy, the banking system, and the trade of every nation, which is eligible to join them. Therefore it will be logical to call for a Unified European Army, and this is actually described in Revelation 17:12-18. The ten horns are ten kings, which will have one mind (This means that they will unify into the Common Market). They will give their power and strength unto the beast, which is the kingdom of the Antichrist. This means they will give their economic power, and their military strength to the Antichrist because he will be the leader of the Common Market.

The Pentagon believes that all of the nations in Western Europe, or the NATO nations, will be their Allies, and will support them militarily when the Russian army invades Western Europe. This will not be the case, however. When the ten Common Market leaders give their power and strength to the kingdom of the Antichrist, this will essentially be the same as joining the Warsaw Pact nations. This means that the reason for the Pentagon to defend Western Europe will evaporate.

Now because of this, and the 100 million soldiers in the army, it is very important to get the US military out of Europe as soon as possible. This is necessary so the Pentagon will not have the chance to use the fear of the Russian army and their nuclear arsenal against the people.

In Daniel 7:21, Daniel 7:25, and in Revelation 13:7 the Antichrist will make war with the saints and overcome them. This means he will take all of Europe. In Daniel 7:25, and Revelation 13:5 he will occupy Europe with his army for 42 months, which is three and one half years. It will take this long to force the mark of the beast on everyone in Europe, and in Revelation 13:16,17 the Antichrist will use his man-made famine to do this. This is also written in Revelation 6:5-8, and Zechariah 5:1-11.

If the Pentagon is caught in the middle of this, there will be a major war. Some of the armies in Western Europe will fight against the US military. There will be rioting and panic everywhere, and about 25 million American troops will be killed within one year. You must realize that 25 million American troops against 100 million soldiers in the army of the Antichrist will be no match at all. If the Pentagon loses this many troops, they will call for a nuclear war against the Antichrist. If the Pentagon destroys the 100 million soldiers in the army of the Antichrist, there will also be a total nuclear war. It is also true that if the Pentagon uses the neutron bombs against the Russian tanks, it will be like saying: Yes, we know that you are the most evil person ever to live on earth, but we are going to use the neutron bombs anyway.

The Antichrist will be the last person that you want to be involved in a nuclear war against because he will use total nuclear retaliation against the USA.

This is why the President must order the Pentagon to close all of the US military bases in Europe now. He should order the removal of all nuclear weapons, which are owned by the US military, and he should order the US troops in Europe to come back to the USA. There are several reasons why the Pentagon cannot interfere with the unified armies of Europe, and I have explained them in the chapter titled, Spiritual Principles of World War III in this book.

In Revelation 9:15-21, and Ezekiel 38:21 the Russian tanks will be used to kill 66.7 million soldiers in the army of the Antichrist. If the Pentagon destroys the tanks, they will create 66.7 million more soldiers to fight against in the Middle East. If the Pentagon interferes with the destruction of the army of the Antichrist, then that army will not be destroyed. The army of the Antichrist will be created to come against the land of Israel to punish it for the sins written in the Old Testament, and in the New Testament when they crucified Christ.

This army will also destroy Rome, Italy because the Roman Emperors killed or crucified 100,000 Christians during the years 95 AD to 305 AD. The American people must convince the President to close the US military bases in Europe. The bases in Japan, Korea, and England should also be closed. Then America will not have to defend half of the world against the Antichrist. In Revelation 6:8 he will own one fourth of the land area on earth. In Daniel 11:24 he will own the world oil supply. In Daniel 11:22 he will own all of Europe. This is verified in Daniel 7:21, Daniel 7:25, and in Revelation 13:7. In Isaiah 26:20, Psalm 23:4, and in Revelation 13:10 we are told to stay out of World War III.

SATAN'S BEST WARTIME TACTIC

The politicians of the world will see the terrible suffering in Europe, when the Antichrist declares his famine, and then they will try to intervene. Then this will cause a nuclear war. The politicians thought they were following a righteous cause when they took down the Berlin Wall; but this is what made it possible for the Antichrist to start World War III.

When World War III begins, the political leaders will believe they should send their military forces to Europe because it will seem like a righteous cause. Therefore Satan's best wartime tactic is to cause politicians to follow righteous causes; and he does this by creating thoughts in their minds. This is also Satan's most deadly tactic because people would never think that devils would try to save the people in Europe, and therefore they would never suspect that this is a tactic developed by Satan. This is the same tactic that caused the Berlin Wall to be taken down, and therefore it is proof of my statement.

The first half of Satan's formula for nuclear war has already been accomplished, when the dividing line in Germany was removed. The second half is to cause the President of the USA to send American troops to Germany or to France when World War III begins. This is what the President must be careful to avoid, and it is why the US military bases in Europe must be closed. It will be too tempting to order American troops to fight against the army of the Antichrist, if the US military bases are left open, because it will seem like a righteous thing to do.

There will be hundreds of righteous causes to fight for during World War III, and the political leaders must not intervene for any reason. You see, Satan will cause a war, and then he will include other nations in it by convincing politicians to follow righteous causes; and you can imagine what a wealth of them there will be during World War III. First, in the famine of the Antichrist, the Warsaw Ghetto tactic will be used against the large cities in Europe; then the Antichrist will take the world oil supply; then his army will occupy Israel; and will also fight against Saudi Arabia; and then there will be chemical warfare used in South Africa, Korea, NE China, and Israel. Just think how popular the politicians of the world will be, when they intervene to stop these events. Then there will be a global nuclear war, and everybody on earth will be killed.

DETERRENCE AND THE PENTAGON

Deterrence is the prevention from action by fear of the consequence. In the nuclear age of today, a potential enemy will not initiate an attack because of the threat of unacceptable retaliatory damage. Just when the Pentagon has convinced you that deterrence can prevent nuclear war, you saw this quote from page 20 of the book, *Nuclear War: Opposing Viewpoints*, © 1985 by Greenhaven Press:

"The real utility of limited nuclear war and enhanced counterforce options became apparent in May, 1975 when James Schlesinger finally acknowledged publicly that the USA would consider 'first use' of nuclear weapons to stop a large-scale communist advance with conventional armaments in Europe. This raised cries of indignation from people who had believed that the USA was adhering strictly to the deterrent philosophy. Schlesinger's proclamation was later extended to Korea and was quickly supported by then President Ford. Although Schlesinger admitted at that time that first use of nuclear weapons by either NATO or the Warsaw Pact would pose grave risks of escalating into major nuclear war, that threat to fire first still stands today."[11]

The Pentagon is breaking their own set of rules for nuclear deterrence by using the neutron bombs against the Russian army in Europe.

Then someone from the Pentagon will say that the threat to use limited tactical nuclear weapons against the Russian tanks moving into Western Europe will prevent the USSR from doing this; or in effect, will deter the conventional warfare in Europe. Then I will describe the actual event as it is written in Bible prophecy:

Daniel 11:22: "And with the arms of a flood shall they be overflown from before him, and shall be broken; yea, also the prince of the covenant."

The phrase, "and with the arms of a flood," is a description of the Russian army moving into Western Europe. Since the event is described in Bible prophecy, there is no possible way that the Pentagon can deter it from happening. I found this quote on page 172 of the book, *Nuclear War: Opposing Viewpoints*:

"Meaningful nuclear disarmament is not possible in today's world. Neither the wishful thinking of supporters of a nuclear freeze nor further sacrifices on the altar of unilateral disarmament will alter this fact. The reasons are as clear and as brutal as the Berlin Wall.

The necessary preconditions for reductions in nuclear arsenals simply do not exist. As long as deterrence based on mutual assured destruction (MAD) remains the guardian of peace, the arms race will continue."[12]

Therefore you see two problems here. First, the Pentagon is breaking their own rules in relation to nuclear deterrence (They are planning to use limited tactical nuclear weapons against the Russian army, even with the threat that the USSR will launch a full-scale nuclear retaliatory strike on the USA), and secondly, the very existence of the policy of deterrence makes it impossible to achieve any type of large-scale nuclear disarmament. This means that the entire subject of nuclear disarmament will have to be addressed in a completely different way. On page 312 in the book, *The Nuclear Reader*, © 1985 by Charles W. Kegley Jr., and Eugene R. Wittkopf, there is a quote from an article by Carl Sagan:

"But, comparable dire warnings have been made by respectable scientists with diverse political inclinations, including many of the American and Soviet physicists who conceived, devised and constructed the world nuclear arsenals."[13] Here it says that the same scientists who developed the technology, which was used to build the world's nuclear weapons, could not bring about the dismantling of those nuclear weapons when they tried. This means that the Pentagon is not going to respond to the needs of the American people now or in the future in relation to nuclear disarmament. I will have to add that we don't have any more time to waste in this matter. The people paid for the nuclear weapons through their taxes, then the scientists helped to build them, and yet no combination of the two groups can achieve any success toward nuclear disarmament.

Now, as far as I can remember, no one in America has given the nuclear weapons to the Pentagon in the first place; and if they did, then the ownership of the nuclear missiles and neutron bombs can be transferred to the Church Committee Group through legislation by the Congress, or through a National Emergency Vote by the American people. The people have a right to change the way their government works, especially when there is a national emergency such as World War III starting within six years.

The people can vote for the Church Committee Plan by using the National Emergency Vote, and then the Church Committee Group can work with the same industries that built the nuclear weapons, in order to dismantle them. The Soviet Union can be invited to join in the nuclear disarmament effort, and we can try to include France, Italy, England, China, and other nations. I know already that the Pentagon will interfere with this plan in every possible way, and this is why they will not be included in it. They have always delayed and stalled on this, and now they will be cut off. It is their duty to protect and defend America, and this will be their only responsibility during World War III. Therefore the disarmament project will be done like this: The Church Committee Group and the Nuclear Industries will work together to dismantle the nuclear weapons.

There is a phrase in the Gettysburg Address, which says that, the American people have the right to change the way in which the US Government works because it was created for them. Here is the quote:

"That this nation, under God, shall have a new birth of freedom—and that government of the people, by the people, for the people, shall not perish from the earth."[14]

In addition to this, the American people have the right to take away the offensive military power from the Pentagon, and give it to the Church Committee Group. This is written in the Preamble to the US Constitution. Here is the quote:

"We the people of the United States, in order to form a more perfect union, establish justice, ensure domestic tranquility, provide for the common defense, promote the general welfare, and secure the blessings of liberty to ourselves and our posterity, do ordain and establish this Constitution for the United States of America."[15]

The phrase, "provide for the common defense," says that the duties of the Pentagon and the US military should be directed toward defending America, instead of causing a nuclear war in Europe. Since the Pentagon is preparing for an attack on the Russian army when it invades Western Europe, the American people should know that this will cause the nuclear destruction and desolation of the USA. This means that the Pentagon is violating the laws of the Constitution.

The power to provide for the common defense is described in Article I, Section 8, of the US Constitution, and that power is given to the Congress.[16] Therefore the Congress has the right to act on behalf of the American people, and take away the offensive military power from the Pentagon, and give it to the Church Committee Group. I must say here that the only way to accomplish full-scale nuclear disarmament quickly enough to survive World War III can be done by the Congress, which can give the ownership of the nuclear weapons to the Church Committee Group. Since we are pressed for time in this matter, I will recommend that the Congress should take one year for the transfer of ownership, and if the matter cannot be resolved, then the American people should have the opportunity to use the National Emergency Vote for full-scale nuclear disarmament through the Church Committee Group.

I must assure you that America will not survive World War III with the Pentagon using the strategy of deterrence against the Antichrist. In Revelation 6:8 his army will control one fourth of the land area on the earth, which means that all foreign US military bases will have to be closed; and in Revelation 9:16 his army will have 200 million soldiers. Do we really want to let the Pentagon fight against them? No. It will not be possible to fight against the army of the Antichrist and protect America at the same time.

I found this quote in the text of the Declaration of Independence, and even though it refers to the British military, it is still an accurate description of the way the Pentagon has been operating in relation to nuclear disarmament over the past 30 years:

"Has affected to render the military independent of and superior to the civil power."[17]

Even with the protests about nuclear weapons, and with the books and articles written about nuclear war and nuclear winter, the Pentagon has still refused to engage in large-scale nuclear disarmament. In effect, the Pentagon has declared that they are better than the people and the Congress, which pay their appropriations. This is no longer acceptable, and the American people should demand that the Congress should vote for the Church Committee Plan, and that they should give the ownership of the nuclear weapons to the Church Committee Group. Then and only then can we achieve large-scale nuclear disarmament. This is the only way to do it without wasting the 8 to 10 years that the Pentagon and the President will waste through their infamous disarmament treaties. You know, the ones where they didn't get the terms they wanted, etc.

FIRST NUCLEAR WAR

The Antichrist will use nuclear missiles to destroy Rome in the first year of World War III. It will be a localized attack in that city, and this is described in Revelation 18:9,10, and in Revelation 18:15-19. The men in these verses would not stand there and watch Rome burn if the attack continued throughout Italy. This nuclear attack will happen as a result of the judgment of Rome in Revelation 17:1-6. It will happen when the Pope and the Vatican try to interfere with the gathering of millions of troops into the army of the Antichrist, or the Unified European Army. The Pope will try to unite all of the Christian people in Europe against the Antichrist. This is written in Revelation 13:7, where the Antichrist will make war with the saints, and he will overcome them. This means that he will destroy Rome first, and he will overcome the armies of the saints later.

Revelation 18:4: "And I heard another voice from heaven, saying, Come out of her, my people, that ye be not partakers of her sins, and that ye receive not of her plagues."

If you live in Rome, Italy, or anywhere else in Europe, you should move somewhere else before World War III starts to avoid the nuclear attack, and the famine of the Antichrist. He will use a famine to force the 800 million people in Europe to receive the mark of the beast, which will be the swastika. This is written in Revelation 6:8, and in Revelation 13:16,17.

The nuclear attack on Rome will happen as a judgment on the city, which is described in Revelation 17:1-18. The emperors in Rome killed 100,000 Christians from 95 AD to 305 AD. In Revelation 17:9 Rome is the great whore, which sits on the seven mountains. The time of this nuclear attack is generalized in Revelation 17:12,13, which says the unification of the Common Market in Europe is the time indicator. In Revelation 17:13 the ten kings, or the ten Common Market leaders, will be unified under the Antichrist, who will be the leader of the Common Market. In Revelation 9:16 the Unified European Army will have 200 million soldiers at the end of World War III. This is why the Pentagon must close all of the US military bases in Europe now.

The Common Market in Europe will be unified in 2006 to 2008, and here is a list of events, which will happen. In Revelation 6:2, Daniel 8:25, and Daniel 11:21 the Antichrist will take Europe peacefully at first. Then in Revelation 6:4 he will cause war: and in Revelation 6:5,6, and Revelation 6:8 he will declare his famine in Europe. The Pope and the Vatican will object to the famine, and the size of the army of the Antichrist. In Revelation 17:14 the ten Common Market leaders will make war against Christ, and in Revelation 17:15 they will want to destroy Rome because of the power and the influence of the Pope. Then in Revelation 17:16, and Revelation 18:1-19 the Antichrist and the ten Common Market leaders will attack Rome, and destroy it with nuclear missiles. In Revelation 17:16 the phrase, "shall eat her flesh," means to loot the city. In Revelation 18:19 the city of Rome will be made desolate in one hour, which could only be done through a nuclear attack.

The judgment on the city of Rome is described in Revelation 17:1-6, and in Revelation 18:1-19. It will happen in the first year of World War III, and the Pentagon will probably retaliate against the Antichrist, since they have US military bases located in Italy. This will include the USA in a nuclear war.

LIMITED TACTICAL NUCLEAR WAR

On page 32 of the book titled, *Disarmament Negotiations and Treaties*, © 1972 by Scribner Publishers, there is a battle scenario for Europe with limited tactical nuclear war.[18] This study was done in 1967 by 12 experts who worked at the request of the United Nations Secretary General. It is called a war game, but it will be much more than that when the real battle occurs. I will guess that the number of troops on each side in the war game is 400,000, and that the Russian army has 10,000 tanks. This is a good approximation, and then the number of American troops will be 400,000. The reason for this scenario is to estimate the total megatons, of the limited tactical nuclear weapons used by both sides. The battle described on page 32 in the book has 20 to 25 megatons altogether.

Now I will extrapolate this figure to a more realistic level. Since there will be 100,000,000 Russian and Eastern European troops in the real battle, you should divide the total number of troops, which is 800,000, into the 100,000,000. You will get a factor of 125. This means that the real battle at the start of World War III will be 125 times larger. Therefore when you multiply the 25 megatons by the factor of 125, you will get 3,125 megatons. To verify the 100,000,000 soldiers in World War III:

Revelation 9:16: "And the number of the army of the horsemen were two hundred thousand thousand: and I heard the number of them."

This is how large the Unified European Army will be in 2022; and it will start out at 100,000,000 soldiers in the year 2012. Therefore the 3,125 megatons will be used in Europe in 2012. When the Pentagon tells the people in Europe that it will be a limited tactical nuclear war, they will not realize just how large the army of the Antichrist will be. This is why the President of the USA must close the US military bases in England, and in Europe now.

On page 32 of the book, the number of civilians killed is put at 1,500,000.[19] Multiplied by the factor of 125, this is 187 million people in Eastern and Western Europe who will be killed in this battle. The people who live in Europe will be very interested in this, especially if the Pentagon still calls it a limited nuclear war.

On page 34 of the book titled, *Blundering Into Disaster*, © 1986 by Robert S. McNamara there is another description of a war game in Europe.[20] It was a study of nuclear war, which was done by a group of experts, who were assembled at the request of the UN Secretary General in 1980. Since this study was done by the UN Secretary General, as was the one done in 1967, I will say that the number of troops is the same as before, which is 400,000 on each side. Then the factor of 125 is the same.

In this study they said that 1,500 nuclear artillery shells, and 200 nuclear bombs were used by the two sides against each other's military targets. The experts concluded that there would be a minimum of 5 to 6 million immediate civilian casualties, and 400,000 military casualties. When you multiply the factor of 125 times the 5 million civilian casualties, you get a total of 625 million people who will be killed in the resulting nuclear war.

I think Robert S. McNamara's study of the war games is more realistic, since it was done in 1980 by the experts for the United Nations; and McNamara himself was the Secretary of Defense for John F. Kennedy, and for Lyndon B. Johnson.

This nuclear war will be caused when the US military uses neutron bombs against the Russian tanks invading Western Europe. This invasion is described in Daniel 11:22, and it will happen within six years. The neutron bombs are described in the book titled, *Missile Envy*, © 1984 by Helen

Caldicott. On page 194 of this book, the neutron bomb is to be used against invading Russian tanks on the battlefield.[21]

The neutron bombs are designed to kill the soldiers who are inside the Russian tanks because the neutrons from them can penetrate any kind of structural material, including armored tanks. In Daniel 11:22 the phrase, "And with the arms of a flood shall they be overflown from before him," is a description of the invasion of Western Europe by the Unified European Army, which will be the army of the Antichrist. The total number of troops in the army will be 100,000,000 in the year 2012 and it will consist mainly of Russian and Eastern European soldiers. When the Antichrist offers $600 dollars per month to the soldiers who join his army, millions of them will enlist immediately. Now in early 2001 most of the soldiers in Russia don't even receive a paycheck because of the failed economy there.

THIRD NUCLEAR WAR

In Revelation 13:4 the beast is the kingdom of the Antichrist, which will include all of the nations on the entire continent of Europe. This is written in Revelation 6:8, where his army will control one fourth of the land area on the earth. In Revelation 9:16 his army, which will be called the Unified European Army, will have 200 million soldiers at the end of World War III. This is verified in Revelation 13:4, in the phrase, "Who is like unto the beast? who is able to make war with him?"

The importance of these facts cannot be overstated because the Pentagon has US military bases all over the continent of Europe. In Revelation 13:5 the Antichrist will spend 42 months trying to subdue all of the armies of the independent nations in Europe which try to resist him; and in Revelation 13:7 he will succeed in doing so. Then if the Antichrist will succeed in conquering the entire continent of Europe, how can the Pentagon protect the US military bases there? The truth is that they cannot do so without causing a global nuclear war against the Antichrist.

The only way to prevent this is by telling the President and the Congress to order the Pentagon to close all of the US military bases in Europe. I have written a description of every single nuclear confrontation between the Pentagon and the Antichrist in these pages because the failure to anticipate even one of them will result in a global nuclear war. The present nuclear deterrence strategy of the Pentagon means that there will be nine nuclear wars between the USA and the Antichrist during the 11 years of World War III.

FOURTH NUCLEAR WAR

There will be a catastrophic nuclear attack on America before World War III even begins, as a result of any major buildup of US troops in the United States. If the Antichrist believes that America is trying to assemble an army of 10 to 25 million troops, in order to fight in the ground war in Europe, then he could use an all-out first-strike nuclear attack on the USA to prevent it. Of course he will use any available Soviet satellites to spy on America to watch for troop movements.

This is why it is so important to vote for the Church Committee Plan. If the Church Committee Group takes the offensive military power from the President and the Pentagon, then there will not be any major troop buildup in America. I think that the US troops which return to the USA after the closure of the US military bases in England, Europe, Japan, Korea, and the Middle East should be stationed on US military bases in such a way that they can protect the coastline on the Eastern, Southern, Western, and Northern US border areas. Then these troops will be able to protect America against an invasion by the army of the Antichrist.

It is important to station the US troops along the Eastern, Southern, and Western coastlines, and along the northern border with Canada, since this will be seen as a defensive troop pattern, as opposed to an offensive one. The Church Committee Group and the American people can put pressure on the President and the Pentagon to force them to station the US troops along all of the US borders in America. It is very important to do this, in order to avoid an all-out first-strike nuclear attack by the Antichrist.

FIFTH NUCLEAR WAR

Adolf Hitler didn't use a naval blockade against England very effectively during World War II, but the Antichrist will in World War III. When you realize that Satan improves the tactics from one world war to the next one, then you know that the Antichrist will improve on the tactics used by Hitler. This means that England will have to fight to the death in World War III against the Antichrist, and it means that a nuclear war could be the end result. If you know this before it happens, then you can keep the nuclear war limited by closing all of the US military bases in England, Scotland, and in Europe before World War III starts. In effect, the Pentagon will have to close all foreign US military bases except those on US possessions.

No matter how obligated the President, the Congress, and the Pentagon feel about protecting England, Europe, or any other nation during World War III, they cannot do it and protect America at the same time. The instructions for the US Government to follow in order to help America to survive World War III are written here:

Isaiah 26:20,21: "Come, my people, enter thou into thy chambers, and shut thy doors about thee: hide thyself as it were for a little moment, until the indignation be overpast.

For, behold, the Lord cometh out of his place to punish the inhabitants of the earth for their iniquity: the earth also shall disclose her blood, and shall no more cover her slain."

This is verified in Zephaniah 2:3, Amos 5:13, Ecclesiastes 9:12, and in I Thessalonians 5:3. The Church Committee Group will follow these instructions during World War III, and this is why the people should vote for the Church Committee Plan.

SIXTH NUCLEAR WAR

The army of the Antichrist will occupy the land of Israel for seven years during World War III. This is written in Daniel 8:9-14, Daniel 11:27-32, and Revelation 11:1-7. The word Gentiles in Revelation 11:2 refers to the army of the Antichrist. They will tread the holy city under foot for 42 months, and then the two prophets in Revelation 11:3-7 will make war against them for 1260 days. The total time involved is seven years.

Since the US military has always taken it upon themselves to protect Israel, there will be a problem when the army of the Antichrist occupies the land there. The President of the USA will probably order the Pentagon to send battle groups of ships to the Mediterranean Sea, and he will order the US Air Force to send fighter airplanes to the area, and then the war will include the USA. At the beginning of the war the Antichrist will have about five million soldiers in the Middle East, and if the Pentagon uses their limited tactical nuclear weapons to kill them all, then America will be involved in a global nuclear war against the Antichrist.

There is another danger here because the Antichrist will use chemical or biological warfare against Jerusalem. This is described in Daniel 11:29-31. It is verified in Ezekiel 5:16. The problem arises because of the large number of soldiers in the army of the Antichrist, and the use of these weapons. There is the additional problem of US troops trying to protect their own military forces or bases during this war. Any one of these factors could include the USA in a nuclear war. The way to avoid this is to close the US military bases in the Middle East now.

SEVENTH NUCLEAR WAR

There are now thousands of US troops in the Middle East protecting the world oil supply. The Antichrist will move his army into that area during World War III, and he will take the world oil supply. This is written in Daniel 11:23-25. In Daniel 11:23 the phrase, "a small people," means the small number of people in Saudi Arabia, Oman, Yemen, Kuwait, and the other rich oil nations.

In Daniel 11:24 the phrase, "the fattest places of the province," means the oil fields and the banks in these nations. The key phrase is: "and he shall do that which his fathers have not done, nor his fathers' fathers."

The political leaders of Germany during World War I and World War II did not take the world oil supply, but the Antichrist will. This is verified in the next phrase in Daniel 11:24: "he shall scatter among them the prey, and spoil, and riches." This means that the Antichrist will divide the riches from the oil nations among the soldiers in his army.

The problem will arise when the US military tries to protect the oil supply in Saudi Arabia and the other nations. You can see from Daniel 11:23-25 that the Antichrist will take the world oil supply, and the USA will become involved in a nuclear war if the Pentagon does try to protect it. Instead of doing this, the USA should try to convert to Natural Gas fuel before World War III even begins. This strategy will keep America out of a global nuclear war against the Antichrist. I have already drawn up the plans for the nation-wide fuel conversion, and all that is needed is a Federal Order to convert.

EIGHTH NUCLEAR WAR

This nuclear war will be fought between the Pentagon and the army of the Antichrist, and it will start when the Antichrist tries to take the world oil supply. There are US military bases and US troops in the Middle East now, and they are there to protect Kuwait and Saudi Arabia. The Antichrist will move his army into that area in the second or third year of World War III. The fact that the Pentagon sent 540,000 troops to Kuwait in 1991 to drive the Iraqi army out proves that the US military will fight against the army of the Antichrist over the world oil supply.

The verses that describe the movement by the army of the Antichrist into the Middle East are in Daniel 11:23-25. In Daniel 11:24 the phrase, "He shall enter peaceably even upon the fattest places of the province," describes the movement of the army itself. If you go back to Daniel 11:23 the phrase, "and shall become strong with a small people," says that the Antichrist will gain favor with the rich oil nations, and this will make it possible for him to move his army into that part of the Middle East.

When this army moves into Kuwait and Saudi Arabia, the US military will be forced to fight against them for two reasons:

•To protect the world oil supply
•To protect the US military bases in the Middle East

If the Antichrist takes the world oil supply, and if the Pentagon lets him get away with it, then there will still be a nuclear war between the USA and the Antichrist because the Pentagon will still have to protect the US military bases in the Middle East. It is extremely important to understand this because the failure to anticipate even one confrontation between the Pentagon and the Antichrist could result in a global nuclear war. The way to prevent it is to close all of the US military bases in the Middle East now. The reason is written in Revelation 9:16. The army of the Antichrist will have 200 million soldiers at the end of World War III. In Revelation 13:4, no nation on earth will dare to fight against it. This means the Pentagon will have to withdraw all US troops back into the USA before World War III starts.

NINTH NUCLEAR WAR

When the CIA gathers intelligence information about the Antichrist and his appearance in Germany and in the Common Market, they will take the information to the President and the Pentagon. Then the generals in the Pentagon will probably recommend that the CIA should kill the Antichrist, so that World War III will go away. They will think that the CIA should end the war before it starts.

There are two problems with this logic: The first is described in Daniel 11:41-45. In these verses the Antichrist will be alive at the end of World War III, which means that the CIA could not have killed him at the beginning of the war. This is verified in Revelation 19:19-21. Here the Antichrist is called the false prophet, and he will be destroyed by Christ at the battle of Armageddon.

The second problem rests in the fact that the Antichrist will not forget that the CIA tried to kill him. If they try and fail, then the USA will be punished by the Antichrist later during World War III, when he has fully gathered all of his military forces. This is described in Revelation 9:16. The army of the Antichrist will have 200 million soldiers at the end of World War III.

Therefore the CIA's attempt to kill the Antichrist will result in a full-scale invasion of the USA during the later years of World War III, or the USA will be included in the major nuclear war between the Antichrist and China at the end of World War III. In fact, this blunder by the CIA could cause a nuclear war at any time during the war. For these reasons the CIA will have to be restricted to anti-terrorism activities in the USA and in North America before and during World War III.

This nuclear war will happen in the tenth year of World War III, and it will include about 10 to 20 nations in Europe, all of Russia, China, and Korea. The Antichrist will expand to the east, and to the Pacific Ocean to include Japan in his kingdom. This is written in Matthew 24:7,8, where nation will fight against nation, and kingdom against kingdom. A kingdom is a group of nations, and the Antichrist will have 41 of them in his. When he tries to expand to the east, all of Korea and Northeast China will become involved in a ground war against him. In Revelation 9:16 the Antichrist will have 200 million soldiers in his army, and no other army on earth will be able to defeat him. When China loses the conventional war, they will retaliate with nuclear missiles against Russia and Germany. In Daniel 11:44 the Antichrist will receive the news about China's nuclear attack, and he will be very angry. This is the meaning of the verse:

Daniel 11:44: "But tidings out of the east and out of the north shall trouble him: therefore he shall go forth with great fury to destroy, and utterly to make away many."

The tidings from the east and the north refer to Northeast China, and their nuclear attack against the Antichrist. In Daniel 11:44 the phrase, "Therefore he shall go forth with great fury to destroy," means that the Antichrist will use total nuclear retaliation against China and Korea.

The nuclear war and the fallout could kill 1.7 billion people, and the only way to stop it will be to have the people in Northeast China and Korea move to South China before it starts. Then China and Korea won't be involved in the conventional war, and they won't have to use nuclear missiles against Germany and Russia.

The United Nations Organization can help to convince China and Korea to avoid the ground war and the nuclear war. The 1.7 billion people killed worldwide is the reason for the phrase, "great tribulation," in Matthew 24:21. All of the nations in the world should warn their people about this major nuclear war, and they should tell them to store enough distilled water in one-gallon plastic containers to last for one year. In Revelation 8:11 nuclear fallout is more deadly in drinking water than in any other form, and it could remain in the rivers and lakes for several months.

In Matthew 24:22 this nuclear war will be so widespread that it could destroy all flesh, or the entire human race; but Christ will return to the earth early to stop it. This is the meaning of the phrase, "for the elect's sake those days shall be shortened," in Matthew 24:22. This means that the major nuclear war between the Antichrist and China will happen at the end of World War III. The verse in Daniel 11:44 also places this nuclear war at the end of the war because it happens before the Antichrist comes to the end of his days in Daniel 11:45.

This nuclear war is described in Revelation 8:10-12. In Revelation 8:10 the phrase, "burning as it were a lamp," means that the nuclear explosion and the mushroom cloud will resemble a table lamp. This is already true. There will be nuclear fallout and nuclear winter in this war, which will kill millions of people. This is the meaning of the phrase, "and the third part of the waters became wormwood, and many men died of the waters because they were made bitter," written in Revelation 8:11. This is a description of the nuclear fallout, which will contaminate one third of the drinking water on the earth. Thousands of rivers and lakes will be contaminated, and millions of people will die when they drink it. This is why the United Nations Organization should help all of the nations store millions of gallons of distilled water.

In Revelation 8:12 there will be a nuclear winter, which will darken one third of the sun, moon, and the stars. One third of the daylight will be lost, which will cause crops to die. It will also cause freezing temperatures, which means that you will need more fuel to keep your house warm. This will happen in the tenth year of World War III. Look at the verse that describes it:

Revelation 8:12: "And the fourth angel sounded, and the third part of the sun was smitten, and the third part of the moon, and the third part of the stars; so as the third part of them was darkened, and the day shone not for a third part of it, and the night likewise."

The Bible is a very modern book when you read it enough to understand what it says. This verse has been here for the entire 60 years since the atomic bomb was developed, and yet no one noticed it.

I know that the Pentagon thinks they have to control world events in some way or another, but anyone who tries to do this during World War III will endanger the entire human race. The Pentagon must not try to interfere with the Antichrist during these years, or he will use total nuclear retaliation against America. To repeat what I said at the beginning of this paper, the Pentagon, the CIA, or any other group, which tries to assassinate or kill the Antichrist, will have their homeland destroyed with nuclear missiles.

Japan will form an alliance with the Antichrist. Then the USSR and Japan will both invade Manchuria, and North and South Korea. The total land area seized in NE China will be 604,000 square miles. This will include all of Manchuria, all of North and South Korea, and 44,000 square miles in addition to these nations.

Manchuria is called Tung Pei by the Chinese, which means, "north east." This relates directly to this verse:

Daniel 11:44: "But tidings out of the east and out of the north shall trouble him: therefore he shall go forth with great fury to destroy, and utterly to make away many."

The description of events in this verse is chronologically after the USSR and Japan invade NE China, and after their armies take Manchuria, and all of Korea. Therefore the phrase, "But tidings out of the east and out of the north shall trouble him," means that China will kill millions of soldiers from the army of the Antichrist. I will guess that China will use chemical weapons, or limited nuclear weapons to kill the soldiers. Then the phrase, "therefore he shall go forth with great fury to destroy, and utterly to make away many," means that the Antichrist will use total nuclear retaliation against China. This is the large-scale nuclear war described in Revelation 8:10-12.

All of this will happen because the Antichrist will want to rebuild the Soviet Navy fleet in the Pacific Ocean, which is located in Vladivostok. The name for this city means, "ruler of the east," in Russian. The Antichrist will be the ruler of the east, only if he makes an alliance with Japan, and then takes Manchuria and Korea. He will have to use the Chinese Eastern Railway for the large military buildup in Vladivostok; and this will be much easier to do, if he makes an alliance with Japan, and then conquers NE China.

I watched a TV News video about Vladivostok in August 1996. The Soviet Navy fleet there is gathering rust, and it is not very well maintained. Some of the ships and submarines there are no longer in working order, and this will be an even greater problem.

The Antichrist will order the rebuilding of the Soviet Navy fleet in Vladivostok. Some of the nuclear waste from the factories, which make the nuclear fuel for the Soviet nuclear submarines, is being dumped into the Sea of Japan. The life expectancy of the people who work at these factories is about 40 years old. The people there are exposed to nuclear radiation for 12 hours per day. Those who eat fish from the Sea of Japan also die from radiation poisoning.

There is another detail about this area, which is important. The people from China are said to be continually claiming the land around Vladivostok, and they also try to change the location of the border between the USSR and China. This is known as a border dispute, and the nation with the largest military force usually claims the land. Since the collapse of the USSR in

1990, China is still in control; but this situation will change when the Antichrist forms the Unified European Army.

For the people in NE China and Korea who do not want to be killed in all of the fighting in Manchuria and Korea, they should move to South China by the year 2018. The nuclear war will happen in the year 2022, and China can minimize the nuclear war itself by ordering the people to evacuate Manchuria and Korea by the year 2018. If the political leaders of China do not wish to order the evacuation of their people from Korea and Manchuria, I will remind them that the Antichrist will force the swastika on the people in NE China, just like he did with the people in Europe. In Revelation 14:11 the people who accept the swastika will go to the Lake of Fire at the judgment. In Revelation 20:14, Psalm 19:4, Psalm 21:9, and Matthew 25:41 the Lake of Fire is the sun. I will now explain the theology about the move to South China.

If the people refuse to move to South China, and if they accept the swastika, then they will go to the Lake of Fire. If the people in Manchuria and Korea refuse to convert to Christianity, then they will go to the Lake of Fire. Therefore the best way for the people to save themselves is to convert to Christianity now, and then to move to South China by the year 2018.

For the people in Japan, the theology is the same because their political leaders will force them to join the Antichrist, and then they will be forced to accept the swastika. This will happen by the year 2016. If you don't believe this, then you should think again, since the political leaders of Japan may do it because of their envy and their hatred for America.

This means that the Japanese people must convert to Christianity to be saved, and they must move away from Japan by the year 2014. These people must not be fooled into believing that they will achieve world domination with the Antichrist. In Daniel 11:45 he will be destroyed, and in Revelation 19:20 he will go to the Lake of Fire. Then in Revelation 14:11 anyone who receives the swastika, or the mark of the beast, will go to the Lake of Fire, and then their souls will burn in the fires of the sun forever.

Korea is an important nation with a population of 68 million people, and it is bordered by China on the north, and by the USSR on the northeast. Korea is less than 200 miles from Japan, and this will be the main reason why the Japanese will help the Antichrist take Korea and Manchuria. Korea was occupied by the Japanese from 1910 to 1945. The Korean way of life changed after Japan took control in 1910. They took the farmland away from the farmers. The Japanese people today basically hate the Koreans, and they treat them as an inferior race of people. This will be another reason why Japan will help the Antichrist take Korea and Manchuria.

The main reason why the Antichrist will take Korea is to get more seaports to accommodate the Soviet Navy's Pacific fleet, when he expands it. Right now the only Soviet Navy seaport in the Pacific area is in Vladivostok. There is one other Soviet seaport to the north named Nakhodka, but it is used for commercial activities. Here is a list of the seaports in Korea:

North Korea:	South Korea:
Chongjin	Chinhae
Kimchaek	Inchon
Nampo	Masan
Unggi	Pohang
Wonsan	Pusan
Ulsan	

The Antichrist will probably use the mineral resources of North Korea for his shipbuilding, and the agricultural resources of South Korea to feed his shipbuilding crews. Japan will probably furnish workers to help the Antichrist rebuild his Soviet Navy fleet in the Pacific Ocean. Japanese fishermen will use the commercial fishing ports in Korea to their advantage. Korea ranks high in fish production. Japan controlled all of Korea from 1910 to 1945, and they will do it again with the help of the Antichrist.

The Antichrist will need petroleum to fuel his ships, and he will use the oil from the Sung-Liao basin in Manchuria to do it. South Korea is a leading nation in the production of steel and ships, and these are exactly what the Antichrist will need to rebuild his Soviet Navy's Pacific fleet. Iron and steel are two of the exports from North Korea.

Another factor of importance here is the cold winter temperatures at Vladivostok, where the Soviet Navy fleet is located. The cold winters in Siberia could be replaced by somewhat warmer temperatures in Inchon, Pusan, Masan, and Chinhae in South Korea. For all of these reasons the Antichrist will transfer his shipbuilding industry southward, where there will be warmer temperatures, and many more Seaports for his Navy fleet.

I've written about Korea and Manchuria so the world will understand the reasons for the large-scale nuclear war at the end of World War III.

This nuclear war is described in Daniel 11:44, and in Revelation 8:10-12; and it could kill 1.7 billion people. The total population of Korea and Manchuria is 168 million people. Therefore it would be better to move these people to South China, than to let the nuclear war kill 1.7 billion people. For these reasons I hope that the United Nations Organization will try to save the people in China, Japan, and the USSR who will die in the large nuclear war;

and they can do this by asking China to let the people in Korea and in Manchuria move to South China.

PREVENTION OF NUCLEAR WAR

To avoid a first-strike nuclear attack by the Antichrist, the Church Committee Group and the United Nations Organization can begin to negotiate with the Soviet Union and China to dismantle 99% of the nuclear missiles in the USA, if Russia and China will do the same thing. This dismantling can begin now, and it can be completed in the USA, Russia, and China by the year 2009.

The reason is that the Antichrist will have control of all of the nuclear missiles in Russia, France, and Italy when his army takes control of Europe in the first year of World War III. I have already proven that he will cause a global nuclear war with China at the end of World War III, and the nuclear fallout from this war will kill 1.7 billion people. In Daniel 11:44 the tidings out of the east and out of the north refers to NE China; and the phrase, "therefore he shall go forth with great fury to destroy," means that the Antichrist will use total nuclear retaliation against China. Then the phrase, "and utterly to make away many," means that he will try to kill everyone in China and Korea.

This is the major nuclear war described in Revelation 8:10-12, and it will kill 80% of the people in Russia and China. In Revelation 8:11 the phrase, "many men died of the waters because they were made bitter," means that millions of people will die because of the nuclear fallout in the rivers and the lakes in their nations. It will contaminate the drinking water, and it will kill millions of people. In Revelation 8:12 the nuclear winter could kill four billion people.

If you will look closely at Revelation 8:12, then you will see that it is a perfect description of nuclear winter. In Matthew 24:21 the phrase, "For then shall be great tribulation, such as was not since the beginning of the world to this time, no, nor ever shall be," means that there will be a global nuclear war just before the Second Coming of Christ. In Matthew 24:22 the phrase, "and except those days should be shortened, there should no flesh be saved," means that the entire human race would be destroyed in the nuclear war at the end of World War III, except that Christ will return to earth early to stop the war and save mankind. Then the phrase, "but for the elect's sake those days shall be shortened," means that the days of the nuclear war will be shortened to save mankind.

Christ will reduce the effectiveness of the nuclear war by stopping it early; and mankind can do the same thing by eliminating as many American, Russian, and Chinese nuclear missiles as possible, before World War III starts. The Russian and Chinese nuclear weapons are the ones that the Antichrist and China will use against each other in the big nuclear war. It is in the interest of all mankind to dismantle as many of them as possible before the Antichrist gains power in Germany, and in the Common Market. After that time it will be too late to stop him.

The Church Committee Group should make it clear to the Soviet Union and to China that America wants to reduce the number of nuclear missiles in the USA before World War III begins. This could reduce the nuclear fallout in the big nuclear war by half, and it would save the lives of 850 million people, most of whom now live in Europe and China. To do this, the USA, Russia, and China must eliminate 99% of their nuclear missiles before World War III starts to reduce the fallout and the nuclear winter in the nuclear war between the Antichrist and China.

You can see in Matthew 24:22 that Christ will reduce the effectiveness of the nuclear war by shortening the time of the war. The people in the USA, Russia, and China can do the same thing by dismantling 99% of their mainland nuclear missiles. Since the negotiations to dismantle the nuclear missiles could save 850 million lives, serious efforts should be made to approve this plan.

To this end the Church Committee Group can announce to Russia and China that they will voluntarily dismantle 10% of the active nuclear missiles in the USA. They can do this without imposing any conditions on Russia or China, and then they can invite Russian and Chinese nuclear missile experts to watch the dismantling. Then the Church Committee Group can seriously negotiate with Russia and China to do the same thing. The nuclear missile dismantling could be done at the rate of 15% of the nuclear missiles in each nation every six months.

America will benefit from this plan, even if 100% of our mainland nuclear missiles are dismantled, and only 75% of Russia's and China's are. One reason is that the Antichrist will not have any reason to use a first strike nuclear attack against America, if our mainland nuclear missiles are dismantled. The other reason is to reduce the nuclear fallout in the big nuclear war by half, which would save 850 million people in Europe and China. About 220 million of these would be in Russia, and 600 million lives will be saved in China.

I have described the 9 possible nuclear wars in World War III, and the task now is to prevent them. This will save lives in America too.

A FOOLPROOF NATIONAL DEFENSE

The Star Wars defense or SDI is orbiting around the earth, and it can be destroyed by Electromagnetic Pulse or EMP, which is caused by one or two nuclear explosions in the upper atmosphere. This means that SDI is vulnerable.

An ABM defense on mainland America would be good, except that it would not destroy the Russian nuclear missiles until they are above the USA. Then the nuclear fallout would settle in our lakes and rivers, and it would kill millions of people. One good part of the ABM defense however, is that it would be within the USA, and it could be defended.

If the Pentagon tried to build floating platforms in the Atlantic and the Pacific Oceans, with ABM defensive missiles on them, they would be vulnerable to attack. These platforms would be stationary, and therefore their coordinates could be put into a Russian guidance computer. The most important requirement for America's National Defense for World War III is this: It must be defendable, and it should be foolproof, so that it cannot be destroyed.

Therefore I will recommend using battleships, Guided Missile cruisers, destroyers, and submarines, which can station themselves in the middle of the Atlantic and Pacific Oceans. These ships can carry ABM defensive missiles, which they can use to destroy any incoming Russian nuclear missiles. The ships can patrol in a north and south pattern, about 1000 to 1500 miles away from the East and West Coasts in the USA. The ships can also patrol in an east and west pattern in the Gulf of Mexico. Therefore America would be protected from nuclear attack from the east, west, and the south.

The Pentagon can get the permission of the Canadian Government to build ABM defensive missile facilities in Northern Canada, in order to protect Canada and the USA. These ABM missiles would get a 1000-mile head start in destroying any incoming Russian nuclear missiles. Then the USA would be protected on the northern side.

There are several advantages to using ships in the Atlantic, Pacific, and Gulf Oceans. First of all, they can intercept the incoming Russian nuclear missiles at 1000 to 1500 miles before they fly over the USA, in the case of the ships in the Atlantic and Pacific. This means that the Russian nuclear missiles would explode over the oceans, instead of exploding over the USA. Therefore the nuclear fallout will settle into the oceans, instead of in America. This is very important when you are trying to save as many lives as you can.

Another advantage of using ships is that they can move, which makes it impossible to program their coordinates into nuclear missile computers in Russia. Therefore they cannot be destroyed as in part of a first-strike nuclear attack by the Antichrist. You see it is always part of a first-strike nuclear attack to destroy as many mainland nuclear missiles in their Silos as possible, and to destroy as much of the defense as possible. The ships in the middle Atlantic and Pacific Oceans would overcome this strategy because they can move. This is why the Pentagon built the MX missiles on 60-mile tracks in the northwestern USA in the 1960s or the 1970s. They wanted to change the location of the missiles by moving them on 60-mile tracks. The ships will improve this idea by 1000% or more because they can move over a distance of thousands of miles.

The ships can also protect themselves against missiles, or against aircraft, or other ships. In fact there could be Aircraft Carriers with enough Jet Airplanes on them to defend the patrolling ships. It will be very important to keep the ships at least 800 to 1000 miles away from Europe; and it will also be a strict rule that they can never try to help or defend England or Ireland during the famine and the blockade of these nations.

Another advantage of ABM defense on ships is that they will have a 1000-mile head start, and therefore if they fail to destroy any incoming nuclear missiles, then they will have a second chance to launch more ABM missiles to destroy them. On the other hand, an ABM defense on mainland USA would not have another chance, if it failed to destroy 3 or 4 nuclear missiles coming from Russia. These nuclear missiles will have about 10 warheads each, and if you multiply this times 4 missiles, you will get 40 nuclear explosions in America. Then you can see why ABM defense on ships would be better.

I just realized that ABM defense on ships in the Atlantic or Pacific Oceans could possibly destroy the Russian nuclear missiles before their warheads go into MIRV, or separate from the missiles. If this is possible, it would be the greatest advantage of having ABM defense on ships in the oceans. The reason is that it would only take 4 ABM missiles to destroy 4 incoming Russian nuclear missiles if they reached them before the warheads separate from the Russian missiles. If they reach them after the warheads separate, then it would take 40 ABM missiles to destroy them.

The number of ships in each patrol group should be: two battleships, four Guided Missile cruisers, four destroyers, two aircraft carriers, and six submarines. The groups of ships should never be greater than this because a battle group of 40 ships would be an open invitation to war. These 12 ships with six submarines should patrol in a north and south parallel pattern in the Atlantic and Pacific Oceans, about 1000 or 1500 miles from the USA if possible.

If it were possible to put ABM missiles on submarines, this would be the best type of defense to use. The submarines cannot be seen by the enemy, and therefore they will not pose a threat which could start a war against the Antichrist. In fact the submarine ABM defense will also conform to the theology of Matthew 5:39-45, simply because they do not pose a threat to war. Therefore they could not cause aggression to escalate, or to cause a war, which would involve the USA.

It may also be possible that submarine based ABM defense could be shielded or protected from EMP, since they stay underwater. This could possibly mean that the water in the ocean might prevent the EMP from interfering with the electronics on the submarines. This means that their computers and electronics will still work, long after the electronics on the ships or airplanes fail. Therefore the Pentagon should do research on submarine based ABM defense immediately.

To review these advantages:

1. The ships can move, which makes it impossible to program their coordinates into a Russian nuclear missile computer.
2. The ships can be defended because they can defend themselves.
3. They can intercept the Russian nuclear missiles at 1000 miles before they fly over the USA. Then the nuclear fallout will go into the ocean, and not into the USA.
4. They will have a 1000-mile head start in destroying the nuclear missiles coming from Russia. Therefore if they miss three or four of them, then they will have a second chance to launch more ABM missiles.
5. The ABM missiles on ships might possibly be able to destroy the Russian nuclear missiles before they go into MIRV. Then one ABM missile will destroy one nuclear missile with 10 warheads. In other words, they could destroy the Russian missiles before the warheads separate from them. This would be the greatest advantage of all because it would mean fewer nuclear explosions in the USA.

I hope that the Pentagon can research these ideas, during the years before World War III begins, and that they can provide America and its people with the best possible defense. This means a defense that can be defended, and one that is as foolproof as is possible. Since I've recommended that the $400 billion dollars per year allocated to the Pentagon should be reduced to $80 billion per year, I also said that the Church Committee Group would give $25 billion dollars per year to the Pentagon for national defense. This way the money will be used for defense, instead of being used for something else.

There have been 3 movies about EMP, or Electromagnetic Pulse, which I know of, and they are:

1. *A View to a Kill*, ©1985 with Roger Moore as James Bond[22]
2. *Goldeneye*, © 1995 with Pierce Brosnan as James Bond[23]
3. *Broken Arrow*, © 1996 with John Travolta[24]

In the movie titled, *A View to a Kill*, there was a discussion about microchips that were immune to the effects of EMP. This will be a requirement for the ABM defense in my plan for a Foolproof National Defense. First of all, the anti-ballistic missile defense systems will be put onto diesel and on nuclear submarines, which will patrol the Atlantic Ocean. The electronic ABM systems on the submarines will be immune to any EMP in the air because the ocean water will stop the electromagnetic field. Since water acts as a ground for electricity, it will also protect the submarines from the EMP, as long as they are 300 to 500 feet underwater. The US Navy can test the depth required for the submarines to be immune to the EMP.

The only time when the ABM missiles will suffer from the EMP will be the time from the launch to the impact with a nuclear missile. This means that the microchips and the electronic technology on the ABM missiles will have to be hardened, so that they are immune to the EMP during flight. I will ask the Pentagon to order the US Navy to perform tests on conventional and on nuclear submarines to determine how deep they have to run to be immune from the EMP. The Pentagon can also order the US Navy to refit these submarines with ABM defense systems. Then the submarines can begin patrolling the Atlantic Ocean, and a few of them can patrol the Pacific Ocean.

They can patrol far enough out to get an advantage time wise over any nuclear missiles, which are launched towards the USA. At the end of World War III, the Antichrist will launch nuclear missiles from Russia to destroy NE China and Korea. This is written in Daniel 11:44. At that time I will recommend that the USA should have more ABM defense submarines patrolling in the Pacific Ocean because that is where the nuclear war will be. The USA must use defense only in this war.

The people may not appreciate my Foolproof National Defense very much at first, until they realize that America will be faced with 11 years of survival against the Antichrist during World War III. He will be the most evil person ever to live on the earth, and he will have the nuclear arsenal of the USSR to use. The American people should also realize that the USA and the USSR have just spent 50 years gearing up for a global nuclear war. The Pentagon may have other ways of describing this, but everyone in the USA knows the truth already. The question is, what is the Pentagon going to do now, with the appearance of the Antichrist in Europe, and World War III starting soon?

In the book titled, *Blundering Into Disaster*, © 1986 by Robert S. McNamara, on page 157, the Star Wars or SDI space defense will not be 100% effective.[25]

This is why I have devised a better and more practical way of providing a national defense against nuclear missiles from the Antichrist during World War III. What the American people must do about the current policies of the Pentagon is this:

1. They must demand that the Star Wars defense or SDI should be stopped.
2. They must demand that all NASA rocket launches be stopped now, along with the funding for NASA itself.
3. They must demand that the US military bases in Japan and Korea be closed by the Pentagon, as well as those in England, Europe, and the Middle East.
4. They must demand that the Pentagon should gradually withdraw all US military troops and activities back into the USA.
5. They must demand that the Pentagon should use my Foolproof National Defense, and that they should test it, and have it 70% operational by the year 2010.

If you are wondering why I have this authority, it is because Christ has given it to me. To find out about the nuclear wars, which will happen within the next 20 years, you should read this chapter. I can keep the USA out of all these nuclear wars, if the President, the Pentagon, and the Congress will work with me to keep the USA neutral throughout World War III.

I will also point out to the American people that the Pentagon will have several reasons to kill me, even though I can keep the USA out of 9 nuclear wars. These reasons are:

1. I will tell the Pentagon that they cannot use their stockpile of nuclear toys, after they spent 50 years developing them.
2. I will help to set up the Church Committee Group, which will take $320 billion dollars per year from the Pentagon.
3. I will help to shut down NASA completely.

Therefore in the event of my death by a contract killer, the Pentagon should be suspect. This is the real reason why people try to kill the prophets, as they did to Christ, and the prophets in the Old Testament. They think to themselves, if we can just get rid of him, then everything will be back to normal. What they don't realize is that four billion people on the earth will burn in the fires of the sun forever, if everything is back to normal. About four billion people are in false religion.

THE 1972 ABM TREATY

When the US President takes the offensive military power away from the Pentagon, what is the first thing they have to do?

THEY MUST DEFEND AMERICA

This is something they haven't done in 50 years. There is proof of this in the speech given by Ronald Reagan in 1981, as reported in the International Herald Tribune of October 21, 1981.[26]

On Page 34 of *Missile Envy*, by Helen Caldicott: "and the only defense is, well, you shoot yours and we'll shoot ours."[27] Was he serious? On page 118: "One billion people would be dead, with one billion more seriously injured, since there is no defense against strategic intercontinental nuclear weapons."[28]

Dr. Helen Caldicott made this statement about nuclear war between the USA and Russia. It almost seems like the Pentagon wanted to pass the 1972 ABM Treaty, so they could get funding for Star Wars or SDI. On page 118: "The USA has been working on this space-based, (SDI) anti-missile technology."[29]

In other words, the Pentagon, with the help of Reagan, has spent money on the Star Wars defense to avoid breaking the 1972 ABM Treaty. This Treaty must be eliminated for the USA to avoid nuclear war, and to protect America from nuclear attack.

In the past the US President and the Pentagon have relied on nuclear threats, simply because they don't have an anti-missile defense system for America. This will be fatal during World War III, especially with the Antichrist in Europe.

When you try to eliminate the 1972 ABM Treaty, you must tell all of the nations that World War III is described in the Nuclear War chapter and everyone must build anti-missile defense systems to protect themselves from the Antichrist.

By the time the Church Committee Group negotiates for a Summit meeting to discuss the elimination of the ABM Treaty, all nations can read about the danger which they will be in during World War III. There will be an advantage for America in the negotiations because the President will not have to threaten the Antichrist with nuclear missiles during World War III, if the USA has an ABM defense.

On page 183: "When military planners discussed the use of anti-missile defense systems to defend the MX converted Minuteman Silos, this would defy the ABM Treaty of 1972."[30] In other words, it is illegal to protect America from incoming nuclear missiles, but it is legal to destroy the entire earth with them. This is the logic behind the 1972 ABM Treaty, and it must be eliminated now.

The President of the USA has little or no control over nuclear weapons research and development.

On page 88: "President Carter left office as he had entered: warning about the threat of nuclear war."[31]

On page 89: "He was a good man, but not strong enough to avoid being outmaneuvered by the hawks—a handful of hostile men who had gained enormous power in a political vacuum..."[32]

The problem here is that you never find out about these things until it is too late. Then the President himself will not be able to stop the hawks in the Congress, and the Pentagon because they will use fear as a tactic to start a nuclear war. There was not a war when President Carter was outmaneuvered; but during wartime the Pentagon will have 100 times more power over the people, and they will be unstoppable. This is why the Church Committee Group must take the offensive military power away from the Pentagon now, before World War III starts.

If there is an inherent problem in the US military, the Pentagon, or in the US Congress when World War III starts, it is already too late to correct it. This is what the nuclear deterrence strategy of the Pentagon is.

When the President orders the Pentagon to protect America with anti-missile defense systems, they can build them on the Atlantic, Pacific, and Gulf Coasts. They must do this so the USA will be protected from the Antichrist. This is very important because he will be the most evil person who has ever lived on earth.

This gives proof of how stupid it is to rely on nuclear weapons: The USA is going into World War III with no anti-missile defense, against the most evil person who has ever lived.

Now you can see why the Pentagon must give their offensive military power to the Church Committee.

The Congress will have to work out the details of this legislation. Then the Pentagon can work on national defense for America, while the Church Committee will prevent nuclear war.

The Pentagon should not be allowed to use SDI or Star Wars as an excuse, and they must not be allowed to use fighter aircraft as their only defense because there is a chance of human error, which could kill 50 million people in America.

The fundamental problem with nuclear weapons is that you have to be more evil than your enemy, so that he will back down when you threaten him with nuclear missiles. This explains why the 9 nuclear threats were all made by the USA, and it was always the US President that made the threat. This is written on page 173 and 174 of *Missile Envy*.[33]

This will not be possible with the Antichrist. You cannot possibly be more evil than the son of perdition, or the son of damnation. You could even call the Antichrist the son of Satan.

This is why the Pentagon will have to go through World War III according to the principles in the Bible.

If the US military refuses to do this, the entire human race will be destroyed.

The inherent problem with the Pentagon concerning nuclear weapons is that they always rely on nuclear threats and superiority, instead of anti-missile defense. If they do this with the Antichrist, they will get:

TOTAL NUCLEAR RETALIATION

The function or purpose of a man in this world is to work, and to go out and explore the world. This is why you see the phrase, "Space, the Final Frontier." It is why the Pentagon and NASA are spending so much money on rocket launches, satellites, and space exploration. This is not necessarily the correct thing to be doing, and it is a perfect example of the wisdom of mankind. This is described in I Corinthians 2:4-6, and in I Corinthians 2:13. In I Corinthians 1:20 it is written that God has made foolish the wisdom of this world, and you will know what this means in just a minute. This is verified in I Corinthians 3:19.

Now if you will imagine that space exploration is a waste of time and money, except for satellite technology, I will explain this. In Matthew 24:35 Christ said:

Matthew 24:35: "Heaven and earth shall pass away, but my words shall not pass away."

This phrase was spoken by the Son of God, and in effect he said that space exploration has no future. The rapture of the church will happen by the year 2025. Then after the 1000 years, or the millennium, the earth and the universe will be destroyed by the year 3025. This is written in II Peter 3:10-13. Therefore space exploration in this universe has no future.

Now if you will permit me this folly, I will show you what the phrase means in I Corinthians 3:18: "If any man among you seemeth to be wise in this world, let him become a fool, that he may be wise."

Now just imagine that there are millions of tentacles in America, which come from the pockets of every tax-paying citizen, then go to the Congress, and then to the Pentagon. These work much like vacuum cleaner hoses, and they suck all of the money out of everyone's pocket, funnel it to Congress, and then to the Pentagon. In the final stage, the Pentagon shoots the money into outer space. Then the movie and TV industry in Hollywood are making billions of dollars selling Star Trek Deep Space Nine, Star Trek Voyager, 2001, Alien, and hundreds of movies and TV shows. The people in America are being ripped off by the Pentagon, and the movie industry in Hollywood makes everyone enjoy it. This is a perfect example of the phrase:

I Corinthians 3:19: "For the wisdom of this world is foolishness with God."

The Pentagon officials could believe they are working for a better future, but I think the 1972 ABM Treaty proves they aren't. This treaty made it illegal to protect America with anti-ballistic missile defense in 1972. I think the 1972 ABM Treaty was passed to pave the way for SDI.

Now you can see what I mean. Space exploration has no future because the entire universe will be destroyed by 3025. This is written in Matthew 24:35. The rapture of the church will happen by 2025. We must take our money back from Congress, and give it to the Church Committee, which will use it to prepare for World War III, and we must do it quickly. On page 157 of Robert S. McNamara's book, *Blundering Into Disaster*, is this quote: "It is generally accepted by the technicians supervising SDI that such a leakproof defense is not a realistic goal."[34]

Here are some quotes from Dr. Helen Caldicott's book, *Missile Envy*, and some of my observations about this and World War III.

On page 37: "If push comes to shove they will rely on the ability to deter the Russians by threatening to have a limited nuclear attack."[35]

The people in the USA must realize that the people in the nuclear weapons industry are the real enemy here, and not necessarily the Russians. They have spent 50 years and trillions of dollars on nuclear weapons, and the US military will use them in World War III. The Air Force Generals and the Pentagon believe they can threaten to use nuclear weapons against Russia, but this will cause total nuclear retaliation by the Antichrist in World War III.

The Antichrist will own 41 nations in Europe, the Middle East, Japan, Korea, NE China, and South Africa. He will use nuclear weapons against Rome, Italy. He will probably use chemical warfare against Korea and South Africa. He will not be afraid of nuclear war because he will not care about his people. This is verified in Revelation 6:8, and in Revelation 13:16,17, where he will declare a famine throughout all of Europe. He will give the souls of 800 million people to Satan, and this is why he will not be afraid of nuclear war.

This is why the US President and the Pentagon cannot threaten to use nuclear weapons against the Antichrist. He will be the most evil person ever to live on earth, and he will use total nuclear retaliation if he is threatened. This is why the Church Committee Plan must be used by the USA in World

War III. The theology for this is written in Matthew 5:39. When you don't retaliate against evil, the aggression from the other nation stops. If Russia fired five nuclear missiles at the USA and the Pentagon worked out a plan to defend America against nuclear war and destroyed the missiles, then the 500 church ministers could pray for Russia according to Matthew 5:44. Now before you laugh at this, this is the only way to prevent global nuclear war. It is what the Bible says to do, and in Matthew 5:43-48 are words spoken by Christ, himself. You should also remember that Christ will return to earth early to stop the nuclear war, and this is written in Matthew 24:22.

The verses in Matthew 5:43-48 give instructions for the Christian, so that he can overcome the evil in the world, which is caused by devils. If he retaliates against evil and kills someone he is then a murderer, and he has not overcome the evil. This theology is also true for the nations, and this is why the 500 church ministers will stop nuclear war. I'm very well acquainted with the theology in Matthew 5:43-48 because I've been plagued by devils for 37 years. I haven't retaliated against evil during these years, and I can personally say that the aggression stops when you do not use evil against evil.

During a nuclear war between the USA and Russia there would be evil used against evil. You would not be delivered from Satan in this situation because he uses evil to destroy people. However, if you do not retaliate against the evil, but follow the theology of Matthew 5:43-48, you actually use good against evil, and the aggression stops. This is how the nations can prevent nuclear war during World War III. You must also remember that our Lord Jesus Christ has already won World War III, and what we must do is to go to the churches of Christ by the millions in order to defeat Satan.

On page 42: "The pulse in outer space is clearly different from the terrestrial EMP (Electromagnetic Pulse), but even stronger, about one million volts per meter, driven directly into the satellite's electronic heart. A relatively small explosion of two megatons just outside the upper atmosphere at an altitude of 50 to 75 miles would damage an unprotected satellite in geosynchronous orbit 22,300 miles above the earth. The kill range could easily be extended by increasing the size of the bomb."[36]

The EMP or Electromagnetic Pulse from one nuclear explosion above the earth could blanket the USA, and shut down all power and communication in America, including the national defense. This means the Star Wars defense will be nullified by a few nuclear missiles sent high into the stratosphere. The US military cannot rely on Star Wars or SDI (Strategic Defense Initiative) during World War III. I know that President Bill Clinton formally ended SDI as a project in 1993, but the Pentagon could still try to use some of it during World War III. This would be a disaster. We cannot let them have more than

$80 billion per year because they will cause a war against the Antichrist, which would escalate into global nuclear war.

The EMP from the Russian missiles would render the Star Wars system of the Pentagon completely useless. If this happens, then what is the backup plan? The US military will have to develop an anti-missile defense system that will operate even with the EMP threat. I've also made yearly payments from the Church Committee to the Pentagon to be sure that the anti-missile defense system will be built before World War III. I did this to stop any arguments, which may occur, and to protect the people.

On page 47: "The bombs are our bombs, made with our money, and the Pentagon is our department, and the military are our servants."[37]

Now the people of America and of the other nations in the world will see whether their military forces really do serve them. If they do serve the people, then they will have no problem giving offensive military authority to the Church Committee Group. The US Pentagon can be the example for the other nations because they will do it first. As I wrote here, there will be nine nuclear wars during World War III.

With this kind of tension in the world, only 500 church ministers will be able to prevent nuclear war. We must not allow any kind of macho attitude in the military forces of the world to destroy the human race in a nuclear war. This attitude is what caused the nuclear arms race to start with, and it is also why the USA has no defense against Russian nuclear missiles. On page 38: "In the eighteen-month period from January 1979 to June 1980, there were 3,703 alarms, most of them were routinely assessed and dismissed, but 152 of them were serious enough to have represented a potential attack."[38]

All types of nuclear errors will be avoided with the Church Committee Plan. If the Pentagon can work in such a way as to have permission given or denied by the 500 church ministers within only a few minutes, they will give nuclear authority to the churches to stop nuclear war. There will be no fear of computer errors, human errors, military mistakes, sabotage, or any other such problems. The way to do this would be to install a hot line from the White House to the Church Committee building, and a hot line from the Pentagon to the Church Committee building. During any time of crisis in World War III the 500 church ministers will stay in their Church Committee building. At other times they can have at least 100 ministers there to have a vote in case of an emergency during World War III.

On page 84: "The Soviets were planning to fight and win a nuclear war, and the only way we could prevent this was to regain American nuclear superiority."[39]

This is an example of the macho attitude with the US nuclear hawks, who are the people which evaluate the nuclear arms buildup by Russia, and its nuclear war capability. They are the people who will convince the US President to launch nuclear missiles during World War III. These hawks always assume the worst possible case for Russian motivations and weapons developments.

On page 117: "And so continues the deadly arms race, fueled by macho men who do not understand conflict resolution."[40]

This is proof of what I said about the nuclear hawks. They are the people who counter a Soviet nuclear arms buildup with a US nuclear arms buildup. Therefore the USA has no defense against nuclear missiles. If 100 Soviet missiles were fired at the USA, 100 missiles would land in the USA. There is something wrong here, and the American people should find out what it is.

The macho attitude leads to this type of strategy: The US military always counters a nuclear weapons advance by Russia with the development of more offensive nuclear missiles. They never put any defensive missiles in place because they are macho men. They do not care about the lives of all the people, and they build more weapons of destruction instead of protecting the nation. The question is now, Will the people sit by and let them fight a nuclear war against the Antichrist, or will they replace them with the Church Committee?

On page 84: "The American Security Council made a film called, The Price of Peace and Freedom. One of the arguments presented was that the Soviets never abide by their treaties. Despite alleged infringements of treaties however, there have been no proven substantial violations by either party."[41]

This is an example of a US military organization brainwashing the American people. The title of the film makes you wonder what they mean. The people must put pressure on the US Congress and the President to pass legislation in favor of the Church Committee Plan, and to have it made legal by January 1, 2007.

The nuclear hawks can influence the thinking of scientists who build nuclear weapons, and the Pentagon which uses them.

The American people can shut them down by demanding that the Church Committee Plan should be adopted.

On page 90: "The American press has misrepresented events in foreign countries, so it has been difficult for the American people to know the truth about international affairs."[42]

You can see the evil, which is present in the thinking of the nuclear hawks, the attitude of the press, and the nuclear weapons industry in the USA. The people in the USA must rely on the truth of Christ to get through World War III, and they must not let the military and the nuclear weapons industry in the USA lie to them anymore. I've found the verse in the Bible, which describes this situation.

I John 1:8: "If we say that we have no sin, we deceive ourselves, and the truth is not in us."

It is a sin to build nuclear weapons, which will destroy all life on earth. When the nuclear weapons industry does this, they always say that they are protecting the USA. This is where the lie is because they haven't made anti-missile systems to protect America; and even if they did, they have still sinned grievously.

The problem is that these people will never admit that they have sinned, even when they have made weapons, which could destroy the entire human race 10 times over. You see, the government will never admit that they have sinned, and this is why the Church Committee Plan should be adopted by every free nation in the world to prevent nuclear war.

On page 91: "The CIA was able to bribe its journalists, subsidize its politicians, conspire with military factions, subvert the labor movement, and engage in propaganda campaigns."[43]

This was all done by the CIA in Brazil. This means they can disregard the sovereignty of any nation. Now imagine what would happen if they did this in Germany during World War III. They would cause a global nuclear war. The American people should vote to have the CIA confined to America, and assigned to anti-terrorist activities. World War III has already been won by Christ, and we don't want the CIA to ruin it, and cause a nuclear war in America.

With World War III on the horizon, remember that we have to get through the war without fighting in it. The USA will not be involved at all if we rely completely on Christ, instead of the military and the CIA. The US military has always interfered with the politics and economics of Third World nations, and this must be stopped before World War III starts. If the US military sends the CIA into Brazil to start a military coup, the Antichrist may not like it, and he might send 50,000 troops there to oust the CIA. As you can see, any foreign activity by the CIA or by the US military could invite the Antichrist into our section of the world. This is why the US foreign policy should be isolationist throughout the war.

On page 104: "The Soviet Union was unhappy that the shah, with American influence, was invited to participate in Afghani affairs."[44]

You can see here that any American involvement in the affairs of another nation always causes intervention by Russia. The new danger in this area will be caused by the Antichrist, who will have 200 million soldiers in his army. This is written in Revelation 9:16, and the USA must have an isolationist foreign policy to avoid any clash with him. We don't want the CIA or anyone else to invite him to our section of the world.

On page 101: Daniel Ortega Saavedra of Nicaragua in 1981: "blackmail with the presence of the United States fleet in our territorial waters, military interventions, the landing of Marines, and the imposition of corrupt governments and one-sided economic treaties."[45]

The US Government should find a way to apologize to South America, and negotiate with them to form SAFTA, or the South American Free Trade Agreement. We need to have good neighbors and free trade during World War III. This means that the CIA will not be allowed into South America again. SAFTA will allow an expansion of trade, without any military involvement, and therefore it will produce good neighbors. On page 108: In, "The USA—Japan—China alliance," Russia will take NE China, Korea, and Japan; and, " the USA—Japan—China alliance will become the USA—China, and the USSR—Japan alliances."[46] The military involvement of the USA must be kept as close to none as possible. Then we will not have to protect anyone, and we will not be drawn into World War III.

On page 109: "The US Navy's primary mission in the 1980s has been shifted from a defensive one of protecting vital sea lanes to an offensive one of force projection against the Soviet fleet."[47]

The US Navy will have to go back to protecting sea lanes during World War III. The merchant ships will have to be restricted within areas of the Atlantic and Pacific Oceans closer to the USA because of Russian submarines.

On page 114: "Obviously the major motivation behind the enormous growth in arms sales in the USA and other Western nations is profit. Probably a similar motivation exists for the Soviet Union."[48]

This pattern can be described by this verse in the Bible:

John 8:34: "Jesus answered them, Verily, verily, I say unto you, whosoever committeth sin is the servant of sin."

The nuclear weapons industry makes weapons and missiles to sell to the Pentagon and the Department of Defense in the USA. That seems to be fine, except that the Pentagon has not protected the USA from a nuclear attack. Now in more recent years however, the nuclear weapons and conventional weapons companies have sold weapons to other nations for profit. These companies now sell weapons to nations that are the enemies of the USA. They find that they like the money so well that they sell the weapons to almost every nation that wishes to buy them. This is the meaning of John 8:34, but with governments and weapons manufacturers they will not admit that they have committed sin. This is where the danger of going into World War III is because the people who are in power now, such as the US military, don't think they have committed a sin, when they have weapons which can destroy the earth 10 times over. If we don't change this system fast, the earth is doomed, with all human life on it.

On page 118: "In 1983 six countries had nuclear weapons: The USA, USSR, Britain, China, France, and India.

By the year 2000, it is predicted that Egypt, Saudi Arabia, Iraq, Iran, Pakistan, South Korea, Taiwan, Philippines, Japan, Mexico, Brazil, Argentina, West Germany, Sweden, Italy, Spain, Canada, and Australia could have nuclear weapons."[49] The total is 18, and added to the other six nations it is 24. This increases the danger for nuclear war during World War III because someone might panic and fire missiles. This is what happens when the USA, USSR, Britain, and France sell weapons to Third World nations.

Suddenly the neighbors of these countries have modern weapons, and then they start building nuclear bombs to protect themselves. The USA should begin talks in the United Nations to eliminate as many nuclear weapons as possible before World War III begins. All arms sales by the USA, USSR, Britain, and France must be stopped.

On page 114: "for a world to become more and more dependent on arms sales which will lead to death and destruction, and could lead to nuclear war, when two thirds of the children are malnourished and starving, is evil and immoral."[50]

The nations of the world can keep their armies at home, and spend their money on food for their people. The need to store dry food for a seven-year famine will be expensive, but the free nations will not have to fight in World War III. Only the nations in Europe, the Middle East, NE China, Korea, Japan, and South Africa will be invaded by the Antichrist. The other nations in the world can stay at home, and use the money that they would have spent on their military to feed their own people during World War III.

We can't fight against the Antichrist because it could start a nuclear war. All of the nations should also realize that they couldn't fight a war against the 200 million soldiers, which will be in his army. Christ has already won World War III, and we must use the Church Committee Plan to be saved.

On page 127: "Of the total US conventional forces, half are allocated to help Western Europe if there is a war with Russia."[51] The USA must stop this war strategy now because the American troops in Europe will be killed by the army of the Antichrist. This would probably lead to a nuclear war because the Pentagon would retaliate against them.

On page 130: "This huge number of US bases has been developed over the years following World War II, but the number has increased from 323 in 1974 to 359 in 1984."[52]

The number of military bases which the USA has overseas is really too many, and should be reduced as soon as possible. President Clinton cut the number of bases in the USA in 1993, and the same thing should be done with the bases overseas. I think the number of bases closed in 1993 was 130, and the number of bases closed overseas should be 368. The logic here is: The less we have to protect, the less chance that America will be involved in World War III.

The military bases in Europe will have to be closed now. These are in: Belgium, West Germany, Greece, Italy, Korea, Netherlands, Portugal, Spain, Turkey, and the United Kingdom. The ones in England are critical, and the British and Scottish people will have to move to the USA. All US military bases in Korea, and Japan must be closed immediately. The USA will not have the economic power to close these bases, and bring the trucks, tanks, and airplanes home after World War III begins because of the Stock Market crash.

The US bases, which can be left open, are in: Puerto Rico, Wake Island, and all US Territories.

The American people should realize that if the Pentagon has $400 billion dollars a year to spend on weapons and war, they will cause a war against the Antichrist, which will lead to nuclear war. The USA should cut back on military spending, close military bases overseas, and call for the Church Committee Plan to take control of all offensive military action.

On page 138: "One purpose of conventional weapons is to deter a conventional war."[53]

This statement was made by Dr. Helen Caldicott, and it is true for that one purpose. The problem is that Army generals and the US military buy weapons to fight wars, and not to deter them.

On page 138: "Nuclear weapons are also being built and deployed in Europe to deter or prevent a conventional war from occurring."[54]

This is ridiculous. All of the arms sales by the USA, Russia, England, and France have now caused more nations to make nuclear weapons to protect themselves from the nations with modern weaponry. The companies that sold modern weapons to Third World nations thought they could get away with making billions of dollars with no risk to the USA and Russia, but they were wrong. By the year 2000, 18 Third World nations will have nuclear weapons, and this will increase the chance of nuclear war during World War III. This is why we must cut the nuclear weapons companies and the conventional weapons manufacturers out of our government. And it is also why the US Government must ban the sales of all types of weapons right away.

On page 138: "Deterrence is a vague, esoteric theory, which says that the possession of nuclear weapons will prevent nuclear war."[55]

As I just said, the US military generals buy weapons to fight war, and not to deter it. They use a lie to convince the people that they are protecting them from attack. Now when World War III starts, the more weapons everyone has, the more nations will be involved in the war, and this is the truth. Then it could escalate into a global nuclear war, simply because a nation panicked, and fired nuclear missiles. Now you can see why I've advised the USA, and all free nations to use the Church Committee Plan. This means that all nations not in Europe, the Middle East, Japan, Korea, or South Africa can avoid nuclear war by using this plan. It will stop nuclear war over 75% of the earth.

On page 209: "In 1960 Herman Kahn wrote the book, On Thermonuclear War. In the book he said that nuclear war would increase the number of children born with genetic defects, but 4% are born that way anyway."[56]

If you look closely at his statement, you can see that he is trying to justify a nuclear war, which would destroy the entire human race. The weapons manufacturers and the military lie to the people about nuclear weapons to get approval for their weapons contracts. James Newman wrote: Kahn's book was, "a moral tract on mass murder, how to plan it, how to commit it, how to get away with it, and how to justify it."[57]

The people in the world are being deceived by the weapons manufacturers and the military. They will have to act quickly to get control of the military forces in their nation before World War III. The people and the churches must put pressure on the political leaders to use the Church Committee Plan during World War III. The military people could say that they need lots of money to protect their nations, but it is more important to feed and clothe them. To win World War III the people must go to the churches of Christ by the millions. Then if anyone is killed their souls will be saved for Christ.

The USA and Russia must dismantle as many nuclear weapons as is physically possible right away. The reason is that World War III is coming soon, and the more nuclear weapons that are destroyed, the less chance and the less severe will be the destruction of the earth.

On page 140: "Conventional weapons should be used only for national defense."[58]

This is a quote from Dr. Helen Caldicott. She said that this and a nuclear weapons freeze, a nonintervention treaty, a reduction in NATO and Warsaw Pact forces, an end to development of conventional weapons, and a call for nuclear disarmament would lead to peace. Russia collapsed in 1990, but the USA must still call for nuclear disarmament.[59] The use of conventional weapons for national defense will be the only military action to be used by the USA and by the other nations during World War III. Then the nations can store food for a seven-year famine, and feed their people during the war, instead of spending money on weapons.

On page 155: "The annual budget and staff for the NSA (The National Security Agency) far exceeds that of the CIA or FBI. It operates in a highly technical field, and it is free to define its own goals."[60]

In other words the NSA, CIA, and FBI make up their own rules. This could be fatal for the USA during World War III. Any kind of a mistake by these agencies could cause a confrontation with the Antichrist.

On page 162: "During the incredible fear, and emotion during a nuclear war, nothing and nobody would work according to plan."[61]

The US military and the American people must realize the danger of having a technological advantage over Russia, caused by their collapse from 1990 to 1998. This collapse will fool the people into believing that we don't have to prepare for World War III. It could also fool the military into believing that we can fight during World War III. The truth is that the Antichrist will take the world oil supply and our military vehicles will have no fuel. It doesn't matter how advanced our weapons are, they will not work if they are out of fuel. This is why the US military should be limited to defend America during World War III. They cannot be allowed to fight in any other nation during the war.

On page 162: " Missiles once launched cannot be recalled or aborted."[62]

This means that nuclear weapons cannot be stopped once the missiles are launched.

On page 162: "The military has resisted installing safety devices like self-destruct mechanisms."[63]

These people have the ability to destroy the entire human race, and they would rather do this than destroy their nuclear missiles.

The US Government can order the Pentagon to put self-destruct mechanisms on the nuclear missiles.

The most formidable resistance to peace for the USA during World War III will be from the Rand Corporation, Boeing, Lockheed, McDonnell Douglas, and the other companies, which make military weapons. These powerful corporations will lobby in Congress, and they will give great sums of money to government agencies, in order to get US military weapons contracts. If the American people want to get through this war alive, they will have to cut the weapons manufacturers out of the government now. The only way to do this is to take $320 billion dollars per year away from the Pentagon. If they don't have any money, then how can they start a war against the Antichrist?

On page 184: "In November 1982 I was lobbying around the halls of Congress. The halls were full of Pentagon lobbyists from weapons manufacturers, but I saw no American people or their children."[64]

You should notice that the Pentagon lobbies in Congress, as well as the companies that make weapons. The nuclear weapons industry lobbies in Congress, and the people must put pressure on the US Government to adopt the Church Committee Plan, which will give the people back their government. If the Pentagon has $400 billion dollars a year during World War III, they will start a war against the Antichrist.

On page 174: "Hence the use of nuclear blackmail has been an American ploy."[65]

This is something that cannot be allowed to happen during World War III. The US President will not be able to threaten Russia with nuclear war, if the Church Committee has authority over all offensive military action. Then the President would have to get approval for any offensive military action from the 500 church ministers. This will include nuclear war, and therefore the President could not make any kind of threat like nuclear attack. Of the nine times when nuclear threats were made, it was always the US President who made the threat against another nation. This is very important to know because the Antichrist will not be afraid of nuclear war. He will give the souls of 800 million people to Satan. He will not care about his people, and this is why nuclear war won't scare him at all.

On page 183: "Because of the MX's vulnerability, military planners have discussed the use of anti-ballistic missile systems to defend the MX converted Minuteman Silos. Such a move will openly defy the Anti-Ballistic Missile Treaty signed by Russia and the USA in 1972."[66]

The USA and Russia have built nuclear weapons, which could destroy the earth 10 times over, and in 1972 they apparently agreed that they would not protect their nations from them. Why are these missiles so valuable that the US military and the Russian military will destroy the entire human race to protect their missiles? When I look at some of the logic in these military plans, I can see that devils have influenced the thinking of the people who made them. For example, why have these people spent trillions of dollars on nuclear weapons, and yet they have no defense against incoming nuclear missiles from Russia? And then why did the USA and Russia have a treaty in 1972, which made it illegal to protect their nations?

On page 192: "Cynical public relations firms using modern psychology are hired to convince people that nuclear weapons are good for them and their children."[67]

This kind of tactic was used during Reagan's years. Dr. Helen Caldicott pointed this out on pages 143,176,181,182,183,191, and 192 of her book, *Missile Envy*.[68]

Not only do these companies make weapons that are evil, they also use tactics that are evil to convince the people that these weapons are good for

WORLD WAR III: NUCLEAR WAR

them. This is where the lie is, and it goes into the government when the nuclear weapons companies lobby in Congress.

The nuclear weapons companies lie to the people in order to get weapons contracts. But the important thing to remember is that neither these companies nor the US Government will admit that they have committed sin, even when they have made weapons that will destroy all life on earth. This is why we must change the system of our government, and put people there who admit the truth about sin, and have asked the Lord Jesus Christ to forgive them. These are the people who will work in the Church Committee Group.

On page 195: "Neutron bombs are designed to be used against invading Russian tanks in Western Europe."[69]

The US military must not interfere with the Antichrist in Europe. The troops that we have in Europe must be brought home now. The people who live in Western Europe will follow the Antichrist, and they will applaud him just like they did with Hitler in World War II. He will bring economic prosperity to Europe, and people will accept the mark of the beast by the millions. Then the Antichrist will build his army of 200 million soldiers.

This is why the US President and the Pentagon should close all of the US military bases in Europe. The USA will not be able to do this later because of the fuel crisis and the loss of economic strength. The Antichrist will attack the USA with nuclear missiles if the US military is still in Europe when World War III begins. On page 196: "The neutron bomb is a trip wire between conventional and nuclear war."[70]

This means it will cause both, and it is why it will be used in Europe. The neutron bomb is a good weapon to be used against tanks, and the US military will use it when the Russian tanks roll into Western Europe. The people in the USA cannot let the US military do this, and the only way to stop it is to put pressure on the US Government to adopt the Church Committee Plan.

The phrase, "trip wire," also means a snare, and it will be the type of snare, which will cause a nuclear war. The US Government must get all US military forces out of Europe now. If the neutron bomb is used against Russian tanks and troops, a full-scale nuclear war will result.

On page 198: "The US emphasis on security access to the Persian Gulf is to protect US energy companies in the processing and global marketing of Persian Gulf oil, and European access to the oil. To this end, the US military and political leadership may be prepared to start a nuclear war."[71]

If you don't believe this, you should remember what happened in Kuwait when Iraq tried to take the oil there. This is why the people in America should try to change the system in Washington DC. They should also put pressure on Congress and the President to build the 50,000 Natural Gas refill stations in the USA, so we can convert our vehicles to Natural Gas fuel. Then we won't need the oil in the Persian Gulf, and we won't have to defend it against the Antichrist.

On page 200: "For 38 years the nuclear doctrine of the USA has been to attack Russia first with nuclear weapons, if the USA disapproves of any Soviet incident or war."[72]

This is probably still the case. The Soviet doctrine is to retaliate with massive numbers of nuclear weapons, when the USA launches its missiles. This strategy must be changed by the US President and the Pentagon. There is going to be fear and tension during World War III, which has never been seen before. This is written in Matthew 24:12, Matthew 24:21, and in Luke 21:26. The Church Committee Plan will take the human errors, the fear, and the emotion out of the nuclear weapons theater, and then the people will be safe from nuclear war.

On page 201: "American scientists are totally out of touch with reality, desperately dreaming up schemes to use their nuclear weapons in a limited way without provoking massive genocide. This is schizoid thinking. (A split between reality and perception of reality)."[73]

This quote is like a prophecy because it is what the scientists will do when World War III starts. They will be desperate, and they will run here and there trying to invent new ideas and weapons. Because these people control the Pentagon and the President to some degree, we must cut them out of Washington DC now by starting the Church Committee Plan. If the American people don't change the system there, the entire earth will be destroyed in a nuclear war.

On page 204: "We have grasped the mystery of the atom, and rejected the Sermon on the Mount. We know more about war than we do about peace. We know more about killing than about living."[74]

I think this book project by Dr. Helen Caldicott was done so that I could study her book in order to write a chapter on the US military. Her material was excellent, and it gave me great insight into the US Government and the Pentagon. I had already written the Church Committee Plan before I read her book, and you can see how well it fits with her descriptions of the military in the USA. There are probably 50 ways in which the Church Committee Plan will stop nuclear war.

On page 206: "The supplemental costs of a 20 year program to provide essential food and for health needs in all developing countries would be $80 billion dollars. This would be available if all nations were to redirect 12% of this year's military spending."[75]

This can be done now and throughout World War III. All nations must stay out of World War III, and then it will only be fought in Europe and in the Middle East. It will not do any good to fight against the 200 million soldiers in the army of the Antichrist; and this is why the free nations should spend their money on food for the seven-year famine, instead of buying weapons. Feed the poor people in your nation, and tell the people to go to the churches of Christ. This is how to win World War III, and how to overcome Satan.

The nations that want to be saved by Christ will have to feed their poor people. Your nation will not be saved if you let your poor people starve. This is written in Matthew 25:41-46.

On page 206: "In the 5 years from 1984 to 1988, the Reagan administration planned to spend $1.8 trillion dollars on military."[76]

President Reagan shafted the USA for the next 50 years, but he is still considered a hero by the people. Yet people like me who work for peace are ridiculed. I will follow the example of Christ because he was ridiculed before he was crucified. The verses in Matthew 5:11,12 say that I'm doing this the right way because I get harassed like the Old Testament prophets.

The atomic bomb is evil. President Roosevelt authorized its construction. Edward Teller was the inventor of the hydrogen bomb, which is 10 times more deadly than the atomic bomb. He destroyed the career of Oppenheimer, and by simple competition he created the most evil device ever known to mankind. These weapons came into the world through the tree of knowledge of good and evil, written in Genesis 2:9, and in Genesis 3:1-7. If you think about this for a minute, you will see that scientists search for knowledge in order to develop new technology for weapons. Then it is no surprise that the most evil nuclear weapons are created by them. This is the meaning of the phrase, "the tree of knowledge of good and evil." The scientists search for knowledge to create nuclear weapons, and they find that knowledge through the tree in Genesis 2:9.

On page 212: "The scientific labs distrust arms control, and provide protection and strong opposition to any measures that might limit nuclear weapons development."[77]

It is the people who work in these labs that will oppose anything that will bring peace to the world. They have the backing of corporations, which have billions of dollars, they have advertising departments that convince people that nuclear weapons are made for peace, and not for war, and they will oppose the right of the people to have the US Government serve them. In other words the scientists control the government as it is now, instead of the people controlling it. This will be fatal during World War III.

On page 213: "The labs have access to classified information and they are extremely powerful and influential within government circles. Over the years these labs have opposed all nuclear arms cut-backs and test ban treaties."[78]

The people in the USA must take the power away from these scientists by forcing the US Government to approve the Church Committee Plan. These people are, "mad scientists," in every sense of the word, and the people should know that they would rather destroy mankind than to destroy their nuclear weapons.

On page 216: President Reagan: "Let us turn to the strength in technology that started our industries."[79]

Here is where I will give a warning to the people: If you rely on these scientists and their technology during World War III, the USA will be destroyed. It was Satan who brought evil into the world through the tree of knowledge of good and evil, and the scientists study and work to improve the evil, which comes through the tree. They have developed weapons that could destroy the earth 10 times over, and they will not admit that they have committed sin.

Do you want the future of the USA to be left in the hands of people who will not admit that they have committed sin, and who do not tell the truth? I don't.

If the military strong point of the USA and other nations is evil, then how will the nations be delivered from Satan? This is why mankind cannot rely on science and technology to save them during World War III. Satan can deceive mankind during war because it is evil. The Lord Jesus Christ can save us because he overcame Satan; and the way to do this is to honor Christ, read the Bible, and go to church. The people must have faith in Christ, and they must believe that only Christ can save the USA. This is the only way to get through World War III without fighting. If any free nation fights against the Antichrist, there will be a nuclear war.

The people must realize that all of the nuclear weapons created over the past 50 years were made for one reason: To be used in World War III. That is exactly what the US military will do if they are not stopped.

There is a verse in the Bible, which describes this:

Matthew 7:15: "Beware of false prophets, which come to you in sheep's clothing, but inwardly they are ravening wolves."

The nuclear scientists come to the people in sheep's clothing because they pretend to be working for peace. But inwardly they are ravening wolves because they are really working to create war, and to get a nuclear advantage over Russia.

The scientists lie to the people to get approval for their weapons contracts. And if they lie to us during World War III, it will be fatal. In John 8:44 Jesus said that Satan is a liar, and the father of lies because he was the first to tell a lie in the Garden of Eden, when he deceived Adam and Eve. When he did this, Satan murdered the entire human race. If the people let these scientists lie to them during the war, the entire earth will be destroyed. These decisions are extremely critical, and Christ warned us six times in Matthew 24:4-27 so that we will not be deceived.

If the free nations want to survive World War III, they will have to refocus their efforts on mercy for their people by providing food, housing, and medical aid for them. The governments can also work for the judgment of Christ by telling their people to go to the churches of Christ during World War III.

The Pentagon has convinced the people that they are working for national security. This situation will change during World War III because they can't win a war against the Antichrist, no matter what they do. If they even try to start a war against him, there will be a nuclear war in the USA. The US military should know that only Christ can win a war against the Antichrist. Only Christ can destroy him and his army. This is written in Revelation 16:16, Revelation 19:11-16, and in Revelation 19:17-21.

The people in the USA must regain control of their government, and use their tax money to prepare for World War III.

On page 222: "The administration of military spending has been staffed, especially in wartime, by executives and officials from the defense industry."[80]

This means the companies, which make the nuclear weapons, can put their own executives into the government agency, which hands out the money for contracts. This means they have a lock on billions of dollars of the tax money, which is paid by the American people. They can spend this money on nuclear weapons, instead of food and housing for the people during World War III.

On page 223: "America does not have a working democracy in the area of defense."[81]

This means the people have almost no power over the defense industry.

On page 241: "It will take a highly motivated, well educated, and determined movement of good American people to shift society toward life and away from death and nuclear war."[82]

To move toward life is to live for Christ, and not for scientific technology and war. The only way to do this is to take the money away from the Pentagon.

On page 241: "Almost the whole financial network of the USA is involved in the weapons industry, and what's more, is working actively to support and represent it."[83]

I believe that the only way to change this type of monopoly on weapons buying and selling, finance, advertising, and lobbying is to cut the cancer out of the government, and replace it with a safe alternative. The Church

Committee Plan will do this, and it will stop nuclear war over 75% of the earth.

The Defense Industry corporations can direct their efforts and technology into helping the people prepare for World War III. Some of the things which will be needed will be: Geiger counters, gas masks, grain silos, anti-missile missiles, food warehouses, greenhouses, welder's goggles, water tanks, and travel trailers.

These corporations can work for the Church Committee, instead of the Pentagon.

The Church Committee Plan will take $320 billion dollars away from the Department of Defense. It will also take the lobbying, the political power, and the false advertising away from the defense industry. Then the people will have control over their government again. This is the one critical step to prepare for World War III. It must be made legal by Congress by January 1, 2007. You must remember what Dr. Helen Caldicott said; the normal means of allocating money in Congress must be changed. This means the House and Senate Armed Services Committees, Defense Appropriations subcommittees, and some other committees may have to be changed.

These could be replaced by other members of Congress who are Christians.

The $80 billion dollars, which is left in the Department of Defense budget, can be used by the Pentagon to pay for thousands of anti-missile missiles on the East, West, and Gulf Coasts in the USA to defend America against nuclear attack. The Pentagon can also use the money to convert the Army, Air Force, and National Guard vehicles to Natural Gas. If there isn't enough money to do this, the Church Committee can give them money from the emergency funds. If there are 10 million vehicles which belong to the military, and it costs $2000 to convert each one, the total cost would be $20 billion dollars to convert them to natural gas. This will be a one-time cost.

On page 336: "We need to create the political climate that will channel government money into peaceful industry, and abolish appropriations for weapons production."[84]

This is what the Church Committee Plan does, but the ways of allocating the money in Congress must be changed, in order to make sure that the system cannot revert to the way it was. This is why the House and Senate Armed Services Committees must be abolished, along with the Defense Appropriations subcommittees, and other agencies. They will have to be replaced with a Committee of Congressmen who are Christians, and who will appropriate the money for the Church Committee.

The American people can join into groups of 100 people, and spend $2000 dollars each to have a construction company build a fallout shelter for them.

The total expense would be $200,000 dollars. It should have a distilled water tank with 15,000 gallons of water. It should also have a few tons of dry food, a few Coleman stoves, a kitchen stove with an oven, a quiet electrical generator, toilet facilities, a television, a fax machine, a telephone, a pool table, books, cards, and recreation, and beds, tables, and clothes closets.

The Church Committee can buy 13 million travel trailers per year, and store them on military bases, with guards to protect them. The US Government can help to get the travel trailers at a discount price. The thirteen million travel trailers per year would cost $156 billion dollars. After six years there will be 78 million of them in storage to be given to the 75 to 100 million homeless people during World War III.

This is what I mean by having one million people march on Washington DC to lobby in Congress, in order to get them to use the Church Committee Plan. The quote from page 336 sounds almost like a prophecy. The Church Committee is a system that will sustain the life process for the people in the USA. The people will have a food supply, housing for the homeless, Geiger counters, fallout shelters, gas masks, and several other things which they will not have if the Pentagon is still in charge of the money in Congress.

When the USA spent 40% of the total money on the military in 1983, how is the economy going to keep up with world markets? The bombs, missiles, and nuclear weapons will sit on shelves in warehouses and will not even be used. The problem is that they will not benefit society. I think the Pentagon already has enough nuclear weapons to protect the USA during World War III; and now the $320 billion dollars from their budget can go to the Church Committee to help the people in America prepare for the war.

On page 326: "It also could be acknowledged that prevention of nuclear war is the ultimate patriotic act."[85]

This is what I'm trying to do here.

On page 331: "The arbitrary decisions of the Pentagon, the fraud and corruption of the nuclear industries and Congress, and the psychic numbing which is present in the public."[86]

These are the various problems with the system as it is now. The people say to themselves, we know that the military and the Defense industry are lying to us about the nuclear weapons, but we will block it out so we won't have to think about the consequences. The people don't have a choice now, with World War III coming. The US military and the nuclear weapons industry have been out of control for 50 years, and now we must stop them to get through World War III alive.

Nuclear war is part of the evil, which came into the world because of Satan. This happened when he lied to Adam and Eve in Genesis 3:1-7. They ate from the tree of knowledge of good and evil. When a person knows what

113

evil is, it becomes a part of them. The people must realize that nuclear weapons will kill everyone on earth, and we must work to dismantle as many of them as we can before World War III starts.

In I John 1:8 the people who say they have no sin are deceiving themselves, and the truth is not in them. This is where the lie is in the nuclear weapons industry, the Pentagon, and the US Government. It is a sin to build nuclear weapons that could kill everyone on earth.

This is where the protest should be made by the people: Get the lies out of the US Government, and rely on the truth of our Lord Jesus Christ during World War III.

Here are some quotes from the book, *Blundering Into Disaster*, written by Robert S. McNamara, who was Secretary of Defense in the USA, under John F. Kennedy and Lyndon B. Johnson.

On page 5: There were 50,000 nuclear weapons in the world in 1986, and a few hundred of them could have destroyed the USA, USSR, and almost the entire earth.[87]

There are still thousands of these nuclear weapons, and the USA and Russia must try to dismantle as many of them as possible before World War III starts.

On page 13: "The Hot Line,"[88] It stopped a nuclear war in 1967. I don't know how this will work in World War III. The Antichrist will be the ruler over Europe, and it will probably be best for the USA to remain neutral and isolated from world politics. The more that the politicians say, the closer America will be to nuclear war. It will be dangerous to talk to the Antichrist over the Hot Line.

The US Government must honor Christ during World War III, and they must change the way that their military works. If the Pentagon has $400 billion dollars per year during World War III, they will cause a war against the Antichrist, which will result in a nuclear war. The only way to stop them is to take their money away from them, and then they will not be able to start a war.

On page 14: In a crisis like World War III, each side will feel pressure to delegate authority to fire nuclear weapons to their battlefield Commanders. As the tension increases, these Commanders will face a desperate dilemma: Use them or lose them.[89]

This kind of statement really gives you confidence in the military doesn't it?

This is a very good reason to give the offensive military authority to the Church Committee during World War III. Then the Pentagon will have to get permission from them before they can start a war.

On page 21: Nuclear weapons replaced the conventional defense by NATO in Western Europe because of financial and manpower reasons.[90]

In other words, it is easier and less expensive to push a button than to send troops and tanks to the battlefield. After the buttons are pushed, then the horrors of nuclear destruction will be left.

On page 28: In 1986 the Soviet writers and politicians declared: "There will be no victors in a nuclear war."[91]

The nuclear hawks in Washington DC and the nuclear weapons industry in the USA told us that Russia was determined to win the nuclear arms race, and they did it to get approval for their weapons contracts. Yet this doesn't quite fit with the statement made by Soviet politicians. You can see here that the people in the nuclear weapons industry and in the military lie to a certain degree to the people in the USA. This cannot be allowed to happen during World War III. We must replace them with the Church Committee.

When the people in America and the other free nations come to Christ by going to church, then we will have defeated Satan. Then the souls of these people will go to Christ. The theology of World War III can be seen by looking at what the Antichrist and Satan will do in Europe. In Revelation 6:8, and in Revelation 13:16,17 the Antichrist will use a famine to give the souls of 800 million people to Satan. Therefore you can deduce that the way to defeat Satan is to have all of the people in all free nations go to the churches of Christ by the millions. Now the situation in Europe is different. The people there must move to another nation out of Europe to be saved.

On page 33: Helmut Schmidt on Tactical nuclear weapons: "Tactical nuclear weapons will not defend Europe, but destroy it."[92]

The US military must remove all nuclear weapons from Europe now, including the neutron bombs. All US military bases in Europe must be closed immediately as well. The Antichrist will have 200 million soldiers in his army, and the US military personnel in Europe will be killed if they don't return to the USA.

On page 34: "The USA has allocated 400 of its submarine based Poseidon nuclear warheads for use by NATO. The Soviet Union, it is believed, envisions as many as several hundred of its ICBM's being used against Western Europe."[93]

This means that Western Europe will be the hot spot during World War III. Of course the Russian ICBM's will be retargeted for the USA, as soon as the Russian Army joins the Antichrist. The USA must call back the nuclear warheads, which were to be used by NATO, in order to prevent any kind of error during World War III. Again, the US military must get out of Europe now, and they must never interfere with the Antichrist there or anywhere else.

On page 35: "NATO strategy relies on the threat of first use of nuclear weapons. The Soviet Union and the USA do not wish to have war. But dangerous frictions between the Warsaw Pact and NATO will develop in the future."[94]

This will happen during World War III, and the USA must withdraw from NATO now, while we have the economic strength to bring our troops home. We cannot fight against the Antichrist. In Revelation 13:10 anyone who fights in World War III will be destroyed. In Revelation 19:19-21 Christ will destroy the Antichrist and his army at Armageddon.

On page 36: "If deterrence fails and conflict develops, NATO's first use stance and strategy carry with them the high risk that Western civilization, as we know it, will be destroyed.

This is the unplanned, and to me, unacceptable result of the long series of incremental decisions taken by the military and civilian leaders of the East and West during the first 50 years of the nuclear age. Can we work ourselves out of this position during the next 50 years?"[95]

Unfortunately we now have only six years, instead of 50. World War III will start in 2012, and with that in mind, the USA must withdraw from NATO now. The President should advise the United Nations Organization to dissolve NATO, so there will not be any conflict when the Antichrist appears, and gains power in the Common Market in Europe.

The people in the USA should remember that Robert McNamara was the secretary of Defense for the US Government for seven years, and that he is very knowledgeable in the field of nuclear weapons. The first use stance by NATO will cause a nuclear war, when the Russian troops and tanks move into Western Europe. This can be prevented only if the USA recalls its troops from Europe, its Poseidon nuclear warheads from NATO, and drops out of the NATO Organization now.

On page 44: "The Air Force, without any intention to deceive, had simply interpreted ambiguous data in ways that supported their weapons programs."[96]

These nuclear weapons have been researched and developed over the past 50 years for one reason: To be used in World War III. The people in the USA must stop the Pentagon now by supporting the Church Committee Plan. If we take $320 billion dollars away from the US military, they will not be able to start a war with the Antichrist. Therefore America will not be in a nuclear war.

This is why anti-missile defense should be used during World War III:

On page 175: "An ABM is an anti-ballistic missile, which is designed to intercept and destroy attacking nuclear missiles and warheads."[97]

Even though the ABM Treaty of 1972 prohibits building and use of nationwide ABM systems, the US military should use them for national defense during World War III. This can be done by the Pentagon because they will still be in charge of America's defense during the war.

Here are some notes, which I've written about the results of nuclear war, which I got from Dr. Helen Caldicott's book, *Missile Envy*.[98] Some of the things, which will be needed after the nuclear attack, will be:

1. Increase the number of doctors for nuclear care by 25%.
2. Scatter and increase the morphine supply to states, which have large cities or populations, and to states that will be nuclear targets. Military guards will have to protect the morphine during World War III.
3. Increase the number of trained medical technicians who will help the burned or injured people; and build more storage facilities throughout the USA, so the technicians will have better access to the drugs and the medicine during World War III.
4. Find safe storage throughout the USA for vaccines and antibiotics, where they will be safe from nuclear attack, and fallout. Some of the vaccines that will be needed are for these diseases: Polio, tetanus, whooping cough, measles, influenza, typhus, smallpox, and diphtheria. There are diseases, which will spread because of the death and destruction after the nuclear attack, and they will spread because people will not be immune to them. These are: cholera, malaria, typhoid fever, yellow fever, dysentery, botulism, food poisoning, hepatitis A, meningitis, pneumonia, tuberculosis, and bubonic plague. The bubonic plague is the most serious threat to mankind because of the increase of rats after nuclear war.
5. Increase the protection of nuclear reactors in the USA by using anti-missile missiles.
6. Instead of evacuating people in the cities, you could use parking garages under the tall buildings for temporary fallout shelters. The evacuation of the people is an open invitation to nuclear war because of Soviet satellites.
7. Radiation doses will be lower in rural areas than in the cities. This is why the people in small towns should stay inside their houses. The nuclear fallout will be in the air outside; therefore the people should stay inside their houses for two weeks after nuclear attack.
8. The ventilation systems in fallout shelters will be blocked when the electrical power system fails. This means they will need electrical generators in the fallout shelters with gasoline in storage. The ventilation systems will also need air filtration facilities that will filter the alpha and beta radioactive particles out of the air. The US Government should order

117

the research and development of air filtration systems that will take nuclear fallout out of the air, which goes into fallout shelters.

9. The hospitals in the cities will have power failures, and will also need backup electrical generators. In fact every hospital in the USA should already have one.

10. Although I do not recommend building elaborate, expensive fallout shelters, I do recommend that the people in large cities should tell the mayors there to work out a plan to put large steel doors on rollers just on the inside of the parking garages in the city. These doors can be left open until a nuclear war happens, and then the parking garages can serve as fallout shelters. The storage rooms in them should have first aid kits with bandages, hydrogen peroxide, and other necessary items to help treat the people who have burns, injuries, or other medical or health problems.

11. Suicide is forbidden no matter what the circumstances are.

12. The people will need to cook food even if the propane or natural gas system fails. The way to do this is to buy Coleman stoves now, and the fuel for them. The new ones have propane cylinders, and they are the best to use. The older ones use white gasoline, which is somewhat dangerous in confined spaces. You will have to keep the Coleman stoves in the storage rooms in the parking garages.

13. The canned food is the best to use after a nuclear attack because the nuclear fallout cannot contaminate it. The fallout is like dust, and it cannot get into the cans. The best food to put into storage is dry food because it will last longer. You must put it into Ziploc bags to keep the alpha and beta particles out. The dry food can be: beans, rice, macaroni, dry pasta, dry nuts, and other types. You can buy most types of dry food in the supermarkets now, and ask how long they will last in storage in Ziploc bags. You can also buy food freezers, and put food in them yourself, but I think the frozen food will only last two years before it spoils. You should be careful to follow directions, and ask how long each type of food will last after it is frozen, or stored in Ziploc bags.

14. It is of the utmost importance to prepare food for storage because it will be nearly impossible to grow food after a nuclear attack. The nuclear fallout will contaminate any food, which is grown outside after the nuclear attack. This is also why the USA and other nations must protect their soil in greenhouses. The Third World nations in South America, Mexico, Africa, India, China, Asia, and others must prepare millions of tons of dry food. It can be stored in grain silos and in food warehouses, where it can be protected from water and weather conditions. The normal food supply in Third World nations will last one or two months at most, and millions of people will starve unless the nations store food for a seven-year famine.

15. The farm tractors in all nations will have to be converted to natural gas because the petroleum fuel will be taken by the Antichrist. This is very important because the food supply depends on it.
16. The US Government should develop a plan to teach the people in cities how to grow crops, and they can grow food if the farmers are killed during a nuclear attack. Only 6% of the US population is involved in farming. The government should also tell the farmers and feed stores to store seeds for all food types in underground warehouses, in steel bank vaults, and in other places where they will be protected from nuclear attack and fallout.
17. Any food crop, which is eaten after a nuclear attack, will almost certainly have nuclear fallout on it, unless it is from a storage area in a house or in a fallout shelter. If you wash the food, it could be contaminated if the water has fallout in it. This is why the people will need Geiger counters. And this is why it is important to store food for a seven-year famine; and it is also important to store millions of gallons of distilled water in tanks, and in one-gallon plastic containers. This water can be used to cook the food.
18. About 50% of the livestock will be killed because of the fallout, and 25% of the cattle will die when they eat grass, alfalfa, or other food, which is contaminated with fallout. The farmers and cattle ranchers should have an emergency plan to contact people or freezer locker companies to slaughter the cattle before the fallout kills them. The beef can be stored in freezers if there are electrical generators there to keep the freezers working. Another idea is to cover the haystacks with plastic tarps during World War III, so the feed for the cattle will not be contaminated by fallout. These tarps must cover all of the hay bales, and should be left in place until the hay is removed to feed the cattle. The cattle ranchers will have to move the cattle from the grass fields, so they will not eat grass or alfalfa, which has nuclear fallout on it. The cattle can be moved to feed lots, and they can be fed with hay bales, which have not been contaminated. Steel buildings would be best to protect the cattle. The cattle ranchers will have to change the water troughs or cover them, so the nuclear fallout in the air won't contaminate the water. The US Government can order companies to build or invent new water troughs for the cattle, which will cover the top of the trough, and protect the water from nuclear fallout. Put these in the steel buildings.
19. The nuclear missiles will release 5000 tons of nitrous oxide per megaton. The nitrous oxides would be carried by the fireball and the mushroom cloud into the stratosphere, where they will combine chemically with the ozone molecules, and destroy them. The ultraviolet light radiation could

increase tenfold in the northern hemisphere within three months after a nuclear war, and double in the southern hemisphere for up to two years. The loss of ozone will cause these:

A. Blindness in mankind, animals, birds, and insects. This will cause a collapse of the ecosystem.

B. Sunburn and skin cancer on mankind.

C. The bacteria, plankton, and algae would be killed by the increase in ultraviolet light, and because they produce much of the oxygen that replenishes the ozone layer, the ozone would never re-accumulate.

D. Crops and plants could also be damaged by ultraviolet light.

The way to protect mankind from blindness like this would be to produce millions of pairs of welder's goggles, which they can wear to protect their eyes while outdoors. Sunglasses would be inadequate because they don't screen out the ultraviolet light. They cause dilation of the pupils, thus allowing the eyes to absorb more light. The welder's goggles screen out the ultraviolet light from the welding, so the person will not be blinded. It is a very serious thing to be made blind, therefore the USA and other nations should order companies to produce millions of these welder's goggles for the people.

The people will have to wear long sleeve shirts, gloves, hats, pants, socks, and shoes while they are outside. The use of white shirts will not protect the skin completely; therefore two shirts may be needed. The increased ultraviolet light will cause severe sunburn within 10 minutes, and a third-degree sunburn in 30 minutes. This will restrict the outside activity of the people, unless they wear protective clothing.

20. The US Government can order engineering companies or the US Air Force to replenish the ozone in the stratosphere above the earth. They could build massive balloons, which could be filled with ozone, and lifted into the sky with hot air balloons, or with B-52 Airplanes. The B-52 could fly over an airfield with a cable and a hook, which could be used to catch another cable connected to a large balloon filled with ozone. The B-52 could lift the balloon up into the stratosphere, and the balloon itself could be punctured by means of remote control from the airplane or from the earth. These ideas can be researched, and used after a nuclear war to replace the ozone in the stratosphere. Then the ecosystem on the earth would be protected from ultraviolet light. Then there would not be blindness, sunburn, or climate changes. The scientists already measure changes in ozone gases in the upper atmosphere with instruments on

aircraft, and balloons. The Air Force can use these ideas to replace the ozone with balloons and aircraft.
21. There will be a nuclear winter, and it is described in Revelation 8:12. The nuclear wars are described in Revelation 8:10,11, and in Revelation 18:1-19. The sky will be darkened because of the smoke from forest fires, urban fires, and burning oil wells. This will cause starvation and death from hypothermia or cold. These conditions will last at least one year. It will be difficult to grow crops with the reduced sunlight of the nuclear winter.
22. It is possible that the human race will be destroyed from the earth, and this is written in Matthew 24:22. Christ will return to earth early to save mankind.

Matthew 24:22: "And except those days should be shortened, there should no flesh be saved: but for the elect's sake those days shall be shortened."

This is why we should not rely on science and technology during World War III. If it were left to mankind all life on earth would be destroyed. It will take a divine intervention by Christ to save us.

In I Thessalonians 4:15 St. Paul said that we who are alive on earth must not prevent them who are asleep. This means that we must not interfere with the resurrection of the dead, and that we should try to prevent nuclear war. This is why the 500 church ministers should be given authority over all offensive military action, including nuclear war. The church ministers already work for Christ, and for the resurrection of the dead, and the rapture of the church. Therefore they will stop nuclear war before it starts.

Here are some events in the present and the future of America, which will cause nuclear war, if they are not corrected:

1. If Congress takes more than one year to pass the Church Committee Plan.
2. If the US military bases in Europe, Japan, and Korea are left open.
3. If neutron bombs are used against the Russian tanks in Europe.
4. If NATO continues to have access to the 400 nuclear warheads from the US submarine based missiles.
5. If the US military continues to be the leader of NATO.
6. If the USA fails to move England, and Scotland to America.
7. If the USA fails to move Israel to America.
8. If the US Pentagon continues to have $400 billion dollars per year.
9. If the Pentagon is in charge of all offensive military action during World War III. The $3 trillion dollars and 50 years of research with nuclear weapons were spent for one reason: To be used in World War III. And this is what the Pentagon will do if they have the chance.

10. The SDI or Star Wars defense system may not even work, and the only way to test it would be to start a nuclear war.
11. Fail to convert the fuel in America to natural gas.
12. The human errors, computer errors, military mistakes, and other problems will cause nuclear war in the USA. This can be avoided with the Church Committee Plan.
13. The US President could threaten to use nuclear weapons against the Antichrist. This can be avoided if the Church Committee Group has power over nuclear war.
14. The pride and arrogance of the people in the USA or in any other nation will include them in nuclear war. Your nation must honor Christ to be saved. You can do this by having your people go to church.
15. If the USA intervenes in South America or in any other nation in World War III. The Antichrist may bring his army and navy there.
16. Devils will cause military mistakes or nuclear errors.

The greatest danger in World War III will be:
TOTAL NUCLEAR RETALIATION BY THE ANTICHRIST.

This is why the military problems will be so sensitive during World War III. There are 50 other ways that nuclear war can happen, and only the Church Committee Plan will prevent it.

The people in the USA and the free nations of the world should be aware of this fact:

All of the scientific research and the trillions of dollars were used to develop nuclear weapons for World War III. If the people let the Pentagon and the nuclear weapons industry go into World War III with more than $80 billion dollars per year, the USA will be in a nuclear war. The Pentagon must also give all offensive military power to the Church Committee members, and then nuclear war can be avoided.

The US President will have to give his offensive military authority to the Church Committee members. Then he will have to get their approval to declare war on another nation. Therefore the Church Committee will have authority over all offensive military action, including nuclear war. On page 174 of Dr. Helen Caldicott's book, *Missile Envy*, is the quote: "Hence the use of nuclear blackmail has been an American ploy."[99] Of the 9 times when nuclear threats were made, it was always the US President who made the threat against another nation. This is why the US President must give all authority for offensive military action to the Church Committee members. Then they will be able to stop nuclear war. It would be fatal to make any kind of threat against the Antichrist because he will not be afraid of nuclear war.

He will give 800 million souls to Satan, which means that he will not care about the people in Europe. To threaten him would be very dangerous.

These are provisions that the US Congress must put in the legislation for the Church Committee Plan. I know that Congress takes forever to agree on anything, but this legislation must be approved by January 1, 2007. The US Government has delayed the publication of my books by 8 years already, since Bill Clinton and his wife decided to try and steal my book royalties.

Here are some quotes from Dr. Helen Caldicott's book, *Missile Envy*, and some of my observations of the US military and the nuclear weapons industry in the USA.

On page 33: "There is no defense against nuclear weapons. If Russia launches 100 missiles at 100 US cities, 100 missiles will land."[100] Therefore the USA has no defense against a nuclear attack. This quote by Dr. Helen Caldicott tells us that the US military and the Pentagon are not very good at protecting the USA from nuclear attack. Someone should tell them that the Russian missiles explode when they hit the ground, just like ours do.

On page 34: "and the only defense is, well, you shoot yours and we'll shoot ours."[101]

This quote from President Ronald Reagan tells us that the US military and the Russian military are playing macho with each other, which could destroy all life on earth. This logic was developed by devils, and it is called, "doctrines of devils." This is written in I Timothy 4:1. The one most important goal of Satan is to avoid the judgment of Christ, so the devils won't have to go to the Lake of Fire. And they will destroy the human race to do it.

On page 35: "In this society anyone who contemplates murdering a single individual is considered either mentally unstable or a potential criminal. But the people within this administration are making statements about nuclear war that contemplate the death of hundreds of millions of human beings."[102]

This is the way that the Pentagon operates, and they will use an all-out nuclear attack to retaliate if Russia launches nuclear missiles at the USA. Then 1.5 billion people could be killed.

On page 35: "The same moral and legal restraints should be applied to these people as to ordinary citizens who contemplate the death of only one human being."[103]

The moral and legal restraints mentioned here are included in my plan to put 500 church ministers in charge of all offensive military action by the US Pentagon, including nuclear war.

This is a moral restraint, and the US Congress can pass legislation to make it legal during World War III. The Pentagon can build defensive missile systems on the East, West, and Gulf Coasts of the USA to protect America from nuclear attack during World War III.

The Pentagon will be in charge of all defensive military action in World War III. There will be a nuclear war in Europe, and the USA must stay out of it. In Matthew 24:22 Christ will return to earth early to stop the nuclear war. This is the nuclear war, which can be avoided by changing America's military system.

On page 37: "What is dangerous is that these characters will think that they can do it, that they have the capabilities for controlling a nuclear war and they don't."[104]

This is the real danger in World War III because the Antichrist will use total nuclear retaliation against the USA.

Japan will join the Antichrist to get fuel for their nation and technology. The Antichrist will help them take NE China and Korea, and then Japan will be his strength in the Pacific Ocean. This is the same agreement that Japan had with Hitler in World War II. The Antichrist and the Japanese military will use chemical warfare against Korea and NE China. The Korean and Chinese people can prepare for this by moving to South China.

It is possible that Japan could attack Hawaii or Alaska with either conventional or nuclear weapons. The time for this will depend on what year Japan joins the Antichrist.

The Antichrist will help Japan take Korea and NE China to get the much needed petroleum fuel for Japan; and for shipbuilding for Russia's fleet. It is also true that Korea has farmland, while Japan does not.

This will cause China to use nuclear weapons against the Antichrist in Europe, and it is the nuclear war described in Matthew 24:22. China is the only neighboring nation, which could fight a nuclear war against the Antichrist; and they will have the motive to do it when the Antichrist helps Japan take NE China and Korea.

In Job 2:4,5 Satan said that Job would curse God to save his own life. This explains the phrase, "doctrines of devils," in I Timothy 4:1. This is the reason for the famine of the Antichrist. In Matthew 24:8, Matthew 24:12, and in Matthew 24:21 the suffering in World War III will be horrible, but we can win it by coming to Christ and the Church.

FOOD STORAGE

The USA and the free nations in the world will have to develop their own policy on food storage for the seven-year famine. They should ask food production companies what kinds of food will last seven to ten years in storage. I think the best kinds of food will be dry beans, rice, wheat, dry peas, dry nuts, and other types of dry food.

This food can be wrapped in plastic packages just like in the food stores, and then it should be put into 55-gallon sealed plastic barrels and put into food warehouses. While studying on the subject of food storage, I called food production companies, food dehydrator companies, and freezer storage companies; and I found that none of these types of food would last seven to ten years in storage. The canned food will not last, the dehydrated food will not last, and the frozen food will not last. They all last from one to two years, but no longer. This is why I recommend dry food for storage for the seven-year famine.

The real problems with society will happen when the people think that their food supply is in danger. This means rioting, looting, and murder. This is why the US Government must order companies to do some research to find what kinds of food will last 7 to 10 years. There will be a need to build millions of food warehouses, and grain silos to use for food storage. The Congress can start a National Hunger Foundation to raise money for food storage. I have allocated $64 billion dollars per year in the Church Committee Funding List to be used for food storage.

The US Government should do an experiment with one supermarket in one small town; to see how long the food supply will last if the people know that the food supply is going to be cut off. The rioting and looting will occur when the food supply is in danger, so this project must be given top priority.

The US Government can give incentives for food companies to develop better preservatives for food, so it will last longer. This could be in the form of tax breaks. The governments in all free nations should know that if the food supply is cut off because of the fuel crisis, (no fuel for farm tractors or trucks) or because of chemical warfare, their food supply would last only 60 days or less. In Revelation 8:10-12 the nuclear war, nuclear fallout, and nuclear winter will also threaten the food supply. This is why the free nations in the world must develop their own national policy on food storage.

The US Government can use an incentive plan to convince food companies to develop ways to store food, and they can also do this to expedite the natural gas conversion plan. These incentives or tax breaks can also be used with trucking by reducing the road tax from $52,000 dollars per year to $10,000 dollars per year. Then the US Government will have the full cooperation of the trucking industry during World War III. This plan can be used for every critical part of the functioning of America during the war.

There are three or four snares involved with the natural gas fuel conversion plan. These are:

1. The mechanics will not train to convert the vehicles if the natural gas refill stations are not built. Therefore the US Government can pay them $800

dollars per month as an incentive to train. They can go to training school for three months, and then get a certificate.
2. If the mechanics don't get training, then the shops won't stay open.
3. If there are no natural gas refill stations, then the new car, truck, and farm tractor companies will not convert their new vehicles.

The US Government has to be aware of these problems.

The US Navy has a phrase to describe their activities, which I think is interesting: A battle group of ships was in the Mediterranean Sea, and the news reporter said: "The group of ships were on training maneuvers." My question is why did they have to go 5,000 miles to the Mediterranean Sea to have training maneuvers? They may have had a US military base nearby, but these bases must be closed right away. This kind of carefree attitude by the US Navy will cause a war with the Antichrist. This will result in a nuclear war, and therefore our military forces around the world will have to change their policies completely to a more isolationist type stance and to defense only. The US Navy will no longer rule the Oceans, and they will not have any fuel to do it anyway. This is why the bases must be closed as soon as possible.

If the US Navy, Army, and Air Force are out of fuel, then how will they defend 360 military bases? Another question is, how will the US military defend the bases, and the nations where they are located, without causing a war with the Antichrist? When he takes 250 of our bases overseas, then America will want revenge, and the Pentagon will use nuclear weapons. The attitude of the US Armed Forces must be to bring everything home, while they have the fuel to do it with.

The US Navy will have to protect the shipping around North and South America, and they may have to set up the moving ABM defense on Guided Missile cruisers, battleships, or on US submarines; But if a US Navy Commander orders a battle group of ships to go to the North Atlantic Ocean near England, the Antichrist will see this as an act of war.

This is why it will be so dangerous to flaunt any kind of military power near Europe. This warning is for the US Navy, and the Air Force.

The News media will be dangerous for the US President and Congress during World War III. The Antichrist could make a statement in Germany about politics, and the US President will hear it within two hours on cable news network in the USA. When he has the chance to respond, he must remember that a nuclear war could happen because of what he says. If he ever threatens to use nuclear weapons, the Antichrist will launch missiles right then. There is a verse, which tells us what to do:

126

Amos 5:13: "Therefore the prudent shall keep silence in that time; for it is an evil time."

This verse says that the US President should not make any statement at all. There is a way to safeguard the Press, which is to give authority to the Church Committee to review the comments of the President, the Congress, and Pentagon, before the tapes can be released to the news media. It will be so critical and important to do this because nuclear war could happen because of one wrong statement. Therefore the Church Committee can be a safeguard for the US Government and the news media.

The only alternative to this would be to have the US Government become completely isolated from world politics, and to ignore any comments or actions by anyone in Europe, or anywhere else in the world.

THE HAWKS

The people who are referred to as hawks in the US Senate and the House of Representatives in Washington DC are the more aggressive Senators and Representatives, and they are probably the ones who are on the House and Senate Armed Services Committees, and the Defense Appropriations subcommittees. I found nothing about the hawks in the Library. Dr. Helen Caldicott's book, *Missile Envy*, describes them on pages 88, 89, and 212.[105] If it weren't for this, I wouldn't have known about them at all. They are the main force for nuclear war in Washington DC, and they are above the law. This is written on page 759, Volume 3 of the World Book Encyclopedia, © 1960.[106] This is also verified by a statement made by Dr. Helen Caldicott: On page 223: "America does not have a working democracy in the area of defense."[107]

The hawks outmaneuvered President Carter in 1980, and they influenced President Reagan to spend $1.8 trillion dollars on national defense.

The US Government should take the hawks completely out of the House and Senate, and give them two years of paid leave to work somewhere else. This will be necessary because of their enormous power, and because they are the main force for nuclear war, along with the US Air Force. The hawks cannot be allowed to interfere with the Church Committee after it replaces the House and Senate Armed Services Committees, and the Defense Appropriations subcommittees in Congress.

The hawks must be removed from Congress because they are the link between the nuclear weapons industry, the money appropriated for defense by Congress, and the Pentagon.

The hawks helped get the approval for SDI. They helped get the money for the Pentagon to use for the Star Wars project. They are also the people who created the macho attitude in the US military, which left the USA without a missile defense system.

On page 248 of *Missile Envy*, if the hawks are removed from Congress, and the funding for research is stopped, the nuclear arms race will cease.[108] The most important reason for removing the hawks is that they will aggravate the Antichrist, and cause him to begin his own nuclear arms buildup in Europe. This is what they do best. The hawks are the one group of people who are against peace for America during World War III because they will try to use their nuclear weapons. They must be removed from Congress to avoid a nuclear war. The trillions of dollars spent on nuclear weapons over the past 50 years will be used to cause a global nuclear war during World War III. If they stay in Congress, they will declare war against the Antichrist. He will be the most evil person who ever lived on the earth, and the hawks will declare war against him, simply because they want to use the trillions of dollars worth of nuclear weapons which they bought during the last 50 years. If they ask why they must resign, I will say, "Now it's your turn to make a sacrifice for America."

The hawks have influence in the nuclear weapons industry, the US Pentagon, Congress, and over the President. If they are removed from the military system, then the main force for nuclear war will be gone. The US Congress can use their power to impeach the hawks, with full pay for one year. This should be done right away. These people shafted the US economy for the next 50 years, when they convinced President Reagan to spend $2.2 trillion dollars on defense during his 8 years in office. They made these weapons for World War III, and you must know that they will use them. The US Government can prevent nuclear war by cutting this cancer out before World War III starts.

The nuclear weapons industry and the corporations are all able to sell weapons to other nations without restraint, probably because of the power of the nuclear hawks.

I could see that no one can prosecute or stop the people who sell weapons, probably because of the power of the hawks. How do they get away with this? There will be 18 more nations with nuclear weapons as an indirect result of the arms sales.

The entire nuclear weapons system should be disconnected now, before the Antichrist gains power in Europe. He will not start a nuclear war with the USA because of our Poseidon submarine based nuclear missiles, which cannot be tracked or destroyed. These warheads alone can destroy Russia and

Western Europe, and they will deter a nuclear attack by the Antichrist during World War III.

We must take the nuclear missiles in the USA away from the hawks and the US Pentagon. If the hawks aren't removed from Congress, they will seize power again, and they will use the power of Congress to declare war against the Antichrist. The power of Congress to declare war should actually be taken away, and the Church Committee Group should have this power and authority given to them. This should also be one of the provisions put into the Church Committee Plan legislation.

When the nuclear hawks are fired, there should be 50 church ministers, or more if needed to replace them. These ministers will be given the power to appropriate money for the Church Committee Plan. This money will be given to the Church Committee proper, which will consist of 500 ministers. They will use the $434 billion dollars every year to help the people in America prepare for World War III.

World War III will cause 75% of the people on earth to lose everything they have: Their jobs, houses, cars, and food. This will be a major tragedy, and it is described in Matthew 24:8, and in Matthew 24:12. On page 602, Vol. 14, of the World Book Encyclopedia, 4 billion people could die because of the famine caused by the nuclear winter described in Revelation 8:12.[109] Therefore it is mandatory for the nations to store food for a seven-year famine.

The people in the USA and the other free nations in the world now have this choice:

1. The Church Committee Plan will provide housing, food, fallout shelters, gas masks, Geiger counters, welder's goggles, clean water, and other necessities to survive World War III.
2. The military establishment in each nation will cause a war with the Antichrist, which will cause a global nuclear war.

Now it is up to the people to decide which they would rather have. If they choose to follow the Church Committee Plan, they should let their political leaders know this by organizing rallies. When the people go back to the churches to pray, the faith of our Lord Jesus Christ is the key to salvation.

THE EVIL TREE

The tree of knowledge of good and evil is like a doorway through which evil comes into the world. Because of the name of the tree, the more knowledge you have about something evil, the more evil it becomes. This is why nuclear weapons are so evil because more research was done on them than on anything else in the history of the world. Nuclear weapons are evil because they can destroy the entire earth within 20 minutes. This is the definition of evil, and the USA and Russia have enough of them to destroy the earth 10 times over.

There has been 50 years of research done by the USA and Russia on nuclear weapons. Each nation spent trillions of dollars on this research. Therefore it will be difficult to stop nuclear war because of the time, money, and manpower spent on research by the USA and Russia. The nuclear weapons industry and the Pentagon in the USA will be opposed to the idea of taking offensive military power away from the US military because of their investment in research. Therefore the corporations in the nuclear weapons industry and the US Pentagon will try to protect the investment in research, which is what makes the nuclear weapons evil to start with. What this amounts to is an investment in evil. They believe that the best way to survive war is to counter evil against evil. This is where the good people of America should stand up for Christ, so our nation will be saved.

The truth is that good is opposed to evil in the tree of knowledge of good and evil, and it is the Bible, which brings good into the world. In fact the Bible tells us how good and evil come through the tree in Genesis 2:9. In Genesis 1:1-31 the Word of God is written in the Holy Bible, and the Word of God created the world. This is also written in John 1:1-5. Therefore the way to overcome the evil in nuclear weapons is written in the Bible. This is written in Matthew 5:39-42, and in Matthew 5:44-48. If the USA does not retaliate against the Antichrist during World War III, then we will not be involved in a nuclear war.

We must have faith in the Lord Jesus Christ, and we must follow his word in Matthew 5:44. In Matthew 5:45 the evil and the good both exist in the world at the same time, and the Lord God Almighty will save us if we love him, and if we are perfect like him. This is true for entire nations, and it is why the Church Committee Plan will stop nuclear war. The church ministers work for the Lord God, and they serve Christ, who will stop nuclear war in Matthew 24:22.

The American people should realize that the nuclear weapons industry and the Pentagon will try to protect their trillions of dollars, which they invested in nuclear weapons, and that they will lie to do it. After all, this is a lot of money to protect. Dr. Helen Caldicott's book, *Missile Envy*, describes this tactic and how it is used by the Pentagon and the nuclear weapons industry. These lies almost always come in the form of promises to protect America. Some of them are written on these pages: 172-178, 180-224, and 236-262.[110]

There has been immorality, corruption, campaign bribery, revolving doors from the Pentagon to the nuclear weapons industry, esoteric language, paranoid delusions, and crazy plans for limited nuclear war.

All offensive military power should be given to the Church Committee Group including nuclear war, and the power to declare war on another nation. On page 144 of the book, *Missile Envy*, the US President has the power to launch nuclear missiles, in accordance with the Atomic Energy Act of 1947.[111] This law must be changed before World War III starts because there will be hundreds of times when Satan and his devils will influence the President to start a nuclear war. America will be safe with my Church Committee Plan, and the Pentagon will still be in charge of national defense.

Then the US President and the Congress would not have the power to declare war on another nation, until they get approval for it from the Church Committee Group. This would provide a safeguard, so America can remain neutral during World War III. Therefore the people should support the Church Committee Plan, and try to get Congress to approve it. Again, the trillions of dollars and the scientific research on nuclear weapons was an investment in evil, and the Pentagon will use it in World War III if we don't stop them.

The idea of not retaliating against the Antichrist is the subject of this entire chapter, and the theology for it is written in Matthew 5:39-42, and in Matthew 5:44,45. On page 148 of the book, *Missile Envy*, there will be extreme difficulty in dealing with a nuclear war, if the President of the USA were killed.[112] And if he had any thoughts about not retaliating against the Antichrist, they would probably die with him. Then there would be emotional and irrational demands for all-out retaliation. This is why the Church Committee Plan should be used to provide a guarantee that all-out retaliation will not happen.

The people in the Pentagon can redirect some of their first-strike technology and weaponry into their work for national defense. This is what the nuclear weapons industry and the Department of Defense have been telling the people in the USA for 50 years: That their technology will be used to protect the United States. And now they can do it by providing national defense for America during World War III.

MISSILE SILOS

The Pentagon has been operating under the power of darkness for 50 years, and they didn't even know it. Darkness exists because the truth is not there. The US military used the fear of Russia's nuclear capability to get more appropriations for their evil nuclear weapons from 1945 to 1995. This entire system was based on lies by the nuclear weapons industry and the Pentagon, which did it supposedly to protect America. This system worked for 50 years, and it will not change very easily now. It is my responsibility to stop nuclear war.

The danger in World War III will happen when the Pentagon tries to convince the American people to let them use limited nuclear war against the Antichrist in Europe; and they will use fear in the minds of the people to accomplish their objective. Therefore the Pentagon will use the power of darkness to cause a nuclear war. This is actually the power to lie to the people. The Pentagon spent 50 years building up their nuclear weapons arsenal; and they did it for one reason, to use them in World War III. This is exactly what they will do if the American people don't stop them.

The truth is that the USA doesn't have to fight against the Antichrist because Christ has already defeated him. This is written in Revelation 19:19-21. The problem is that the hawks in Congress will convince the Pentagon and the President that the US military must take action during the war. They are the main force behind the nuclear arms buildup in America, and they will not let the people rest while the Antichrist is in Europe. This means that the hawks will be the main force working for the power of darkness during World War III.

They used fear and lies to get money for their nuclear weapons, and they will use fear and lies to use them. The House and Senate Armed Services Committees, and the Defense Appropriations subcommittees must be disbanded, and then replaced by the Church Committee Group.

In the disarray of the Russian military, the Antichrist will not want to have a nuclear confrontation with the USA. Therefore the Pentagon can shut down the missile silos in the United States. Then the Antichrist will go south to the Middle East according to Daniel 11:21-31. He will go there to take the world oil supply, and he will stay there off and on for 7 years. This is written in Daniel 12:11, Daniel 8:13,14, and in Revelation 11:1-4. He will do this as long as the US military leaves him alone.

The nuclear missile silos in the USA must have a lockout mechanism after they are shut down, so they cannot be reactivated by anyone for any reason. I've also written another method for the prevention of nuclear war. The Church Committee can select military chaplains to live at the military bases where nuclear missile silos are located. They can be given authority over missile launches by giving them a voiceprint command sequence before missiles can be launched. The number of chaplains needed would depend on the number of silos and military bases.

If the chaplains use keys to activate the launch sequence, the military personnel could use force to take them away, and then launch the missiles themselves. This would happen in the form of a military protest during a critical stage of World War III. These kinds of problems must be considered to find the best way to prevent nuclear war. If computers are included in the launch sequence, then the Church Committee voiceprints should be a part of that process too. If there is an effort to forcefully take the voiceprints or to record them and use them later, the chaplains could have a lock out system. Even this would not be 100% effective to stop Neo-Nazi takeover, and there will be problems like these after the Antichrist appears in Europe.

There will be Neo-Nazis who will get into the US military, or they will become traitors while in the military when they see the Antichrist. Therefore the best way to prevent nuclear war will be to shut down the missile Silos completely. This will eliminate forceful military takeover, sabotage, computer errors, human errors, and any other problems. If this is done now, then the Pentagon will not be able to use the Antichrist scare tactic to cause a nuclear war in Europe. They will not be operating with the power of darkness during World War III, and the USA will avoid nuclear war.

The Antichrist will not start a nuclear war with the USA as long as our Poseidon and Trident submarines are at sea with their nuclear warheads. Even if the Antichrist completely destroys the USA with a first-strike nuclear attack, the nuclear warheads on our submarines could still destroy every large city in the USSR and Western Europe. This means that our nuclear submarines will deter the Antichrist from using his nuclear weapons against us. Therefore the US Air Force nuclear missile silos in the USA must be shut down, and our US Navy's submarine missiles will remain in use during World War III. The President will have authority over these, so that the Pentagon will have to contact him before launching them.

The people in the USA will have to be reassured that they will be safe without the use of the US Air Force's nuclear missiles. The theology for this is written in Matthew 5:39-42, and in Matthew 5:44. It is also based on the fact that Christ has already won World War III, and this is written in Revelation 19:11-16, and in Revelation 19:19-21. The people in the USA and the other free nations of the world can overcome Satan by going to Christ and the church. This is the most important thing to do during World War III.

The Pentagon can help to reassure the people by building anti-missile defense systems on the East, West, and Gulf Coasts of the USA. The military forces in other nations not in Europe can do this to protect their people, but the use of nuclear missiles is forbidden by any nation. If the Pentagon is allowed to keep their offensive military power, and their nuclear missile silos, then they will be in Satan's pocket throughout World War III. They used the power of darkness to get appropriations for nuclear missiles, and they will use it to cause a nuclear war, if we don't stop them.

The system used by the Pentagon will not change very easily, but with the support of the American people it can be done. The only sure way to stop the power of darkness is to get rid of the hawks, and shut down the US Air Force's missile silos. The hawks can be replaced by the Church Committee Group; then the Church Committee can take away the President's power to launch nuclear missiles, and Congress's power to declare war on another nation.

The US Navy's nuclear submarines will deter the Antichrist from causing a nuclear war.

DANGER

In the normal way which world events occur, the Pentagon will fail to close their 368 overseas military bases, including the ones in Europe; and then when the Russian tanks roll on Western Europe the US military will use neutron bombs against them. (The neutron bombs are limited tactical nuclear weapons, and they work extremely well against tanks and armored vehicles). As you can see, on pages 86 and 87 of *Missile Envy*, the neutron bomb was developed specifically by scientists for the Pentagon to use against Russian tanks, when they use a blitzkrieg on Western Europe.[113] And as Dr. Helen Caldicott said on page 87: "It therefore must be considered a possible trigger for nuclear war."[114]

The military importance of these weapons can be seen by the way in which they kill people. Neutrons can penetrate any sort of structural material, including armored tanks; then they kill the soldiers inside them. The soldiers who are not killed immediately by the nuclear blast will receive such high doses of radiation that they will die within two days. On page 196 of *Missile Envy*, the neutron bomb as a battlefield weapon in Europe is considered by some military people to be more acceptable than an ordinary hydrogen bomb.[115] It therefore blurs the distinction between conventional and nuclear weapons, and could thus cause a nuclear war.

On pages 194 and 195 of *Missile Envy*, President Reagan decided to let the US military stockpile fully the, "enhanced radiation," neutron bomb for use in the 8 inch artillery projectile, and the Lance nuclear battlefield missile.[116] By 1986 the 155-millimeter nuclear artillery projectile will also be made for use in Europe. All three of these neutron bombs will be used in World War III.

This will anger the Antichrist, and he will use total nuclear retaliation against the USA. This is the most serious threat of nuclear war to America, and to the rest of the world. Therefore the people in the USA must be sure that the Pentagon closes the US military bases in Europe, Japan, Korea, and England.

Now I will prove that the Antichrist will use the Russian army to take Western Europe. In Revelation 6:4 the great sword represents the 60 million troops in the Russian army, and the large number of tanks in that army. In Revelation 9:17 the phrase, "as the heads of lions," means that the Russian tanks will devour Western Europe, like a lion devours its prey. In Revelation 9:17-19 the phrase, "and out of their mouths issued fire and smoke and brimstone," refers to the gunfire coming from the cannon on the front of the tank. The word, "their" in these verses refers to the tanks. With this knowledge you won't confuse the descriptions of the tanks with the descriptions of the rockets or the guns. In Revelation 9:19 the phrase, "for their power is in their mouth, and in their tails," refers to the cannons on the front of the tanks, and the rockets on the back of them. The phrase, "for their tails were like unto serpents, and had heads," refers to the Russian rockets mounted on the back of the tanks. The phrase, "their tails" refers to the back of the tanks; and the phrase, "like unto serpents, and had heads," refers to the rockets. On the Russian version of the Apache helicopters, the rockets have a conical head, which is four inches in diameter. This is the meaning of the phrase, "and had heads," in Revelation 9:19.

These rockets have a long narrow tail, and a four-inch conical head, and they resemble serpents. This is the reason for the phrase, "like unto serpents." In Revelation 9:19, the phrase, "and with them they do hurt," means that the rockets kill and destroy when they are fired from the tanks. These types of rockets can be found only on Russian tanks, which proves that the Antichrist will use the Russian army to take Western Europe, and then the Middle East, and with it the world oil supply.

The reason for this Bible research is to prove that the Russian tanks will move into Western Europe. If the US military bases in Europe are left open, then the Pentagon will use neutron bombs to destroy these tanks, and a global nuclear war will result. It doesn't matter if the Pentagon has nuclear superiority over Russia, the Antichrist will not be afraid of anybody. The people in the USA must ask the President and the Congress to take the offensive military power away from the Pentagon now, and then Congress can adopt the Church Committee Plan to prevent nuclear war.

To avoid the loss of 25 million American troops, a nuclear war, and violent public anger in the USA for 12 years, the Pentagon must do these three things:

1. Close all US military bases in Europe, England, Japan, Korea, and in the Middle East. Bring all of the troops, equipment, and weapons back to America. The responsibility of the Pentagon during World War III should be national defense only.
2. The Pentagon must give their offensive military power to the Church Committee Group.
3. The Pentagon must give $320 billion dollars from their annual budget back to the Congress, which can keep it in reserve until they pass the legislation for the Church Committee Plan. If the Pentagon has only $80 billion dollars a year during World War III, they won't have enough money to start a war against the Antichrist.

The US military bases in Europe must be closed while the Pentagon has enough money to bring their troops and weapons home. These three things are what are known as safeguards. In the first one, the Pentagon will not have a foundation in Europe to use to fight against the Antichrist, if all of the US military bases there are closed. In the second one, the Pentagon will not have the legal right to start a war. In the third one the Pentagon will not have the money to start a war.

I must tell you here that the Joint Chiefs of Staff and the Pentagon will probably say that some of the information in this chapter is outdated or obsolete because the neutron bombs in Germany and in Europe may have been removed from service, and the number of tactical nuclear weapons there may have been reduced. But I will say that the important thing to realize about the subject of tactical nuclear weapons in Europe is that the Pentagon has been planning to use them against the Russian army to destroy the Russian tanks as they are invading Western Europe; and the Pentagon has been planning to do this for about 50 years. When you ask why this is important, I will quote this verse to you:

Revelation 9:16: "And the number of the army of the horsemen were two hundred thousand thousand: and I heard the number of them."

The army of the Antichrist will have 200 million soldiers in it at the end of World War III. This is verified in Daniel 11:40. And there will be about 100 million soldiers in it in the first year of the war. When the Pentagon gives the order to use tactical nuclear weapons against the Russian army, or the army of the Antichrist, a global nuclear war will be the result.

You should also know what the Pentagon, and the Joint Chiefs of Staff, who have never even met me, think about the prophet sent by the Almighty Father of our Lord Jesus Christ to save America from the Antichrist and from World War III. Here are some quotes from the book titled, *In Search of Captain Zero*, written by Allan C. Weisbecker:

"Since Christopher's bolt from Montauk there were at first sporadic postcards from down South. Rambling, arcane, disjointed but ultimately insightful, his missives, like his life, contained flashes of brilliance but no discernible structure. Then came that last one, the signature in Christopher's hand: 'Capitan Cero'—Spanish for 'Captain Zero.'"[117]

The US Government has been blocking the publication of all of my books from 1992 to 2004. And as a result I have made exactly zero in royalties for all of my work. And as if that is not enough, President Bill Clinton, the Congress, and the Pentagon expect me to mail all of my book manuscripts to the very government, which is blocking publication of them. In my opinion, therefore, this is the real reason for the book title, *In Search of Captain Zero.*

I have made zero for all of my work, and the government is in search of a person like me to mail the book manuscripts to them, so they can steal the royalties, and then say that America will be saved.

I found this book while searching for books on nuclear war, which is why I have included some quotes from it here. I must say, however, that there is very little about nuclear war in it. On pages 168 and 169 there is a reference to a man named Teddy Carlton, who used to help build the nuclear-powered submarines in Groton, Connecticut, and who then found that he no longer wanted to do that, and moved to Guatemala in Central America, where he planned to build a bordello, or a whorehouse.[118] It seems strange to me that he didn't consider the latter a sin, while he did the former. On the front book flap it says he was an ex-nuclear engineer. And while this doesn't really qualify it to be in the nuclear war category, it does place it in the, "Cover your ass" section of the Pentagon's propaganda machine.

Here is the last quote from the final pages of the book, *In Search of Captain Zero:*

"Allan Weisbecker is a novelist, screenwriter, lifelong surfer, and award-winning photojournalist whose work has appeared in Smithsonian, Men's Journal, Popular Photography, American Photo, Sailing, Surfer, Surfing, and The Surfer's Journal. He is the author of Cosmic Banditos, a novel said by reviewers to 'out-gonzo Hunter S. Thompson.' Weisbecker lives in Long Island, New York."[119]

Anyone whose work has appeared in the Smithsonian will be noticed by the Pentagon. Then there is, Popular Photography, and Men's Journal.

There is another book with propaganda titled, *The Pentagonists* written by A. Ernest Fitzgerald, a former engineer and cost expert at the Pentagon. Even though he was called a, "whistle blower," he was still a Pentagon official, which may explain why he allowed the propaganda to be put into his book. The quotes in it are in the Table of Contents. And the chapter titles which appear to be aimed at me are:

GARY L. WILSON

Contents

In my opinion the "Contract" described here is my persecution by the FBI agents. The "Let Him Bleed," comment means that the persecution will continue. The, "Kangaroo Court" means that no matter what I do, there seems to be no justice. The, "Dr. Doom," refers to the idea of a prophet of doom, as in Revelation prophecy. The phrase, "I Will Never Lie to You" is ludicrous. And the final chapter title, which refers to me, is, "The Santa Claus Coup" which conveys the idea that I should play Santa Claus and mail all of my book manuscripts to the US Government.

Then there are the quotes on the book cover on the back of the book:

"'Ernie Fitzgerald is one of the reasons why America is great. As long as we have free speech, an independent Congress and courageous officials like Fitzgerald, who are willing to tell the truth about how the government spends the taxpayer's money, our nation will be strong.'

—Senator William Proxmire (D., Wisconsin)

'I would like to give my highest recommendation to Mr. A. Ernest Fitzgerald, who would make an excellent Comptroller General of the United States.'

—Representative Jack Kemp (R., New York)

'Fitzgerald paid an enormous personal price for teaching us that military airplanes were collections of overpriced spare parts flying in close formation. He showed how the Pentagon made stealing legal.'[121]

—Representative John Dingell (D., Michigan)"

What these Congressmen and Senators did not tell you is that in 1989 there was a National Debt of $2.857 trillion dollars; and the US Congress spent all of the money by giving it to the other branches of the government. And then they were paying $240 billion dollars as the interest on the national debt in 1989. I found this information on page 109 of the 1998 World Almanac.[122]

The national debt has gone much higher since then, up to $7.4 trillion dollars, and the interest on it has also gone up. By the way, this is the secret the government is hiding. It is the reason for the continuing government cover-up of the truth behind the assassination of President John F. Kennedy. And even I was not ready for what happened next. I mailed a total of 140 letters to the US Congress right after the terrorist attacks on September 11, 2001, warning them about World War III, and I got no response from them! Here are copies of some of the letters, which I mailed to the Congress from November 5, 2001 to March 7, 2002:

Congress

There is something very important which I must tell you in relation to my books about World War III that you should remember. As you well know, the US Pentagon has been preparing for a war against the Russian army, as it tries to invade Western Europe, for almost 50 years. The Pentagon has nuclear weapons in several delivery types at US military bases in Germany and in other nations in Europe. Knowing this, you should be aware of the fact that the use of these nuclear weapons could cause a nuclear war between the United States and Russia.

Now I will explain the problem. Look at this verse:

Revelation 9:16: "And the number of the army of the horsemen were two hundred thousand thousand: and I heard the number of them."

The army of the Antichrist will have 200 million soldiers in it at the end of World War III. I have estimated that the same army will have about 80 million soldiers at the beginning of the war, since the Antichrist will be the leader of the Common Market when he puts the army together. It will be called the Unified European Army, and it will have predominantly Russian and Eastern Bloc European soldiers in it at first. The Antichrist will pay the soldiers $600 dollars per month to join, which is ten times what some of the underpaid soldiers are getting now.

Now look at this:

Daniel 11:22: "And with the arms of a flood shall they be overflown from before him, and shall be broken; yea, also the prince of the covenant."

This verse describes the nations of Western Europe as they are being overrun by the army of the Antichrist. There will be several battles in this war between the US Pentagon and the Antichrist, and I have calculated that at least 9 of them will lead to global nuclear wars if they are allowed to take place. The nuclear wars will be fought over:

1. The US military trying to protect Western Europe.
2. The Pentagon trying to protect the US military bases in Europe.
3. The Pentagon trying to stop the famine of the Antichrist.
4. The Pentagon trying to retaliate for the nuclear attack on Rome, Italy.
5. The US military trying to protect England.
6. The US military trying to protect Israel.
7. The Pentagon trying to protect the world oil supply.

8. The Pentagon trying to protect the US military bases in the Middle East.
9. The Pentagon retaliating for the major nuclear war between the Antichrist and China at the end of World War III.

The Antichrist will own all of the nuclear weapons in all of the nations in Europe when he takes control of the entire continent in the first year of World War III. This is why it is so important to allow my books on World War III to be published as soon as possible. Then the United States, Russia, China, and the United Nations Organization can dismantle all of the nuclear weapons in Europe, before the Antichrist takes control of them. I am now asking you to tell the FBI agents in this project to allow my books on World War III to be published.

Congressmen

I know that America suffered a tragic loss on September 11, 2001. And I realize that the American people are afraid of the use of the anthrax by the terrorists who have been sending it in letters. Yet I must warn you of an even greater threat to the United States. People often think of Iraq or Afghanistan when they talk about the use of weapons of mass destruction, yet there is an evil threat just over the horizon, which is almost beyond comprehension.

There is a good reason for Bible prophecy, and it almost always comes just before a major war. I have written three books about World War III, which prove that the coming Antichrist will take control of all the nuclear, biological, and chemical weapons now in the possession of all of the nations on the mainland continent of Europe. He will own everything there, including the conventional military weapons. This is verified here:

Revelation 13:5: "And there was given unto him a mouth speaking great things and blasphemies; and power was given unto him to continue forty and two months."

The Antichrist will spend 42 months taking control of all of the nations in Europe. Look at this verse:

Revelation 13:16: "And he causeth all, both small and great, rich and poor, free and bond to receive a mark in their right hand, or in their foreheads."

The Antichrist will force everyone in Europe to accept the mark of the beast; and the beast will be the kingdom of the Antichrist. I have written three books about World War III, which have the descriptions of these events, and President Bill Clinton blocked the publication of them for eight years. Now I am asking the US Government to allow my books to be published, so the United States will have enough time to prepare for the coming World War III.

It is obvious that the nations of the world need to have enough time to eliminate all of the nuclear, biological, and chemical weapons in the USSR, and in the other nations in Europe before World War III begins, and this cannot happen with the US Government blocking the publication of my books.

Congress

I did Bible study and evangelism from 1983 to 1992, and there is a prophecy about me in Isaiah 41:15-29. The description in Isaiah 41:15 is that of a harvester. In Matthew 13:37-43 the harvest will occur at the end of the world. This means that the Second Coming of Christ is near. In Isaiah 41:16-19 there is a description of the letters of evangelism, which I mailed to churches from 1983 to 1992. The whirlwind is used to scatter them, and it is the symbol for the prophet Elijah in II Kings 2:11. This means that the Almighty Father has given the spirit of Elijah to me, and he has told me to announce the Second Coming of Christ to the world.

In Jeremiah 23:18-20 the whirlwind of the Lord shall come forth in the latter days, which is now. In Isaiah 41:25 the Lord will raise up a prophet from the north, which means North America, and I am the prophet. In Isaiah 41:26 there is no one who knows the events of the end of the world, or of World War III, except the Lord God Almighty. In Isaiah 41:27 the first prophet is me; and the phrase, "Behold, behold them," refers to the letters of evangelism which I mailed to the churches. The phrase, "and I will give to Jerusalem one that bringeth good tidings," refers to the Second Coming of Christ because Christ will bring the Good News to Jerusalem at his Second Coming.

Here is a list of the things, which are included in my books:

1. My books announce the Second Coming of Christ.
2. My books have proof that immortality with Christ is real.
3. My books have 5 prophecies from the book of Revelation.
4. My books have the cure for AIDS.
5. My books have an accurate interpretation of the book of Revelation.
6. My books will prevent 9 nuclear wars between the Pentagon and the Antichrist.
7. My books have a prophecy about the Second Death, which proves that the Lake of Fire described in Revelation 20:14 is the sun.
8. My books should be published as soon as possible to give America enough time to prepare for World War III. I will not mail my book manuscripts to anyone else, since that would cause me to be condemned to the Lake of Fire.

You can see here that the US Government is so afraid I will find the truth about the John F. Kennedy assassination and write books about it, that they are willing to let America go into 9 possible nuclear wars against the Antichrist during World War III instead of allowing my books to be published in my name. And even though the book titled, *The Pentagonists* was published in 1989, three years before I began writing my books, the US Government has had a desire to steal my books ever since Lyndon B. Johnson became President on November 22, 1963 because he worked with the CIA to kill John F. Kennedy.

I have tried to imagine how the President, the Congress, and the Pentagon will think about World War III during the years leading up to it, and the only possible answer is that they will look at it the same way as they did World War II. The Pentagon has already made preparations for World War III in Europe because they have neutron bombs and limited tactical nuclear weapons deployed there to help them stop the Russian tanks as they invade Western Europe. This is the reason for the NATO Pact, which is designed to protect the nations in Western Europe from any and all attacks by the USSR and the former communist nations in Eastern Europe.

The problem is that the Pentagon has already made plans to fight in World War III, without even knowing any details about the war itself. There is a list of 9 nuclear wars which the Pentagon will be involved in because of their present military strategy in Europe and in the Middle East, and they will be included in them because they plan to use the US military to fight in the ground war in Europe during World War III.

These pre-conceived notions about World War III will cause the President, the Pentagon, and the Congress to completely ignore the instructions given to them by Christ through Bible prophecy in my books titled: World War III: The Nations and World War III: The People. The President and the Pentagon will panic when they find out that the Antichrist will control 25% of the land area on the earth. Yet in Revelation 6:8 it says that he will. The Pentagon will not believe that Christ will win World War III for us, yet in Revelation 19:11-21 he will.

This is why the Joint Chiefs of Staff must be required to make televised monthly reports to the American people before and during World War III. The people will get the chance to learn how the Pentagon officials think about World War III, and how they plan to keep America neutral during the war.

Since there are so many things that the Pentagon has to do before World War III begins, I think the American people should demand that the Joint Chiefs of Staff make Televised monthly reports in which they say what has been done to that date. This will make the Pentagon much more accountable to the American people both before and during World War III. I cannot overstate the importance of this because it will eliminate most of their efforts to stonewall me, and the people concerning the war.

I can submit a list of questions to the Pentagon on the first of each month, and then they can try to answer them on the fifth day of the month on their televised monthly report. The list of questions can be read on TV by the Pentagon as they answer them; and then I will make comments about their answers when the Pentagon officials are finished with the monthly report.

One very good reason for the televised reports is that the American people will always have an idea as to the thinking of the Joint Chiefs of Staff and the Pentagon concerning World War III by using them. If the Pentagon refuses to close the US military bases in Europe, England, Japan, Korea, and the Middle East, then the American people will hear about it in the televised monthly reports. If the Pentagon plans to send 25 million US troops to fight in the ground war in Europe during the first year of World War III, then the American people will hear about it. If the Pentagon plans to use limited tactical nuclear weapons in Europe or in the Middle East, then the American people will hear about it. If the Pentagon plans to retaliate against the Antichrist when he uses nuclear weapons to attack Rome, Italy, then the American people will hear about it in the monthly reports.

If the Pentagon refuses to make the televised reports every month, then the American people should call for the resignation of the Joint Chiefs of Staff. If the Congress doesn't think the charges are sufficient for their impeachment, then the Joint Chiefs of Staff should be forced to resign. Since there is a total of nine possible nuclear wars which the Pentagon will be involved in during World War III because of their present military strategy in Europe and in the Middle East, the American people have the right to force the Joint Chiefs of Staff to make the televised monthly reports.

I have just finished doing seven years of study and research while trying to solve all of the strategy problems for the US military and the Pentagon, in order to keep America neutral during World War III. If the Pentagon gets away with their efforts to stonewall me, then all of that work was done for nothing. I know that the Pentagon could use propaganda and fear to try and convince the American people that the US military should fight in the ground war in Europe during World War III, but here is the reason why they cannot do so:

Revelation 9:16: "And the number of the army of the horsemen were two hundred thousand thousand: and I heard the number of them."

The army of the Antichrist, or the Unified European Army, will have 200 million soldiers at the end of World War III. This is why the Pentagon cannot fight against that army in Europe, and protect America at the same time. The

US military will have to save all of our troops to protect America during the war. If the Pentagon loses 25 million US troops in the first year of World War III, then there will not be enough soldiers left to protect us later.

Again, the Pentagon will refuse to believe what is written in my books about the army of the Antichrist because they will get to keep their money and their power by doing it. The reason for the televised monthly reports is to force them to communicate their status, and their ideas in regard to World War III.

CHAPTER IV

Nuclear Winter

Not only were Carl Sagan and his fellow scientists correct about their descriptions of nuclear winter, and not only is it described the same way as they predicted it, but it will happen as the result of a large-scale nuclear war between Russia and China in the last year of World War III.

Revelation 8:12: "And the fourth angel sounded, and the third part of the sun was smitten, and the third part of the moon, and the third part of the stars; so as the third part of them was darkened, and the day shone not for a third part of it, and the night likewise."

The phrase, "Nuclear Winter," means the severe cold and dark conditions caused in the aftermath of a large-scale nuclear war, as the result of the massive amounts of smoke and dust which will be thrown up into the stratosphere by the nuclear blasts, and the fires in the cities and in the forests. These conditions are described in Revelation 8:12, where one third of the earth will be covered with the smoke and dust clouds for an unknown duration of time. This will cause prolonged darkness, abnormally low temperatures, violent windstorms, toxic smog, and persistent radioactive fallout. The temperatures in the Northern Hemisphere could drop as much as 25 degrees centigrade, which could produce killing frosts in July. The smoke clouds could be as large as entire continents, and in Revelation 8:12 they will cover one third of the earth. In the World Book Encyclopedia, © 1997, Volume 14, on page 602, it is written that nuclear winter could kill 4 billion people.[123]

There has long been a controversy between people of religion and the people of science on the subject of creationism, and on some other points as well. This is noted on page 131 of the book titled, *Fire and Ice*, ©1990 by David Fisher.[124] I think that both of these groups will be pleased to learn that religion and science do not really oppose one another as subjects of study. They are both designed the same way to be revealed to mankind slowly over long periods of time. The scientists themselves can verify this with their subject of study by pointing out the dates of various scientific discoveries, such as the radio, the television, the telephone, and others. Most Christians will say that this is also true about the discoveries in the Bible concerning theology. The mysteries in the Bible are what keep the people interested, and then they continue to read it, and they are therefore, still saved by Christ. If you will read this verse, then you will see that the Bible says that religion and science are not opposed to each other:

I Timothy 6:20: "O Timothy, keep that which is committed to thy trust, avoiding profane and vain babblings, and oppositions of science falsely so called."

The profane and vain babblings which sometimes come through people are caused by devils; and the phrase, "oppositions of science falsely so called," means that religion and science do not really oppose one another. It would appear as if devils also cause the arguments between the creationists and the scientists, or they magnify it by various means. This is why St. Paul told Timothy to avoid profane and vain babblings, as well as oppositions between science and religion. Then in the next verse, which is I Timothy 6:21, he said that any Christians who say that science and religion are opposed to each other have erred concerning the faith.

The reason why St. Paul gave these instructions to Timothy is that he had received the gift of prophecy from the Lord Jesus Christ. This is verified in I Timothy 1:18, and in I Timothy 4:14; and it is the meaning of the first phrase in I Timothy 6:20: "O Timothy, keep that which is committed to thy trust."

Prophecy is so valuable that St. Paul gave very precise instructions to Timothy concerning various aspects of it. I am explaining these things now because the Pentagon will try to use pro-Pentagon scientists to confuse the nuclear winter issue with me, in just the same way that they did it with the nuclear winter scientists.

Here are some of the events, which caused the TTAPS Group to study Nuclear Winter.[125] This group of scientists and the initials from their last names spells the TTAPS: Richard Turco, Brian Toon, Tom Ackerman, James Pollack, and Carl Sagan.

1. With the discovery of Shoemaker-Levy-9, which was a comet or an asteroid which had broken up, and which then impacted with the planet Jupiter: The cloud from one impact explosion rose 2,000 miles from the surface of Jupiter, and the dust remained in the atmosphere for one year

afterwards. This indicates on a different scale that a nuclear winter could last for a year or more after a global nuclear war on the earth.

2. In 1908 a 10 Megaton asteroid explosion occurred near Tunguska, Russia. The explosion actually flattened the forests for about 100 miles in all directions. There is a very real danger that large asteroids exploding in the earth's atmosphere could be mistaken for nuclear explosions, and could therefore cause a full-scale nuclear retaliation by the USA, USSR, or China during World War III. Since the falling asteroids are described in Revelation 6:13, and according to this verse they will fall in great numbers, I will urge the United Nations Organization to call for a Zero Tolerance policy toward nuclear warheads in all nations of the world.

3. Ed Tagliaferri said on the TV Video called, Fire From the Sky, that there are 25 asteroid high altitude detonations reported by the US military Distance Early Warning Satellites which scan for nuclear missile launches (I think he said that there are 25 of these every day).[126] In the film, Fire From the Sky, the scientists predicted that a major asteroid collision with the earth would cause a cloud of dust so large and so high in the atmosphere that it could cause a "nuclear winter" scenario, which could last for a year.[127]

These major asteroid collisions could cause tidal waves in the oceans, which could be up to one mile high, if they impact there when they hit the earth.

Now I will explain the ways in which the Pentagon used their scientists to sabotage the nuclear winter scientists. Look at these quotes from the book titled, *Fire and Ice*, ©1990 by David Fisher. On page 129 it says:

"The editors of the National Review stated that: The idea of nuclear winter was invented in 1982 by anti-nuclear strategists who felt the political need to hype their cause."[128]

Why would the editors of this magazine make such a statement? Here is another quote from page 129:

"Despite the fact that nuclear winter was a fraud from the start, and was widely known to be a fraud in the scientific community, it had a successful run with the general public."[129]

What this article doesn't say is that the scientific community described here is really made up of pro-Pentagon scientists. With both of these quotes, the editors of the National Review were trying to discredit the work of Carl Sagan and the 1983 TTAPS study. In fact it almost seems that these editors were trying to sweep the results of the TTAPS study under the rug, before anyone had the chance to evaluate them. On page 130 of the book, *Fire and Ice*, it states that the editors of the National Review misquoted Freeman

Dyson, a well-respected physicist, in order to further discredit the TTAPS findings.[130] Then on page 131 of *Fire and Ice* is this quote:

"The Review article states that, Nuclear winter isn't science, it is propaganda."[131]

To prove that the National Review articles are lies, read this quote on page 131 of the book, *Fire and Ice*:

"The willingness of prominent men of science to debase themselves and their calling for the cheap thrills of political notoriety is a scandal."[132]

To eliminate any confusion here, look at this quote on page 132:

"The United States Department of Defense was not pleased with the theory of nuclear winter, to no one's surprise, for if it were true it meant that our immense stockpile of nuclear weapons is worthless: To use them would be to commit national and global suicide."[133]

Then right after this statement it says that the Department of Defense requested a study by the National Academy of Sciences. The National Academy later endorsed the TTAPS study. You should notice that when the Department of Defense and the Pentagon are against the wall so to speak, they always call for a study to examine the results being discussed. This is known as stalling for time, and it is a very good tactic, since it causes public interest to subside over great periods of time. Then after the results of the National Academy of Sciences study are in, the Pentagon simply does nothing; and they get away with this because the public has lost interest in the subject.

Then further down on page 133 it says that Edward Teller, a pro-Pentagon scientist, said that the TTAPS study was an exaggeration of the effects of a nuclear war.[134] Now wait just a minute here; wasn't Edward Teller the man who was instrumental in the creation of the hydrogen bomb? Wasn't he the man who effectively multiplied the power of the atomic bomb by a factor of 10? Yes, Edward Teller was an ambitious scientist. He was so ambitious that he was the prime government witness in the Oppenheimer case, which means that he destroyed the career and the life of the scientist who trained him in the field of nuclear physics. Then if Edward Teller multiplied the power of the atomic bomb by a factor of 10 into the nuclear bomb, then it would seem obvious that he is lying for the Pentagon, since they are the people who give large government grants for scientific research.

The Pentagon and the military-industrial complex are driven by greed. They have gotten $265 billion dollars per year in their budget for almost 20 years, and they plan to keep it that way. They will try to discredit my books and me, they will have their scientists ridicule me in the TV News and in the press, and if they think it is necessary, they will kill me. Unfortunately this will cause America to be included in nine nuclear wars during World War III.

I should recommend that when the Pentagon uses these tactics against me, when they have their people ridicule me in the TV News, and when they try to discredit my work, and when they try to harm me in any way at all, the American people should stop paying federal taxes.

The scientists who study the effects of nuclear war and nuclear winter are trying to save mankind while the Pentagon and the military-industrial complex are in the group of people, which will eventually destroy the human race. It is their job to kill people after all, and you should never forget this. They argued against the findings of the TTAPS study, the United Nations SCOPE study of 1985, and several others in order to protect their annual budget.[135] If the Pentagon were to eliminate a large number of their nuclear weapons, then their annual budget would be cut in half. This is another detail, which you should never forget, since the battle over nuclear winter always takes place in the minds of the public.

The real reason why the Pentagon ignores every book and magazine article about nuclear arms reduction is that their annual budget would be cut in half if they were to comply with the demands of the public. This is why the Pentagon dismisses the idea of nuclear winter as being irrelevant.

Again, the reason is that the Pentagon and the military-industrial complex are driven by greed. This is why they discredit every book on nuclear arms reduction.

It is time that we stop paying the Pentagon to destroy the human race. The American people should vote to take $320 billion dollars per year out of the Pentagon's budget, and then the money can be used by the Church Committee Group to provide food and housing for the people in the USA during World War III. Of course the Pentagon will say that nuclear weapons are needed to preserve the peace, but in reality they are needed to preserve the annual budget of the Pentagon. Many of the American and Soviet physicists who conceived, devised, and constructed the world's nuclear arsenals have given dire warnings to the policy makers in the Pentagon and in the US Government, concerning nuclear war and nuclear winter, but they have been ignored. The very scientists who built the nuclear weapons find that they cannot dismantle them, even with the full support of the people. This is one reason why President Dwight D. Eisenhower warned the American people about the growing power of the Pentagon and the military-industrial complex.

The Pentagon will do anything to preserve their annual budget, including lying to the American people. Even though I have the advantage of knowing what motivates the Pentagon, I know that they will ignore me too, just like they did with Carl Sagan, and the other prominent scientists who studied nuclear winter. This is why I have devised the National Emergency Vote, and it is the only possible way that the American people can bypass the immense power of the Pentagon, and the military-industrial complex. This is the only method that the people of the USA can use in order to be served with their own tax money during World War III.

Now if you will go back to the first pages in this chapter, where I explained the theology of I Timothy 6:20,21, you will realize that St. Paul gave instructions to Timothy and to me, so I would know in advance that religion and science are not opposed to one another as subjects of study. You see, I have to know this to understand why the editors of the National Review tried to discredit the TTAPS study; and I had to know it to understand why Edward Teller did the same thing. They did it for the Pentagon, but I would not have known this without the instructions in I Timothy 6:20,21. I would have been confused just like the nuclear winter scientists were. If I were opposed to scientists as a group, then the Pentagon and their supporters would be able to take advantage of my confusion, and I would then be discredited.

The Pentagon will try to use the Christian versus scientist angle against me, but it will not work because I know that religion and science are not opposed to each other. Then they will try to confuse the issue like the National Review did, but that won't work either. You should realize that there will be two groups of scientists, the Pentagon, the TV news media, and myself involved in the argument over nuclear winter; and this is why St. Paul gave me specific instructions through Timothy.

In fact the Pentagon used their power in the media to use some statements made by two other scientists, Starley Thompson and Stephen Schneider of NCAR (The National Center for Atmospheric Research), to try to discredit the term nuclear winter itself. On page 136 of the book, *Fire and Ice* is this quote:

"The newer results have been referred to by Thompson and Schneider as, 'nuclear autumn,' rather than winter... A lot of media coverage emphasized the mistaken notion that the concept of nuclear winter had been disproved by the later studies."[136]

This media coverage came from the Pentagon, and the newspapers, magazines, and TV reporters who work for them in various ways. You should notice how well this worked to discredit the TTAPS study. The Pentagon will use their own scientists to disagree with me, or they will use the results of other groups of people to discredit the concept of nuclear winter a second time, when this book is published. I read the article written in *Foreign Affairs* magazine written by Thompson and Schneider, and the language in it sounded very much like Pentagon jargon. The date of the article's publication was June 1986.[137] There is another point, which is important here, and it is that the Pentagon is working from a position of power, since they are assured of getting $400 billion dollars each year, in their annual budget. This is the very thing, which allows them to do the things that they do to people, and get away with it. This also allows them to ignore the wishes of the American people, when the subject of nuclear disarmament comes up.

The very scientists who built the nuclear weapons find that they cannot dismantle them, even with the full support of the American people. The policymakers in the Pentagon ignored the warnings given by the same scientists who made the nuclear weapons! This is why the people should use the National Emergency Vote to give the offensive military power of the Pentagon to the Church Committee Group. The people can also vote to give the nuclear weapons, which by the way, were paid for with the tax money given to the US Government by the American people, to the Church Committee Group; and then they can work with the United Nations organization toward large-scale nuclear disarmament.

I will say now, that the Pentagon and the President will try to make promises concerning nuclear disarmament when my books about World War III are published, but you should always remember that President Bill Clinton tried to use Federal power to steal my books before they were even published, and when I went to testify against him in January 1999, the Congress would not give me an appointment to do so. The Pentagon and the President will try to stall, or delay the nuclear disarmament process; and they will try to make promises to the American people, but they will only waste more time. This is the cause and effect of the idea of working from a position of power.

This means that the Church Committee Group should eliminate all of the ICBM warheads in the land based missile silos in the USA, which would in itself eliminate a large number of targets, and therefore would eliminate some reasons for a Soviet first-strike nuclear attack; and then the Church Committee Group should eliminate all of the tactical nuclear weapons in Europe; and then they can leave only 200 nuclear warheads on the US nuclear submarines at sea. I believe that the Church Committee Group and the United Nations Organization can convince the Soviet leaders to dismantle their nuclear warheads down to a similar level, and some of the other nations with nuclear weapons can dismantle a large part of theirs as well.

I know already that most of the people in America want to eliminate the possibility of a global nuclear war between the USA and the USSR; but the danger is far greater with World War III coming about six years from now. The nuclear arms race has gone out of human control from 1952, when the hydrogen bomb was constructed, until now. This is described on page 92 of the book, *The Long Darkness*.[138] The Pentagon used the fear of nuclear weapons to stockpile more of them. The problem with all of the efforts toward nuclear disarmament is that nothing major ever happens to make it come to pass; or if it does, then the next President calls for more nuclear weapons to be made. This is also caused by the immense power in the Pentagon's annual budget.

I have noticed in reading the books and magazine articles about nuclear winter that some of the scientists believe in altruism, and in adaptation and creative solutions to difficult problems. This is written on page 65 of the book, *The Long Darkness*.[139] However, this is a major mistake when lust for power, and greed are involved in the situation. The very fact that the Pentagon has done nothing to further large-scale nuclear disarmament, and the fact that they use the media to discredit people, indicates that greed is involved. Another problem exists because of the fact that the Pentagon can use their immense budget to influence the President. They did this in 1983 to 1987, when President Ronald Reagan approved the construction of the neutron bombs, which are now in Europe. Several nuclear disarmament treaties had been signed before Ronald Reagan came into office, but he gave the Pentagon his permission to build more nuclear weapons anyway.

The Pentagon will use every available resource to make sure that disarmament never happens, since they will lose half of their annual budget if it does. When the Pentagon is put into the position of answering to the American people over an issue, they will always call for a study, or they will say that they have to arrange for high-level talks on the issue. These tactics tend to pacify the American people, until they forget what the issue was. I know for a fact that there will have to be a major change in the US Government to affect large-scale nuclear disarmament; and the Church Committee Plan is the way to make it happen.

I spent three years trying to inform Bill Clinton about World War III, and the nuclear wars which will be caused by it, and about the appearance of the Antichrist in Europe; and I told him about the fact that the Antichrist will have control of the nuclear weapons of the USSR, France, Italy, and other nations in Europe, and he decided to steal my books instead of saving the USA. Once again, the US Government has failed to cooperate. Now you can see why I don't believe in the concept of altruism where the US Government is concerned. I think the Church Committee Group will have this quality, if the American people vote to put them in the Congress in place of the nuclear hawks, whereas the President and the Pentagon never will. On page 96 of the book, *The Long Darkness* is this quote:

"The spiritual aberration that I call nuclearism: the exaggerated dependence upon, and even worship of nuclear weapons."[140]This is the nature of the problem, which the US Government has, and it will cause a global nuclear war with the Antichrist within six years. Believe me, it is time to clear up the aberration now, before the Antichrist comes into power in Europe. The best way to do this is through the Church Committee Group because church ministers worship Christ, and not nuclear missiles. They know how to save the American people, since Christ himself will win World War III for us, when he returns to the earth. On page 106 of the book, *The Long Darkness* is this quote:

"Our nuclear warheads and the ballistic missiles on which they are mounted are failing to provide us with the security that is their ostensible purpose."[141]

How much more will this be true when the Antichrist takes power in Europe? Of course the Pentagon will say that they will need the nuclear missiles to protect America from the Antichrist; but in reality the nuclear weapons will have to be dismantled to protect the entire world from the large-scale nuclear war, and the severe nuclear winter, which the Antichrist will cause. The nuclear winter is described in Revelation 8:12, and one third of the sun will be blocked out by it, for an unknown duration of time. This means that one third of the earth will be covered with the dust and smoke particles in the stratosphere, caused by the nuclear war between the Antichrist, when he uses nuclear missiles against China in the last year of World War III.

If the greater part of the nuclear weapons in the USA, the USSR, and China are not dismantled now, then the nuclear winter described in Revelation 8:12 could cover 95% of the earth, instead of 33% of it.

This was one of the findings of the TTAPS study, that one hundred million tons of smoke injected into the stratosphere during a nuclear war would block out 95% of the sunlight on the earth. This is written on page 126 of the book titled, *Fire and Ice*.[142]

Another very important question is this: Can America rely on security based on nuclear deterrence with the Antichrist in control of half of the nuclear weapons on the earth? Probably not, but I am sure that the Pentagon will find some ingenious way to make everyone believe that they can. In the Church Committee Plan the Pentagon will still have their defensive military power, which means that they can still protect America during World War III.

If the Pentagon tries to keep their nuclear weapons, then they will still rely on nuclear deterrence, and they will not use an ABM defense to protect America from nuclear missile attack by the Antichrist. In the past 50 years, the defense against nuclear attack has not existed because of the theory of nuclear deterrence. In this nuclear age, the measure of national security becomes a matter of judgment, and those people who make the judgment are the President and the Pentagon. Usually the American people have no say in the matter, even though they pay the salaries of everyone in the US Government. Here are some notes from pages 109 and 110 of the book titled, *The Long Darkness*:

"Objective estimates of national security include such uncertainties as the assessment of the level of international tensions, predictions of the likelihood of nuclear war, the chances of its escalation should a small nuclear war begin, or the possibility of surviving one. Because the estimates of these are so uncertain, we are led to rely on more subjective criteria in judging the success or failure of national security policies. National security then becomes a state of mind."[143]

So far the Pentagon has fooled everyone on the national security issue, since they have not provided a defense against nuclear missile attack for 50 years.

Robert S. McNamara pointed this out in his book titled, *Blundering Into Disaster*.[144] On page 120 of the book, *The Long Darkness*, it says that, "Most reasonable people seem to have thought that the Star Wars missile defense scheme would have been laughed out of existence because of its sheer absurdity when viewed from economic, strategic, technical, moral, or practical angles. But such thoughts fail to reckon with the depth of the public's gullibility and blind acceptance of technological solutions to human problems."[145]

This is where Pentagon propaganda steps in together with the help of the Hollywood film industry, in the Star Wars movie. Have you noticed the success of these films, or have you noticed the lines of people waiting to get tickets for them? While everyone waits for the next Star Wars movie to be released, the Pentagon rakes in another $500 billion dollars of your tax money! It is not an accident that the Star Wars defense has the same name as the Star Wars movie: This is called Pentagon propaganda!

Most Americans think that President Reagan was a hero, not even realizing that he signed a blank check for the Pentagon's annual budget. In 1984 about 68% of the American people agreed that it is only a matter of time before a global nuclear war happens because of the fact that more nuclear weapons are being built every year. The strange thing about the arms race is that the Pentagon uses the fear of nuclear weapons to get the money to build more of them. Fear and lies fall under the works of darkness, which means that Satan and his devils could cause a nuclear war to escalate by creating more fear when it occurs. On page 111 of the book, *The Long Darkness*, "Nuclear weapons are a direct threat to our national security and to world peace, and to all human life."[146]

The Pentagon says that the USA must have enough nuclear weapons to obliterate the USSR during a nuclear war. Then the USSR must have at least as many nuclear weapons as the USA, in order to deter a nuclear war. Therefore the Pentagon says that the USA is secure from a nuclear threat because the US military has enough nuclear weapons to prevent the USSR from using a first strike nuclear attack. When you look at a map of the targeted areas in the USA and the USSR however, you will see that the only safe places to live on the earth are in the nations that have no nuclear weapons at all. This obviously means that someone in the Pentagon is lying about the security, which nuclear weapons are supposed to give to America.

There is another important point about national security as it applies to the USA, with the Antichrist in power in Europe. It is this: The more nuclear weapons that the USA and the USSR dismantle now, the less ABM defense our nation will require to keep us secure during World War III. Of course I am talking about my Foolproof National Defense, which is described in the Nuclear War chapter.

This ABM defense will be built into US submarines, which will patrol the Atlantic and Pacific Oceans throughout the war. The Pentagon will say that it will be too expensive to build, but it will not be if the US Government dismantles most of their nuclear weapons, and if they convince Russia to do the same. In response to this idea, the US Government will go into their bureaucratic inertia stage, which can last for years; and believe me, I am speaking from personal experience when I say this.

I should tell the American people what the Pentagon will do in response to the issues which I have described in this chapter. There are thousands of people who could be assigned to think up ways to refute everything I have said. This is what they did to the nuclear winter scientists, and I will explain how it was done. When the TTAPS study was finished in 1983, between 300 to 400 people in the Pentagon were assigned to read the report to make their own comments about it, and to have a large group discussion about the TTAPS report itself. After this was done, several people were assigned to call the National Review magazine, with stories they had thought up to discredit the TTAPS scientists. There were probably 150 different magazines and newspapers, which were influenced by the Pentagon group, as well as several TV News stations. I would say that the TV news media is where they hit the hardest. They also called Edward Teller, and asked him to disagree with Carl Sagan about the concept of nuclear winter.

This is probably how the Pentagon creates propaganda. The people should realize that there is no federal law against lying, and this is what these people do when they have to. Since the Pentagon has all of that money, you should know that they would use it on propaganda to keep their nuclear weapons. Most of the money for this will be spent on the TV news media. You will get a chance to see this when my book is published.

After reading articles from several magazines, I have a better idea of how the Pentagon has reacted to the nuclear winter concept. In the *Foreign Affairs* magazine from June 1986 is this quote:

"It is reasonable to ask why the scientific basis of the theory of nuclear winter still provokes such divergent scientific opinions."[147]This comment came from Starley Thompson and Stephen Schneider. Instead of asking, I will tell you why. The Pentagon gets enough money every year to spell the success or failure of every physicist or scientist in the USA. Therefore they have several hundred of "their" scientists to disagree with the nuclear winter theory. In the same article it says that the bulk of the news media coverage of the nuclear winter debate in late 1983 concentrated on the more dramatic conclusions and criticisms of the theory. The Pentagon can influence the news media too. You should notice that popular interest in nuclear winter topics decreased after this.

On page 317 of *Science News* magazine from November 12, 1983 is this quote:

"Those of you familiar with the scientific enterprise know that to get more than 50 scientists to agree—with no significant dissent—to a broad set of conclusions is unusual. To get them to agree on conclusions that bear on a problem of great and current public concern is extraordinary. But the group was absolutely unanimous in its conclusions, Ehrlich said:

'With all of the uncertainties and so on, if there is a full-scale nuclear war, odds are you can kiss the Northern Hemisphere goodbye.'"[148]

This is the group of scientists who told the truth about nuclear winter, and you can see that they did agree on how serious the implications would be if it happened. This group is opposed by the scientists who are influenced by the Pentagon. I will use the present tense here because the nuclear winter debate will happen all over again when my book is published. I must warn the American people not to expect any positive action by the Pentagon after this debate is finished. Where greed is concerned, the truth takes a second chair. This is why the phrase, "nuclear autumn" was invented. Pro-Pentagon scientists used it to discredit the concept of nuclear winter. The phrase is described in the *Discover* magazine article from November 1989, on page 26. It says:

"This new scenario earned the deceptively comforting name nuclear autumn."[149]

The name nuclear autumn was intended to be deceptive, and it was described in several magazine articles, and several of the books about nuclear winter. In *Newsweek*, March 31, 1986, on page 65 is the quote:

"For nuclear strategy, the implications of even modified nuclear winter theory are profound. Behind the scenes in the Pentagon, it has touched off an intense debate."[150]

You can see that after 18 years nothing has come of the "intense debate" in the Pentagon, and nothing ever will. If they seem to react favorably to the views of American citizens, it is done only to placate them. In reference to this debate however, the more truthful slant would be that they used 400 people in the Pentagon to debate on how to sabotage the nuclear winter theory. On page 986 and 987 of the *Foreign Affairs* magazine from June 1986 are these quotes:

"Given that the total yield of 100 megatons could trigger nuclear winter, the implication was that the level of superpower arsenals would have to be reduced to about one percent of their current value. Thus, the call for a policy of drastic cuts in strategic arsenals was directly linked to the threshold concept (of nuclear winter)."[151]

Notice what happened next!

"Ironically, just when the strategic implications of the threshold concept were starting to be debated in the strategic policy community, the strongest scientific arguments against the concept emerged."[152]

Now you can see that the Pentagon does influence scientists to discredit the nuclear winter theory. It was no accident that it happened the way that it did. Carl Sagan said it was imperative to reduce the world's nuclear arsenals to a level safely below that sufficient to trigger nuclear winter, and then pro-Pentagon scientists tried to discredit his threshold concept. You should remember that the Pentagon is working from a position of power, and all that they had to do in these instances was to invent the term, "nuclear autumn" to replace nuclear winter; and then to argue that Carl Sagan's threshold concept was not valid. On page 1002 and 1003 of the June 1986 *Foreign Affairs* article are the quotes:

"The Soviet Union has, to many Western observers, appeared steadfast in its ostensible acceptance of the absolute horrors implied by the earliest nuclear winter scenario. Remarks by Soviet spokesmen have especially emphasized the idea that nuclear winter 'retaliation' would be automatic following a nuclear strike by either side."[153]

This should have been the reaction of the people in the Pentagon, but it wasn't. Now if you will stop and reflect for a minute, try to remember the way that the Pentagon used the fear of Russian propaganda to get more money for the production of nuclear missiles in the 1950s and 1960s. Then look at this quote, in reference to the one above:

"The Soviet position, however, is frequently believed to have been adopted for its propaganda value, presumably in the hope that US and West European public opinion could be used to pressure the USA into arms control negotiating positions more favorable to the Soviets."[154]

Now the Pentagon will try to make us believe that suspicion is involved when the USSR tries to negotiate for nuclear arms reductions based on the nuclear winter theory. Then further down on page 1003 it says:

"It is well known that differing perceptions of technical and political problems often contribute to the difficulties the superpowers have in coming to agreements on strategic issues."[155]

This is always the argument that the Pentagon uses. Then they say that the potential for nuclear winter is another reason to support the continued modernization of US strategic forces with smaller, more accurate nuclear warheads. This is written on page 983 of the *Foreign Affairs* article.[156] I thought they were supposed to dismantle the ones that they already have? They can always do one thing better than anything else, and it is to spend money. Then next they say that nuclear winter is a good reason to pursue Star Wars defense, or SDI. This is also written in *Time* magazine from December 24, 1984, on page 56:

"Science adviser George Keyworth and other members of the Reagan Administration are citing nuclear winter as further justification for developing the Star Wars defense system."[157]

There was an argument about it then by Theodore Postal and many other nuclear strategists, that Star Wars would cause the Soviet Union to build more advanced nuclear weapons, and thus increase the threat of global holocaust. That doesn't matter to the Pentagon though because they like to spend money, and it is their job to kill people, after all. You have to remember that there is evil and good in the world, and it is the responsibility of the prophets to tell you where the evil is, and how to get rid of it. This is what Jesus did in John 2:13-17. He also upbraided the scribes and Pharisees in Matthew 23:1-36. He came to give immortality to the people of Israel, and they killed him trying to take it.

Moses repeatedly warned the Hebrews to purge the evil from among them in Deuteronomy 13:5, Deuteronomy 17:7, Deuteronomy 17:12, and in Deuteronomy 19:19. The key phrase in all of these verses is:

"So thou shalt put the evil away from among you."

In the case of America this means to dismantle the nuclear missiles, which the Pentagon now has. This is also written in Jeremiah 18:11, in the phrase, "return ye now every one from his evil way, and make your ways and your doings good." If the reaction of the Pentagon is to waste time, to spend more money, to debate the issue, or to use fear against the American people, then this is the meaning:

Jeremiah 18:12: "And they said, There is no hope: but we will walk after our own devices, and we will every one do the imagination of his evil heart."

If you really look at the Pentagon in relation to the nuclear disarmament issues, then you will probably agree that this verse describes their actions perfectly. They have walked after their own devices. Christ described this in:

Matthew 7:15,16: "Beware of false prophets, which come to you in sheep's clothing, but inwardly they are ravening wolves.

Ye shall know them by their fruits. Do men gather grapes of thorns, or figs of thistles?"

The thorns and thistles described here are nuclear missiles. The people in the Pentagon are described as ravening wolves because they have gotten $265 billion dollars per year for almost 20 years.

In Matthew 7:17 is the phrase, "But a corrupt tree bringeth forth evil fruit." Then in:

Matthew 7:20: "Wherefore by their fruits ye shall know them." What are the fruits of the labor of the Pentagon? Nuclear missiles. They have no defense against nuclear missile attack by another nation. They only have nuclear missiles. In Matthew 7:15 the Pentagon's way to confront World War III is wrong. They are called false prophets. They will use nuclear threats against the Antichrist during World War III, and America will suffer nuclear retaliation from him. The true prophets can see evil where it is, and the reality of sin in governmental institutions, just as Christ did when he was in Israel. This is described by St. Paul in this verse:

Ephesians 6:12: "For we wrestle not against flesh and blood, but against principalities, against powers, against the rulers of the darkness of this world, against spiritual wickedness in high places."

The phrase, "against spiritual wickedness in high places," means Bill Clinton trying to steal my books, and it means the Pentagon getting $400 billion dollars in their annual budget, while refusing to dismantle their nuclear missiles. You see, they have to hold onto the nuclear missiles, or their budget will be cut. This is the meaning of the phrase, "spiritual wickedness in high places." The deceit is what causes them to refuse nuclear disarmament. This is why the Pentagon will have to give their offensive military power to the Church Committee Group. Then they will use the taxpayer's money to provide food, housing, gas masks, and other services to the American people throughout World War III.

Isaiah 1:17: "Learn to do well; seek judgment, relieve the oppressed, judge the fatherless, plead for the widow."

This is what the Church Committee Group will do. They will help the oppressed people in America. They will also follow the instructions of Christ in Matthew 5:39-48. Look at this example to avoid a global nuclear war:

Steve throws a rock at Bill.
Then Bill throws a rock back at Steve.
The escalation proceeds.
Or

Steve throws a rock at Bill.
Bill does nothing.
The escalation stops.

This is the reason for the theology in Matthew 5:39-48. If you follow the instructions of Christ in these verses, you will avoid a nuclear war. This is the most important responsibility of the Church Committee Group. On page 64 of the *Atlantic Monthly* magazine from November 1984 is the quote:

"The military solution to the nuclear winter problem is a much larger number of much smaller, extremely accurate weapons that would allow targets in cities to be destroyed without burning down the cities around them."[158]

The Pentagon is always good at spending money, aren't they? This is why they are called ravening wolves in Matthew 7:15. Therefore when the Pentagon wants to fund another project, or spend money on more advanced weapons in response to my book, you already know that their approach to the problem is wrong. A good example of this is using Edward Teller, the inventor of the hydrogen bomb to refute the nuclear winter theory. I am really amazed that no one noticed this before. On page 59 of the same article in the *Atlantic Monthly* is the quote:

"When the TTAPS group presented its findings at a highly publicized conference in Washington, the response from the White House and the Pentagon was virtual silence."[159]

This will probably be their reaction to my book as well, but this too is wrong. The only correct solution is the Church Committee Plan.

On Saturday March 30, 1997, I returned from the Easter Vigil at All Saints Catholic Church in Puyallup, Washington. I had another revelation from the Lord God Almighty, which I received at church. The first three Bible readings today were from Genesis 1, Exodus 14, and Isaiah 55:7-13, and I have just finished reading and highlighting the copies from 18 magazine articles about nuclear winter, after having read copies from five books on the same subject. I have been reading about the absolute horrors that would follow a major nuclear war, and I have made notes and references to the death that it would cause. I will describe this first, and then the revelation afterward. These quotes are from the book titled, *Nuclear Winter*, ©1985 by Owen Greene, on pages 3 through 6:

"The effects of nuclear war

1. Nuclear explosions would send dust, radioactivity, and various gases into the atmosphere.
2. The explosions would ignite fires, burning cities, forests, fuel, and grasslands. The total area covered could be vast.

3. The fires would send plumes of smoke and gases tens of thousands of feet into the atmosphere.
4. Some of the dust, radioactivity, and smoke would be carried by the wind, around the earth.
5. The zone for the smoke and dust clouds would be in the Northern Hemisphere.
6. Under the clouds of smoke and dust, daylight could be reduced to near darkness.
7. Temperatures would drop on land under the clouds of smoke and dust. The average temperatures would probably not return to normal for more than a year.
8. Some of the smoke and dust would settle to the ground after the main nuclear attacks, and it will bring radioactive fallout with it. When the smoke and dust clears, the earth's surface will be exposed to damaging ultraviolet radiation."

"The effect of the ultraviolet radiation is comparable to being in a microwave oven. The biological effects of the items listed above are:

1. Very little plant growth for months in the Northern Hemisphere.
2. Harvest failure throughout the Northern Hemisphere.
3. The death of countless wild plants and animals.
4. The collapse of advanced agriculture.
5. The collapse of medical and public health services.
6. The death from famine and epidemics of more people than those who died in the nuclear war itself.

In short, human suffering would be worldwide, and on a scale almost beyond comprehension."[160]

This is a picture of man destroying the earth. Now look at Genesis 1:1-31, where the Lord God Almighty created the earth. Then if you will read my Church Committee Plan chapter, and compare it to these verses:

Isaiah 55:6-12: "Seek ye the Lord while he may be found, call ye upon him while he is near:

Let the wicked forsake his way, and the unrighteous man his thoughts: and let him return unto the Lord, and he will have mercy upon him: and to our God, for he will abundantly pardon.

For my thoughts are not your thoughts, neither are your ways my ways, saith the Lord.

For as the heavens are higher than the earth, so are my ways higher than your ways, and my thoughts than your thoughts.

For as the rain cometh down, and the snow from the heaven, and returneth not thither, but watereth the earth, and maketh it bring forth and bud, that it may give seed to the sower, and bread to the eater:

So shall my word be that goeth forth out of my mouth: it shall not return unto me void, but it shall accomplish that which I please, and it shall prosper in the thing whereto I sent it.

For ye shall go out with joy and be led forth with peace: the mountains and the hills shall break forth before you into singing, and all the trees of the field shall clap their hands."

This is a prophecy about my Church Committee Plan! These are instructions for the US Congress to use the Church Committee Plan before and during World War III. The ways of the Lord God are higher than the ways of men, and his thoughts are higher because he created the earth. This means that he knows how to save the earth as well. I spent almost five years working on the Church Committee Plan, and I followed the instructions in the Bible in regard to the aspects of the carnal man vs. the spiritual man. It would be better to have the spiritual man in control of the offensive military power of the USA because he would not be tempted to put US troops into Europe, or to use a first-strike nuclear attack against the Antichrist. This also follows the instructions of Christ in Matthew 5:39-48. Now while I am writing the Nuclear Winter chapter, I find that Isaiah 55:6-12 is a prophecy about the Church Committee Plan. This proves that Christ is working through me to save America.

Now I will write a list of the magazine articles, which I have read, about nuclear winter. They were all on microfilm at the Tacoma Library:

The Atlantic	11-84	page 53
Discover	1-85	page 24
Discover	11-89	page 26
Foreign Affairs	6-86	page 981
Popular Science	7-85	page 12
Newsweek	3-31-86	page 65
Newsweek	9-14-87	page 12
Science	12-23-83	page 1292
Science	12-23-83	page 1293
Science	1-12-90	page 166
Science News	9-14-85	page 171
Science News	11-12-83	page 314
Science News	12-22-84	page 397
Science News	4-19-86	page 249
Scientific American	8-84	page 33

Scientific American	2-85	page 60
Time	12-24-84	page 56

The article in *Scientific American* from 2-85 on page 60 is about the SALT Treaties.[161] In *Science News* from 9-14-85 on page 171 is an article titled, *Nuclear Winter*: Shutting Down the Farm? The report says that starvation will be the greatest cause of death following a nuclear war.[162] An unseasonable cold snap, or a summer freeze, could wipe out the entire harvest of crops in the Northern Hemisphere. Low light levels would reduce the net primary productivity in surviving plants. Reduced rainfall would occur after a nuclear war, and when it does rain it could contain pollutants such as nitrogen oxide, ozone, carbon monoxide, and sulfur dioxide. This would produce acid rain, which would kill crops. The bees and insects, which pollinate the flowers on seed crops, would be killed in a nuclear winter, and then those crops would not develop. The pyrotoxins produced in a nuclear war, as well as the radioactive fallout, and the increased ultraviolet light levels would kill insects, birds, animals, plants, and humans on a catastrophic scale. Insects, animals, and humans who survive will be blinded by the increased level of ultraviolet light.

Not a nice picture, is it? There have been thousands of scientists who have done research work on nuclear winter, and have even left their own fields of study to devote countless hours to prove that it will happen after a nuclear war. Then the Pentagon ignores them. I know how it feels. President Bill Clinton was working from a position of power, and he would not allow my books to be published, after I did 10 years of evangelism and Bible study, and then seven years of book writing. The Pentagon is also working from a position of power, and they ignore the results of the nuclear winter studies. In Ephesians 6:12 this is called spiritual wickedness in high places. If you will think about these situations for a minute, then you will realize that the scientists were discriminated against just like I was. This is why St. Paul gave me the instructions in I Timothy 6:20. This enabled me to look at the situation from the point of view of a scientist, and then I could recognize the discrimination that they faced.

The articles written by Carl Sagan, Richard Turco, Brian Toon, Thomas Ackerman, James Pollack, Mark Harwell, Janet Raloff, and several nuclear winter scientists were very valuable. In the *Science* magazine from 12-23-83 on page 1293 the scientists said that their concern was to save the two to three billion people who are not killed if a major nuclear war occurs.[163] This is why they studied the possible effects of nuclear winter. They also said that food resources would become scarce throughout the world in a very short time, and that agriculture as we know it, would for all practical purposes, come to an end during nuclear winter. If no food were put into storage by nations throughout the world, then three billion people will starve to death.

This is why I recommend the building of food warehouses, and the storage of food by every nation in the world starting now. These nations should also put seeds for all crops into storage as well, and then they can use them after the nuclear winter is over. Tractor fuel and fertilizers will also be in short supply, especially when the Antichrist takes the world oil supply in the year 2014. For this I recommend that all nations convert to natural gas fuel now; and they can put fertilizers into storage too. These instructions do not apply to the nations in Europe because the people there will have to evacuate to be saved. I also recommend that nations with cattle, sheep, pigs, and other livestock should give their farmers subsidies to build large steel buildings during the years 2012 to 2016 to cover five acres, with properly slanted roofs that will not collapse because of the buildup of snow. These could be used to protect their animals from nuclear fallout, pyrotoxins, increased ultraviolet light, and cold weather. I will also recommend that the nations call for a buildup of livestock herds during the years 2008 to 2018; and then they can use the large-scale slaughter, cutting, wrapping, and freezing of beef, lamb, pork, chickens, turkeys, and other meats in preparation for the nuclear winter. In the years from 2017 to 2021 the nations can build thousands of cold storage buildings to accommodate the freezer meats. On page 1298 of the *Science* magazine article from 12-23-83, it says that no irrigation, lack of rainfall, and frozen lakes and rivers will hamper any efforts toward farming.[164] These are more good reasons for the steps, which I have outlined. On the same page it says that there will be large forest fires and brushfires caused by multiple airbursts of nuclear weapons. This could lead to catastrophic flooding, especially with the heat generated by the nuclear explosions and the forest fires. Then the flooding will cause erosion, which will take some of the topsoil needed for crops. There will also be major dust storms because of the violent windstorms caused by nuclear winter.

On page 33 of the *Scientific American* article from 8-84, the TTAPS group said that the authoritative studies available on the added threats of delayed radioactive fallout, depletion of the ozone layer, and adverse changes in the climate after a nuclear war, had played down their importance.[165] The term, "authoritative studies," means those of or influenced by the US Government. On page 38 of the same article, there are more than 1,000 missile silos in the USA, and 1,400 of them in the USSR, and two nuclear warheads are targeted to hit each one. This means that there will be 4,800 nuclear explosions in the world if there is a major nuclear war between the USA and the USSR.[166]

Just imagine that there were large eruptions of 4,800 volcanoes on the earth at the same time. On page 39 of the article, it says that the nuclear dust calculations are consistent with observations of volcanic phenomena.[167] The eruptions of El Chichon in Mexico in 1982, Tambora in 1815, and Krakatau in 1883 are mentioned here, and global dust veils were used to test and calibrate the climate models. Violent eruptions can lead to a significant climatic cooling for a year or more. This was mentioned in the book, *Fire and Ice*, © 1990 by David Fisher, on page 33.[168] Because of the large eruption of the volcano Tambora in 1815, 1816 became known as, "the year without a summer." The dust from this volcano went so high into the stratosphere that there was no rain to wash it out of the air, and back down to the earth.

From 1983 to 1990 intensive research markedly improved the TTAPS group's understanding of the physical aspects of the nuclear winter theory. On page 166 of the *Science* magazine article from 1-12-90 it says that midsummer land temperature decreases average 10 degrees centigrade to 20 degrees centigrade, with local cooling as large as 35 degrees centigrade, and subfreezing summer temperatures in some regions.[169] The atmosphere circulations caused by the solar heating of soot in the smoke clouds is found to stabilize the upper atmosphere against overturning, thus increasing the soot lifetime. This means that the smoke will stay in the stratosphere longer because of the fact that the sun will heat the soot and cause it to rise higher. This will also accelerate the movement of the smoke clouds to the Southern Hemisphere, and then nuclear winter will happen there too. Serious new environmental problems are mentioned in reference to soot injection, including disruption of monsoon precipitation and severe depletion of the stratospheric ozone layer in the Northern Hemisphere. For this I will recommend that welder's goggles should be manufactured, and every man, woman, and child in every nation in the world should buy a pair of them. In fact every government should make sure that enough of them are available for the people. Then when depletion of the ozone layer happens, the people can wear welder's goggles, as well as long sleeved shirts, coats, and gloves. They can also wear ski masks if necessary.

On page 166 of the *Science* article from 1-12-90 it says that enough smoke could be generated during nuclear war to decrease solar intensity or sunlight by 50% or more on a hemisphere scale.[170] This means that the Northern Hemisphere would be darkened by as much as half. Sooty smoke from urban fires is the major contributor to nuclear winter. Upper layers of this smoke could be heated by as much as 100 degrees centigrade. Make a note of this fact, for when smoke or air is heated, it rises, and this will cause it to go up into the stratosphere, where there is no rain to wash the smoke out of the air. This could cause it to stay in the sky for two or three years, instead of one. You should notice that the scientific language in the TTAPS group articles is difficult to understand even if you have studied Physics, Calculus, and

Engineering at the college level. The articles are: *Science*, 12-23-1983, page 1293;[171] *Scientific American*, August 1984, page 33;[172] and *Science*, 1-12-90, page 166.[173]

This is one factor, which made it easier for the Pentagon and their scientists to sabotage the nuclear winter theory. This is why they thought up the term, "nuclear autumn." Why should a person try to understand the language in the articles, if nuclear winter is changed to nuclear autumn? This proves that the effort to sabotage the TTAPS group findings was organized; and it probably happened in exactly the same way that I described it: The Pentagon selected 300 to 400 people to read the TTAPS report to write down their comments, and then to have a large group discussion about it. When it was decided what should be done, several people were assigned to call pro-Pentagon scientists, and magazine editors to write about the nuclear autumn idea.

A good example of this is the article written in *Foreign Affairs*, in June 1986, on page 981, by Starley L. Thompson and Stephen H. Schneider. The title for the article is Nuclear Winter Reappraised, and this alone suggests that it was meant to sabotage the TTAPS findings. The two scientists worked at the National Center for Atmospheric Research, which is a government agency. Thompson was an atmospheric scientist, and Schneider was the Deputy Director of NCAR. After reading the article I found that Thompson and Schneider refuted and verified the TTAPS group findings at the same time. They had to write down the scientific proof of the nuclear winter theory, but they had to refute the theory for the Pentagon too. In the following quote:

"We intend to show that on scientific grounds the global apocalyptic conclusions of the initial nuclear winter theory can now be relegated to a vanishingly low level of probability."[174] Thompson and Schneider said here that they were going to make the nuclear winter theory go away. This is what the phrase, "to a vanishingly low level," means. This is why they invented the phrase, "nuclear autumn." It made the nuclear winter theory go away and it was then called nuclear autumn instead. If you will look at Revelation 8:12 however, you will find that nuclear winter did not go away.

Revelation 8:12: "And the fourth angel sounded, and the third part of the sun was smitten, and the third part of the moon, and the third part of the stars; so as the third part of them was darkened, and the day shone not for a third part of it, and the night likewise."

I should warn the American people that the Pentagon will deliberately mock the words written in the Bible to make me angry, in order to cause me to leave Washington, D.C. Then the people will have no one to deliver them from World War III during the critical times. This is the reason for the Church Committee Group because they will always be there for the American people. This is the reason for the National Emergency Vote, which will take the power away from the nuclear hawks, and give it to the Church Committee Group.

I will not tolerate any additional studies on nuclear winter, any bureaucratic inertia, any disagreements over nuclear disarmament, or any additional spending for more advanced weapons. The only way to deliver the American people from World War III is by using the Church Committee Plan. The Pentagon is working from a position of power, and their power has to be taken away. The proof of this is written on pages 48 and 49 of the US Government Budget Supplement for 1997.[175] The Pentagon is going to spend $4 trillion dollars on the Joint Strike Fighter, and on the other military weapons listed in this booklet during the next 20 years. This will mean that 100 million Americans will be homeless and starving by the year 2014. The Church Committee Group will provide the food and housing for the people, and the Pentagon will make weapons. You will see that prophecy is meant to save lives, and military forces are meant to kill. The most tragic thing of all is that the Pentagon will jeopardize the safety of the American people by fighting against the Unified European Army, or the army of the Antichrist.

Revelation 9:16: "And the number of the army of the horsemen were two hundred thousand thousand: and I heard the number of them."

Believe me, you don't want to invite those 200 million soldiers to America, and this is what the Pentagon will do. To find out what the Pentagon has to do in relation to World War III, you should read the Spiritual Principles of World War III chapter. They have to provide a national defense, and they have to build an ABM defense on their submarines at sea. This will not be very expensive if the USA and USSR lead the way in large-scale nuclear disarmament.

There is another thing which should be analyzed by the American people, and it is the bureaucratic resistance of my Church Committee Plan in other US Government agencies, and perhaps even in the Congress itself. In the *Science News* article from April 19, 1986, on page 249 is this quote:

"Before publishing the report, the GAO or General Accounting Office, sent around copies of a draft for comment by US agencies involved in nuclear winter research. One of the primary criticisms it received came from the OSTP or the Office of Science and Technology Policy. According to the GAO, the OSTP argued that the report's discussion of policy issues was giving more validity to the nuclear winter theory than was warranted. OSTP therefore suggested that the tenor of the report be changed. The GAO disagreed and left those discussions in its report."[176]

Once again a government agency tried to sweep the nuclear winter theory under the rug. I would say that the OSTP could be influenced by the

Pentagon because of the annual budget of $400 billion dollars. On the same page in the article from *Science News* it says: "The GAO says that some scientists argue that, 'given the range of likely consequences in nuclear war,' such biological studies should be conducted along with the existing physical and chemical research. However, others including officials in the White House Office of Science and Technology Policy, 'think that biological implications have secondary importance.'"[177]

In other words, someone in the US Government decided that you should starve to death in a nuclear winter, if by accident you did survive the nuclear attack. Biological implications mean food crops. Here is a quote from *Discover* magazine of January 1985, on page 26:

"Paul Crutzen's insight may turn out to be one of the best of all scientific contributions to human welfare. If his predictions turn out to be correct or reasonably probable, we are at last free of the threat of full-scale nuclear warfare."[178]

People have dreamed about a world free of nuclear war for 54 years, and with the Pentagon in power, that is all it will ever be. When greed is in the formula, the welfare of the people is not important. You have to face the facts, and you have to realize that a profound change in the US Government will have to happen before nuclear disarmament will occur. This is why the Church Committee Group will have to lead the way with the United Nations Organization and the major nuclear powers, in order to effect large-scale disarmament throughout the world.

If the United Nations SCOPE study could not influence the President of the USA to call for large-scale disarmament, then the best and only way is for the Church Committee Group to do it after they are voted into the Congress by the American people. I wrote letters to Bill Clinton about World War III, the Antichrist, and nuclear war for three years, and I even advised him to call for major nuclear disarmament policy, and then he decided to steal my book and the royalties. This is why I know that anyone who expects the US Government and the Pentagon to dismantle their nuclear weapons is being too altruistic. With these kinds of abuses in the US Government, it is time to stop dreaming, and take action; and this is the very reason for the Church Committee Plan. It will save me years of arguments with people who would never change no matter what I do.

In the *Science News* article from 11-12-83 on page 314 is the quote:

"The two to three billion people who are at least able to stand up after the last nuclear weapon goes off are going to be—at least in the Northern Hemisphere—starving to death in a dark, smoggy world."[179]

This is a reality that the Pentagon has ignored for 22 years, and they will ignore it for another 20 years in order to preserve their $400 billion dollars per year. They don't care about the survivors of a nuclear war because it is their job to kill people, not to save them. In the same *Science News* article it says about the sunlight in a nuclear winter:

"Light could prove to be insufficient to sustain photosynthesis, noted plant physiologist Joseph Berry of the Carnegie Institution."[180]

This means that plants will die because there won't be enough sunlight to keep them alive. If the cold and the frost do not kill the plants, then the lack of sunlight will. On page 316 of the *Science News* article from 11-12-83 it says under the diagram:

"Minimum explosive yield needed, (from a nuclear weapon) to inject material such as smoke and dust into the stratosphere is about 300 kilotons. The dust from high yield ground bursts—at nuclear missile silos or other hardened facilities—is largely injected into the stratosphere."[181]

It should also be noted that the nuclear warheads needed to destroy hardened targets such as nuclear missile silos would have to be one megaton to be effective. Then looking back at the 1,000 silos in the USA, and the 1,400 in the USSR, with 2 warheads targeted at each one, this equals a yield of 4,800 megatons in a minimum first and second strike nuclear exchange. This is why the TTAPS group used a baseline case of 5,000 megatons for the nuclear war scenario on page 316 of the 11-12-83 *Science News* article.[182] Therefore I was right when I compared it to the eruptions of 4,800 very large volcanoes. For this scenario, the sunlight in the Northern Hemisphere would drop to 1% to 5% of its former level. This means it would be very dark and cold. On the same page in the *Science News* article it says that with the aid of the smoke in the urban firestorms resulting from a nuclear attack on the cities in the USA and USSR, a payload or yield of only 100 megatons used on a total of 100 cities could trigger an effect about as bad as the 5,000 megaton scenario. This means that a first and second strike attack by the USSR and the USA on missile silos and on 100 cities would send the smoke from about 10,000 volcanos, which erupted at the same time, high into the stratosphere. You must remember that the nuclear winter is real, that it is described in Revelation 8:12, and that it will happen as a result of a nuclear war between Russia and China. This is also described in Daniel 11:44 where the Antichrist will be angry at China, and he will use total nuclear retaliation. This is the meaning of the phrase, "therefore he will go forth with great fury to destroy, and utterly to make away many." To make away many means to kill many people. This means that the Antichrist will target the major cities in Korea and in China with nuclear warheads. This is why the Church Committee Group and the United Nations Organization should work together to dismantle nuclear missiles on a large scale. Another important point is the 10,000 nuclear warheads, which the Pentagon has stockpiled, which are not even shown in the books. These are described in Robert S. McNamara's book, *Blundering Into Disaster*, © 1986 on page 41. I would think that the USSR has a similar number stockpiled as well.[183] This is another good reason for the United Nations to use the International Court of Law to hold the USA, USSR, and China if possible to the Zero Tolerance rule. The other nuclear powers can participate too.

On page 57 of the *Time* magazine article from 12-24-84 is the quote:

"Paul Crutzen and John Birks said that at least 386,000 square miles of forest could burn during a nuclear holocaust."[184]

The enormous columns of smoke rising into the stratosphere would be enough to block out almost all of the sunlight in many areas for weeks or maybe months. In 1950 a giant forest fire in Alberta, Canada burned an area of 10,000 square kilometers. The smoke from this fire covered about half the land area of the USA, and as it spread to Great Britain, it was seen by aircraft pilots at 35,000 feet. This is described on page 54 of the *Atlantic Monthly* magazine from November 1984.[185] The smoke from the firestorm at Hiroshima, Japan was sent up into the atmosphere by the 12-kiloton atomic bomb, and then returned to the ground as black rain. You should note that the hydrogen bomb is capable of much more damage than an atomic bomb, and it can send dust and smoke as high as 20 kilometers into the stratosphere. One of the pro-Pentagon people said there was not a nuclear winter after Hiroshima and Nagasaki, but there is no comparison between these 12-kiloton small yield atomic bombs and the more powerful hydrogen bombs.

On page 58 of the *Atlantic Monthly* magazine is the quote:

"Nuclear weapons, especially when detonated in the air, produce an intense thermal pulse that can ignite fires simultaneously over vast areas. Any city attacked with nuclear weapons will burn, and many of these burning cities will generate firestorms whose gigantic smoke columns will carry soot particles into the upper atmosphere, where they might stay for months."[186]

Now I will use some of the quotes from these five books, which I have read about nuclear winter:

Nuclear Winter, © 1984 by Mark Harwell
Nuclear Winter, © 1985 by Owen Greene
Fire and Ice, © 1990 by David Fisher
The Long Darkness, © 1986 by Yale University
A Path Where No Man Thought, © 1990 by Carl Sagan

On page 65 of the book, *Nuclear Winter*, by Mark Harwell, it says that urban or city fires will cause the greatest problems after a nuclear war because of the very sooty smoke which they will produce.[187] On page viii of the foreword in the same book it says:

"The air bursts over cities could ignite flammable materials and cause vast fires producing sooty smoke."[188]

On page 126 of the book, *Fire and Ice*, by David Fisher, is the quote:

"If most of the smoke particles are black and sooty, as is expected from the sort of flammable materials found in cities, they would absorb more sunlight than they will scatter away. This means that the cloud will get hot and the heated air will then rise extending its atmospheric lifetime."[189]

Then the smoke particles will remain suspended high up, and sunlight will be cut off below. On page 127 of *Fire and Ice*:

"Daylight would not return for many months—a 95% cut in sunlight would give days about as bright as moonlit nights."

"The world would be subjected to prolonged darkness, abnormally low temperatures, violent windstorms, toxic smog, and radioactive fallout."[190]

On page 24 of Carl Sagan's book, *A Path Where No Man Thought*, is the quote:

"Because cities and petroleum repositories are so rich in combustive materials, it doesn't require very many nuclear explosions over them to make so much smoke as to obscure the entire Northern Hemisphere and more."

"The resulting environmental changes from this may last for months or years."[191]

On page 201 of the same book it says that the more cities and petroleum facilities are in flames, the worse the climatic damage is.[192] On page 41 of this book it says that there could be thousands of fires caused by nuclear explosions in cities, forests, and oil and gas fields.[193] On page 65 of Carl Sagan's book, it says that nuclear winter will have a disproportionate climatic impact compared to that which caused the Ice Age because of how much darker sooty smoke is than the dust created by the impact of an asteroid.[194] It is also true that: Smoke will stay up in the stratosphere longer because it is lighter than dust. On page 54 of the book, *Nuclear Winter*, by Owen Greene, is the quote:

"The height to which the smoke from fires rises depends mainly on the rate at which it produces heat, that is its power, W. The formula is:

Top= .25 W to the one fourth power
Base= .15 W to the one fourth power

Heights are measured in kilometers, and power in megawatts."

"Usually, the more powerful the source of heat, the more the air is heated and the higher it goes."[195]

On page 55 it says:

"Because fires started by nuclear weapons are ignited almost simultaneously over a wide area, they are much more powerful than normal fires."[196]

On page 58 the most intense city fires will send plumes of smoke to the greatest heights.[197] The danger is that smoke clouds which reach the stratosphere will stay there for a year or more because there is almost no rain there to wash the particles back down to the earth. This is written on page 122 of the book, *Fire and Ice*.[198] On page 37 of the book, *A Path Where No Man Thought*, by Carl Sagan, is the quote:

"In many cases significant amounts of smoke reach the stratosphere, sometimes to 15-30 kilometers altitude even without self-lofting (heating of the smoke by sunlight making it rise through the air)."[199]

On page 84 of the book, *Nuclear Winter*, by Owen Greene it says that higher smoke produces more cooling at the earth's surface, and it stays up longer.

"If it is in the post nuclear stratosphere, it may stay up for months or years rather than a week or two—typical of the troposphere."[200]

On page 66 of the book, *Nuclear Winter*, by Mark Harwell, it says that about 500 million tons of smoke would be injected into the atmosphere because of city fires in a 5,000 megaton nuclear war.[201] On page 126 of *Fire and Ice* it says that the TTAPS group estimated that more than 100 million tons of smoke could be generated in a nuclear war involving less than half of the total strategic weapons of the USA and USSR.[202] It also says here that Paul Crutzen estimated a value of about 300 million tons of smoke. On page 89 of the book, *Nuclear Winter*, by Owen Greene it says that overall the production of smoke in the severe nuclear war scenario would be four times that of the baseline 5,000-megaton scenario. It also says that 25% of the smoke will be in the post nuclear stratosphere.[203] On page 32 of the same book is the quote:

"There are about 2260 urban centers (cities plus their surrounding urban conglomerations and suburbs) in the world with population of more than 100,000 people."[204]

In a severe nuclear war scenario almost all of these cities would be hit with nuclear warheads, and they would burn. Then on page 33 is the quote:

"The scale of many of these fires would be quite unprecedented. Even if only 2/3 or less of each of the affected cities were actually within the ignition zones, many of the largest city fires would be ignited almost simultaneously over more than 400 square miles. It is very likely that in many of these cities the fire would spread, and the secondary fires would lead to even larger burned areas."[205]

The area of 400 square miles is 20 miles times 20 miles, and many large cities really do have this much land area. This is why a nuclear attack on cities would cause so much smoke, and so much damage to the ecosystem of the earth. On page x of the foreword in the book, *Nuclear Winter*, by Mark Harwell is the quote:

"Even a comparatively small nuclear war can have devastating climatic consequences, provided cities are targeted."[206]

This was the most striking and unexpected finding of the TTAPS study done in 1983. On page 13 of Mark Harwell's book, he wrote that in the baseline case of 5,650-megaton nuclear war, there would be 5,000 cities targeted worldwide.[207] On page 197 of the book, *A Path Where No Man Thought*, by Carl Sagan is the quote:

"A small nuclear war in which hundreds of cities are burning is likely to generate a much more severe nuclear winter than a large one in which thousands of hardened targets are attacked."[208]

You should note on page 202 of Carl Sagan's book that nuclear attacks on urban centers and petroleum refining and storage facilities are targeting strategies seldom discussed.[209] I know that he was talking about the Pentagon here; and I think they invented the phrase, mutually assured destruction or MAD, so they would never have to talk about the targeting of cities again. On page 270 of Carl Sagan's book is the quote:

"City targeting remains a ghastly and hateful necessity, but it is intrinsic to the very nature of nuclear weapons."[210]

On page 330 of Carl Sagan's book is a quote from General David C. Jones, former Chairman of the Joint Chiefs of Staff, in testimony before the Senate Armed Services Committee on March 30, 1987:

"I first became involved in nuclear targeting in 1954. What came home clear to me at the time was the easiest thing to do was to destroy cities…Conversely, the hardest thing to do was to protect cities from attack. I estimate that 2% of the force of either side, impacting on the cities of the other side, would do catastrophic damage to most of the urban-industrial area. It takes only a few hundred nuclear weapons, probably not more than a couple hundred, to impact and make very, very great damage."[211]

On page 203 of Carl Sagan's book:

"Urban and petroleum targets are characterized by high concentrations of flammable materials in a relatively small area. This is why they have the potential to create a global nuclear winter with a modest number of detonations."[212]

On page 350 of Carl Sagan's book:

"Some of the cities in the USA with populations over 100,000 that contain strictly military targets and are likely to be targeted in a counter force nuclear war:

Phoenix, Tucson, Arizona
Little Rock, Arkansas
San Diego, Stockton, California
San Francisco, Oxnard, California
Long Beach, Sacramento, California
San Jose, San Bernardino, California
Sunnyvale, Concord, California
Denver, Colorado Springs, Colorado
Washington, D.C.
Jacksonville, Tampa, Florida
Miami, Fort Lauderdale, Florida
Honolulu, Hawaii
Chicago, Illinois
Fort Wayne, Indiana
Des Moines, Iowa
Wichita, Kansas
New Orleans, Louisiana
Springfield, Massachusetts
Detroit, Michigan
Duluth, Minnesota
Kansas City, St. Louis, Missouri
Omaha, Nebraska
Las Vegas, Nevada
Albuquerque, New Mexico
Columbus, Dayton, Cincinnati, Ohio
Oklahoma City, Oklahoma
Pittsburgh, Pennsylvania
Charleston, South Carolina
Knoxville, Tennessee
Amarillo, San Antonio, Fort Worth, Texas
Salt Lake City, Utah
Arlington, Chesapeake, Newport News, Virginia
Norfolk, Alexandria, Virginia
Seattle, Tacoma, Washington
Milwaukee, Wisconsin
This list is incomplete."[213]

I got the list on page 350 of Carl Sagan's book, and it contains 53 cities in America that would be hit with nuclear warheads in a Soviet attack, simply because they contain military targets.[214]

You should notice that several very large cities in America are not on this list, such as New York, Boston, and Atlanta. These cities will also be targeted in a large-scale nuclear war because of the (MAD) mutually assured destruction concept developed by our own Pentagon. On page 123 of Carl Sagan's book is the quote:

"Efim Slavsky in July 1968 told Andrei Sakharov 'If the imperialists use nuclear weapons, we'll retaliate at once with everything we've got and destroy every target necessary to ensure victory.' Sakharov concluded from this, 'So our response would be an immediate, all-out nuclear attack on enemy cities and industry, as well as on military targets.'"[215]

This targeting plan will still be in effect when the Antichrist takes control of the nuclear weapons in the USSR at the beginning of World War III. This is why the American people should demand that the US military system be changed now, while we still have time to get rid of the threat of global nuclear war, and the nuclear winter that will follow it. I should warn the people in America that the Pentagon will very seriously damage the nuclear disarmament efforts prior to World War III because their system is motivated by greed. For this reason you cannot trust them to hold high level talks, conduct studies or research, negotiate treaties, or anything else of this nature. You have to change the US military system to keep America out of 9 nuclear wars. This is the only way: The Congress and/or the American people must vote for the Church Committee Plan.

The targeting of cities is also a high priority for nuclear strategists in China. On page 346 of Carl Sagan's book it says:

"Zhang Aiping, one of those responsible for Chinese nuclear weapons, is quoted as indicating that, 'the ability to destroy urban areas or soft military targets in a retaliatory strike is what matters.'"[216]

Quote from, *China Builds the Bomb*, © 1988 by John W. Lewis, and Xue Litai.

On the subject of targeting it is very important to know that China will be involved in the large-scale nuclear war against the Antichrist. There will be approximately 1.7 billion people killed in this nuclear war, and in the nuclear winter that will follow it two billion more will die. This war is described in Revelation 8:10-12, and in Daniel 11:44, and it is in the Nuclear War chapter. The Antichrist will deliberately target the cities of China and Korea, in order to kill as many people as possible. For this reason China and Korea can be important voices in the United Nations Organization's Zero Tolerance Policy toward nuclear weapons.

When looking at the causes of nuclear winter it is important to look at oil refinery fires. On page 123 of Carl Sagan's book, "high priority is still directed to petroleum refineries... Cities and petroleum depots continue to be so heavily targeted that the threat of nuclear winter is not reduced by the latest US targeting doctrines."[217]

This was written in 1990, when Carl Sagan's book was published. On page 203, "the petroleum refineries exhibit the greatest climatic sensitivity for the least number of detonations (even for tactical—that is, about 1 to 10 kiloton yields—rather than strategic weapons)."

On the same page:

"The British and French nuclear forces (with about 1,000 and 700 strategic warheads respectively), when their present modernization is completed, are seen to be capable of causing a marginal and perhaps even a nominal nuclear winter with only about 1/3 of the warheads dedicated to urban targets in the Soviet Union."[218]

This "nominal nuclear winter" is described on page 194 of Carl Sagan's book.[219] On page 347 it says:

"Some 450 oil refineries (and 3,000 oil pipelines) are on hypothetical, nearly identical target lists published both in the USA and in the USSR. However, most storage capacity is concentrated in a small number of large refineries and depots."[220]

On page 119 is the quote:

"The petroleum stores of the warring nations and their suppliers are alone sufficient to cause major climatic disturbances—with the expenditure of only a few hundred small warheads or fewer out of a global nuclear arsenal of nearly 60,000. This sensitivity follows because petroleum refining and storage facilities are highly localized, extremely vulnerable to nuclear detonations, produce enormous clouds of black oily smoke, and offer strategically critical targets to the war planners."[221]

You should also know that the oil well fires in Kuwait in 1991 couldn't even be compared in scale to the oil refinery fires, which will happen in a nuclear war because of the power of the fires caused by nuclear detonations. Look again at the formula for the height of the smoke in these fires:

Top= .25 W to the one fourth power

If the temperature generated in the explosion of a 100-kiloton nuclear warhead is 20 million degrees Fahrenheit, then this will cause the fire in the oil refinery to leap right into a super-fire category as soon as the explosion occurs. This will also happen in the large city fires caused in a nuclear war. The extreme heat generated in these explosions occurs in the air burst cases, and almost all cities and petroleum refineries are targeted with these types of warheads. I should note that I found almost no reference to the extremely high temperatures in the 18 magazine articles, and the 5 books, which I read about nuclear winter. The extreme heat generated by these air burst nuclear warheads will cause thousands of super-fires in the 5,000-megaton baseline nuclear war scenario. On page 28 of the book, *Nuclear Winter*, by Mark Harwell, there are 419 cities in the USA with populations of 100,000 or more; and these cities will be attacked by air-burst nuclear weapons in a large-scale nuclear war. In addition to these fires, there will also be fires in cities in or near military facilities, as well as forest fires, and fires in oil refineries.[222]

On page 519 of the Encyclopedia Americana, © 1993, Volume 20, I found this quote:

"In the case of a 1 megaton bomb, so much energy is released into such a small volume that the temperature can rise to about 100 million degrees Kelvin—about 5 times hotter than the temperature at the center of the sun."[223]

When I looked on pages 976 and 980 of the 1997 World Book Encyclopedia, Volume 18, I found that the sun has temperatures of 27 million degrees Fahrenheit in the inner core.[224] This means that the temperature in a 1-megaton nuclear explosion can be higher than 135 million degrees Fahrenheit. Conventional frame houses could be ignited and destroyed by fire at 8 to 10 miles from a 1-megaton nuclear detonation.

On page 520 of Encyclopedia Americana is the quote:

"By the time the fireball reaches its maximum diameter of several thousand feet, each section of its surface is radiating about three times as much heat and light as a comparable area of the sun itself."[225]

This is equal to 110,000 degrees Fahrenheit. At 2.5 miles the temperature would be the same; and at 6 miles from ground zero it would be 11,000 degrees Fahrenheit.

It is very important to know that the extreme heat generated in these fires will push enormous volumes of smoke higher into the stratosphere. This is why the nuclear winter caused by a 5,000 megaton nuclear war could last for one or more years. It doesn't rain in the stratosphere, and there would be no precipitation to wash the smoke back down to the earth for this same reason. Thus it would stay up there longer, and block out the sunlight and the heat, which warms the earth.

Another important difference between these nuclear fires and ordinary ones is that there would be nobody to fight them. As in the case of the 1906 fire in San Francisco, and the 1871 fire in Chicago, when there is no one to fight a large city fire, it will burn most of that city to the ground. This will also be the case with urban fires caused in a nuclear war. On page 44 of the book, *Nuclear Winter*, by Owen Greene, is the quote:

"A high density of ignition points leads to rapid burning. Where the number of established fires approached about one per building, the time of burning of the whole area would be comparable to the time to burn a single building, which is about half an hour to 2 hours for domestic buildings, and rather longer for most industrial and commercial buildings. The heat produced by such rapid burning around the center of the ignition zone would produce high winds throughout the ignition zone, spreading the fires, and increasing the power of the fire still further. This is the mechanism of a firestorm: Its development depends both on the size of the fire zone, and on the density of combustible materials, not just on the latter, as is sometimes suggested."[226]

When you are looking at the density of combustible materials, you also have to take into account natural gas lines, which would be broken by the effects of the blast from the nuclear explosion. You should also include gasoline and diesel storage tanks in service stations, propane storage tanks, and oil in refineries. Smaller individual fires could include gasoline tanks in cars, diesel tanks in trucks, and the heating oil tanks at houses. When the cars and trucks ignite, the plastic door facing and upholstery will burn. The rubber tires on all of the cars will also burn. Just try to imagine all of the houses, cars, and trees burning within a six mile radius in a city; then try to imagine the asphalt streets burning too, sending thick black smoke into the sky. These are in addition to the buildings, which will provide the fuel for the massive firestorms. There are probably more combustible materials in cities that I haven't mentioned. The high levels of damage to structures from blast (thereby exposing fuel for combustion), favor extensive spreading of the fires, and since there will be no one to fight them, they will burn for weeks. It is also true that furniture inside the rooms in the buildings can ignite by exposure to the thermal pulse through windows; and only a few of these room fires are necessary to start mass urban fires.

The fires will spread to other buildings through firebrands, which are, glowing embers carried by the wind. They will also spread by direct contact to the flames, and as I just mentioned, by thermal pulse. The last one is by far the greatest method, since wooden structures can ignite 10 miles from ground zero, in a 1-megaton explosion. On page 44 of the book, *Nuclear Winter*, by Mark Harwell, is the quote:

"With a fuel load of 64 foot pounds to the -2 power in a densely built up commercial industrial center, calculations reveal a potential average energy release of 4 times that observed in Hamburg."[227]

The burning of Hamburg, Germany is, described on page 7 of *Fire and Ice*, by David Fisher.

"On July 27, 1943, nearly a thousand British bombers dropped two thousand tons of bombs on Hamburg, most of them incendiaries. The temperature reached 1000 degrees Fahrenheit, in the center of town, igniting the world's first firestorm. The superheated air rose so fast that it sucked in outside air in the form of hurricane strength winds which force-fed the fire still further. On the outskirts of the storm people were stuck in molten asphalt, suffocating and igniting."[228]

You have to be aware of the fact that military tacticians desire these kinds of events because it is their job to destroy cities, and to kill people. This is why the hydrogen bomb was such a hit with the Pentagon, and it is why they will resist large-scale nuclear disarmament in various devious ways. Unfortunately they caused the USSR to develop a nuclear arsenal equal to that of the USA, and the Antichrist will have control of it within six years.

Now that the military tacticians have found the perfect weapon to cause massive urban firestorms, the scientists have studied nuclear winter from 1982 to 1997, and they have found that the long-range effects of a large-scale nuclear war could cause four billion deaths after the war is over. Then the Pentagon ignored them, and they still have the same number of nuclear warheads and bombs. The city fires in a nuclear war could release four times as much energy as the one in Hamburg, which killed 40,000 people; and this is why the Pentagon will not dismantle their nuclear weapons.

The common mistake that people make here is:

1. Nuclear war between the USA and USSR could kill 155 million Americans and about 140 million citizens of the USSR.
2. The scientists have found that nuclear winter would kill four billion people because of cold, starvation, and other factors.
3. Since these findings are so horrifying, most moral responsible people believe that the Pentagon should begin large-scale nuclear disarmament.
4. Yet this is why the Pentagon resists the disarmament movement because of the ways that nuclear weapons kill people on such a large-scale.

Therefore you will not influence the Pentagon to eliminate nuclear weapons by arguing with them about morality. You have to change the US military system by using my Church Committee Plan. This is the only way to save the valuable time that the Pentagon will waste before World War III.

On page 44 of the book, *Nuclear Winter*, by Mark Harwell is the quote:

"The blast would destroy the physical structure of the area in cities, so that pathways for exit would be obstructed and tortuous flash blindness could be widespread. The local fallout would be greatest at the time when people are trying to flee the fires. Many will be overcome by noxious fumes from burning synthetics, high CO levels, and fatal temperatures from the fires."[229]

On page 48 of Carl Sagan's book, is a list of these pyrotoxins, or poisonous gases:

CO - Carbon Monoxide
HCN - Hydrogen Cyanide
HCl - Hydrogen Chloride
C3H40 - Acrolein
C2H3Cl- Vinyl Chloride

"These compounds are produced through expanding use of plastics and synthetic fibers."[230]

Here is another list:

Formaldehyde
PCBs - Poly-chlorinated biphenyls
Chlorinated benzenes
Poly-chlorinated dibenzofurans
Dioxins

"In a nuclear war the sources of such toxic materials would be widespread. Mass fires in urban areas would introduce unprecedented quantities of pyrotoxins into the atmosphere."[231]

On page 49 of the book:

"At many oil refineries, enormous stocks of sulfur would create a plume of sulfuric acid that would poison the air, and acidify clouds and rainfall far downwind of the refineries."[232] A pall of asbestos fibers would be generated from the pulverization of buildings by the nuclear blast waves. These fine fibers would drift over large areas, exposing multitudes to the long-term prospect of deadly cancer mesothelioma caused by breathing asbestos. There will also be the nuclear fallout, which is in the form of alpha and beta particles, and gamma rays. On page 52 of Carl Sagan's book it says that the radioactive elements in the nuclear explosion tend to condense onto dust particles. Since the dust is swept into the fireball (In a ground burst nuclear weapon), the radioactivity is spread over a large area, as the dust settles downwind of the detonation. This creates an extensive field of fallout.

"For many years calculations of radioactive fallout after a nuclear war were based on the high yield bursts that carried the fallout well up into the stratosphere. From there it took months or years to fall out, which means that the dangerous radioactivity had decayed. Since then the superpowers have reduced the average yield of their strategic weapons. Ironically, this means that the fallout is carried only into the troposphere, and it falls out in weeks, instead of months or years."[233] So the fallout is still deadly when it comes back down to earth. On page 53 of Carl Sagan's book it says that the study of nuclear winter has discovered the error of nuclear fallout calculations, and has made a major contribution toward correcting it.

"Fashionable current estimates are that the prompt fallout from a Soviet/American strategic nuclear exchange would kill 50 million people."

"Many victims that are not killed outright by radioactivity tend to succumb to secondary illnesses that take hold because radiation compromises the human immune system. The people suffering burn or trauma injuries are much more susceptible to death from radiation exposure. Moreover, intermediate and long-term exposure to lower levels of radioactivity—from external gamma radiation, as well as from radioactive materials inhaled with air and ingested with food and water—can induce fatal disease long after the war. All in all, we estimate that the total number of casualties from radioactive effects of all sorts following a major nuclear war could approach 300 million."[234]

Since the radioactive fallout is in the form of dust, and alpha and beta particles in the air it is extremely important to stay indoors in order to avoid breathing it. This is why I recommended staying in the basement or in a central room in your house for up to two or three weeks after a nuclear attack, if you are not in danger of being caught in a city fire. I also recommend that you should now purchase a travel trailer, which you can use to live in after you flee from any city fire near your house. In this case you will have to wear a gas mask to filter the radioactive fallout out of the air, which you breathe. In fact every man, woman, and child in the world should buy one of these special gas masks now, before World War III begins. They can also buy an inexpensive Geiger counter in order to check the radioactivity of the food that they eat, and the water that they drink. It will be particularly important for the people in Italy, Greece, Albania, and surrounding nations to buy these, since the Antichrist will use nuclear missiles to destroy Rome, Italy. It will be a good idea for the people in China, Korea, the USSR, and Japan to have these gas masks, and Geiger counters before the large nuclear war begins at the end of World War III.

I will assign the task of getting the gas masks manufactured the correct way to the National World War III Preparedness Agency. They should be made to screen radioactive fallout, all sorts of pyrotoxins, which I described a few pages back, and fine asbestos particles out of the air, which people have to breathe right after a nuclear war occurs. It would be a good idea to have the US Government pass federal laws to regulate the manufacture of these gas masks prior to World War III, in order to eliminate counterfeit gas masks, which are made improperly. The United Nations Organization can do the same thing on a worldwide scale to make sure that they are made properly. In fact it would be a good idea to designate specific companies in the USA and elsewhere, which are assigned by the US Government and the United Nations Organization to make gas masks, which will:

1. Filter radioactive fallout out of the air.
2. Filter pyrotoxins out of the air.
3. Filter asbestos fibers out of the air.

The US Government and the United Nations Organization can also designate companies to manufacture inexpensive Geiger counters. It should be illegal for any other companies to make gas masks or Geiger counters, other than the ones designated by the US Government and the United Nations Organization. It is very important to pass these laws now, since they could save the lives of billions of people later. There is proof of this in Revelation 8:10-12.

Next on the list of nuclear winter effects is ozone depletion. What happens in this case is that more ultraviolet light (UV-B radiation), can penetrate to the ground, if the ozone is depleted in the upper atmosphere.

On page 57 of Carl Sagan's book:

"There is an additional mechanism by which nuclear war threatens the ozone layer. With massive quantities of smoke injected into the lower atmosphere by the fires of nuclear war, the nuclear winter would not only grip the earth's surface, but the high ozone layer as well. The severely disturbed wind currents caused by the solar heating of smoke would, in a matter of weeks, sweep most of the ozone layer from the Northern mid-latitudes deep into the Southern Hemisphere."[235]

This means that the people in the USA, USSR, Europe, Japan, Korea, North East China, and Canada would suffer from blindness and severe sunburns because of the depletion of the ozone in the Northern Hemisphere. I will recommend that everyone in these nations should buy welder's goggles because they will protect your eyes from the UV-B ultraviolet light rays. Anyone living in the Northern Hemisphere should buy them and they will have to wear long sleeved shirts to avoid the sunburns. The manufacture of the welder's goggles should also be regulated by the US Government and the United Nations Organization. I went to a welding shop and put on a pair of goggles, and I found that the rectangular lens was the best, and it is very important that you can see well enough to walk while you have them on. I could see just fine with goggles, which have a darkness rating of 5.

The penalty for making improper gas masks, Geiger counters, or welder's goggles should be death, since the lives of billions of people would be at risk because of it.

At this point I should say that the construction of major government funded fallout shelters for the civilian populations in the large cities would be enormously expensive. This is why I recommend using underground parking garages for shelters in large cities.

Not only would it be too expensive for the governments of the USA and the USSR to build effective fallout shelters for their citizens, but the effects of the nuclear war and the related nuclear winter will mean that fallout shelters will have to be built in Third World countries which are not even involved in the nuclear war. This is one of the moral arguments developed by the scientists, but as I explained earlier, only a change of the US military system and the Pentagon will work. To be precise, the people have to vote for the Church Committee Plan. Only then will the people in Third World countries be safe from the effects of nuclear war and nuclear winter.

Instead of spending billions or trillions of dollars on fallout shelters, the US Government should use the Travel Trailer Plan of the Church Committee Group. These are mobile, and they can be given to the survivors of a nuclear attack. In one of the descriptions of the firestorm in Hamburg in 1943, when the doors to the fallout shelter were opened two days after the bombing had stopped, the inrushing oxygen from the outside air caused the entire inside of the shelter to burst into flames. On page 7 of *Fire and Ice*, it says that the temperature in that firestorm reached 1,000 degrees Fahrenheit in the center of town. Then it should be obvious from these descriptions of massive firestorms that anyone in a fallout shelter in the middle of a city ablaze will die from extreme temperatures.[236]

This is why it would be a better idea to have the Church Committee Group purchase 100 million travel trailers, which they can give to the American people during World War III. This will eliminate the problem of homelessness on a very large scale, and it will enable millions of Americans to simply relocate after a nuclear attack. It would be better to live in a travel trailer somewhere else, than to bake in a fallout shelter near your home. Again, the people who move will have to wear gas masks to filter the nuclear fallout from the air that they breathe.

On page 184 of the book, *Nuclear Winter*, by Owen Greene, it says that 3 forest fires in America, 50 in the USSR, and 74 in Europe will be caused by a nuclear exchange between the USA, USSR, and Europe.[237] This totals 127 forest fires, which will add to the smoke injected into the atmosphere. On page 53 of the book, *Nuclear Winter*, by Mark Harwell, it says that 19,000 to

160,000 square miles of forest and rangelands could be consumed by fires after a nuclear war.[238] Then on page 38 of Carl Sagan's book, is the quote:

"The smoke pall from the Alberta, Canada forest fires in 1950 lowered surface temperatures in Washington, DC by 4 to 6 degrees centigrade. In Ontario, more than 1000 kilometers from the fires, it was dark as midnight near noon."[239]

"Alan Robock of the University of Maryland has analyzed satellite-based meteorological records of forest fires in Canada, China, California, and Wyoming and finds cooling of up to 20 degrees centigrade beneath the smoke from the fires."[240]

This is cooling which is very substantial. In a nuclear winter this could last for a year or more. In the book, *Nuclear Winter*, by Mark Harwell there is an evaluation of the biological consequences of nuclear war and nuclear winter. On page 104 of this book, there is a diagram, which explains how the earth's water or hydrologic cycle works:[241]

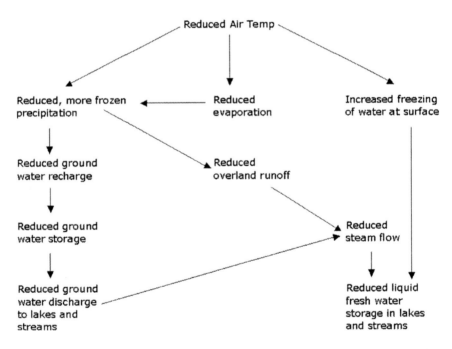

From this you can see how nuclear winter and cold weather would affect the earth's water system. There would be less rainfall, less stream flow, less water in lakes and streams, and most importantly more frozen water in lakes. This will make it more difficult for animals to drink water, and more difficult for farmers to irrigate their crops. On page 104 of Mark Harwell's book:

"For the earth as a whole, there are about 13 million of these smaller lakes, holding 2000 cubic kilometers of water, and averaging about 3 meters in depth. These lakes' small volumes make them more susceptible to significant freezing. In so far as the surface area of the lakes represent opportunity of access, these small lakes are extremely important, making up about 2/3 of the total lake surface area on earth."[242]

On page 122 of Mark Harwell's book:

"Combined, the decreased sunlight and lower temperatures could reduce rainfall because of the change in available energy needed for the hydrologic cycle. Further, most surface water would be frozen and thus unavailable for humans, crops, and livestock."[243]

On the same page it says:

"Alter temperature, rainfall, or any other basic resource, and crop yields are severely reduced."[244]

On page 124 of Mark Harwell's book:

"The projected 99% reduction in sunlight would prevent most plants from growing and cause them to deplete any stored reserves of nutrients. Thus, crop production would not be possible if sunlight were reduced 99%; and most crop production would be impossible if sunlight levels were reduced by 50%."[245]

In addition to this is the factor of freezing temperatures, and killer frosts which could wipe out the crops in entire states. On page 123 of Mark Harwell's book:

"Most tropical plants require daytime temperatures of 20 degrees centigrade or higher for growth and fruit formation. The exposure of crops even to low, nonfreezing temperatures for short periods during the growing season will severely reduce crop yields."[246]

On page 122 and 123:

"About 95% of the food energy grown in the USA comes from tropical annual plants, except for the tree fruits."[247]

The quick freeze is what will kill these types of plants, and this will be caused by nuclear winter. On page 124:

"The key question is, of course, how much food could be produced after a nuclear war. The answer is simply very little, if any."[248]

This is why I recommended the large-scale storage of dry beans of several types, dry macaroni, dry noodles, rice, and other dry foods by the US Government. I will also recommend that people should do this on an individual basis. In fact, if you have a travel trailer, or if you can afford to buy one, then you can put dry foods into hundreds of plastic containers; and then seal the lids and store them in the shelves of your travel trailer. Then after you buy the gas mask, the welder's goggles, and distilled water, you will be ready to roll, provided that you have a vehicle to hitch the travel trailer to. You should also store large quantities of dry beans and dry foods in the basement of your house.

On page 126 of Mark Harwell's book:

"Optimistically, perhaps as many as 1/3 of the livestock might survive a winter attack, and be kept in production. However, a summer attack would destroy most of the forage, and leave the livestock severely stressed for food."[249]

This is why I recommended the large-scale slaughter, cutting, wrapping, and freezing of cattle, pigs, sheep, chickens, and turkeys in the years 2020 to 2022. Also on page 126 it says:

"The reduction of temperatures to -25 degrees centigrade would seriously impair poultry and pig production without substantial protection by human-provided shelter and heat."[250]

This is why I recommended the large-scale construction of steel buildings before the nuclear war of 2022. The governments in nations, which produce livestock and poultry, can give subsidies to their farmers from 2008 to 2016 to encourage them to construct steel buildings to protect their animals from nuclear fallout, pyrotoxins, cold weather, and increased ultraviolet light. This will help a greater percentage of the livestock and poultry to survive the critical first year after a nuclear war. It will be very important to construct the steel buildings in such a way that the roofs do not collapse from the buildup of snow. For this reason the governments in each nation should regulate the production of them; and they can also recommend air filters for the windows, which will filter nuclear fallout and pyrotoxins out of the air. For these reasons the governments should provide a list of the construction companies in each state or province of their nation, which will be authorized to construct the steel buildings for their farmers. The list should be made up after the governments have conducted studies on the air filters needed, and on the proper type of roofs for the buildings.

During a nuclear winter there will also be the problems of lack of equipment, fuel, fertilizers, pesticides, some feeds for animals, human labor for crop and livestock production, and seeds for some crops. Without petroleum there will be no fuel for farm machinery or trucks. This is why I recommended the conversion to natural gas fuel by the USA, and by every other nation not in Europe or the Middle East by the year 2009. I wrote an entire plan for this in the Surviving Nations chapter in my book titled, World War III: The Nations. The Antichrist will take the world oil supply in World War III, and this is verified in Daniel 11:23-25. The king of the south here is the king of Saudi Arabia, or the oil emirates, or the United Arab Emirates.

It is not really very difficult to convert used tractors and harvesters to natural gas, and I outlined a plan to have British Petroleum and Texas Natural Gas help provide training for all nations to convert them. This plan is also included in the Surviving Nations chapter of my book. The conversion of all new cars, trucks, tractors, and harvesters can be done at the factories; and these vehicles should be manufactured to use gasoline and/or natural gas. They should all be dual fuel vehicles to eliminate the possibility of bankrupting the manufacturing companies, or of having useless vehicles.

On page 127 of Harwell's book:

"The primary problem would be the impossibility of tilling and planting vast acreages without tractors and fossil fuel energy."[251]

I think the idea here is that 95% of the oil refineries in the USA, USSR, and Europe will be destroyed in the nuclear war. This is why there will be no fossil fuel during the nuclear winter.

Since the Antichrist will take the world oil supply, the farmers will have to convert all of their tractors and harvesters at least 8 to 10 years before the nuclear winter even occurs.

On page 139 of the book, *Nuclear Winter*, by Owen Greene it says that there would be almost no harvest in the Northern Hemisphere after a nuclear war.[252] In the Southern Hemisphere there would probably be poor harvests of crops. This means that starvation would be the fate of hundreds of millions of people in Third World countries. They depend on food imports and food aid as it is now, and that would be cut off during nuclear winter. It is extremely urgent for these nations to build hundreds or thousands of food warehouses now, in order to store dry beans, dry macaroni, dry noodles, and rice in 55-gallon sealed plastic barrels for use during nuclear winter. This is another project which the United Nations Organization could take part in.

On page 76 of Carl Sagan's book:

"The total loss of human agricultural and societal support systems would result in the loss of almost all humans on earth, equally among combatant and non-combatant countries alike."[253]

The food stocks in cities will drop to zero within four weeks, even without rioting and looting. Therefore mass starvation would result in Africa, Asia, and South America. Even if these nations store dry food now, their people will be malnourished in terms of vitamins B_{12}, C, A, riboflavin, calcium, iron, and vitamin D. Here is a formula for nuclear winter from *Nuclear Winter*, by Owen Greene:

Nuclear explosions ➜ dust and fires ➜ smoke ➜ blocking of sunlight ➜ darkness and cold on Earth.[254]

These things will have a profound effect on the earth's ecosystem, which could last for years. There is a summation of all these effects on pages 156 to

160 in the book, *Nuclear Winter*, by Mark Harwell.[255] You can find this book and read it if you call a few large libraries in the major cities. Some of the things, which I haven't described, are: widespread ice formation, and termination of phytoplankton productivity, which would kill the support base for ocean and freshwater fish. The ice formation would kill most of the fish in smaller lakes as well. Reduced rainfall and soil erosion would reduce productivity of crops. Lack of safe drinking water will be a serious problem. This problem will have to be solved on an individual basis, with people buying 1-gallon plastic containers of distilled water by the hundreds, and storing them in the basements of their houses, and in the shelves of their travel trailers. This will be very important for the people in Italy, Greece, and Albania; and for the people in the USSR, China, and Korea. These are the nations where the nuclear fallout will occur.

On page 161 of Mark Harwell's book: "Large scale migrations from pre-war residences will be required to search for food," right at the time when local fallout and extreme cold temperatures occur.[256] There will be difficulties in transportation, lack of good information on where to find food, and rioting and looting where the food is stored. This will be an important concern for the United Nations Organization, the USA National Food Preparedness Agency, and the other governments, which build the food warehouses. They will have to use military troops to protect the food, and so they should build the food warehouses on military bases; or they can use the vacant buildings on these bases for food storage. This is why the 55-gallon sealed plastic barrels should be used because the food will survive better, and then the warehouses can be in used buildings.

On page 65 and 66 of the book, *Nuclear Winter*, by Owen Greene, it says that one of the long range effects on the earth's ecosystem would be the cooling of the oceans during a nuclear winter.[257] They would retain lower temperatures for several years, and this could cause a buildup of ice in the sea, and glaciers on the land. This would influence the nuclear winter, and it would probably limit access to the oceans to some degree. There is a list of some of the targeting categories for nuclear war on page 14 of Owen Greene's book:

1. ICBM - Intercontinental and intermediate range ballistic missile forces, launch facilities, launch command centers, nuclear weapon storage sites, airfields, and nuclear submarine bases.
2. Military and political leadership.
3. Conventional military forces - bases, airfields, ammunition storage facilities, storage yards.

4. Economic and industrial targets - war supporting industry, ammunition factories, tank and truck factories, petroleum refineries, railway yards, aircraft factories, civil airfields, and defense electronics industry.[258]

These add up to 35,000 targets for one side alone, and hundreds of cities will be destroyed as an indirect result of the targets listed above. Not only is the Pentagon intent on keeping their present budget of $400 billion dollars per year, but also they plan to spend $4 trillion dollars over the next 15 years for modernization of the US military weapons. They are listed on pages 48 and 49 of the 1997-Supplement of the US Government Budget.[259] On page 49 there is also a description of the Start I and Start II Treaties.[260] The problem with these treaties is that they take almost forever to implement, and then the political leader of the USA can disagree with the Soviet leader on some of the terms of the treaties. Since the Pentagon gets $400 billion dollars per year, they can influence the President to make decisions that benefit them. Another very important point about nuclear disarmament and the Pentagon is that it will always occur at some time in the future; and yet it never does happen. This has been a fact of life for everyone in the USA for 50 years, and it is now time for a change. The Church Committee Group will dismantle all land based nuclear missiles in the USA, and all tactical nuclear weapons in Europe; and the world's nuclear arsenal can be reduced to 1,000 warheads, with the help of the United Nations Organization.

The Pentagon will say that the nuclear weapons and the modernization funding on page 48 and 49 of the US Government Budget 1997-Supplement are needed to preserve the annual budget of the Pentagon. Here is a list of the modernization-funding plan:

DDG-51 Guided Missile Destroyers
C-17 Strategic Airlift Aircraft
Joint Standoff Weapon
Marine Corps V-22 Tilt-Rotor Aircraft
Navy F/A-18 E/F Fighter
Navy New Attack Submarine
Air Force F-22 Fighter[261]

On page 49 you should notice the phrase, "The budget proposes large investments in research and development for advanced systems that will enter production in the middle of the next decade."[262] These will include the:

Joint Strike Fighter
Army Comanche Helicopter

Marine Amphibious Assault Vehicle
New Navy Surface Ship

These new weapons will enter production just before there will be 100 million homeless and starving people in America, and even this will not stop them from funding their programs anyway. Here is a quote from page 74 of the book, *The Nuclear War Game*, © 1983 by Adam Suddaby:

"Moreover, in the great powers vast bureaucracies have grown up to deal with military matters (As many civilians are paid out of military budgets as there are troops in uniform). Academics and bureaucrats join with the military and defense industries to form an academic-bureaucratic-military-industrial complex intent on maintaining and increasing military budgets and agitating for the use of every conceivable technological advance for military purposes. This complex has so much political power as to be almost politically irresistible."[263]

The fact is that the Pentagon will resist large-scale nuclear disarmament because it will cause their annual budget to be cut in half; and if they do opt for the disarmament in START I and START II, then they will make up for modernization funding as I just described. They are, "intent on maintaining and increasing their military budget." This is why all previous efforts toward nuclear disarmament have failed, and it is very possible that START I, and START II could fail to work. On page 49 of the 1997-Supplement of the US Government Budget it says that these treaties will bring Soviet nuclear warheads to 1/3 of their Cold War level; but the supplement book was published in 1997.[264] These treaties take too long to implement. We do not have enough time to wait for them. We have to eliminate the bureaucracy from the military system, and this means eliminating the nuclear hawks on the Senate Armed Services Committee, and the Defense Appropriations subcommittees. These people will be replaced by the members of the Church Committee Group, who will then appropriate money to help the American people survive World War III. They will fund the programs written on the Church Committee Plan Funding List, which means that they will provide food, housing, gas masks, and other essentials for Americans, and not for military weapons. The taxes that are paid to the US Government are from the people, and therefore the people can vote to use the Church Committee Plan.

The Pentagon will try to sweep the entire concept of nuclear winter under the rug a second time, when this book is published. They will try to discredit me, and they will try several new tactics to make the people lose interest in my ideas; nevertheless, I will use some quotes from the book titled, The Effects of Nuclear War, © 1979 by the Office of Technology Assessment. On page 3 is the quote:

"As to whether people would die from blast damage, or from starvation during the following winter."[265]

This sounds like a description of nuclear winter! Then on page 4: "additionally, the possibility of significant long-term ecological damage cannot be excluded."[266]"The impact of even a 'small' or 'limited' nuclear attack would be enormous."[267] Some of the differences in vulnerability of the USA and USSR to nuclear attack:

"Vulnerability of agricultural systems, vulnerability of cities to fire."[268]

On page 5 is the quote:

"This postwar damage could be as devastating as the damage from the actual nuclear explosions."[269]

Then on page 8:

"Millions of people might starve or freeze during the following winter."[270]

On page 9 is the quote:

"A 1975 study by the National Academy of Sciences addressed the question of the possibility of serious ecological damage, and concluded that while one cannot say just how such damage could occur, it cannot be ruled out."[271]

These are descriptions that match the ones made by the hundreds of scientists who studied the effects of nuclear winter, and the book written by the Office of Technology Assessment was published in 1979. This was three years before the concept of nuclear winter was even discovered!

Then on page 94 are the quotes:

"The effects of a large Soviet attack against the USA would be devastating."[272]

"The Department of Defense 1977 study estimated that 155 million to 165 million Americans would be killed by a large scale attack if no civil defense measures were taken, and all weapons were ground burst."[273]

For the past 50 years the Pentagon has forced the USSR to develop a nuclear arsenal comparable to that of the USA. The Antichrist will control the nuclear weapons of the USSR, France, and Italy within six years, which means that the Pentagon has played right into his plan for world destruction. This is yet another reason to vote for the Church Committee Plan because it will accomplish large-scale nuclear disarmament before the Antichrist even appears. The Pentagon is playing Russian roulette with nuclear missiles instead of a gun, and when the Antichrist is in control of the nuclear weapons in Europe, there might be a few explosions.

On page 153 of Owen Greene's book it says that a global nuclear war followed by nuclear winter would lead to the deaths of billions of people.[274]

Then on page 164:

"A nuclear war could kill over a billion people."[275] Then the nuclear winter could kill one or two billion more.

On page 104 of *The Long Darkness*:

"Scientists and other members of the Strategic weapons community focused with intense interest upon the possible inaccuracies in the Turco-Sagan reports."[276]

This happened because the scientists and the other people worked for the military-industrial complex. Then on the same page:

"Largely lost sight of among the scientists in the Kennedy School debate was the fact of nuclear war, its overwhelmingly catastrophic global consequences, and the additional dimension of disaster contained in the nuclear winter analysis."[277]

It is really amazing to me that Turco, Sagan, Toon, Pollack, and Ackerman didn't figure out what was happening here. The other scientists ignored their findings because they were getting paid by the Pentagon, or by Pentagon related research and development. John E. Mack wrote on page 118 of *The Long Darkness*:

"From the economic standpoint, nuclear related industries support millions of jobs and return huge profits to corporate executives and investors."[278]

Then on page 119:

"There are situations in which corporate leaders,…speak out—often after retirement—against the arms race and begin to work toward ending it."[279] Why do they wait until after they retire? They don't want to risk losing their income before retirement. Again on page 119:

"The fact that there are scientific, academic, political, military, and other careers to be made in nuclear weapons—related work is, of course, familiar to everyone."[280]

Then on page 120 is a quote, which illustrates the degree of self preservation of the large annual budget, and the system which the Pentagon uses to do this:

"Once the task of preventing nuclear war is defined as occurring by means of strategic thinking within the parameters of a given system, it is unlikely that much attention will be given to questioning the system itself."[281] The Pentagon says that nuclear weapons deter a conventional war, and that a second-strike nuclear attack deters any use of nuclear weapons in a first-strike attack. In other words, they say that nuclear weapons deter a nuclear war. The very concept of deterrence is what perpetuates the large nuclear arsenals of the USA and the USSR; and the Pentagon wants to perpetuate their large arsenal to preserve their large annual budget. Then on page 107 of *The Long Darkness*: "Security based on nuclear deterrence may become ever more diminished."[282]

This will be immediately obvious when the Antichrist is in control of all the nuclear weapons in Europe. Then on page 107:

"Rather, it is the shift in the order of magnitude of destructiveness of nuclear weapons…and the interlocking nature of the offensive/defensive postures of the nuclear superpowers that have changed everything."[283]

This is why large-scale nuclear disarmament must be done now, before the Antichrist even appears. The nuclear winter scientists were compelled to use moral arguments to convince the US Government to dismantle their nuclear weapons because they did not find a way to change the system themselves. The only logical way to do this is with Bible prophecy. You see, I know exactly what the Antichrist will do during the 11 years of World War III, and I know how the Pentagon can avoid a global nuclear war against him. I know how to change the US military system and how to change the bureaucracy in Washington, D.C. I learned all of these things by reading and studying the Bible; and the most important thing is that the Lord Jesus Christ will destroy the Antichrist and his army at the end of World War III. This is written in Revelation 19:11-21; and I described exactly what the Pentagon has to do in relation to Bible prophecy to avoid a war against the Antichrist in Europe, in the chapter titled, Spiritual Principles of World War III. The American people must demand that the Pentagon follow the instructions written there, and they should demand that the Congress use the Church Committee Plan. On page 204 of Carl Sagan's book:

"Massive reductions in the nuclear arsenals is something we do for ourselves and for the human species."[284]

On page 146 of the same book:

"A single surviving ballistic missile submarine on either side could obliterate any nation on earth.

The widely acknowledged dissuading influence of such small invulnerable retaliatory forces is a kind of minimum deterrence. It already exists without nuclear winter."[285]

This will be enough to deter the Antichrist from attacking the USA.

I should point out that the Pentagon and the US military are not mentioned in the prophecies about World War III in the book of Revelation, Daniel, Ezekiel 38, Ezekiel 39, Matthew 24, Mark 13, Luke 21, II Thessalonians 2, or anywhere else. Therefore the people of America should ask themselves these questions:

1. How is it possible for the Pentagon to have US military bases in Europe, and not have to defend them against the army of the Antichrist? Answer: The US military bases in Europe, England, Japan, Korea, and the Middle East must be closed by the year 2009.

2. How is it possible for the Pentagon to maintain a global military readiness plan for world security, with the army of the Antichrist in Europe, and in other places of the world? Answer: The US military must withdraw all of their troops back into America to remain neutral during World War III.
3. Can the Pentagon fight against the Antichrist, and protect America at the same time? Answer: No. In Revelation 9:16 he will have 200 million soldiers.
4. How is it possible for Army, Air Force, Marine Generals, and Navy Admirals to resist the temptation to fight against the army of the Antichrist? Answer: They must give their offensive military power to the Church Committee Group.
5. How is it possible for the President of the USA to resist the temptation to threaten the Antichrist with nuclear missiles? Answer: The President must give the power to launch nuclear missiles to the Church Committee Group.
6. How is it possible for the President and the Congress to resist the temptation to declare war on the army of the Antichrist? Answer: The Congress must give the power to declare war to the Church Committee Group.

This is how prophecy works, and this is how the prophets save the nations to which they are sent. The American people will have to put pressure on the US Government to be sure that they follow these instructions.

I have read two more books on nuclear war, and I will quote some of the information here. I am constantly amazed at the ability of the proponents of strategic nuclear thinking to toss around the phrases, which describe their ideas. I believe that strategic thinking itself has become a New Age philosophy in America, with hundreds of thousands of followers in the academic, bureaucratic, research and development, and military sections of the USA. In the book titled, *The Spread of Nuclear Weapons: A Debate*, the author Kenneth N. Waltz, a leading scholar of international politics, said that more nuclear weapons in the smaller nations of the world would mean that: more may be better. This is the title of the first chapter in his book. On page 2 is the quote:

"The world has enjoyed more years of peace since 1945 than had been known in modern history."[286]

"The prevalence of peace indicates a high ability of the postwar international system to absorb changes and to contain conflicts and hostility."[287]

This is one of the main arguments for nuclear deterrence in the strategic weapons community, but it is no longer true when you know that a nuclear war is inevitable, and that it will happen within 20 years. In fact there could be nine nuclear wars within the next 20 years; one will be fought between the Antichrist and Rome, Italy; and one between the Antichrist and China. They are described in the Nuclear War chapter. On page 3 of Kenneth Waltz's book: "'To deter' literally means to stop people from doing something by frightening them."[288]

"Deterrence is achieved not through the ability to defend, but through the ability to punish."[289]

Then on page 21 of the same book:

"Deterrence requires the ability to inflict unacceptable damage on another country."[290]

In response to this I will say that the entire concept of deterrence loses considerable value with at least nine nuclear wars coming in the next 20 years; and deterrence loses even more credibility with the Antichrist gaining control of all of the nuclear weapons in the USSR, France, and Italy within six years. Then on page 11 of Kenneth Waltz's book:

"Where states are bitter enemies one may fear that they will be unable to resist using their nuclear weapons against each other."[291] Then using partial quotes about bitterness:

"But bitterness among some potential nuclear states..."[292]

Then another partial quote:

"Playing down the bitterness sometimes felt by the USA, the USSR, and China..."[293]

"Moreover, those who believe that bitterness causes wars assume a close association that is seldom found between bitterness among nations and their willingness to run high risks."[294]

Now I will quote from the book of Revelation about the bitterness of nuclear war:

Revelation 8:11: "And the name of the star is called Wormwood: and the third part of the waters became wormwood; and many men died of the waters because they were made bitter."

Wormwood comes from the plant Artemisia, and it has a bitter taste.

The bitterness in the waters is nuclear fallout, which will kill about 1.7 billion people in the large-scale nuclear war in 2022; but the reason for the comparison to the bitterness among nations is now obvious. The bitterness between the USSR and China is described on page 11 of Kenneth Waltz's book, and it has existed for hundreds of years.[295] In the year 2016 to 2017 the army of the Antichrist will try to expand his kingdom to the Pacific Ocean, and they will have to use military force to occupy North East China and Korea to do this.

This will be ignored for some time by the political leader of China, but then he will be reminded of the bitterness of the rivalry between the USSR and China, and he will use military force. Then in Daniel 11:44 the Antichrist will use total nuclear retaliation against China.

It should also be noted that the star in Revelation 8:11 is called Wormwood, and that the third part of the waters became wormwood. This is like saying that the star is a nuclear missile, that it contains radioactive materials, and that the radioactivity will be passed on to the rivers and fountains of water. If there are people who are still skeptical about this information, then the real proof of the nuclear missile is written in:

Revelation 8:12: "And the fourth angel sounded, and the third part of the sun was smitten, and the third part of the moon, and the third part of the stars; so as the third part of them was darkened, and the day shone not for a third part of it, and the night likewise."

This is a perfect description of the darkness caused by a nuclear winter, where the smoke from city and forest fires rises high into the stratosphere, where it may stay for months or years, and where it blocks out the sunlight to the earth below. It is very important to notice that nuclear winter as studied by scientists will follow a nuclear war; and it is described the same way in Revelation 8:10-12.

Then on page 16 of Kenneth Waltz's book there is this quote:

"Nuclear weapons do not make nuclear war likely, as history has shown."[296] Unfortunately history is about the past, and the nuclear wars are in the very near future. Another good point is that the entire concept of deterrence is based on threats. The USA will not use a first-strike attack because of the threat of retaliation, and the USSR will not either. The problem with this type of thinking occurs when you realize that you will be facing the Antichrist within six years, and it may not be a good idea to threaten him with nuclear missiles or anything else. There have been nuclear threats used about 9 times in the last 50 years, and it was the US Government that used them every time. I described this in the Nuclear War chapter of this book. This is why the American people should put pressure on the US Government to cause the Congress to use the Church Committee Plan; and then the Church Committee Group can call for large-scale nuclear disarmament before the Antichrist appears in Europe.

There is proof that the current system of the US Government will not accomplish this goal, on page 166 of the book titled, *Nuclear War: Opposing Viewpoints*, © 1985 by Greenhaven Press. Here are some quotes by Jeremy J. Stone about nuclear disarmament treaties and their ratification:

"The USA can ratify agreements only if two-thirds of the Senate will approve. And this requires the support of two political parties in constant rivalry with one another, often to show which is tougher in dealing with the USSR."[297]

Then an interesting question:

"What else can explain the fact that the last three treaties solemnly approved and signed by our executive branch have never been ratified? Among them, the SALT II treaty was said by the Joint Chiefs of Staff to have only nominal effects on the US Force planning. Nevertheless, a host of political complaints killed the agreement."[298] These people keep overlooking the power of the hawks in the Congress.

The people on the House Armed Services Committee, and the Defense Appropriations subcommittees work directly with the Pentagon to appropriate money for use by the US military. They get $400 billion dollars per year, and that money will keep flowing only if there is resistance to large-scale disarmament. This resistance can be camouflaged under the bipartisan political system by the disagreements between the US Government and the Soviet Union, or in many other ways. The one fact that never changes is that nuclear disarmament is scheduled by the US Government to occur in the near future, and yet it never does happen at all.

On page 79 and 80 of the book titled, *Blundering Into Disaster*, © 1986 by Robert S. McNamara is the quote:

"Our current nuclear weapons building program, which is producing 2,000 warheads annually, is the biggest in 20 years. And steps are under way to expand substantially, for the 1990s, both the production of the key nuclear materials—tritium, uranium, and plutonium—and the production of the warheads themselves. At the same time, our weapons laboratories are forecasting large increases in the number of underground tests required for the development of new types of nuclear arms. Officials at the Los Alamos Scientific Laboratory said recently that although in the past only about six nuclear tests were required to develop a weapon, perfecting one of the new, more complex designs we are working on today will require at least 100 to 200 explosions. They say, 'The physics processes are far more complicated than anything we've looked at before.'"[299] I explained earlier in this chapter that arguments about morality will not cause the people in the Pentagon to use large-scale nuclear disarmament, and I was correct. In fact this quote by Robert S. McNamara proves it. You can never expect the Pentagon to follow moral arguments because it is their job to kill people, after all. It is also their job to protect the USA from nuclear missile attack, but because of the principle of deterrence they build more nuclear missiles instead. On page three of the book by Kenneth Waltz is the quote:

"Purely deterrent forces provide no defense."[300]

This is not good strategy at all with the Antichrist gaining control of all of the nuclear weapons in the USSR, France, and Italy within the next six years. And I'm sure that the American people will agree with me. Including the nuclear war which the Pentagon will cause while trying to defend the US military bases in Europe, the USA will be involved in nine nuclear wars within the next 20 years because of the fact that large-scale nuclear disarmament is never achieved. It will be a major mistake to place your faith in the New Age strategic philosophy of the Pentagon because that alone will condemn the USA by bringing all of the plagues described in the book of Revelation upon America. It works like this during World War III: Either your nation chooses to be saved by Christ, or it will be destroyed by the Antichrist. When you honor Christ, and when you have faith in him, then he will protect your nation from the Antichrist.

The question now is, what will happen during World War III if the Pentagon follows its present strategy of nuclear deterrence against the Antichrist?

1. The USA will be involved in a nuclear war while trying to defend the US military bases in Europe.
2. The USA will be involved in a nuclear war because the Pentagon will retaliate against Germany and Russia when the Antichrist uses nuclear weapons to destroy Rome, Italy.
3. The USA will be included in the major nuclear war between Russia and China in 2022. The other nuclear wars are described in the Nuclear War chapter.

As things were before my book was published, the Pentagon didn't know about the nine nuclear wars, their causes, or their dates in the future. With Bible prophecy, I can predict what will happen, why it will happen, and when. The reasons here are that the army of the Antichrist will have 200 million soldiers in Revelation 9:16, the Antichrist will take Western Europe in Daniel 11:22, he will destroy Rome in Revelation 17:16-18, and he will enforce his famine in Europe in Revelation 6:8, and Revelation 13:16,17. World War III itself will last eleven years, so all of these events will happen during that eleven year period. Therefore if I am wrong about the date of the beginning of World War III, everything else can be readjusted when the war itself does begin.

Of course this means that the CIA and the Pentagon will need me to get America through World War III, and for this reason they should not kill me before it starts.

On the subject of nuclear weapons, what is the USA going to do about the nuclear warheads in the USSR, France, Italy, Israel, Iraq, Iran, Saudi Arabia, and South Africa, which the Antichrist will inherit in the years up to 2016? The Pentagon cannot just sit back and ignore this threat to the safety of the world. They cannot just say that deterrence will nullify the strength of these nuclear warheads. This is why the American people must put pressure on the US Government to use the Church Committee Plan. On page 29 of the book titled, The Spread of Nuclear Weapons, is the quote:

"In the desperation of defeat, desperate measures may be taken, and the last thing anyone wants to do is to make a nuclear nation desperate."[301]

In the light of this statement, what will the political leader of England do, after Britain, Scotland, and Ireland are blockaded for one or two years by the Antichrist? I think he will retaliate with nuclear missiles against Germany and Russia; and since England has 1,000 nuclear warheads, the damage to Europe will be considerably great. Another situation very similar to this will occur in France, Italy, and Saudi Arabia. Each of these nations will be invaded and occupied by the army of the Antichrist, and they will also become desperate.

After doing some research, I found out which nations in the Middle East have nuclear weapons, and I made the following list.[302] If you add up all of the nations that the army of the Antichrist will invade and occupy during World War III, they would be as listed chronologically:

1. France in the first year of World War III
2. Italy in the first year of World War III
3. USSR in the third year of World War III
4. England in the third year of World War III

From the third to the tenth year:
5. Israel
6. Saudi Arabia
7. Iraq
8. Iran
9. India
10. Pakistan
11. South Africa
12. China
13. North Korea

The army of the Antichrist will invade all of these nations except India and Pakistan; but the army will be so close to them that they will feel threatened. As you can see, this list of nuclear nations that will be desperate during World War III is a compelling argument for immediate worldwide nuclear disarmament. This is why I urge the United Nations Organization to use all of their power, perhaps even the International Court of Justice to legally bind all of the nuclear nations in the world to follow the Zero Tolerance Directive toward nuclear weapons. It will also be very important to convince the nuclear nations to destroy all of the tritium, uranium, and plutonium that they have, so the Antichrist cannot use it to make nuclear weapons in Europe.

The Antichrist will be the most evil person ever to live on the earth, and even if these nations do not start a nuclear war against him, he will take control of their nuclear arsenals later with the strength of his army. In Revelation 9:16 he will have 200 million soldiers. Now look at this verse:

Revelation 13:4: " And they worshiped the dragon which gave power unto the beast: and they worshiped the beast, saying, Who is like unto the beast? who is able to make war with him?"

If you cannot fight a war against the beast, or the kingdom of the Antichrist, then the only other alternative would be nuclear retaliation if the nations become desperate. The big question for the world is: Will mankind choose to follow good or evil during World War III?

Here is a verse that refers to this question:

Revelation 13:10: "He that leadeth into captivity shall go into captivity: he that killeth with the sword must be killed with the sword. Here is the patience and the faith of the saints."

This means that it will be better to evacuate from Europe, the Middle East, North East China, Korea, or South Africa than to try to fight against the army of the Antichrist. If your nation chooses evil and war, then you will be destroyed by war. This is the meaning of the phrase, "he that killeth with the sword must be killed with the sword."

I got most of the list for the nuclear nations in the book titled, *The Politics and Strategy of Nuclear Weapons in the Middle East*, © 1992 by Shlomo Aronson. I must say that it is difficult to get a list of the nuclear nations in the world, and the types of weapons that they have; and yet this is the first thing that the United Nations Organization has to do to achieve nuclear disarmament throughout the world.

On page 216 of the book, *Missile Envy*, © 1984 by Helen Caldicott, it says there was a profound split in the scientific community over the Star Wars defense or SDI. The most avid proponents were those who worked in the weapons labs, who in effect were the pro-Pentagon scientists. Look at this quote:

"They claim to have all the data and hence discredit anyone who disagrees with them."[303] The Pentagon scientists did this over Star Wars or SDI, and they also did it over the nuclear winter issue. They tell the people that this happens because national security is involved; but it really happens because of their love for money. Look at this verse:

I Timothy 6:10: "For the love of money is the root of all evil."

It is also true that the Pentagon uses its massive economic power against people who are opposed to their principles, and they usually win the battle in the media because of the sheer numbers of newspaper and magazine articles that they call into play. They will do this to me too.

NUCLEAR WINTER FOOD STORAGE

The food supply prepared for the nuclear winter at the end of World War III can be done on a large scale in the ninth and tenth year of the war. From years seven to ten the USA and other nations can build freezer warehouses to store freezer beef and other meats. Then at the beginning of the ninth year of World War III the nations can call for large-scale slaughtering, cutting, and wrapping of their livestock, and poultry to be put into the freezer warehouses. The freezer meats can be double wrapped to make them last longer in storage.

There can also be an increase in the manufacturing of canned fruits and vegetables in the ninth year of World War III. This means that there will have to be an increase of farmland for the production of the fruits and vegetables needed for canning in the food production companies. This will have to occur in year three through year eight of World War III to allow for canning in year nine. It also means that strict regulations concerning the expiration dates of canned foods, and of freezer meats will have to be implemented by the governments of the nations of the world. The canned food and the freezer meats will last two years, and the large-scale nuclear war will happen at the end of World War III, which means in year ten. Therefore the nuclear winter will occur in year ten and year eleven of the war.

All of these things will have to be regulated by the Food and Drug Administration, the US Government, and the Church Committee Group. It may be possible to produce canned fruits and vegetables that will last from three, four, or five years in storage. To do this you should contact the FDA, the USDA, or the food manufacturing companies themselves.

FREEZER WAREHOUSE GENERATORS

The freezer warehouses that will store the beef, pork, and other meats for the nuclear winter will have to be equipped with backup electrical generators to ensure that the meat stays frozen at all times during the nuclear war. If these generators run on diesel, or on gasoline fuel, it may be necessary to leave the tanks empty until the ninth year of World War III, and then fill them up when needed. The reason is that the gasoline will lose its vitality after sitting in a tank for nine or ten years. This is probably true for diesel fuel too.

You should know that gasoline and diesel fuel will be in very short supply in the ninth year of World War III, since the Antichrist will take the world oil supply in the third year of the war. Therefore propane or natural gas will probably be the only fuel available toward the end of World War III. If you decide to use these types of fuel, you will have to put individual tanks on the generators, in case the natural gas lines are broken or destroyed in the cities. It would be a good idea to build large propane and or natural gas refilling stations where you can refill the tanks for the generators.

All of these ideas can be used to help build the freezer warehouses. Then there will be a large supply of food available when all of the crops fail during the first year of the nuclear winter. You should realize that all of the livestock will die from the nuclear fallout, the pyrotoxins, the freezing cold, and the lack of food and water during the nuclear winter anyway, and this is why they must be slaughtered and put into the freezer warehouses in advance.

FOREST FIRES

I have known how to prevent the huge forest fires in the Western states for over eight years, but when Bill Clinton was the President, he was not interested in anything I wrote, other than trying to steal my books.

If you will read my plan to prevent the large forest fires carefully, then you will find that it will also save millions of acres of forests in America, and in the world during a global nuclear war. There will be fires in the large cities, and in the forests; and the way to keep the fires from burning out of control in the forests is to create clear cut boundaries of one half of a mile around every 5,000 to 10,000 acres of trees.

I will include copies of my two-page letter here, in order to tell the President and the American people that there is a way to save the forests, and to prevent the deaths of hundreds of fire fighters every year. This letter is worth $1 trillion dollars each year, since that is how much timber is wasted every year in the huge forest fires in the United States. Therefore you should not be fooled by the lumber industry, when they tell you that the clear-cut boundary plan will not work. And I must tell you here that all of America's forests will burn to the ground in a global nuclear war if my plan is not implemented right away. And there will be a global nuclear war at the end of World War III.

I have known for several years that the way to stop forest fires from spreading is to clear cut boundaries around every area of 5,000 or 10,000 acres to the width of one half mile for each boundary. Then the fire will burn only that 5,000 or 10,000 acres, and no more.

Yet at the same time, I believe that there must be a reason or a motive somewhere in the lumber industry to let the fires burn huge areas, perhaps to keep the price of timber as high as possible for those lumber companies. The way to overcome that type of attitude is to give a Federal order to the Department of Forestry, requiring all heavily forested areas to conform to the clear-cut boundary method of preventing forest fires.

I think the Canadian lumber companies have taken the foreign market away from US lumber companies because of their lower prices. And I believe the Canadian companies are barred from selling their lumber in America. This is one of the methods used by American lumber companies to keep the price of lumber higher. And I believe the huge forest fires burning out of control may be another one. Therefore they may have a motive for keeping things the way they are now, which also means that thinning out the trees in the forests will not solve the problem of huge fires; but the clear-cut boundary method will.

It is of the utmost importance to issue a Federal order to implement that plan. And the width of the clear-cut boundaries must be specified at one half of a mile; and even then the lumber companies could allow the fires to jump over the boundaries by either leaving them too narrow, or by leaving too much timber in those areas. In my very short career as a logger, the company that I worked for had orders to cut all timber down to two feet from the ground. This may also work in the clear-cut boundaries to prevent fires that jump over them.

And the way to convince the American people that this will work will be to tell them that the fire fighting crews can battle future forest fires within the clear-cut boundaries. This will keep the fires contained within that 5,000 or 10,000 acre forested area. The large airplanes with fire retardant chemicals can dump their payloads in the clear-cut boundaries; and the helicopters with buckets of water can do the same.

If you run into opposition to this plan, where people say that it cannot be done because of the uneven growths of trees, then you can tell them that 20 foot trees can be cut down to provide the boundaries, just the same as 100 foot trees can. But the important point is to get the message out that this plan will save the lives of hundreds of fire fighters every year, as well as saving millions of acres of trees.

The lumber companies that make the clear-cut boundaries will of course be given permission to market the trees that they cut down. In some cases they can use it for lumber, and in others they can use it for pulp paper. And if they are faced with a clear-cut project of small trees, then they can cut them down in early December, and sell them as Christmas trees. And in fact they can postpone the projects involving the smaller trees until early December in most states.

I found a small problem with the clear-cut boundary plan, namely what to do about replanting trees in the boundaries themselves. When the newly planted trees are four or five years old, and 10 to 15 feet high, it will be necessary to move the boundary over one half of a mile, into the larger trees. This will enable the boundary areas to replenish themselves, while still preventing the huge forest fires from burning out of control. You can tell the Department of Forestry about this idea.

CHAPTER V

The Joint Chiefs of Staff

I read somewhere that the Pentagon has so much money and so much power that they can destroy a person's career and ruin his life in just a few months. For this reason no timid person would ever dare to take them on or attack them for their corruption or their bad fiscal policies.

Since I am writing books about World War III, and since the USA could be included in nine nuclear wars because of the military policies of the Pentagon, I will ignore the statement above. However, this does explain why there are so few books describing the corruption and the idiotic military policies of the Pentagon. For this reason the American people are naive about what the Pentagon does.

If you look at the historical events of the 1980s, then you will see that there was an attempt to assassinate President Ronald Reagan in March 1981. The assassination attempt was made by John W. Hinckley Jr. Now you can see that President Reagan was shot in 1981, and then he literally turned his pockets inside out from 1983 to 1988. He made his famous Star Wars speech in March 1983. Here is a quote from page 216 of the book, *Missile Envy*, © 1984 by Helen Caldicott:

"In Reagan's Star Wars speech in March 1983, contrary to Eisenhower's warning (to guard against the increasing power of the military-industrial complex), he offered an epiphany to the powers of scientific technology to heal all problems, even those it had created. The President has admitted that he really does not understand anything about computers or high technology himself."[304]

Now doesn't it seem strange that Reagan emptied his pockets for the Pentagon when he didn't even understand the Star Wars or SDI program? Here is a quote from page 206 of *Missile Envy*:

"In the five years from 1984 to 1988, the Reagan administration plans to spend $1.8 trillion dollars (but actually, if hidden costs are included, it will be $2.5 trillion), on 'defense.' In comparison, America has spent only $1.5 trillion on defense over the last 37 years. When Reagan was elected, the administration, Pentagon, military corporations, and scientists, were like little boys let loose in a candy shop. They ordered every single weapon on the shelves."[305]

Now you should look at the events from 1972 to 1983, from the point of view of the Pentagon. The ABM Treaty was signed in 1972, and in effect it made it illegal to use a land-based ABM defense against nuclear missiles. Then as soon as it was signed, the Joint Chiefs of Staff probably formed a group of defense experts, and then told them to analyze the current defense strategy, taking into account the effects of the 1972 ABM Treaty. Then from this group came the idea to build a space-based defense against nuclear missiles.

After the group reported this to the Joint Chiefs of Staff, the Pentagon probably called Edward Teller, and asked him to work out the technical details for a space-based defense, and then report on his findings. Edward Teller then put together a group of scientists at the Lawrence Livermore Laboratory, and began working on the new Star Wars defense, which is now called the Space Defense Initiative.

Now look at the overall set of events. The Pentagon had the 1972 ABM Treaty in place, which justified the need for a space-based defense. The Pentagon also had Edward Teller and his group of scientists at work on the new Star Wars defense from 1972 to 1981. Now the Pentagon needed a President to sign the blank check to pay for the new space-based defense; and in 1981 there was an assassination attempt on President Ronald Reagan by John W. Hinckley Jr.

The only thing needed to make it all work now, was a way of telling President Ronald Reagan why he was shot by John W. Hinckley Jr. The Pentagon could have asked Edward Teller to tell President Reagan that the KGB set up the assassination attempt in 1981; and then Edward Teller could have said that the CIA told him and the Joint Chiefs of Staff in a secret conference that the KGB did try to kill him.

Then of course President Reagan became very angry at the Soviets, and signed a blank check for the new Star Wars defense, or SDI. You should remember that President Reagan called the Soviet Union the "evil empire." This is a phrase from the movie Star Wars, which connects the Star Wars defense to the Star Wars movie; but it also tells you that President Reagan disliked the USSR very intensely.

The very fact that a President would try to sell the American people on the idea of a space-based defense, while using quotes from a movie like Star Wars, should tell you right away that something is wrong. This type of action is called propaganda, and it is very dangerous when used by a President. I looked in the 1999 Almanac the other day, and I found that President Reagan spent nearly $2.2 trillion dollars on defense in his eight years in office.

When you look at all of the events that happened from 1963 to 1983, you will see that the Pentagon probably believed that this set of events would work, simply because of the multitude of assassinations and assassination attempts during that time period. They could have asked the CIA to tell President Reagan that the KGB played a part in all of the earlier assassinations.

Now go back to the quote from page 206 of *Missile Envy*:

"The administration, Pentagon, military corporations, and scientists were like little boys let loose in a candy shop. They ordered every single weapon on the shelves."[306]

If you know a little about theology, then you will realize that the deceitfulness of sin actually caused them to spend more than they ordinarily would have because the plan worked. Here is a quote about the Star Wars defense from page 217 of *Missile Envy*:

"Robert Bowman, former head of the advanced weapons program, said of the various Star Wars schemes, 'All have staggering technical problems. All are likely to cost on the order of a trillion dollars. All violate one or more existing treaties. All are extremely vulnerable. All are subject to a series of countermeasures.'"[307]

The Star Wars defense was built in outer space, which means that the American people could not look at the thing they were paying for with their tax money. In other words, it could be a junkyard in outer space, and no one would even know it. This is what I meant by the naivety of the American people in regards to the Pentagon.

The most important thing to remember about the Joint Chiefs of Staff is that they think in terms of trillions of dollars. If they had anything to do with the assassination attempt on Ronald Reagan in 1981, then this concept explains why. When you think in trillions of dollars, you look at future events, you try to imagine how the events during the present time could result in the acquisition of trillions of dollars in the future, and then you act out those events. This is what the Pentagon does.

The 1972 ABM Treaty made it illegal to use a land-based ABM defense to protect against incoming missiles. When this was done, the Pentagon began thinking about creating a space-based defense against nuclear missiles. Then nine years later President Reagan was shot, and two years after this he emptied his pockets for the Pentagon. On page 216 of *Missile Envy* it says that Reagan didn't consult with the normal defense and national security people, and that he wrote his Star Wars speech only after talking with Edward Teller.[308] Edward Teller was involved in the plot to sabotage the career of Robert J. Oppenheimer. Look at the quote on page 216:

"In September 1982, Teller took his case to the White House and briefed President Reagan on his Star Wars concept. Reagan was entranced and..."[309]Was President Reagan entranced, or was he afraid for his life? If you doubt that the Pentagon had anything to do with the attempt on Ronald Reagan's life, then you should look at their job description. They kill people, and they have possession of nuclear warheads that could kill three billion people or more in a global nuclear war.

There is an oddity about the Pentagon that should be explained here. If you have ever wondered why they do the strange things that they do, such as ignoring the wishes of the American people in reference to the dismantling of their nuclear weapons, and trying to discredit the nuclear winter scientists, then here is the answer: They always think in trillions of dollars, and they do not make any decisions without doing so. The Pentagon refuses to conform to the principles advocated by the American people who want to dismantle the nuclear missiles; and in major wars like World War III they use the concept of patriotism to convince the people to conform to their military policies. Therefore, patriotism can be used as a means of deception by the Pentagon.

This is what they did in the Vietnam War. The US Defense budget was $43 billion dollars in 1960, and it went up to $303 billion in 1989. Here is a quote from the front flap of the book titled, *Military Incompetence*, © 1985 by Richard A. Gabriel:

"After the American withdrawal from Vietnam, the Pentagon embarked on a program of reform to ensure that its forces would never again be defeated. Have we succeeded with a trillion dollars in building our defense? Or have the Pentagon and recent Administrations squandered our security?"[310]Once again, the Joint Chiefs of Staff think in trillions of dollars. Further down is this quote:

"A New York Times editorial commented in May 1985: 'The grave error was simply to throw money at the problem to pour it down the Pentagon's throat without reforming its stultifying inter-service rivalries and non-competitive procurement system.'"[311]

Here is proof that the Pentagon refuses to conform to the principles of the American people. On pages 79 and 80 of the book titled, *Blundering Into Disaster*, © 1986 by Robert S. McNamara is the quote:

"Our current nuclear weapons building program, which is producing 2,000 warheads annually, is the biggest in 20 years. And steps are underway to expand substantially for the 1990s, both the production of the key nuclear materials—tritium, uranium, and plutonium—and the production of the warheads themselves."[312]

Robert S. McNamara was the Secretary of Defense for John F. Kennedy and Lyndon B. Johnson in the 1960s. You should ask the question, Why did McNamara name the title of his book, *Blundering Into Disaster*? Of course this was meant as an insult to the Pentagon because of their idiotic military policies, but why did McNamara do it? I found the answer on page 603 of the book titled, *Kennedy*, © 1965 by Theodore C. Sorensen:

"Less than a week after the new JFK Administration had come into office, McNamara reported to the Cabinet, and then in detail to the President about what he had found in the Pentagon: A strategy of massive nuclear retaliation as the answer to all military and political aggression, a strategy believed by few of our friends and none of our enemies, and resulting in serious weaknesses in our conventional forces.

A strategic nuclear force vulnerable to surprise missile attack, a non-nuclear force weak in combat-ready divisions, in airlift capacity and in tactical air support, a counterinsurgency force for all practical purposes non-existent, and a weapons inventory completely lacking in certain major elements, but far oversupplied in others.

Too many automatic decisions made in advance, instead of in the light of an actual emergency, and too few Pentagon-wide plans for each kind of contingency. The Army was relying on airlift that the Air Force could not supply. The Air Force was stockpiling supplies for a war lasting a few days, while the Army stockpiles assumed a war of two years."[313]

Then after reporting this to the President, Robert S. McNamara requested answers to some questions. On page 604 of the same book is this quote:

"He requested detailed answers to 96 questions of his own (which rocked the Pentagon, and became known as McNamara's 96 Trombones)."[314]You can see here that the Pentagon ridiculed the Secretary of Defense while he was trying to help them improve the US military systems. Then McNamara named the title of his book, *Blundering Into Disaster*, in 1986. Of course you can see another reason for the title because of the ridiculous state in which the US military was when he did his evaluation in 1961.

The one quote that bothers me the most is the one here:

"A strategy (by the Pentagon) of massive nuclear retaliation as the answer to all military and political aggression."[315]

Here is the reason why:

There will be a total of 9 possible nuclear wars, which the USA could be involved in during World War III. They will happen when the Pentagon uses the US military to fight battles over some of the following strategic issues, or when they counterattack against the Antichrist over these issues:

1. Limited Tactical Nuclear War
2. The US troop buildup in America
3. US military bases in Europe
4. The attack on Rome, Italy
5. The blockade of England
6. The occupation of Israel
7. The world oil supply
8. US military bases in the Middle East
9. The CIA trying to kill the Antichrist

The Limited Tactical Nuclear War will occur when the Pentagon uses neutron bombs against the Russian tanks, when they invade Western Europe. This will happen in the first year of World War III. The nuclear war over the buildup of US troops in America will also happen in the first year. The US military bases in Europe will have to be defended, and this will cause a nuclear war.

The Pentagon will retaliate when the Antichrist uses nuclear missiles to destroy Rome, Italy. The blockade of England will lead to nuclear war. The battles in Israel will cause a nuclear war. There will be a nuclear war because of the battles over the world oil supply. The Pentagon will cause a nuclear war while trying to protect the US military bases in the Middle East. If the CIA tries to kill the Antichrist at any time during World War III, then America will be included in the big nuclear war at the end of the war.

These nuclear wars cannot be avoided because of the present policy of deterrence that the Pentagon has. They can avoid them only by closing all of the US military bases in England, Europe, Japan and Korea. However, the Pentagon will not do this because the Joint Chiefs of Staff think in trillions of dollars. This is what they believe will happen, and here are the amounts of money they believe they will lose, in their own minds:

They will lose these amounts:

1. The $1.5 trillion dollars that will be the cost of bringing the US military troops and weapons back to America.
2. The $2 trillion that the Pentagon has invested in Europe since 1970.
3. The $210 to $250 billion dollars per year paid to the US military personnel who work at the bases in Europe and overseas. When you

multiply this by the 20 years leading up to and including World War III, the total is $4.2 to $ 5 trillion dollars.

4. The $4 trillion in modernization and long term procurement, that the Pentagon will not need if they stay out of World War III.
5. The $100 billion needed to dismantle the nuclear weapons that they will bring back to America, and those that are already here.

The total amount is:

$11.8 trillion dollars: minimum, and $12.6 trillion dollars: maximum.

Now you know why the Pentagon will refuse to save America from World War III.

Now I will try to verify each item.

1. On page 131 of *Missile Envy*, © 1984 by Helen Caldicott, it says the US military has 334 total foreign areas that can be considered foreign US military bases.[316] The US Government paid over $600 billion dollars to supply the transport aircraft, jet fighters, ships, tanks, personnel, and all military weapons used in the Gulf War in Saudi Arabia and Kuwait in 1991. I think England and Japan paid part of it, but the fact remains that it cost $600 billion. They would have to pay at least $1.5 trillion dollars to bring all of the US military equipment back to the USA from the 334 bases. On page 24 of the book titled, *America's Defense: Opposing Viewpoints*, © 1991 by Greenhaven Press is the quote:

"Prior to the Gulf conflict, 435,000 US troops were already assigned to 395 major military bases in 35 foreign countries. Accompanying them were more than 168,000 civilian Pentagon employees and 400,000 family dependents."[317]

In this book it says that the Pentagon has 395 major military bases in 35 foreign countries. Therefore I will say it will cost from $1.5 to $2 trillion dollars to close them, and bring the US military troops and weapons back to America. To reduce the cost of doing this, the Pentagon can transport a major portion of its tanks, trucks, personnel carriers, jets, and other equipment on US aircraft carriers, instead of using the transport aircraft to do it.

2. The Pentagon has invested from $2 to $3 trillion dollars in NATO Europe since the Vietnam War.

3. The Pentagon is paying about $150 billion dollars per year to defend the countries in Europe. On page 25 of the book, *America's Defense: Opposing Viewpoints*, © 1991 by Greenhaven Press, is the quote:

"In the 1980s the US annually spent about $160 to $170 billion to defend countries in Europe, $30 to $40 billion to defend countries in Asia, and $20 to $40 billion to protect US access to Persian Gulf oil."[318]

At the minimum here the total cost is $210 billion dollars to $250 billion a year. Even though these amounts are for the 1980s, I would guess that they are very much similar now. The Pentagon will have to cancel all of these expenditures and bring all of the US troops and weapons in all of these areas back to the USA to protect America during World War III. They will refuse to do it since it will cost them $4.2 to $5 trillion dollars.

4. The Pentagon has been allocated $4 trillion dollars for the modernization of their weapons, for long-term procurement, for the Joint Strike Fighter, and for new helicopters and submarines. I heard this announced on the TV News in Tacoma, Washington in 1996 or 1997. It was a Seattle TV news station that made the announcement. Here is a list of the modernization-funding plan from page 48 and 49 of the US Government Budget 1997-Supplement:

DDG-51 Guided Missile Destroyers
C-17 Strategic Airlift Aircraft
Joint Standoff Weapon
Marine Corps V-22 Tilt-Rotor Aircraft
Navy F/A-18 E/F Fighter
Navy New Attack Submarine
Air Force F-22 Fighter[319]

On Page 49 you should notice the phrase:
"The budget proposes large investments in research and development for advanced systems that will enter production in the middle of the next decade."[320]
These will include the:

Joint Strike Fighter
Army Comanche Helicopter
Marine Amphibious Assault Vehicle
New Navy Surface Ship

Of course the Pentagon will have to cancel all of the orders for these weapons to save America from the Antichrist and from World War III; but they will refuse to do it since they will lose the $4 trillion dollars for modernization.

5. The Pentagon will have to pay $100 billion dollars to dismantle the nuclear weapons that they must bring back from Europe, along with the ones that are already here.

The minimum total cost for all of these, or the total amount that the Pentagon will lose is:

$11.8 trillion dollars

The maximum total cost, or the total amount which the Pentagon will lose is:

$12.6 trillion dollars

Since the Joint Chiefs of Staff think in trillions of dollars, they will refuse to save America by staying out of World War III. Of course this means that the Pentagon will have the wrong types of weapons because they don't really know anything about World War III. At this time they don't have an ABM defense against incoming nuclear missiles, and the Soviet nuclear arsenal will belong to the Antichrist within six years. The Pentagon needs to put together a Foolproof National Defense against nuclear missiles by putting an ABM defense on moving ships and/or submarines. I think the subs would be immune from EMP, or electromagnetic pulse because they travel underwater. I wrote about this in the Nuclear War chapter.

The American people should put pressure on the President and the Congress to stop the $4 trillion dollars in funding for the Joint Strike Fighter, the modernization, and the long-term procurement for weapons that the Pentagon has ordered. The problem is that the Pentagon will have the $4 trillion dollars to shuffle around to use in any way they see necessary during the 11 years of World War III. The American people cannot allow this to happen because the Pentagon will use the money to become involved in World War III, which means they will lose 25 million American troops, and then start a global nuclear war against the Antichrist. In the book titled, *Blank Check*, © 1990 by Tim Weiner, it says the Pentagon has a secret budget which has consumed $100 billion dollars in just 3 years. Here is a quote from the front flap:

"Over the past 3 years (before 1990) the black budget has consumed more than $100 billion dollars—$100 million a day."[321]

This isn't the worst part of it. When the Pentagon gets involved in the ground war in Europe in the first year of World War III, they will have to spend from $1 to $1.5 trillion dollars per year to fight there. In other words, it will take $11 trillion dollars at minimum cost for the 11 years of World War III; or it will take $16.5 trillion dollars at the maximum cost. This is the amount of money that the American taxpayers will lose, and then there will be 100 million homeless and starving people in the USA during World War III.

The question to ask now is, what is the Pentagon's current strategy, if World War III were to start within the next six years? In the book, *Military Incompetence*, © 1985 by Richard A. Gabriel it is just to throw money at the problem, and now you know that it will be $11 trillion to $16.5 trillion dollars of your own tax money.[322]

On page 41 of his book, *Blundering Into Disaster*, © 1986, Robert S. McNamara wrote in Table 3 that the Pentagon had 9,500 tactical nuclear weapons altogether in 1985.[323] In her book, *Missile Envy*, © 1984, Helen Caldicott said the Pentagon made plans to build 800-eight inch neutron shells, 380 Lance neutron warheads, and 1,000 of the 155-millimeter neutron shells.[324] These are called neutron bombs, or limited tactical nuclear weapons. On page 195 of her book, Helen Caldicott wrote:

"Neutron bombs are designed to be used against invading Russian tanks in Western Europe."[325]

The invading army and the tanks are described in Daniel 11:22.

Daniel 11:22: "And with the arms of a flood shall they be overflown from before him, and shall be broken."

To learn why the people in Western Europe will be broken, look at this verse:

Revelation 9:16: "And the number of the army of the horsemen were two hundred thousand thousand: and I heard the number of them."

The army of the Antichrist, or the Unified European Army, will have 200 million soldiers in it at the end of World War III. For this reason, the Pentagon's strategy in Europe is wrong. They must evacuate all US military troops there, and they must close the bases. The Pentagon cannot fight against the army of the Antichrist and protect America at the same time.

On page 34 of his book, *Blundering Into Disaster*, © 1986, Robert S. McNamara wrote:

"Have the more modern weapons deployed on both sides in the 1970s changed the likely results of a nuclear war in Europe? Not at all. A group of experts was assembled in 1980 by the UN Secretary General to study nuclear war. They simulated a conflict where 1,500 nuclear artillery shells and 200 nuclear bombs were used by the two sides against each other's military targets. The experts concluded that as a result of such a conflict there would be a minimum of five to six million immediate civilian casualties and 400,000 military casualties, and that at least an additional 1.1 million civilians would suffer from radiation disease."

"It should be remembered that this scenario, as horrible as it is, involves the use of only a small portion of the tactical nuclear weapons deployed in

Europe, and it assumes that none of the thousands of nuclear warheads in the USA and USSR central strategic arsenals would be used."[326]

You should remember what McNamara said here because the tactical nuclear war in Europe will be 125 times larger than the one in the study; since there will be 100 million troops in the Unified European Army, or the army of the Antichrist which will invade Western Europe, instead of 800,000 soldiers that they expect. This can be verified in Revelation 9:16. Therefore the Pentagon will start a global nuclear war while trying to protect Western Europe. You should also know that this is the battle plan, which the Pentagon will use at the beginning of World War III.

For this reason the Pentagon has to close the US military bases in Europe. On page 26 of the book, *America's Defense: Opposing Viewpoints*, © 1991 by Greenhaven Press is the quote about the Pentagon:

"It can reduce its annual military budget to 2/3 or less of its present size. It can cut its nuclear forces by 3/4, and its conventional forces by 1/2. The US can safely reduce by almost a million the number of its active duty military personnel. These reductions should begin with troops in Europe, Japan, South Korea, and the Philippines."[327]

These recommendations were made by someone knowledgeable in the defense field, and they verify my instructions for the Pentagon concerning World War III. They can close the bases, and they can bring the US troops and weapons back to America. Since the Pentagon will refuse to do this because of the $11.8 to $12.6 trillion dollars that they will lose, I have thought of an alternate plan.

THE CHURCH COMMITTEE PLAN

1. The American people should vote for the Church Committee Plan, either by working with the Congress, or by using the National Emergency Vote.
2. Then the American people should vote to give the offensive military power of the Pentagon to the Church Committee Group.
3. Then the Church Committee Group can order the Pentagon to close the US military bases in all foreign countries, including England, Europe, Japan, Korea, and the Middle East.
4. The American people should vote to give possession of the US nuclear missiles and tactical nuclear weapons in Europe and in America to the Church Committee Group.
5. Then the Church Committee Group can dismantle 99% of the nuclear missiles and nuclear weapons, and they can convince the other nuclear

nations in the world to join them. It is very important to do this before the Antichrist appears in Europe.

I described the Church Committee Plan more completely in the chapter about it. Another important reason for using it is that it will keep the USA out of the nine nuclear wars that I described earlier.

In regards to the trillions of dollars that the Pentagon spends, here is a quote from the front flap of the book, *The Pentagon and the Art of War*, © 1984 by Edward N. Luttwak:

"In peacetime, Congress and the media loudly denounce 'fraud, waste, and mismanagement' but they account for only a few percentage points of the defense budget. At the same time, Luttwak argues, we systematically overspend tens of billions of dollars on forces that played a glorious role in past wars but are of scant use today, while neglecting other forces that have become vitally important."[328] The Pentagon has enormous power in the TV news media and in the newspapers and magazines, and they tell the people who work there to start arguments about waste and mismanagement. The Pentagon is also capable of finding the bolt that costs $820 dollars, or the wing nut that costs $943 dollars; and it is them who inadvertently bring these items to the attention of the TV news media. The American people never hear about the $210 to $250 billion dollars that the Pentagon spends while protecting other nations in the world.

When I looked at the US Budget Receipts and Outlays from the US Department of the Treasury, I found that the Pentagon gets about $30 billion dollars per year more than that which they report to the American people.[329] In the fiscal year of 1993: they received $278,586,000,000 for the military, and $29,266,000,000 for the civilian part of the Department of Defense. The total is $307,852,000,000. This is more than $307 billion dollars; and I hope you noticed all of the zeroes here, since your taxes are paying for them. Then in fiscal year 1994 it was: $268,635,000,000 for the military branch of the Department of Defense, and for the civilian branch it was $30,402,000,000. This is $299,037,000,000 altogether. I will tell you plainly that the Pentagon's annual budget will have to be reduced by the amounts that they are now spending to protect Europe, Asia, and the oil nations in the Middle East, or the Persian Gulf.

According to page 25 of the book, *America's Defense: Opposing Viewpoints*, © 1991, this figure is $210 billion a year minimum, and $300 billion a year maximum.[330] They will have to use several billion or possibly $1.5 trillion dollars to close the US military bases overseas, and bring the US troops and weapons to America. I think they can reduce this amount to $500 billion dollars or less by using US Aircraft carriers to bring the tanks, trucks, personnel carriers, artillery guns, jet aircraft, and other weapons back to America. You see, with transport airplanes you use fuel to lift the tanks and trucks into the sky; while the water in the ocean does the lifting for you with aircraft carriers. They are called aircraft carriers because they carry airplanes and other heavy objects. If the Pentagon starts doing this soon enough, and if they use all of their aircraft carriers and other available ships, then they can probably reduce the cost to less than $500 billion dollars.

While I am on the subject of military spending, I would like to quote from page 67 of the book, *The Spread of Nuclear Weapons: A Debate* © 1995 by Kenneth N. Waltz and Scott D. Sagan:

"First, military bureaucracies, like other organizations, are usually interested in having more resources: they want more weapons, more men in uniform, more pieces of the budget pie. This could obviously lead to larger than necessary nuclear arsenals."[331]

In fact the nuclear arsenals themselves and the money allocated to building them actually fuel the need for a larger annual budget for the Pentagon. Here is a quote from page 75 of the book, *Missile Envy*, © 1984 by Helen Caldicott:

"It has only been within the last 15 years or so before 1984 that the US cities have become vulnerable to a Russian missile strike that could take place within 30 minutes after launching. This is because the USA failed to stop the arms race in 1960, when it started deploying its first ICBMS."[332]

While thinking about the naivety of the American people concerning the Pentagon, I was driving past the University of California at Berkeley, and as I drove south on the Nimitz Freeway, and then on the MacArthur Freeway in Oakland, I wondered why these admirals and generals receive this kind of glorification by the people. Then I remembered that General Douglas MacArthur was fired by President Harry Truman in 1951 because he continually made unauthorized policy statements to the Press and the News media about President Truman's strategy in the Korean War. MacArthur wanted 300,000 more US troops so he could attack Chinese Communist bases in Manchuria. I read somewhere that MacArthur wanted to get the USA so much involved in the fighting so he could get permission to use the atomic bomb against Red China. Truman believed that the fighting must be confined to Korea, and not be allowed to spread into a possible global war. MacArthur made several public statements criticizing this policy, and then Truman removed him from duty.

You can see in this example that Pentagon generals do not always do what is best for the country. The US military could have lost one or two million troops in the Korean War if General MacArthur had gotten his way, and 10 to 20 million Chinese people could have been killed by the use of the atomic bomb in China.

Yet at the same time President Truman became very unpopular when he removed General MacArthur from duty in 1951. You can see the awe and the popularity of General MacArthur in the eyes of the American people in this example; and this kind of blind patriotism will result in the deaths of 25 million American soldiers in the first year of World War III.

While driving past UC Berkeley on the freeway, I remembered reading the book, *The Spread of Nuclear Weapons: A Debate*, © 1995, and I thought of this quote on page 16 made by Kenneth N. Waltz:

"Nuclear weapons do not make nuclear war likely, as history has shown."[333]

You should brace yourself for these statements. On page 17:

"The use of nuclear weapons by lesser powers would hardly trigger them elsewhere."[334] On page 33 he says:

"The presence of nuclear weapons makes war less likely."[335] The following quote proves without any doubt that Kenneth Waltz has some connection with the Pentagon because he advocates the selling of nuclear weapons to other nations. On page 44:

"The measured spread of nuclear weapons does not run against our interests and can increase the security of some states (or nations) at a price they can afford to pay."[336]

The question is, who is going to sell them? The Pentagon, of course. Then on page 21:

"A thriving arms trade in ever more sophisticated military equipment provides ready access to what may be wanted, including planes and missiles suited to the delivery of nuclear warheads."[337] Obviously this statement is meant to justify the selling of military weapons by the Pentagon to other nations. The question now is why did they choose a Professor of political science at UC Berkeley? It seems to me that an organization steeped on propaganda would use this kind of tactic to try and obliterate the truth. The Pentagon lost the Vietnam War—there were protests at over 100 college campuses over it, but UC Berkeley was one of the loudest and most active. Here is the formula:

1. UC Berkeley protested over the Vietnam War.
2. Now UC Berkeley advocates the use of conventional and nuclear weapons.

The Pentagon does things like this because the Joints Chiefs of Staff always think in trillions of dollars.

It is true that the Pentagon gives large monetary grants to colleges and universities. Here is a quote from Scott D. Sagan on page 47:

"Waltz is by no means alone in holding this position, as a number of other political scientists have jumped onto the pro-proliferation bandwagon."[338]

This is called Pentagon propaganda. To stop it you must vote for the Church Committee Plan. Look at this quote from page 42:

"The strongest way for the USA to persuade other countries to forego nuclear weapons is to guarantee their security."[339] The problem here is the age old one: The Pentagon makes money either way. The Pentagon will make money ensuring their safety, or by selling them conventional or nuclear weapons. The Pentagon spent about $200 billion dollars on the Vietnam War, which they lost, and then afterwards they embarked on a program of spending so they would never lose another war. Don't you see it now? The one common thing about their programs is that they always make money either way.

The Pentagon budget will have to be reduced to less than $100 billion dollars per year, so they will not be able to fight against the 200 million soldiers in the army of the Antichrist during World War III.

Edward Teller

Encyclopedia Britannica © 1997, Vol. 11, pg. 619: Edward Teller was an understudy of Robert J. Oppenheimer in the early 1950s and later he developed the world's first thermonuclear weapon, and he became known as, 'the Father of the H-bomb.' Teller's stubborn pursuit of the weapon in the face of skepticism, and even hostility from many of his peers played a major role in the bomb's development.

"At the U.S. government hearings held in 1954 to determine whether Oppenheimer was a security risk, Teller's testimony was decidedly unsympathetic to his former chief. After the hearings' end, Oppenheimer's security clearance was revoked, and his career as a science administrator was at an end. Although Teller's testimony was by no means the decisive factor in this outcome, many prominent American nuclear physicists never forgave him for what they viewed as his betrayal of Oppenheimer."[340]

There is something else about Edward Teller that you should know, since President Ronald Reagan gave hundreds of billions of dollars to the Pentagon for development of the neutron bombs, or the limited tactical nuclear weapons to be used in Europe. Here is the quote from the same page:

"Teller was instrumental in the creation of the United States' second nuclear-weapons laboratory, the Lawrence Livermore Laboratory, in Livermore, California, in 1952. For almost the next four decades it was the United States' chief factory for making thermonuclear weapons. Teller was associate director of Livermore from 1954 to 1958 and from 1960 to 1975, and he was its director from 1958-1960."[341]

Edward Teller had a strong motive to try and convince President Ronald Reagan to empty his pockets for the Pentagon. His laboratory in Livermore, California probably played a big role in making the neutron bombs, which President Reagan helped pay for. If this is true, then Edward Teller and the Pentagon did exactly what President Dwight Eisenhower warned the nation about in 1961. He warned the USA to guard against the acquisition of too much influence by the military-industrial complex in congressional budget allocations.

Now after reading this chapter, there are some questions which we must ask:

1. Will the Pentagon and the US military try to find ways to keep their military bases in Europe and in the Middle East open, by starting conflicts between US troops and the troops of other nations, or between US troops and terrorists in the years before World War III begins?
2. Will the Joint Chiefs of Staff decide that they must kill me to guarantee that their US military bases throughout the world can stay open?
3. Will the Joint Chiefs of Staff decide that they will have to wiretap the office of the President of the United States to find out exactly what I am saying to him about World War III?
4. Will the Joint Chiefs of Staff decide that they must kill the President of the United States to guarantee that he will not give the order to close all of the foreign US military bases in the world?

We, meaning myself, the President, and all of the people in the United States, must ask these questions because the Joint Chiefs of Staff and the people in the Pentagon always think in terms of trillions of dollars.

When a group of people think that way, then the lives of other people are not very important to them at all. Yet the lives and the souls of every person in America are important. And if the Pentagon refuses to follow the instructions of Christ before and during World War III, then this is what will happen:

Revelation 9:16: "And the number of the army of the horsemen were two hundred thousand thousand: and I heard the number of them."

The army of the Antichrist will have 200 million soldiers in it at the end of World War III, and they will invade the United States if the Pentagon loses 25 million US troops at the beginning of the war. They will invade America if there are no troops left to defend it. Then this will happen:

Revelation 14:11: "And the smoke of their torment ascendeth up for ever and ever: and they have no rest day nor night, who worship the beast and his image, and whosoever receiveth the mark of his name."

The army of the Antichrist will force everyone in the United States to receive the mark of the beast, or the swastika, and then their souls will burn in the fires of the sun forever. This is written here:

Psalm 19:4: "In them hath he set a tabernacle for the sun."

The Lake of Fire in Revelation 20:14 is the sun. Look at this:

Matthew 25:41: "Then shall he say also unto them on the left hand, Depart from me, ye cursed, into everlasting fire, prepared for the devil and his angels."

The everlasting fire described here is prepared for the devil and his angels, and it is the fire of the sun. And everyone who is forced to receive the swastika will also go there. After their bodies vaporize because of the extremely high temperature, their souls will burn in the fires of the sun forever. This is what will happen if the Pentagon refuses to follow the instructions of Christ before and during World War III.

CHAPTER VI

The Church Committee Plan

The Church Committee Group that works in the Congress will have to learn all of the duties performed by Congressmen, since they will serve in the same capacity as they do. This of course means that the Church Committee Group will have to study books about the duties of the Congress. Although it is difficult to find up-to-date books on the subject, I did find a few. They are:

Lawmaking and the Legislative Process © 1996

Congress A to Z © 2003 by the Congressional Quarterly Inc.

Congressional Quarterly's Guide to Congress © 2000

I did my research by reading these books, but the Church Committee Group will have to study the working of the Congress more completely than I did, however. These books can be found in a large City's Library, or you can write to this address to order them:

Congressional Quarterly Inc.
1414 22nd St. NW
Washington, D.C. 20037

I should point out here that the book titled, *Lawmaking and the Legislative Process*, © 1996 is a book on the procedure of State Lawmaking, but it is almost the same as in the US Congress.

The Church Committee Group should study all aspects of the working of Congress, from lobbying to legislative staff to the passage of bills. I got the following quotes from the book titled, *Lawmaking and the Legislative Process*, © 1996. On page 28:

"Lobbying occurs at every stage of the process, from ideas for legislation to drafting, introduction, committee consideration, floor consideration, and votes on final passage."

"A major factor in the legislative process is the role of lobbyists. Lobbyists are major players in the game of legislation. They are in the same category as legislative staff when it comes to making decisions about whether a bill will be introduced, and in voting on a proposal. Making final decisions about voting is something that only members of the legislature can do."[342] The Church Committee Group must remember that they are working in the Congress to be the major lobbying interest for the American people prior to and throughout World War III. You have probably heard the expression:

"All of the major corporations have lobbyists in the Congress, but the American people have none."

This statement will no longer be true when the Church Committee Group starts to work there. This means that the Church Committee must make this basic decision before voting in the committees and on the floor of the Congress:

Is this bill going to work for the American people, or against them?

This consideration should be about 90% of the determining factor for the voting of the Church Committee Group. The Church Committee members should always remember this when voting.

For this reason the Church Committee Group must look at the lobbyists in the Congress as their enemies in most cases when it comes to getting support to pass legislation. This is why I put ten more Church Committee Group members than the regular members on the Committees. On page 28 I found this quote:

"Like legislative staff, lobbyists may have considerable influence in the lawmaking process. Hired to represent the interests of a group, a business firm, or even an individual,"[343] I stopped the quote here to point out something very important. If the powers of lobbyists are similar to those of the legislative staff, then the Church Committee members can hire expert legislative staff to help overcome the influence of the lobbyists in the Congress. To continue the quote:

"In some instances, during sessions of the legislature, lobbyists follow legislation that might affect the special interests of their clients and seek to influence its passage or defeat."[344] The Church Committee Group can tell some people on their legislative staff to serve as watchmen to watch the incoming legislation, and to alert the Church Committee when a new bill is introduced, which will be very harmful to the interests of the American people. It may be necessary to put 30 or 40 members of the Church Committee's legislative staff on this permanent assignment. The churches in

America will pay the costs of the salaries for the Church Committee Group, their legislative staff, and for other necessities. On page 29 is the quote:

"In earlier times it may have been possible for legislators to become familiar with the details of the proposals they were called upon to consider. Now, however, it is unrealistic to expect a legislator to become an expert on every subject that comes before the legislature. Now the most effective legislators are those who concentrate on becoming experts in one or two subject areas. On legislation outside their area of expertise they rely on other members whose knowledge and judgment they respect, on legislative staff, and on non-members with expertise—including lobbyists."[345]

Starting from the top, the Church Committee Group will have to hire perhaps 200 professional legislative staff people. They can help the Church Committee Group to become experts on subjects like appropriations for spending on military weapons, weapons systems, long-term procurement, and other Department of Defense related fields. The Church Committee Group will have to know how the legislation works on these projects in order to defeat any Pentagon spending programs. The Church Committee Group members will work on the House and Senate Armed Services Committees in the Congress, and then they will divert all of the money for those projects back to projects that serve the interests of the American people.

The projects related to the national defense of the USA can be paid by the Church Committee Group members, and I think the funding for this project should add up to about $100 billion dollars or less. This will include the costs for building an ABM Defense system, which will have to be done according to the plans outlined in my Foolproof National Defense. The part of the Church Committee Group that will work on the House and Senate Armed Services Committees will probably need twice as many legislative staff people to support them as the other committee people will. The reasons for this are outlined in the jurisdiction language for the Armed Services Committees themselves:

JURISDICTION

"Aeronautical and space activities peculiar to or primarily associated with the development of weapons systems or military operations; the common defense; the Department of Defense, the Department of the Army, Navy, and Air Force. The maintenance and operation of the Panama Canal. Military research and development; national security aspects of nuclear energy; naval petroleum reserves, except those in Alaska; pay, promotion, retirement, and other benefits of members of the Armed Forces, including the overseas education of civilian and military dependents; selective service system; and strategic and critical materials necessary for the common defense."[346]

This information can be found in The Congressional Standing Committee System, Congressional Research Service, in the Library of Congress. The Senate Subcommittees for the Armed Services Committee are:

Acquisition and Technology
Airland Forces
Personnel
Readiness
Seapower
Strategic Forces

When the Church Committee Group members work on the House and Senate Armed Services Committees, they will have to ask the committee members to give them on-the-job training. Most importantly, they will have to ask the Armed Services Committee members to separate all of the offensive military projects from the defensive military projects; and then gradually they can begin to phase out the offensive projects. To give you an idea as to how this can be done, any military action, which is not designed to protect the USA, should be eliminated. Of course this rule will not be 100% accurate, but it gives you a basic idea. You should also know that all of the US military bases in Europe, England, Japan, Korea, and the Middle East must be closed now. If any of these bases remain open, then America will be forced to fight in the ground war in Europe. We will lose 25 million American troops, and we will be involved in a global nuclear war against the Antichrist.

This is why the Church Committee Group has to work on the House and Senate Armed Services Committees and subcommittees. I would think that a period of one year could be devoted to the on-the-job training project for the Church Committee Group members who will work on the Armed Services Committees and subcommittees. I have no idea now as to the numbers of people who work on the subcommittees, but they can also work with the members of the Church Committee Group, and they can learn through on-the-job training too.

To go back to the language in the Jurisdiction of the Senate Armed Services Committee, I will explain what programs can be eliminated.

"Aeronautical and space activities primarily associated with the development of weapons systems or military operations."[347]

This project can be stopped. I think that it includes the Star Wars defense or SDI.

I cannot overstate the importance of eliminating the SDI. This should be one of the goals of the Church Committee Group; and then they can work with the Pentagon to build the Foolproof National Defense according to the plan that I wrote in my Nuclear War chapter. This will be an ABM defense that can be built on US ships and submarines. Since it will be a mobile defense, it cannot be targeted by the ICBM's in the Soviet Union.

The next project to be eliminated is:

"Military research and development."[348]

The projects associated with research are conducted at the Los Alamos and the Livermore labs in New Mexico and in California. If these projects are allowed to continue, the Pentagon will try to tell the laboratories to develop special weapons to enable them to kill the Antichrist in Germany. This will include the USA in a global nuclear war; and in Daniel 11:37-45 the Antichrist will still be living at the end of World War III.

The next project to be eliminated is:

"The overseas education of civilian and military dependents."[349]This will no longer be needed because the US military bases in Europe, England, Japan, Korea, and in the Middle East will be closed. As soon as the bases are closed, this project can be stopped.

The next project to be cancelled is:

"The selective service system."[350]

This must be eliminated to make it impossible for the President and the Pentagon to involve America in the ground war in Europe. The reason for this is written here:

Revelation 9:16: "And the number of the army of the horsemen were two hundred thousand thousand: and I heard the number of them."

The army of the Antichrist will have 200 million soldiers at the end of World War III, and they will invade the USA if the US military fights against them in Europe. You should also know that this army will have 100 million troops at the beginning of World War III, and it will be called the Unified European Army. It is also described in this verse:

Revelation 13:4: "And they worshiped the dragon which gave power unto the beast: and they worshiped the beast, saying, Who is like unto the beast? who is able to make war with him?"

The beast is the kingdom of the Antichrist, and no army on earth can defeat its army, as described here. The instructions for the USA in relation to World War III are:

Revelation 13:10: "He that leadeth into captivity shall go into captivity: he that killeth with the sword must be killed with the sword. Here is the patience and the faith of the saints."

If American troops fight in World War III, then America will be killed by the sword, or by the army of the Antichrist. The next project to be eliminated is:

"The strategic and critical materials necessary for the common defense."[351]

Of course this refers to uranium, plutonium, nuclear warheads, and chemical and biological weapons. I think this is the reason for the veiled language in this last phrase. The number one priority in all of the projects for the Church Committee Group must be to pass the legislation that will transfer the ownership of the strategic and critical materials back to the American people whose taxes paid for it. Of course the Church Committee Group will be the group representing the American people, and therefore the ownership of these materials will go to them.

After this is done, the Church Committee Group can work with the United Nations Organization, which can try to arrange a worldwide effort to destroy 95% of the nuclear warheads, and all of the chemical and biological weapons. It is extremely important to realize that all of these weapons owned by the USSR will be used against the people in Europe in World War III to force them to accept the swastika. This includes the hundreds of tons of chemical and biological weapons in Soviet Russia today. The Church Committee Group should tell the United Nations Organization about this right away.

The other committees in the Congress that will need Church Committee Group members in a supervisory role, and in voting capacity are, in the Senate:

Senate	Church Committee Group:
30 - Senate Appropriations Committee	40 members
20 - Senate Foreign Relations Committee	30 members
23 - Senate Intelligence Committee	33 members
18 - Senate Armed Services Committee	28 members

The Senate Armed Services Committee and the Armed Services subcommittees must be completely overruled after one year of on-the-job training. While the training is in progress, the number of Church Committee Group members on the Senate Armed Services Committee and on the subcommittees must exceed the number of Congressional members on them by at least ten (except in the case of very small subcommittees, where it can be five), and all of the Church Committee Group members on all of the committees will be allowed to vote on every bill and on every project. This will apply to every committee that is relevant to World War III and the American people.

In the House of Representatives:	Church Committee Group:
60 - Appropriations Committee	70 members
46 - International Relations Committee	56 members
56 - National Security	66 members
? - Armed Services Committee	?

As you can see, these committees will have 10 more Church Committee members than the number of Congressional members already on them. The House Armed Services Committee and the Armed Services subcommittees must be overruled after one year of on-the-job training. While the training is in progress, the number of Church Committee Group members on the House Armed Services Committee and on the subcommittees must exceed the number of Congressional members on them by 10. All of the Church Committee Group members will be allowed to vote on every bill, and on every project.

On page 32 of, *Lawmaking and the Legislative Process*, © 1996, it says how the process of writing and passing a bill in the legislature works.[352] The Church Committee Group will have to learn all of the basics involved in this process. After the Church Committee Group is formed by selecting part time or retired church ministers, which can be done by contacting some of the church associations, then a class can begin in which a teacher can instruct them how the legislative process works in the Congress. The teacher can be found by talking to some of the legislative staff people who work in the Congress. Either one of them can do the part time teaching, or they can direct you to someone who will.

On page 34 it says the Speaker of the House and the majority leader in the Senate are very powerful positions.[353] It also says the committee chairmen are powerful. Further down on page 34 it says that the money committees are the most influential in the Congress.[354] On pages 36 and 37 of the book, *Lawmaking and the Legislative Process*, © 1996, it describes eight examples of how bills originated as ideas and were then introduced in the legislature.[355] Although this book is on state legislatures, it is very similar to the Congress. I will recommend to the Church Committee members that they study this book and others on the legislature. On page 39 there is a generalized description of how an idea becomes a law.[356] On pages 42 and 43 there are more descriptions of the 8 examples of prospective bills.[357] Here is a quote from page 45:

"On paper, the lawmaking process is simple: Introduction of a bill, committee consideration, floor action by both chambers of the legislature, final passage, and the President's signature or veto. In practice, it is not so simple. The power structure—the leadership and the personalities of the individual members—plays a major role. An understanding of how legislatures really work is essential for anyone who wants to make a difference."[358]

This is why the Church Committee Group must attend the class on legislative knowledge. Again on page 45:

"The process begins with an idea that is drafted into a bill. Theoretically, anyone may write a bill. Writing proposed legislation, however, requires specialized legal knowledge. That is why most bills are written by the legislature's staff attorneys who are experienced drafters. Bills drafted by anyone outside the legislature must be reviewed by the legislature's legal staff to ensure that they are in the correct form for bills."[359]

The Church Committee Group will have to hire their own legislative staff people to help them learn the process, and to help them write bills for the legislature. Then on page 45 it says:

"The next step in the process is the actual introduction of a bill. Bills can be introduced only by members of the legislature—not by private citizens, or lobbyists, or even the President. Anyone other than a member who wants a bill introduced must persuade a legislator to sponsor it."[360]

Although the Church Committee Group will not have the power to introduce bills in the Congress at first, they should be given the power as they gradually learn their positions through the on-the-job training. On page 18 of the book, Congress A to Z, © 2003 by the Congressional Quarterly Inc., there is a description of how the work of appropriating money works in the Congress.

"One of the Congress's most important duties each year is to pass bills appropriating money to operate government agencies and programs."

"Appropriations bills provide legal authority to spend money previously approved in Authorization bills, but they need not provide all of the money authorized."[361]

On page 27 is the quote:

"Authorization bills create legal authority for new programs."

"Authorization bills do not themselves provide money; that requires separate action through the appropriations process. Congressional rules state that programs must be authorized before money can be appropriated for them..."[362]

Back on page 18 it says:

"Each year Congress must pass 13 regular appropriations bills."

"Each of the 13 regular appropriations bills covers one governmental function, such as defense, or more than one function..."[363]

Since the Church Committee Group will eventually work with the House and Senate Appropriations Committees, they should learn as much as possible about the appropriations process. On page 19:

"The House Appropriations Committee is the largest standing committee in the Congress, and one of the most powerful. Its members play a crucial role in the annual process by which Congress determines funding levels for government agencies and programs."

"By custom, all spending bills begin in the House of Representatives."

"The full Appropriations Committee looks to its subcommittees to make most of the important decisions. The recommendations of the subcommittees—one for each of the customary 13 annual spending bills—are generally accepted by the full committee without substantial change."

"The real work of the Appropriations Committee is done in the subcommittees. Subcommittee members each year listen to many hours of testimony from government officials, who come to explain the dollar amounts requested for their agencies in the Federal government's budget as prepared by the President."[364]

In the case of the House and Senate Appropriations Committees, the Church Committee Group must have its members on all of the subcommittees that work on appropriations, and they should have a majority of members, plus 5, on each subcommittee. On page 20 is the quote:

"Service on the Appropriations Committee continues to be one of the most sought-after positions for House members."

"The Appropriations Committee does not have the power to prepare legislation which establishes government programs. Instead, members have the opportunity to steer funds to activities that are important to them or their constituents."[365]

One of the key roles of the Church Committee Group will be to steer funds to World War III projects which will benefit the American people. To learn how much money is needed for what projects, the Church Committee members on the House and Senate Appropriations Committees must refer to the chapter about the Church Committee Plan, and then look at the Funding list. I think the total funding each year for the Church Committee Plan will be $434 billion dollars.

There is a description of the activities of the House Armed Services Committee on page 23 of the book, Congress A to Z, © 2003 by the Congressional Quarterly Incorporated;[366] and there is a description of the activities of the Senate Armed Services Committee on page 25.[367] The Church Committee Group members who are assigned to these committees will have to do a lot of studying to learn everything they need to know.

The same is true for the Church Committee Group members who serve on the House and Senate Intelligence Committees, since they will have to know about any illegal actions by the CIA, FBI, NSA, or any other intelligence agencies that work for the United States Government. There are descriptions of the activities of these committees in the book, Congress A to Z.[368]

On page 540 of the book titled, Congressional Quarterly's Guide to Congress, © 2000, there is a list of the Standing Committees in the House and the Senate, and a list of the dates when they were established.[369] It will be a good idea to learn the history of the Congress too because it proves that the House and the Senate have made changes in their structure and their procedures in the past, in order to better serve the American people. Here is a quote from page 539 of the book, Congressional Quarterly's Guide to Congress:

"But as the nation grew and took on more complex responsibilities and problems, Congress had to develop expertise and the mechanisms to deal with the changing world. And so, from a somewhat haphazard arrangement of ad hoc committees evolved a highly specialized system of permanent committees."[370]

The Congress will have to adapt to the changes described in this chapter to be sure that America can survive World War III. If the elected members try to ridicule the members of the Church Committee Group who are assigned to work there, then it will be obvious to all of the American people that the Congress does not want the USA to survive the war. This will eventually lead to rioting and looting in every major city in America from the West to the East coast, and I am sure that Washington DC will be the first city to suffer from it. On page 535 of the book, Congressional Quarterly's Guide to Congress, there is a description of the shape of power in the Congress.[371]

The Church Committee Group members should learn this inside out, since the members of Congress will probably try to put roadblocks in your way, while you are trying to save the USA. I know that Bill Clinton and Hillary Clinton tried to steal my books, and when I went to Washington DC to testify in his impeachment trial, the House Judiciary Committee would not give me an appointment. This was planned by the Congress, since I had been writing letters to them for five years; and I had written letters to the House Judiciary Committee for two years.

One good way to overcome the roadblocks will be to hire very good Congressional staff people. I know this will be expensive, but I will ask all of the Christian Churches in America to contribute money to the Church Committee. Here is a quote from page 581 of the book, Congressional Quarterly's Guide to Congress:

"The influence of congressional staff is vast."[372]

Then it says that critics complain that the staff exercises too much power and costs too much money. Then here is the next quote:

"Legislators need staff to provide the expertise that one person alone simply could not master."[373]

The Christian Churches in America can set a good example for everyone by contributing a little money each to the Church Committee Group's 1-800 telephone number. Then the Church Committee Group can use the money to begin their studies of the legislative system of the Congress. On page 581 it says:

"There are nearly 20,000 aides who work directly for Congress."[374]

They can help the Church Committee Group members.

ARMED SERVICES COMMITTEES

The people in the Church Committee Group who take the places of the people on the House and Senate Armed Services Committees can learn how to perform their duties by means of on-the-job training. They can work with people in the House and Senate who can teach them what to do. This is how the newly elected Representatives and Senators learn how to do their job, and the Church Committee members can do it too.

When the Church Committee members replace the people on the Armed Services Committees, they will have to replace them on the other committees where these people also worked. They can learn through on-the-job training there as well.

One of the new responsibilities for the Church Committee Group will be to convince the Pentagon to build an ABM defense to protect America from nuclear missiles fired by the Antichrist during World War III. I described this in the pages, A Foolproof National Defense. The Church Committee Group will have to fund this project, but they must encourage the Pentagon to build it. The Church Committee Group can also ask the manufacturing companies that make chemical and biological warfare gas masks to make 250 million of them for the American people.

One of the first things that the Church Committee Group will notice is that the Pentagon claims to be performing jobs that they are not really doing. They claim to be protecting America from nuclear missile attack, while they do not have an ABM defense. They claim to be doing research on the defensive aspects of chemical and biological warfare agents, while they have not issued any gas masks to the American people. They claim to be preparing for a war like World War III, while they have not built any food warehouses or grain silos.

The Pentagon also claims to be spending $400 billion a year protecting the USA, when they are really spending about $300 billion dollars per year in the defense of Western Europe, the Middle East, Korea, Japan, and other nations. This means that they are spending less than $100 billion per year protecting the USA. The Church Committee Group will be the deciding factor in changing these things, and they will serve the American people who pay the taxes to the United States Government.

IMPLEMENTATION OF THE CHURCH COMMITTEE PLAN

I've thought of a very fast way to implement the Church Committee Plan, which will cause the least problems for the US Government. The Congress has to voluntarily elect 300 to 500 church ministers, who will replace the hawks in the Senate and the House of Representatives; and they must appropriate $434 billion per year to give to the Church Committee Group. I look at it this way: If I can save $324 billion per year by postponing the payment of interest on the National Debt, then the Congress should give $434 billion per year to the Church Committee Group.

By implementing the plan this way, the Congress will avoid having four or five million people march on Washington DC to force the United States Government to make a decision. You see, this will cause rioting, and it could be very dangerous.

When the American people read this book, then they will wait to see what the Congress is going to do. The longer the delay in making a decision, the more angry the people will be. This is why I have done so much work on these problems to make it easier for the United States Government to prepare for World War III by providing housing, food, gas masks, natural gas fuel conversion for the vehicles, and other things for the people.

It is possible for the United States Government to remain neutral throughout World War III, and by doing this they will be able to take care of their own people, instead of fighting for someone else in Europe. This is what the Church Committee Plan does, and I hope that the Congress will support the Plan 100%. In fact the Congress can play a major part in getting the President and the Pentagon to conform to the Church Committee Plan.

If the Church Committee Plan is not adopted by the Congress, then the US Pentagon will become involved in World War III in Europe. They will either cause a nuclear war against the Antichrist, or they will send 25 million American troops to fight in Europe, along with their vehicles and weapons. The cost for this will be $1 trillion per year. Those are the only two choices for the Pentagon. This will leave no money for the needs of the American people during World War III, and there will be 100 million homeless and starving people in the USA. Since World War III will last 11 years, these people will be homeless for about ten years.

In Proverbs 10:21 the lips of the righteous feed many people. This is why I have developed the Church Committee Plan. In Proverbs 12:11 if the people follow the Pentagon, then they are void of understanding. This is also written in Proverbs 28:19, where the people who follow after vain persons shall have poverty enough. The key verse here is:

Proverbs 13:23: "Much food is in the tillage of the poor; but there is that which is destroyed for want of judgment."

The phrase, "Much food is in the tillage of the poor," means that much food must be put into storage to survive in times of famine. All of the nations will have to do this to survive World War III. Then the phrase, "but there is that which is destroyed for want of judgment," means that the food will not be put into storage at all, if the American people allow the Pentagon to continue to spend $400 billion dollars per year on the United States military. This will lead to the spending of $1 trillion per year during World War III.

In Proverbs 29:7 the righteous consider the cause of the poor, but the wicked do not care. The American people must regain control of their money now by telling the Congress to adopt the Church Committee Plan. The quicker this is done, the more food and housing there will be for the American people throughout World War III.

This plan will take $434 billion from the Congress, and give it to the Church Committee Group. If the Congress will not do this, then the American people should have a National Emergency Vote as soon as possible to establish the Church Committee Group. This group should have the power to freeze $434 billion in the Congress, and then take the money to help the people prepare for World War III. Since the national emergency is World War III, the Church Committee must have the authority to take the money from Congress.

The Church Committee Group must take the offensive military power away from the Pentagon, or they will start a nuclear war against the Antichrist in Europe.

As soon as they are established, the Church Committee Group will write these ballots for a vote:

1. Freeze $434 billion dollars in the Congress to use for World War III.
2. Take the offensive military power from the Pentagon, and give it to the Church Committee Group. The Pentagon will keep their defensive

military power, and they will provide national defense during World War III.

3. Take the offensive military power from the President, and give it to the Church Committee Group.
4. Take the power to declare war from the Congress. The President and the Congress must have the approval of the Church Committee Group to use these powers.
5. Take the power to launch nuclear missiles from the President.
6. The Church Committee Group must have the power to shut down all US mainland nuclear missile silos.
7. The Church Committee Group must take the ownership of America's nuclear missiles, which were paid for with the taxes of the American people, and then they should work with the Soviet Union, the United Nations Organization, and other nations to dismantle as many nuclear weapons as possible, before the Antichrist gains power in Europe.
8. The Church Committee Group must take the ownership of the chemical and biological warfare agents from the Pentagon, and then they should work with the other nations in the world to destroy as much of these as possible before World War III starts.

The nuclear warheads on all US nuclear submarines will remain in operation as a precautionary measure to prevent a first-strike nuclear attack. The US Government will be exactly the same as it was before, so the American people will not have to worry about anarchy. The main focus of change will be in the war powers of the US Government. Here are some more notes:

1. The Pentagon will still take care of national defense.
2. The House and Senate Armed Services Committees will have to allow members of the Church Committee Group to sit in on their meetings, so they can learn what to do through on-the-job training.
3. The money allocated in the budget for the Pentagon cannot exceed $80 billion per year. If the Pentagon has $400 billion per year during World War III, they will cause a war against the Antichrist, and America will be involved in a global nuclear war.
4. Since the Congress will never take the $320 billion per year away from the Pentagon, some of the Church Committee Group members will have to sit in on the House and Senate Appropriations Committee meetings, as well as the appropriations subcommittee meetings, in order to learn what to do there, and how to take money to fund their projects.

5. The Defense industry corporations which make weapons of war can now help the American people prepare for World War III by making these products: anti-ballistic missile defense systems, gas masks, Geiger counters, food warehouses, grain silos, and travel trailers.

Here is a list of the departments in the US Government that can give money to the Church Committee Group, their budgets for the year 2003, and the amounts of money they can give to the Church Committee Plan:

Fiscal Year 2003:	Amount to be Given:
Department of Defense:	$267 billion
Military: $408 billion	
Civilian: $40 billion	
National Aeronautics and Space Administration:	$14 billion
$14.8 billion	
Department of the Treasury: $324 billion	
Internal Revenue Service: $47 billion	
Interest on the National Debt:	$324 billion
TOTAL FUNDING:	$591 billion[375]

The Department of the Treasury will not have to pay the interest on the National Debt for the next 25 years because of World War III and the national preparations for it. Therefore they can give $324 billion per year (which is the interest as of 2003) to the Church Committee Plan.

With this plan, the American people can prepare for World War III, the famines caused by it, the homelessness problems, and the nuclear wars. The US Government will serve them instead of science and technology; and the Pentagon will not have enough money to start a nuclear war against the Antichrist. If the strength of your national defense is the evil of nuclear war, then how will your nation be delivered from Satan during World War III? The Church Committee Plan must be used so the government will have to rely on Christ and the Bible, and then the USA will be able to win the victory over Satan.

The US Government and the Church Committee Group will have to move 32 million people from England, Scotland, and Israel to the USA as soon as possible. They should clear this through the US Immigration Service after my books about World War III are published. Most of the people who move to the USA can live in RV parks in Arizona, California, New Mexico, Oregon, Nevada, and Texas. The details about these parks are written in the chapter titled, The World War III RV Park Project, in my book titled, World War III: The People.

The Church Committee Group will have to post their travel trailer telephone numbers with the British, the Scottish, and the Israeli governments. In other words, they can help these governments give the travel trailers to the people who move here from these countries, after they make a large down payment for them. If only 20 million people move to the USA from these nations, then the extra RV park spaces can be used by the American people during World War III. Here is a list of the projects that will be required to prepare America for World War III, and the funding needed for each one:

Natural Gas wells	$5 billion per year
Natural Gas pipelines	$4 billion per year
Natural Gas refill stations	$10 billion per year
Grain Silos	$10 billion per year
Food Warehouses	$40 billion per year
Food for storage	$64 billion per year
Travel Trailers	$156 billion per year
Recreational Vehicle Parks	$40 billion per year
ABM Missile defense	$30 billion per year
Steel buildings	$10 billion per year
Biological agent test kits	$2 billion per year
Chemical agent test kits	$2 billion per year
Gas masks	$5 billion per year
Ozonization plants	$14 billion per year
Water tanks	$2 billion per year
Welder's goggles	$1 billion (one time cost)
Geiger counters	$4 billion (one time cost)
Move Israel to the USA	$35 billion (one time cost)
TOTAL EXPENDITURES:	$434 billion dollars

Since the total funding for the Church Committee Plan is $591 billion, and the total amount for expenditures is $434 billion, there will be a surplus of $157 billion per year. This money should be used for anti-ballistic missile defense first, and then for any other project on the list which may require additional funding.

Of the other projects, first priority should be given to the construction of at least 50,000 natural gas refill stations in the USA, at 1000 per state. The President should do this immediately, even before the Church Committee Plan is in effect. He can call for an evaluation of the natural gas wells and pipelines to see if any additional construction may be needed in that area.

The President can order a 20% increase of farmland in America before World War III starts to provide more food for storage. Then there should be major construction projects on food warehouses and grain silos. The Church Committee Group must have authority in these plans because the US Government will cause delays.

The USA will need 13 million travel trailers per year at $12,000 dollars each, and the cost will be $156 billion dollars per year. These can be stored on US military bases, and they should be scattered throughout the USA, so they will not be destroyed in a nuclear attack. The best way to do this would be to store them on US military bases that have been closed; and then the US military should provide soldiers to protect them. These men will work in shifts of eight hours each, for 24 hours every day, and they will have to bring weapons to protect the travel trailers. The weapons will have to be sufficient to perform the task, which means that they may have to have laws rockets, automatic rifles, and maybe even a US Army tank.

The Church Committee Group can order the construction of five million grain silos, and 20 million food warehouses per year. They can also pay subsidies to the farmers for a 20% increase in farmland through the Department of Agriculture. Before this is done however, you will have to build the food warehouses and the grain silos.

With a project of this magnitude, where you have to store enough food for 270 million people for a seven-year famine, you would have to build 20 million food warehouses, and five million grain silos each year for seven years. The total would be 140 million food warehouses, and 35 million grain silos. These calculations take into account the problems with food storage, such as rodents, insects, mold, mildew; and other problems such as theft, or rioting, which may destroy the buildings and the food. Therefore you can see that my calculations are correct in terms of the buildings needed for the food storage (I made sure that enough of them would be built, plus 20% in excess).

While doing the calculations for the cost of the food warehouses, I noticed that it would cost about $2 Trillion each year for the construction costs alone for 20 million food warehouses per year; and this assumes that the cost of each one will be $100,000 dollars. With this in mind, I came to the conclusion that land and buildings will have to be donated for the project, both by individuals and by corporations. Another good idea would be to use the buildings on US military bases in America that have been closed. As long as the dry food is stored in 55-gallon sealed plastic barrels, I would think that it could be stored there. In fact this is why I thought of this method to start with to save money by using older buildings to store the food in. If the plastic barrels are made thick enough, then no rodents, insects, or moisture will get into them.

I think it would be cheaper to build the grain silos than the food warehouses, but the manner of storage and the vertical pressure from the 55-gallon plastic containers will cause problems. The Church Committee Group, the US Government, and the World War III Food Preparedness Agency can hire engineers and food storage experts to figure out how the 55-gallon plastic barrels can be stored in the grain silos.

The corporations in America can be of great help in building the food warehouses and the grain silos by contributing buildings and money for the project. For these reasons, there should be foundations set up in every state to collect money for the World War III food project. They can use 1-800 telephone numbers to collect the money; and they can coordinate their efforts with those of the World War III Food Preparedness Agency.

If anyone has any ideas about the storage of food for World War III, they can either call the Church Committee Group, or the World War III Food Preparedness Agency. I am hoping at this time that the Congress will help establish the Church Committee Group in Washington DC, so that they can begin working on these projects. I have provided all of the logistics free of charge for the Congress, the President, the CIA, the FBI, and the Pentagon; and all they have to do to save the American people is to follow these instructions.

To move the people of Israel to the USA, there will be 1.4 million travel trailers at $12,000 each, which is $16.8 billion. Then 1.4 million RV park spaces can be built for $2000 each, which is $2.8 billion. The total cost is $19.6 billion, and this is a one-time cost. Some of the land can be donated by the US Government, or by the States, and they should contact the Church Committee Group to do this. The project to move Israel should begin as soon as possible, so they can move before World War III starts.

To prevent a nuclear war in Europe, the people in England and in Scotland must move to the USA. The British and the Scottish governments can make a down payment of $50 billion now, since this will start the construction of the RV parks for them. They will have to pay for 15 million travel trailers at $12,000 each, which is $180 billion; and they will pay for 15 million RV park spaces at $2000 each, which is $30 billion. The total amount needed to move 30 million people from England and Scotland to America would be $210 billion.

The Church Committee Group can build 80 million RV park spaces for the American people who become homeless during World War III. To do this, they should follow the instructions in the chapter titled, The World War III RV Park Project. The construction cost will be $160 billion at $2000 per RV space; and the Church Committee Group will have to set up telephone numbers to collect money to pay for the land. Then they can buy land for the

RV parks. The Church Committee Group can use advertising to collect money for the land. They can do this by setting up 1-800 telephone numbers, and they can use a title, like the World War III RV Park Land Project. They can also ask the US Government, the States, and corporations to donate land for the RV parks, as well as money for the RV park construction. Therefore when the people and corporations contribute money for this, it will be used for the American people.

To fund the Church Committee Plan you need $434 billion; and since there is a total amount of $591 billion per year, there will be a surplus of $157 billion per year. There are other surpluses as extra funds, since $40 billion in the first year is for one time cost payments. You should refer to the Funding list to see what these items are. The most important use for these extra funds will be for the construction of anti-ballistic missile defense for the USA, since the Antichrist will be in control of the nuclear weapons of the Soviet Union, France, and Italy within six years; and he will start World War III within that time as well.

Now I will make a list of the projects in order of importance:

1. Anti-ballistic missile defense
2. Natural gas refill stations
3. Food warehouses
4. Grain silos
5. RV park construction
6. Gas masks
7. Construction of natural gas wells
8. Construction of natural gas pipelines
9. The annual order of 13 million travel trailers
10. Food for storage
11. Place the orders for welder's goggles, and Geiger counters
12. Construction of ozonization plants

It is important to know the order of importance of these projects because it may take five years to build an anti-ballistic missile defense for America; and this is why it must begin right away. The USA will be paralyzed during World War III, if there aren't enough natural gas refill stations. This could also happen if the President fails to issue a federal order to convert to natural gas fuel for the automobile, truck, tractor, and farm vehicle manufacturers. This is why it is second on the list of importance.

There is $40 billion allocated for the construction of food warehouses per year, and $10 billion for grain silos. These can be built on the US military bases in the USA, which have already been closed, and the US military can provide soldiers to protect them. They will work in 8-hour shifts to protect these buildings 24 hours per day, and they will be armed with weapons suitable for the task. They will have automatic rifles, laws rockets, and US Army tanks.

The US Government can issue a federal mandate to increase the farmland in the USA by 20% before World War III starts (This can be done only when the food warehouses and grain silos are built, so there will be a place to store the food). In the case of farm subsidies, they should be paid only for food crops which can be stored up as dry food: For example, dry beans, rice, wheat, dry macaroni, dry pasta, dry peas, and other foods which can be stored for at least 10 years. This food will be stored in 55-gallon plastic barrels in the food warehouses. This food will all be put into storage to prepare for the World War III Stock Market crash in the first or second year of the war, and the famine that will occur with it. Grain silos can be used to store food too.

NATIONAL EMERGENCY VOTE

When the American people know that World War III will start soon, and when the Congress does nothing to help them prepare for it, they can use this plan to take control of their own money, and their government. There can be a National Emergency Vote to elect the Church Committee Group, which can help the people prepare for the war. This can be done on January 1, 2007 if the Congress hasn't done anything by then. By using this plan, the American people will be provided with travel trailers for mobile housing, RV parks to move them to in case of nuclear attack; and they will be provided with gas masks, welder's goggles, Geiger counters; they will have dry food stored in grain silos, and in food warehouses, and they will have all of the things they will need to survive World War III.

The Church Committee Group will work in the Congress to make sure that America remains neutral throughout World War III; and they will prevent the nine nuclear wars that the Pentagon will otherwise be involved in. The President, the Congress, and the Pentagon will have to get the permission of the Church Committee Group to take any type of offensive military action during the war. They will not be able to threaten the Antichrist with nuclear missiles because they will not have the power to launch them.

The ballots for the Church Committee Plan can be drawn up and approved by a vote of the American people after the Church Committee Plan has already been approved by the National Emergency Vote. Then the ballots can be voted on by the people on June 1, 2007.

The best reasons for using the National Emergency Vote are those involving the actions of our own federal government. President Bill Clinton and his wife blocked the publication of my books for 8 years, while trying to steal the royalties from them. When I went to testify against Bill Clinton at his impeachment trial in January 1999, The House Judiciary Committee would not give me an appointment. Henry Hyde's secretary acted as if she was afraid for her life, as if she believed that she would be killed if she were to give me an appointment.

When I asked her what I should do with my written notes, she told me to go to the House Deputy's Office, which was down the hall, and to the left. When I went there I was refused by three secretaries, none of whom would give me an appointment.

You can see therefore, that our own federal government is really forcing us to use the National Emergency Vote to save America from the Antichrist, and from World War III. This is why I devised that plan to start with. I spent the entire 8 years of Bill Clinton's two administrations writing and adding more material to my books on World War III, and this is when I wrote the pages on the National Emergency Vote. If the federal government is going to be an obstacle to the salvation of the United States, then we must use the National Emergency Vote to do it ourselves.

CHURCH COMMITTEE ELECTION

Here are some of the problems that could occur when the Church Committee Group tries to set up a national election for the Church Committee Plan:

1. You will have to get the vote set up at every state election in the USA. Most states have elections every 2 years, and this is too long to wait, since World War III is a national emergency.
2. The hawks in the Congress will not want the election to succeed, which means that they will try to use advertising to sabotage the Church Committee Plan.
3. The hawks in the Congress will put other items on the ballot, which may try to destroy the Church Committee Plan.

If the Church Committee Group tries to set up the election by using the TV news media, then the Congress will say that the results are not legally binding. Therefore it would be a good idea to ask the state legislatures to put the election on their ballots within one year after the publication of my books about World War III. In other words, the states may have the authority to set up a special election, simply because World War III is a national emergency. If this is possible, then the Church Committee Group should contact every state legislature in the USA, as soon as possible to try and convince them to hold a special election.

If the state legislatures will not do this, then the Church Committee Group should go to CNN, ABC, NBC, and CBS news, and ask them if it is possible to set up a national election by using the TV news media.

TIME SCHEDULE

Here is the basic format that the Church Committee Group should follow, when they are preparing to work in the Congress:

1. When first formed, the Church Committee Group will take classes on the Legislative process, and the working of the Congress.
2. After the National Emergency Vote has taken place, the Church Committee Group will report to the House of Representatives, and the Senate, just as if they are newly elected Congressmen. Then they will serve the first year through on-the-job training.
3. After the first year, all of the Church Committee people will be full Representatives and Senators.

The Church Committee members in the Congress will have the power to overrule the people on the Committees in the House and the Senate during their first year, but they should use that power sparingly, until their training is completed.

While the first 400 to 500 Church Committee members are in training for, or are working in the Congress, there can also be another group of 300 church members who can study the legislative process, and the working of the Congress. These people can replace any members whom become ill, or who wish to retire.

US MARSHALS

I believe that the Congressmen in the committee meetings, and in the halls of the Congress will try to harass and ridicule the Church Committee Group members to cause them to quit their jobs, simply because the power structure in the House of Representatives and the Senate is opposed to the Church Committee Plan. The hawks in the Congress will try to cause the Church

Committee Plan to fail, so they will be able to work with the Pentagon to use their nuclear missiles against the Antichrist during World War III.

For this reason, there can be US Marshals to escort the Church Committee Group members to and from their committee meetings in the Congress. They can also sit in on the meetings, and they should have the power to arrest anyone who harasses the members.

The plan to do this can be included on one of the ballots, which the American people can vote on, after the National Emergency Vote has taken place. Then it will be legal to have the US Marshals as escorts, since the American people will have approved it by voting for that plan or idea. This concept has been used before, during the racial integration plan in the southern states in the 1960s. Therefore the US Government itself has proven that it is legal to use military escorts to and from schools to protect the children; and the courts in America already use US Marshals to escort people in and out of the courtrooms. For these reasons, I believe that US Marshals should be allowed to escort the Church Committee Group members to their meetings in the Congress.

INTERNATIONAL EMERGENCY VOTE

There will be several problems in Europe that must be resolved before World War III, and I should help resolve them. Here is my idea to speed up the worldwide approval of the Church Committee Plan, which will give me more time to help in Europe. The United Nations Organization can help to implement this plan, called the "International Emergency Vote." The basic idea for it is described in the National Emergency Vote pages.

The US military has several nuclear missiles, which should be controlled by the people, so the Pentagon doesn't destroy half of the world with them. The Church Committee Plan gives the people this control, and makes it impossible for the Pentagon to start a nuclear war. The offensive military power of the Pentagon will also be limited, in order to avoid a confrontation with the Antichrist. This same thing can be done in all nations not in Europe, so there will not be total panic and military blundering everywhere in the world because this will cause a global nuclear war. Thus the International Emergency Vote will help the free nations to change their military systems to national defense only, while there is still time to prepare for World War III. By doing this, they will not be involved in any offensive warfare, and they will avoid nuclear war.

The implementation of the plan can be done at the UN Organization itself by having the ambassadors from each nation report on the votes of their people, or the votes of the national government itself (this could be done through delegates who work for the government). This will permit more nations to adopt the plan that will reduce the chances of nuclear war during World War III. Therefore the International Emergency Vote will speed up the acceptance of the Church Committee Plan, which will prevent nuclear war.

The United Nations can write a few pages to inform their member nations about this plan, and they can get ideas from the National Emergency Vote plan in this chapter. The individual nations can then choose the Church Committee members to sit in authority over the military forces in their nation by selecting from volunteer church ministers, or by letting the people elect them. The volunteer idea will be the quickest way. I would greatly appreciate the help of the UN Organization with this idea, and then I will be able to spend more time stopping the nuclear war in Europe, and solving other problems.

When the people of the world learn that World War III will start soon, and when their national governments do nothing to help them prepare for it, they can make an appeal to the UN Organization for the International Emergency Vote. This will be a vote to elect Church Committee Groups in all nations, which will have the power to freeze millions or billions of dollars, and then use the money to help their people prepare for World War III. In the case of the US Government, the Church Committee Group can freeze $434 billion in the Congress, and then take the money to pay for the projects written on the Church Committee Funding list in this book. When the Church Committee is elected, they can put ballots up for a vote by the people.

One very important detail in this plan is to have every host nation stop the immigration into its own country immediately, so the nations from Europe will have room for their people to live there. Every Church Committee Group in every nation should have the power to stop the immigration there.

THE SECOND DEATH

In Revelation 20:14 the second death is described as the Lake of Fire. I spent 5 years trying to find the verse, which tells where the Lake of Fire is located. It is described in Revelation 2:11, Revelation 14:11, Revelation 19:20, Revelation 20:10, Revelation 20:14,15, Revelation 21:8, Psalm 21:9, and Matthew 25:41. There are several verses in the book of Revelation where the sun is used for symbolism. These are, Revelation 1:16, Revelation 10:1, Revelation 12:1, and Revelation 19:17. I kept track of all of these verses for five years, until I finally found this verse:

Psalm 19:4: "Their line is gone out through all the earth, and their words to the end of the world. In them hath he set a tabernacle for the sun."

The phrase, "In them hath he set a tabernacle for the sun," means that the devils which followed Satan will actually dwell in the fires of the sun forever. The word, "tabernacle" means a dwelling place. This explains the meaning of the phrase, "everlasting fire" in Matthew 25:41. The fires of the sun will burn for 10 billion years according to scientists, and this is a good description of everlasting fire in my opinion.

Therefore the Lord God Almighty will put Satan and his devils into the Lake of Fire in Revelation 20:10; and he will put the souls of people who do not pass the judgment in the Lake of Fire as well. This is written in Revelation 20:14,15. The only way to pass the judgment is to go to church every week, read the Bible, and worship the Lord Jesus Christ. This is what it means to have your name written in the book of life in Revelation 20:15. Everyone who is not written in the book of life will be cast into the Lake of Fire, and this is why it is so important to read the Bible.

AN EMERGENCY FOR ALL MANKIND

Now since there are about four billion people on earth now, who will go to the Lake of Fire, I will use this title to help the people understand this. In John 14:6 Jesus said, "No man cometh unto the Father, but by me." This means that only the people who have faith in Christ will be saved. Therefore all of the people in other religions will have to convert to Christianity to be saved, and to go into the kingdom of heaven. The Hebrew people stumbled upon the works of the Old Testament law, so the Gentiles would be saved. This is written in Romans 9:32, and Romans 11:11. The word Gentiles here means all people who are not Jews. Therefore the Lord God has called all nations of the world to be saved by Christ.

The churches of Christ throughout the world can help to warn all of the people of the world that the Lake of Fire is the sun. This is written in Revelation 20:14,15, Psalm 19:4, Psalm 21:9, and Matthew 25:41. Everyone who does not convert to Christianity will be condemned to burn in the fires of the sun forever. In Matthew 25:41 the souls of people and the spirits of devils will burn there forever, but will not be destroyed by the fire. This is verified in Revelation 14:11. I know that no one really wants to go there, and with the help of the churches of Christ throughout the world, the people can avoid the Lake of Fire. The TV evangelists can have great crusades, but the people also have to go to church every week to be saved. This is written in Matthew 26:26-30, Mark 14:22-26, and in Luke 22:17-20.

For these reasons I will ask all nations of the world to set up 1-800 telephone numbers in all of their large cities, which can be used to collect money to build more churches. Some of the people who own large buildings can allow them to be used for church services, and the rent can be paid through the 1-800 telephone numbers. Some of the large corporations, which own vacant buildings and warehouses, can donate them to be used as churches. All nations should also know that three or four billion people will die because of World War III, famine, the fuel crisis, the stock market crash, nuclear war, nuclear winter, disease or pestilence, and earthquakes. These events are described in Matthew 24:6-8, and Revelation 8:10-12.

I have also devised a way for the people to attend church seven days a week, so that more of them can be saved with the churches that exist now. The system works in alphabetical order like this:

ABCD —- Sunday		QRST —- Thursday
EFGH —- Monday		UVW —- Friday
IJKL —- Tuesday		XYZ —- Saturday
MNOP — Wednesday		

The people whose names begin with ABCD will go to church on Sunday. Those with names beginning with EFGH will go on Monday, IJKL will go on Tuesday, etc. The church ministers will be responsible for using this system, and for instructing the people on how to use it, when the churches become overloaded with large numbers of new people. The ministers can also have church services 4 times each day, at 10AM, 1PM, 4PM, and 7PM. I hope that all of the people of the world will go to the churches of Christ every week, and that they will all be saved by the Lord Jesus Christ. This is the only way for billions of people to avoid going to the Lake of Fire.

I will also include the prophecy about the second death with this letter, so that you will know that the second death in Revelation 20:14,15 is the Lake of Fire. Then in Psalm 19:4, Psalm 21:9, and Matthew 25:41 the Lake of Fire is the sun. I also wrote about this in The Second Death chapter.

I have found a way to save all of the people of the world who have other religions than Christianity. As with Judaism being the religion of the Old Testament, and Christianity the religion of the New Testament, the Jewish Rabbis can invite Christian Ministers to preach the gospel of Christ in their synagogues. Christ himself preached in the synagogues in Luke 4:14-20. This can also be done with other religions, such as Animism, Buddhism, Islam, Hinduism, etc.

The Priests in the temples of these religions can invite Christian Ministers to preach the gospel of Christ to their people, so that they will be saved by

Christ. This way the Priests will still get paid, they will still be important to their people, and they will be instrumental in saving them. The Christian Ministers will preach every Sunday morning, and every Wednesday and Saturday evening. Then Christianity will replace Judaism in the synagogues, and it can also replace the other religions to help save the people for Christ. This can be done gradually throughout each nation, in the same temples where the people normally go to pray.

All of the people of the world are trying to worship God, but it is Christianity that is the true way to do this. This is written in John 14:6, and in John 4:23,24. In I John 5:20 the Father of our Lord Jesus Christ is the true God and eternal life.

If the Priests in the other religions do not invite Christian Ministers to preach in their temples, then their people will find out that the Lake of Fire is the sun, and they will begin to go to the churches of Christ in their nations. Then the Priests in the temples of these other religions will be deserted by their people, and they will lose their income and their status. Therefore I think that it will be better to tell the truth from the beginning, and to try to save the people by using this plan. Then you can see that I am looking out for the best interests of the hierarchy in the other religions, as well as the best interests of their people. And the best part of this plan is that the people can be saved by the Lord Jesus Christ, and they will avoid the second death in Revelation 20:14,15, which is the Lake of Fire, or the sun.

FAMINES

There will be four kinds of famines during World War III, and I will describe them here:

1. The famine of the Antichrist in Europe. This is described in Revelation 6:5,6, Revelation 6:8, and in Revelation 13:16,17. The Antichrist will use the Unified European Army to starve the 800 million people to death in Europe to force them to receive the mark of the beast, which will be the swastika.

2. Famines in several nations caused when the Antichrist takes the world oil supply in the Middle East. This is described in Daniel 11:23-25.

3. There will be over 200 famines during World War III, one in every nation in the world, which will be caused by high unemployment, and by the failure of the economies in every nation. This is described in Matthew 24:7-12, Mark 13:8, and in Luke 21:11.

4. Famines caused by droughts. These famines will be caused by curses on the nations of the world that do not worship Christ in church during World

War III. This is described in Leviticus 26:18-20, and in Deuteronomy 28:23,24.

Now I will explain the ways that you and your nation can avoid these famines:

1. The only way to avoid the famine of the Antichrist is to evacuate Europe. In Revelation 13:5 the Antichrist will take 42 months to force everyone in Europe to receive the swastika, and he will use the famine to do it with. In Revelation 14:11 every person who receives the swastika will burn in the Lake of Fire forever. In Revelation 20:14, Psalm 19:4, Psalm 21:9, and Matthew 25:41 the Lake of Fire is the sun.

2. Your nation can avoid the famines caused by lack of fuel by converting your tractors, harvesters, and your trucks to natural gas fuel.Every nation of the world should begin this conversion of fuel now by building hundreds or thousands of natural gas refill stations throughout your nation.

3. The way to avoid the famines caused by the failure of each nation's economy is to store vast quantities of dry food in grain silos, and in food warehouses. All of the nations not in Europe or the Middle East will have to do this right away, and they should find ways to rotate the food in and out of the warehouses by using the food before it spoils.

4. The famines caused by droughts can be avoided by having all of the farmers and all of the people in every nation go to church right away to give glory and honor to the Lord Jesus Christ. In Leviticus 26:18-20, and in Deuteronomy 28:23,24 droughts are curses, which are intended to make the people repent of their sins. This is verified in Amos 4:7-9, Haggai 1:5-11, and in Haggai 2:15-19.

Since there will be over 200 famines during World War III, which will be caused by the failure of the economies in every nation of the world, the last thing that you want to do is to complicate this with famines caused by droughts. Since World War III will last 11 years, your people should begin to worship Christ in church now, so that your nation will not be included in the war. In II Chronicles 16:9 the nations that do not worship the Lord God Almighty will have wars. Here is wisdom: Tell all of the people in your nation to worship Christ in church throughout World War III, so you will not be included in the war.

THE WORLD WAR III FOOD PREPAREDNESS AGENCY

It will be absolutely necessary for every nation in the world to establish their own World War III Food Preparedness Agency, so their people will not starve to death during the war. To help them do this, I will describe the two types of food distribution plans. From the beginning to the end of World War III there will be homeless and starving people because of the 50% unemployment rates. These people will call on the government in their own nation to ask for food during the war. Therefore the political leaders in every nation must be prepared; and they must build food warehouses to store dry food in 55-gallon sealed plastic barrels in. The food can consist of dry food in plastic packages, such as dry beans, dry macaroni, rice, dry pasta, dry peas, and other dry foods.

The other type of food storage plan is the one needed to prepare for the nuclear winter, which will occur at the end of World War III. It is described in the Nuclear Winter chapter. In the seventh to the tenth years of World War III, every nation can build freezer warehouse buildings to store large quantities of freezer beef, pork, turkeys, chickens, and other meats. Then in the ninth and tenth years of World War III, the nations can slaughter, cut, wrap, and freeze the meat for storage. The freezer warehouses will have to have electric generators to use in emergency situations, in case the supply of electricity is stopped because of nuclear war.

The United Nations Organization can help convince the nations not in Europe or the Middle East to start their own World War III Food Preparedness Agency. They can work with the FDA, the USDA, and food production companies to find out what kind of dry foods will last 10 years in storage. Then the 55-gallon plastic barrels can have the expiration dates stamped on the top and sides, and the oldest ones will be used first.

FEDERAL ORDER TO CONVERT TO NATURAL GAS FUEL

Here are the steps needed to convert to natural gas:

1. Train people or construction companies to build the refill stations.

2. Build the natural gas refill stations.

3. Train mechanics to convert cars, trucks, buses, and farm tractors for the individual people.

4. Convert the cars, trucks, buses, and farm tractors for the people.

5. The new car, truck, bus, and farm tractor companies must train mechanics and engineers to convert their new vehicles, when the refill stations are built. This is why it is so important to have a federal order to convert to natural gas. Another reason is that the national defense, national peace, the food supply, national employment, fire control, and police departments all depend on the natural gas conversion plan. This is true for all

nations, which are not in Europe or the Middle East. They should convert if there is an available supply of natural gas in their nation or close to it.

The last two steps in this project will be paid for by private consumers because they will pay for the conversions on new cars, and on their own vehicles. Therefore the new car, truck, bus, and farm tractor companies can produce 100% dual fuel vehicles (Gasoline and natural gas, or diesel and natural gas) by 2010. They can do this without any lost revenue because the cost will be paid by the consumer. These companies should make the new vehicles with a toggle switch on the dash to allow the driver to select from two types of fuel.

The Federal Government should advise the consumers that petroleum fuel will not be available during World War III. This is why they should make every effort to buy a new dual fuel vehicle as soon as they can. The new car and truck manufacturers can help minimize the paralysis of their nation by flooding the market with these new vehicles. The trucking industry must be supervised by the federal government because the food supply is vital to the nation. The farm tractors are important for food production and harvest.

There could be a federal task force organized to find out how many wells, pipelines, and refill stations will be needed to fuel the entire USA for 14 years; and they must find out how much natural gas is in reserve in America, and whether it will last through World War III.

1. The task force can have new natural gas wells drilled. They should be very well defended and camouflaged, in underground bunkers.

2. There may be a need for more pipelines ten feet underground.

3. Make synthetic oil and valve lubricant.

Here are some points about funding these projects:

Why build new freeways if the cars are all out of fuel? Take $50 billion from the Department of Transportation budget. What good is it to have ships, tanks, and trucks for defense if they are all out of fuel? Take $100 billion from the Department of Defense for the conversion plan. The Army and National Guard must have their vehicles converted and there must be refill stations in every state in order for them to stop rioting. This is why I recommended 1,000 natural gas refill stations in every state. In places like California there could be 2,000 of them if necessary.

The free nations must convert to avoid paralysis, and they must: Store food for a seven-year famine. Put more land into farming. Protect their soil by using greenhouses. Store distilled water. Make gas masks for their people. Form trade alliances with neighbors. Build fallout shelters, and store food and water.

GAS MASKS

I called several telephone numbers at the Fort Lewis Army base in Tacoma, Washington, in 1998 to try and find out what kind of gas mask to buy, in order to be prepared for chemical or biological warfare during World War III. No one there knew what kind to buy, except for the chemical corps people, who said that the information was classified. They told me to write to the Pentagon.

I called the same telephone numbers in July 1999 to ask the people at Fort Lewis about the gas masks again. Here are the phone numbers that I called:

Air Force Recruiting:	1-253-475-8200
Army Intelligence:	1-253-967-2501
Army Recruiting:	1-253-537-1634
Fort Lewis Public Affairs:	1-253-967-0157
Fort Lewis Community Services:	1-253-967-7166
Fort Lewis Operator Assistance:	1-253-967-1110
Fort Lewis Chemical Corps:	1-253-966-1870

The two recruiting offices are not on the Fort Lewis Army base, but I called them first because I thought that even they would have the information about the gas masks because of the importance of it. At any rate, here is what happened when I made the telephone calls:

When I called the Air Force recruiting office, I got an answering machine. When I called Army Intelligence, they said that they didn't know what kind of gas mask to buy for chemical or biological warfare. Then they said to call 1-555-1212 to get the Pentagon's telephone number. Army recruiting said to call the Fort Lewis Operator, and ask her who to call. The Fort Lewis public affairs office had an answering machine on. Fort Lewis community services said to call operator assistance. When I called operator assistance, the woman there said to call the Chemical Corps, and then she gave me their telephone number. When I called them, the man said that they did not give gas masks to civilians; and then the man laughed, and said that they get theirs from the US military.

With all of this in mind, try to imagine that a biological warfare attack just occurred in the city where you live, and 8,000 people have been taken to hospitals, and 2,500 deaths have been reported. The first thing you would think of doing would be to call the US military base near the city where you live, and ask them for a gas mask. They would tell you the same thing that they told me:

"We do not have gas masks for civilians."

Of course it will take all day to find out about this, since you will have to call from seven to ten telephone numbers; and if you decide to go to the US military base, like I did in 1998, you will have to ask for directions about 10 times to find out where to go.

I have a feeling that the US military bases will be closed after a chemical or biological warfare attack, since they do not give any help to civilians, they know that civilians will panic during an attack like this, and in the case of a biological warfare attack they will not let civilians onto the US military base, since they know that the disease will be spread to military personnel.

After wasting one day calling the seven to ten telephone numbers, and driving to the US military base, you get home and watch the TV news, only to find out that 20,000 people have now been taken to hospitals because of the biological warfare agents; and 7,200 deaths have now been reported. At this point you start screaming, and you pull out your hair because you don't know what to do. You thought the US military had a plan to protect American citizens when this happens.

Then you decide to call a few US Army surplus stores, or in my case it was called a GI surplus store. I drove to one Army surplus store in Tacoma, Washington, but the man said they didn't have any gas masks. He then told me to go to the Foxhole GI surplus store on South Hill in Puyallup, Washington. I went there, and sure enough they had gas masks, and they were the same ones that were used in the Gulf War in Kuwait.

M-17 Gas Mask: Cost: $54.99
2 Filter Pack: Cost: $15.99
Protective Suit: Cost: $40.00 New

The address for the Foxhole surplus store is:

The Foxhole
GI Surplus
12520 Meridian East
Puyallup, WA
98373
1-253-845-6100
1-800-584-0506

The man said that the M-17 gas mask would protect you from both chemical and biological warfare agents. I drove to the Tacoma Foxhole surplus store, and I bought an operator's manual. This is what I found:

Page 2-56

Filter element model number	Connector color	Useable for
M13A2	Green	All known CB agents

Page 2-55 Peacetime replacement for filter element

Climate	Climate categories	Replacement intervals (months)
Tropic	1, 2, & 3	2
Temperate	4, 5, & 6	12
Arctic	7 & 8	24

Page 2-54   Filter replacement criteria for combat
Replace every 30 days
after exposure to toxic chemical operations

The M-17 gas mask was manufactured in 1987 as well as I can determine.

When you buy a gas mask, you must be sure that you get an operator's manual to go with it because they are complicated to use, and your life will depend on whether or not you can use it safely. If the gas mask leaks in combat conditions, then you will die from exposure to toxic chemical or biological warfare agents.

When I went to the Foxhole surplus store to get a manual, the man said that the newest gas mask is the M-42. He also said that it is a controlled item, which means that the US military will not allow civilians to buy them. The Pentagon says that they will save American citizens from chemical or biological warfare attack, they will not give gas masks to civilians, and they use military procedure to prevent the purchase of the latest gas masks by civilians. I really don't understand their thinking here, but I have been in the US military myself. I was stationed in Vietnam for almost five months, and I was in Japan for eight months. You really have to be there to understand what incompetence is. There is no other way to explain it to you.

Now that I'm on the subject, the American people will have to get training on how to use their gas masks, and they will have to get the operator's manual when they get the gas masks. These things will have to be considered by the Church Committee Group, when they contact the companies which make the gas masks, and when they begin to give the gas masks to the American people. The manufacturing companies should make instruction videos, which they can sell for $9.99, and these can help the people to understand the operator's manual. They will also help them to use their gas masks properly.

Going back to my telephone calls, and my expedition to find a gas mask, I realized that under chemical or biological warfare conditions there would be 75,000 rioting people around the Army surplus store. They will all be screaming to get a gas mask, or to get into the store to get one. When you multiply this rioting and looting scenario all across the USA to include 800 cities, then you will find that America will have a major civil war, simply because the Pentagon does not supply gas masks to the people. The US Government agency, which is being paid to protect the USA, will cause the nation to be destroyed in a chemical, or a biological warfare attack, or in the civil war caused by the panic, which they will produce.

If you are wondering why 800 cities will have rioting, it is because people in every city will be worried about the spread of the biological disease, or they will be worried that another chemical or biological warfare attack will occur in the city where they live. The American people will be outraged by the fact that the Pentagon does not issue gas masks to civilians, and this alone could cause rioting and looting in 100 or 200 cities.

Now you can see that the Pentagon is being paid to do a job that they are not really doing. They are being paid to protect the people from chemical and biological warfare attack, while they have not issued one gas mask to the citizens of America, as far as I know.

I did all of this research to find out which type of gas mask the Church Committee Group should purchase for the American people. I had no idea that the Pentagon classifies the M-42 gas mask as a controlled item. It is the latest model as well as I can determine. The M-17 gas mask is available to the American people through the Army surplus stores. The M-17 gas mask protects you from chemical and biological warfare agents, but I'm not sure whether it will protect you from nuclear fallout, pyrotoxins, asbestos fibers, and sooty smoke. All of these substances will be mixed in the air after a nuclear war. These are things that the Church Committee Group will have to ask the gas mask manufacturing companies before they make the purchases.

It may be possible to get some of this information from the 1-800 telephone number for the Foxhole surplus store. You should ask them for the names of the companies which make the gas masks. Here is the address, which was on the operator's manual, which I bought:

Commander
US Army Armament, Munitions and Chemical Command
Attn: AMSMC-MAR-T (A)
Aberdeen Proving Ground, MD
21010-5423

The Church Committee Group can purchase about 50 million gas masks per year over a five-year period, which will provide 250 million gas masks for the American people. The cost for each one at the Foxhole surplus store was about $100 dollars, including the four filters. When you multiply the $100 dollars times 250 million people, you get $25 billion dollars. The Church Committee Group has $5 billion dollars allocated every year to pay for these, and I put this on the Funding list.

This is why you should vote for the Church Committee Plan. The Pentagon is not performing the jobs that they are getting paid to do, and they are incompetent, just like former Secretary of Defense Robert S. McNamara said that they are, with his book title, *Blundering Into Disaster*.[376] I put myself in the place of every citizen in America to do this project the correct way. I made the telephone calls, I went to the US Army base at Fort Lewis in 1998, and I did it all so that you would know what to expect when a chemical or biological warfare attack occurs. I plan to write a book on chemical and biological warfare, how to prepare for it, and how to save the lives of those people who live in the vicinity of an attack.

I called the Chemical Corps at Fort Lewis Army base in Tacoma, Washington several times in September 2002 to update these pages. The number that I called was 1-253-967-0940. The first time I called, there was a female who answered the telephone, and she knew nothing about gas masks, as well as being rude to me. The next time I called, I got an answering machine, which mentioned the name of a Colonel. The next three times I called, I let the telephone ring three times, and no one was there. And then the sixth time I called, a man answered the telephone.

When I asked what kind of gas masks the US Army is now using, the man asked, "Who are you?"

Then I answered, "I am a civilian."

Then he asked, "Why do you want this information (About the gas masks)?"

I answered, "I'm writing a book about biological warfare."

Then he told me that the Army is using the M-40 gas mask. When I asked what kind they were using in 1998, he said that it was the M-40. Then I told him that I believed the M-42 was being used in 1998, and he said that the M-42 is just another version of the M-40.

This means that my original notes here about the M-42 gas masks really refer to the M-40, instead of the M-42. I have to tell you now that the military cannot be relied upon for help during an emergency, like a biological warfare attack.

As a result of this surprise, I went to the Foxhole military surplus store in Tacoma, Washington to find out what the latest gas mask is that is available to civilians.

M-17	$54.99
M-25	$49.99
M-40	$99.99

You can see that there is a contradiction with this information as it relates to the gas masks now being used by the US Army. If the M-42 is another version of the M-40, and the M-40 is now being used by the Army, and both are considered as controlled items by the Pentagon, then the M-40 gas masks cannot be available to civilians. Yet on the shelf in the Foxhole surplus store the M-17, the M-25, and the M-40 gas masks were all listed with their prices, so I would believe them rather than the US Army. This means that the Army is probably using a gas mask other than the M-40 at this time.

The Church Committee Group can also provide protective clothing for the American people. I believe that the cost for this will be from $40 to $60 per person at wholesale price, which will cost from about $10 billion to $15 billion altogether. Then when the gas masks and the protective clothing are manufactured in great enough numbers, the Church Committee Group can work with state and county officials to distribute them to the American people.

THE CHRISTIAN PARTY

I have another great idea, where the Christian Voter's Alliance and the Church Committee Group can both have national offices in Washington DC, and they can collaborate with each other to make it possible to get the Church Committee Group members, who will receive on-the-job training in the Congress, to actually run for office in the states and then replace the Congressmen and Senators who work in the Congress now. In order to make this happen, the Church Committee Group will first have to get 100 members for the Senate, and 435 members for the House of Representatives who are willing to establish residences in the states which they will be running for office in. And the legislative advisors who work for the Christian Voter's Alliance in each state will have to help the Church Committee Group members meet all of the requirements, which are very complicated, to have their names placed on the ballots in the state elections.

It may be a good idea for the Christian Voter's Alliance's offices in each state to hire two people who know the rules of elections, and who know the requirements needed to get a person's name put on a ballot for an election. I will call these people political advisors, who can be hired in addition to the two legislative advisors in every state. And their jobs will be primarily to get

257

the church ministers running for office in their state prepared for the elections. This will be critical, so the Christian Voter's Alliance's offices in every state should make sure that the two political advisors hired by them are, both qualified to do the job, and loyal to the Alliance. They will have to be loyal Christians.

I will add here that the correct age group for the church ministers should be from 60 to 70 years old, since they will be working in the House of Representatives and in the Senate for several years. Of course anyone in the Church Committee Group can resign when they so desire, but when that time comes, it would be extremely important for the church minister doing it to tell the ministers in the Church Committee Group's office about it, preferably one year in advance, so they can get a church minister ready to run for the vacant office left upon retirement.

Perhaps the most important thing in all of these plans would be the formation of a Christian Party in America, much like the Democratic and the Republican Parties. One reason would be to have a convention in election years. Look at this:

"Third party and independent candidates must submit a Certificate of Nomination from a convention..."[377]

The convention could be held by the Christian Party during election years. Another benefit of having a Christian Party would be that the candidates running for office in it could be younger than 60 or 70 years old. I still recommend however, that they should have backgrounds in the Christian ministry, especially with World War III coming soon.

I will repeat it here, that the Church Committee Group and the Christian Voter's Alliance can both have national offices in Washington DC, and they can collaborate with each other, and with the state offices of the Christian Voter's Alliance to get the Church Committee Group members to run for office in the states to replace the Congressmen and the Senators who work in Washington DC now. And the Church Committee Group and the Christian Voter's Alliance can work together to form a Christian Party in America. This can be done with the help of political advisors and legislative staff people who know how the Democratic and Republican Parties are set up, both in the states, and at the national level.

It will be the responsibility of the state offices of the Christian Voter's Alliance to lease and to set up the state offices of the Christian Party, and it will be up to the board of directors to make sure that it is done correctly. What I am doing here is to give them some good ideas on how to do it.

It will be a good idea for the board of directors to send the political advisors working for them to the state offices of the Democratic and the Republican Parties to ask questions about the functions of their offices to get as many pamphlets and as much information about the operation of the Democratic and Republican Parties as they can, and to look at the size and the organization of the offices, so they can get good plans for their own offices when they lease and then furnish them.

They can also ask how many employees and volunteer workers work at the offices during the normal times of the year, and how many of them work there during the times of the Democratic and Republican conventions in the summer and the fall. It will also be a good idea to get as much information as is possible about the conventions, about the work that has to be done to make them possible, and about the materials needed for them. The political aides should also ask what licenses or permits are required to set up a political party in their state, and what must be done to get them.

It will be the responsibility of the board of directors of the state offices of the Christian Voter's Alliance to pay the salaries of the people who will work in the state offices of the Christian Party. I am not sure how this works for the Democratic and the Republican Parties, but this is the only way to make it work for the Christian Party when it is first set up. I will recommend however, that the employees of the Christian Party in America should be paid the same as the people in the other parties.

I found that the 2003 Election Manual for Candidates and Campaigns, given to me by the office of the Pierce County Auditor in Washington state, has a lot of information about the requirements needed to get a person's name placed on the ballot for an election, and I think that the political advisors will have to get the election manuals to know the dates of when to file for an election, when to file financial affairs statements, and when to file the other forms required by law in each state.[378] Of course the two political advisors in each state can help the Christian Voter's Alliance in other ways, but their main responsibility will be to get the church ministers prepared for the state elections so they can run for office to be Congressmen and Senators. There is some information about the requirements needed to run for office in the 2003 Election Manual for Pierce County in Washington State, which is important.[379] The details will vary and the dates will not be the same for any other states, but I will include the information at the end of these pages to let you know how complicated it is to run for office.

The political advisors will have to get the election manual in the appropriate year to find out what the requirements are in their particular state, and it will be their responsibility to telephone the church ministers running for office in their state to tell them exactly what they will have to do, and exactly when they will have to do it, in order to get their names on the ballot and to do it legally in their state. And it will be the responsibility of the members of the board of directors of the state offices of the Christian Voter's

Alliance to make sure that they do it. Here are the quotes from the 2003 Election Manual:

Candidate Filing Guidelines[380]
Where to File Declaration of Candidacy
Any nonpartisan office except judicial and schools shall file in the county that contains the majority of the registered voters of the district.
Reference RCW 29.15.030, 28A.315.380 (3)

Secretary of State:	US Senators & Representatives
Elections Division	State Supreme Court
Leg. Bldg/PO Box 40231	State Senators & Representatives
Olympia, WA 98504-0231	(Districts 2, 26, 31)
(360) 902-4180	State Offices

Pierce County Auditor:	State Senators & Representatives
2401 S. 35th St., Room 200	(Districts 25, 27, 28, 29)
Tacoma, WA 98409	Pierce County Offices
(253) 798-7430	Superior Court & District Court
(800) 446-4979	Court of Appeals, Div. 2, Tacoma Municipal Court; City, Town, Schools contained in Pierce County, Special Purpose Districts, and Precinct Committee Officers

When to File
July 28 - August 1, 2003
Filing Closes at 4:30 p.m. on August 1, 2003
Lot drawings to determine ballot placement will begin between 4:30 PM and 5:00 PM on the last day of filing. All candidates are invited to observe.
Filing Guidelines (continued)

Residency Requirements[381]
US Senate: Candidates must be at least 30 years of age, US citizens and residents of the state for which they shall be chosen. (Reference US Constitution, Article 1, Section 3)
US Representative: Candidates must be at least 25 years of age, US citizens and residents of the state for which they shall be chosen. (Reference US Constitution, Article 1, Section 3)
State Legislature: Candidates must be qualified voters in the district. (Reference State Constitution, Article II, Section 7)

State Offices: Candidates must be qualified electors of the State of Washington. (Reference State Constitution, Article III, Section 25)

Supreme, Superior, District Court Judges: Candidates must be resident electors of their district and admitted to practice law in the courts of record of the State of Washington. (Reference State Constitution, Article IV, Section 17 Article III, Section 25; RCW 3.50, 3.34)

Tacoma Municipal Court Judges: Candidates must be qualified resident electors of Pierce County and admitted to practice law in the courts of record of the State of Washington. (Reference Tacoma City Charter 5.3)

Court of Appeals Judges: Candidates must be residents of the district for not less than one year and admitted to practice law in the courts of the State of Washington for not less than five years prior to taking office. (Reference RCW 2.06)

County Offices: Candidates must be residents and registered voters of Pierce County. County Council candidates must be residents and registered voters of their district for one year prior to filing. (Reference Pierce County Charter 4.30)

City of Tacoma: Candidates for council shall be qualified electors (registered voters) and residents of the City for two years immediately preceding the time of filing, and residents of their district for one year immediately preceding the time of filing. (Reference Tacoma City Charter 2.2)

Filing Guidelines (continued)

Declaration of Candidacy & Filings[382]

A candidate, who desires to have his or her name printed on the ballot for election to an office other than President of the United States and Vice President of the United States, shall complete and file a Declaration and Affidavit of Candidacy. A person filing a Declaration of Candidacy for an office shall, at the time of filing, possess the qualifications specified by law for persons who may be elected to the office. The candidate must be properly registered to vote in the geographic area, district and/or division represented by the office at the time of filing. The officer with whom declarations are filed shall review each declaration for compliance with this law. (Reference RCW 29.15)

When filing for an office, no candidate may use a nickname that denotes present or past occupation or military rank, use a nickname that denotes the candidate's position on issues or political affiliation, or use a nickname designed to intentionally mislead voters. (Reference RCW 29.15)

Filings made by mail for regular candidates and Precinct Committee Officers must be received by the filing officer not earlier than ten working days before the first day of filing or no later than the close of business on the last day of the filing period, irrespective of postmark. Failure to meet the deadline renders the filing invalid and it will be returned. Candidate filings (except for Precinct Committee Officer) must be notarized if mailed in or if delivered by someone other than the candidate. (Reference RCW 29.15; WAC 434-228)

If a candidate files a declaration by fax, the original signed document must be received in the Auditor's Office not later than seven calendar days after the receipt of the fax. If there is a filing fee, it must be paid at the same time of the faxed declaration or it will not be accepted. (Reference WAC 434-208-070,080)

Filing Fees
FILING FEES ARE NOT REFUNDABLE. (Reference RCW 29.15)
•A filing fee equal to 1% of the annual salary at the time of filing shall accompany each Declaration of Candidacy for any office with an annual salary of more than $1,000. (Reference RCW 29.15)
Filing Guidelines (continued)[383]
•A filing fee of $10 will be charged for offices with annual salaries under $1,000. (Reference RCW 29.15)
•A filing fee is not charged for offices without a fixed annual salary. (Reference RCW 29.15)
•A filing fee of $1 shall accompany each Declaration of Candidacy for Precinct Committee Officer. (Reference RCW 29.15)
•Filing fees are not refundable. If a candidate withdraws and re-files for a different position, a second filing fee must be paid for the new position.

Insufficient Assets for Filing
If a candidate's committee and/or candidate lacks sufficient assets or income to pay the filing fee required, he/she can submit a nominating petition with signatures of registered voters from their jurisdiction instead of paying the filing fee. This petition must have at least the number of signatures equal to the number of dollars of the filing fee. The petition must be completed and submitted to the Pierce County Auditor no later than Friday of filing week. Petitions may not be submitted at a later date for a refund of the filing fee. Please remember to allow enough time to check signatures, as no additional signatures may be submitted after the close of filing on Friday. Petitions cannot be combined with money to make up the filing fee. (Reference RCW 29.15)

Filing Guidelines (continued)[384]
Third Party and Independent Candidates
Third party and independent candidates must submit a Certificate of Nomination from a convention held between the last Saturday in June, and not later than the first Saturday in July, for any partisan office. Offices governed by the County Charter permit independent candidates to file without a Certificate of Nomination. (Charter 4.20)
Certificates and petitions for third party candidates must be filed with the Secretary of State except for an office whose jurisdiction is entirely within one county, in which case the certificate and petition are to be filed with the appropriate County Auditor. In order to nominate candidates for the offices of President and Vice President of the United States, United States Senator, or any statewide office, a nominating convention shall obtain and submit to the Secretary of State the signatures of at least 200 registered voters of the State of Washington. In order to nominate candidates for any other office, a nominating convention shall obtain and submit to the filing officer, the signatures of 25 registered voters within the jurisdiction of the office for which the nominations are made. Certificate of Nominations must be submitted not later than one week following adjournment of the convention. If the Certificate of Nomination is found to be valid, candidates will be eligible to file their Declaration of Candidacy with the filing officer to whom the report was filed (along with the appropriate fee) during the normal filing period. For more information, contact the Secretary of State, Election Division, in Olympia, at (360) 902-4180. (Reference RCW 29.24; Pierce County Charter 4.20)

Write-ins
Any person desiring to be a write-in candidate for any regular office or office of Precinct Committee Officer may, if the jurisdiction of the office sought is entirely within one county, file a Declaration of Candidacy with the County Auditor and pay the filing fee (if any) no earlier than the day after the regular filing period and no later than the day before the election. If the jurisdiction of the office sought encompasses more than one county, the Declaration of Candidacy shall be filed with the Secretary of State. Votes cast for write-in candidates who have filed such declarations and write-in votes for persons appointed by political parties, **need only specify the name of the candidate in the appropriate location on the ballot and connect the arrow to the right of the write-in in order to be counted. Write-in votes will not be tallied unless a significant number, which could affect the outcome of the election, were cast for an office.** No person may file as a write-in candidate where: At a general election, the continued person attempting to file either

filed as a write-in candidate for the same office at the preceding primary or the person's name appeared on the ballot for the same office at the preceding primary; the person attempting to file as a write-in candidate has already filed a valid write-in declaration for that primary or election, unless one or the other of the two filings is for the office of precinct committee officer; The name of the person attempting to file already appears on the ballot as a candidate for another office, unless one of the two offices for which he or she is a candidate is precinct committee officer.

2003 Key Reporting Dates for Candidates[385]
PUBLIC DISCLOSURE COMMISSION
711 CAPITOL WAY, RM 206
PO BOX 40908
OLYMPIA, WA 98504-0908   **2003 Key Reporting Dates for Candidates**
(360) 753-1111
TOLL FREE 1-877-601-2828

DATE	ACTIVITY	C-4 REPORT PERIOD
Within two weeks of Becoming a candidate	File a C-1 (non-incumbents also file an F-1)	
Jan 10	File monthly C-4 & C-3, if necessary	close of last report thru Dec 31
Feb 10	" "	close of last report thru Jan 31
Mar 10	" "	close of last report thru Feb 28
Apr 10	" "	close of last report thru Mar 31
May 12	" "	close of last report thru Apr 30
Jun 10	" "	close of last report thru May 31
Jul 1	Begin filing C-3 reports weekly, each Monday, for deposits made during previous 7 days (Monday thru Sunday)	
Jul 10	File monthly C-4, if necessary	close of last report thru Jun 30
Jul 28-Aug 1	Declaration of candidacy filing week	

Aug 26	21 day pre-primary C-4 due [1]	Jul 1 thru Aug 19
Sep 8-15	Campaign books open for public inspection	
Sep 9	7 day pre-primary C-4 due [1]	Aug 20 thru Sep 8
Sep 9-15	Special reports due if candidate receives contributions of $1,000 or more from one source. [2]	
Sep 16	PRIMARY ELECTION DAY	
Oct 10	Post-primary C-4 due [3]	Sep 9 thru Sep 30
Oct 14	21 day pre-general C-4 due	Sep 9 thru Oct 7
Oct 14-Nov 3	Special reports due if candidate receives contributions of $1,000 or more in the aggregate from one source. Unless the contribution is from the **state committee** of a major political party or a minor party, a candidate may not now receive from one source contributions totaling over $5,000 in the aggregate. [2]	
Oct 27-Nov 3	Campaign books open for public inspection	
Oct 28	7 day pre-general C-4 due	Oct 8 thru Oct 27
Nov 4	GENERAL ELECTION DAY	
Dec 10	Post-general C-4 due (and C-3, if necessary)	Oct 28 thru Nov 30

CHAPTER VII

Spiritual Principles
of World War III

The nuclear weapons in Europe will cause the worst public relations disaster in all of history for the President and the US military. They have already been the cause of protests over the last 20 years, and they will be again, when the people in Europe find out that the US Pentagon will be forced to use them against the Russian army.

The President of the United States must work with the UN Organization, and ask them to announce to the TV news that the Pentagon will remove their nuclear weapons from Europe. If this isn't done, the people in Europe will protest at the US military bases, as soon as they hear about the new nuclear weapons' problem. The sooner the President decides to remove them, the fewer problems he will have with the people in Europe.

CENSURE RESOLUTION

As I was watching the events in Bill Clinton's impeachment trial, I noticed that the Democrats in the Congress wanted to adopt a Censure Resolution to punish Clinton, instead of going ahead with the impeachment trial. Then I realized that this might be a good thing to have during World War III. I will explain it with this example.

Just imagine that ten million soldiers from the army of the Antichrist, or the Unified European Army, are moving southward to take the world oil supply in the Middle East. Then imagine that the President and the Pentagon will try to send five to ten million American troops to the area to stop them.

266

When the Congress tells the President and the Pentagon not to give the order to transfer the troops, and when they do it anyway, then what should the Congress do? They will not have enough time to impeach the President or the Pentagon Generals because it takes six months to do it.

The correct thing to do in this case would be to have the Congress censure the President, the Joint Chiefs of Staff, and the other people involved to stop them from giving the order to transfer the ten million troops to the Middle East. To make sure that the Pentagon doesn't transfer them anyway, the Congress will have to send two man teams to every US military base in the world to watch out for any activity such as a large transfer of US troops.

The Congress will have to write the legislation for the Censure Resolution, and when they do it they should make it a treasonable offense for anyone who disobeys the censure by the Congress. They should write the legislation in such a way that the Congress would have the power to remove from office anyone who commits treason by disobeying the censure. This should include the President, the Joint Chiefs of Staff, any person in the US military, in the CIA, the FBI, etc.

Now when the President commits treason by disobeying the censure by the Congress, he can be removed from office without an impeachment trial. The legislation for the censure resolution should be included in the War Powers Act by the Congress.

CHRIST AND THE CONGRESS

The Congress consists of the Senate and the House of Representatives, and it will be the most difficult part of the government to conform to the commandments of Christ. These are:

In Matthew 5:39-48 is the phrase, "But I say unto you, that ye resist not evil." This means that the US Government should not interfere with the Antichrist during World War III.

In Revelation 13:10 is the phrase, "he that killeth with the sword must be killed with the sword." This is a command to remove the US military from Europe, and close the US military bases in Europe, Japan, Korea, and the Middle East.

In Isaiah 26:20,21 the US Government is instructed to withdraw from world politics, and to adopt a policy of isolationism. This is the meaning of the phrase, "Come, my people, enter thou into thy chambers, and shut thy doors about thee: hide thyself as it were for a little moment, until the indignation be overpast." The indignation here is World War III, and this is written in Isaiah 26:20. In the next verse the Lord will punish the people in the nations that follow the Antichrist, and he will also destroy the army of the Antichrist. There is no doubt about the meaning of these verses. They mean to adopt a policy of isolationism in politics, and to withdraw the US military back into the United States. The reason for this is written in Isaiah 26:21, in the phrase, "For, behold, the Lord cometh out of his place to punish the inhabitants of the earth for their iniquity."

This means that the Lord will punish the nations in the kingdom of the Antichrist. This is verified in Revelation 16:1-21, where the 7 vials will bring plagues against the kingdom of the Antichrist. Then in Isaiah 26:21 the phrase, "the earth also shall disclose her blood, and shall no more cover her slain," means that the army of the Antichrist will be slaughtered in Israel. This is verified in Jeremiah 7:32, Joel 2:20, and in Revelation 19:19-21. Christ will destroy them in the ways described in Ezekiel 38:19-23, and Ezekiel 39:1-5. In Ezekiel 39:6 the phrase, "And I will send a fire on Magog," means that the plague of hail and fire from Revelation 8:7 will also happen to the kingdom of the Antichrist.

In Zephaniah 2:3 the phrase, "seek righteousness, seek meekness: it may be ye shall be hid in the day of the Lord's anger," means that the US military will not be killed in the plague of hail and fire from Revelation 8:7, and Ezekiel 38:22, if they are not fighting against the army of the Antichrist in Israel. This is one of the most important points about World War III: The US military must stay out of World War III to avoid getting 10 million American soldiers killed in the plagues. This is the meaning of Zephaniah 2:3.

In Matthew 24:21,22 Christ will return to earth early to stop the nuclear war. This means that total nuclear war is against the laws of Christ. Therefore the Congress must do all they possibly can to keep the Pentagon out of World War III to avoid nuclear war against the Antichrist.

It will be difficult to conform the Congress to the laws of Christ because of the system of checks and balances, which causes Congress to take forever to do anything. This system of government was invented to make a steady form of government, so it would last 300 years. The idea behind this was survival, and now Congress must change very quickly to survive World War III. Without survival, the Congress will not exist. Some of the needed steps are:

1. Get rid of the hawks by giving them one year of paid leave.

2. Get rid of the House and Senate Armed Services Committees, and the Defense Appropriations subcommittees.

The hawks are the groups that will light the matches, when the Pentagon and Congress are standing in the Vat of gasoline. In other words, they will use fear to get approval to use nuclear weapons.

3. If the President has to ratify the bill from Congress to get rid of the hawks, then I will recommend that he should do it.

4. Congress must refuse to declare war against the Antichrist, no matter what happens during World War III. This will help prevent nuclear war.

5. The Congress must set up a Church Committee Group in the Senate, and in the House of Representatives to replace the hawks.

With the US military bases open in Europe, and the neutron bombs waiting to be used against the Antichrist, and the Russian tanks, all the hawks will have to do is to use fear to get permission to declare war against the Antichrist. This is why the Congress must get rid of the hawks. If these steps are not followed by the Congress, then the American people will try to kill the Congressmen, when they have no food or housing to survive World War III.

The US Government was separated into 3 branches, so the President could not become a dictator. The Legislative branch is comprised of the House of Representatives and the Senate, so that one group could not seize all of the power. Therefore the hawks have contradicted the laws of the Constitution by forming powerful groups in both the House and the Senate. This is verified on page 89 of Dr. Helen Caldicott's book, *Missile Envy*. The hawks used their power to out-maneuver the President of the USA, Jimmy Carter, in order to avoid a freeze on nuclear weapons production.[386]

The hawks also have a revolving door into the Pentagon, and into the nuclear weapons industry, which makes them even more dangerous. These people appropriated about $7 trillion of the taxpayer's money to be used by the Pentagon from 1945 to now. Some of this money was used for production of missiles, and the nuclear warheads that they carry. Then you must realize that the hawks are powerful in both the House and the Senate, some of them work in the Pentagon, and in the nuclear weapons industry. This leaves only the President to oppose them, and they can use the fear of the Antichrist and his army to out-maneuver him.

PROOFS OF POWER

When you look at the Antichrist, and the power he will attain, you must first realize that the power will come from several places. Look here:

Revelation 13:1,2: "And I stood upon the sand of the sea, and saw a beast rise up out of the sea, having seven heads and ten horns, and upon his horns ten crowns, and upon his heads the name of blasphemy.

And the beast which I saw was like unto a leopard, and his feet were as the feet of a bear, and his mouth as the mouth of a lion; and the dragon gave him his power, and his seat, and great authority."

The ten horns here represent the leaders of the Common Market in Europe, and it says that they will give their crowns to the kingdom of the Antichrist, which is the beast described in these verses. Then the phrase, "…and the dragon gave him his power, and his seat, and great authority," means that Satan will give the leadership of the Common Market to the Antichrist, since it says in Revelation 12:9 that the dragon is Satan. Now look here:

Revelation 13:3,4: "And I saw one of his heads as it were wounded to death; and his deadly wound was healed: and all the world wondered after the beast.

And they worshipped the dragon, which gave power unto the beast: and they worshipped the beast, saying, Who is like unto the beast? who is able to make war with him?"

The wound described here was the Berlin Wall and the dividing line in Germany; and everyone celebrated when it was removed. Now, the wound is healed, and this is the meaning of Revelation 13:3. In Revelation 13:4 it says the people in Europe will worship the dragon, which is Satan. And they will worship the kingdom of the Antichrist, which is the beast. Therefore the people of Europe, as well as Satan, will give power to the Antichrist. And the members of the Common Market will give power to him.

You should be aware of this while reading these pages, in order to understand completely where his power will come from.

It is very important to understand why the Antichrist will have the power to do the things that the Bible says that he will do. First of all, he will cause World War III, since mankind gave him the power to do it, when they took down the Berlin Wall in 1990. You should always remember that Satan deceived the whole world, when he convinced the political leaders to take down the Berlin Wall. Satan caused World War I, World War II, and now he will cause World War III, with the help of the Antichrist. You should also know that the people in Europe will applaud the Antichrist when he appears, which means that they will welcome World War III yet once again.

The Antichrist is already in Germany, and in II Thessalonians 2:6-8 he will be revealed when the Holy Spirit is removed from Europe. When you study the theology of World War III very closely, you will find that the Lord God will use the army of the Antichrist to punish the people on earth who refuse to go to church to worship Christ. You should always remember this verse:

Proverbs 16:4: "The Lord hath made all things for himself: yea, even the wicked for the day of evil."

If your nation will not go to the Christian churches to worship the Lord Jesus Christ, then you will get the Antichrist and his army. Now I will describe the verses, which explain the proofs of power for the Antichrist.

Revelation 6:2: "And I saw, and behold a white horse: and he that sat on him had a bow; and a crown was given unto him: and he went forth conquering, and to conquer."

This verse describes the Antichrist, who is sitting upon a white horse. The phrase, "and a crown was given unto him," refers to the leadership of the Common Market, which will be given to him by the other Common Market members. This is a power given to the Antichrist by mankind. Here is another verse:

Revelation 6:4: "And there went out another horse that was red: and power was given to him that sat thereon to take peace from the earth, and that they should kill one another: and there was given unto him a great sword."

Power will be given to the Antichrist to start a war in Europe, which will eventually lead to World War III. The reason for this is described in II Thessalonians 2:3-12. The Antichrist is the son of perdition in II Thessalonians 2:3. He is the Wicked one in II Thessalonians 2:8, and in II Thessalonians 2:9 he will work with Satan to start World War III. Then in II Thessalonians 2:10-12 the real reason for this power is explained. The people in Europe will worship the Antichrist like they did with Adolf Hitler before and during World War II; and then the Antichrist will receive the power to bring down fire from heaven. This is the meaning of the verse:

II Thessalonians 2:11: "And for this cause God shall send them strong delusion, that they should believe a lie."

It is described perfectly here:

Revelation 13:13: "And he doeth great wonders, so that he maketh fire come down from heaven on the earth in the sight of men."

Then in Revelation 13:14,15 the Antichrist will deceive the people in Europe with this power. You must understand that it will be an unforgivable sin to applaud the Antichrist like the people did with Hitler prior to World War II, since the whole world saw what happened when they did it the first time. This will cause the wrath of God to come forth in the form of the "strong delusion", described in II Thessalonians 2:11. When the people in Europe believe the lie, or when they believe that the Antichrist is a god, then they will come together to receive the mark of the beast by the millions, which will cause them to be condemned to the Lake of Fire. This is written here:

Revelation 14:11: "And the smoke of their torment ascendeth up for ever and ever: and they have no rest day nor night, who worship the beast and his image, and whosoever receiveth the mark of his name."

This entire process must be understood before you can realize why the Antichrist will receive the power to start World War III. There are some other factors involved in it, such as the power to destroy Rome, Italy; and the Antichrist will receive this power because the Roman Emperors killed and crucified 100,000 Christians from 95 AD to 305 AD. This is described in Revelation 17:1-7, Revelation 17:15-18, and Revelation 18:1-19. In Revelation 17:16 the ten horns are the ten Common Market leaders. This is why they are called ten kings in Revelation 17:12. In Revelation 17:17 God will put it in their hearts to give their kingdoms to the Antichrist, so they can unite their armies to destroy Rome. In Revelation 17:18 the woman is the city of Rome.

The process involved in World War III also includes the occupation of Jerusalem, Israel by the army of the Antichrist during World War III. This is described here:

Revelation 11:1,2: "And there was given me a reed like unto a rod: and the angel stood, saying, Rise, and measure the temple of God, and the altar, and them that worship therein.

But the court which is without the temple leave out, and measure it not; for it is given unto the Gentiles: and the holy city shall they tread under foot forty and two months."

The next verse that describes proof of power is here:

Revelation 6:8: "And I looked, and behold a pale horse: and his name that sat on him was Death, and Hell followed with him. And power was given unto them over the fourth part of the earth to kill with sword, and with hunger, and with death, and with the beasts of the earth."

The army of the Antichrist will receive power to rule over one fourth of the land area of the earth. This will include all of Europe, including the USSR, as well as several other nations. The army will kill with the sword, which means with war; they will kill with hunger, which means with famine. In this case it means the famine of the Antichrist, which will include the 800 million people in Europe. The army will also kill with death, which means chemical, biological, and nuclear warfare; and they will kill with the beasts of the earth, which refers to lions, tigers, and other animals. Here is another verse:

Revelation 13:5: " And there was given unto him a mouth speaking great things and blasphemies; and power was given unto him to continue forty and two months."

The Antichrist will receive power to continue his conquest of Europe for 42 months. This means that the famine of the Antichrist will last that long for those people who resist. Here is another verse:

Revelation 13:7: "And it was given unto him to make war with the saints, and to overcome them: and power was given him over all kindreds, and tongues, and nations."

The Antichrist will have power over all nations, since World War III, and its effects will be felt by everyone in the world. I would say that the most important verses are these:

Revelation 13:16,17: "And he causeth all, both small and great, rich and poor, free and bond, to receive a mark in their right hand, or in their foreheads:

And that no man might buy or sell, save he that had the mark, or the name of the beast, or the number of his name."

This is another description of the famine of the Antichrist, which is also written in Revelation 6:8. The phrase, "And he causeth all...to receive a mark in their right hand, or in their foreheads", means that the Antichrist will force the 800 million people in Europe to receive the mark of the beast, which will be the swastika; and he will use a famine to do it.

These proofs of power tell you that the Antichrist and his army are predestined to carry out certain functions, before World War III even begins.

When you connect these proofs with Ezekiel 38:21,22, Ezekiel 39:1-20, Revelation 9:13-19, Joel 2:2-11, II Thessalonians 2:2-12, Revelation 16:16, Revelation 13:1-18, Revelation 12:17, Isaiah 26:20,21, Isaiah 30:27-33, Jeremiah 7:30-34, Jeremiah 19:6, Daniel 11:21,22, Daniel 11:23-28, Daniel 11:36-45, Matthew 24:15-22, Mark 13:14-20, and other verses, you can see very clearly that the Pentagon cannot become involved in World War III for any reason. The commandment from the Lord God to stay out of the war is stated directly in Revelation 13:10, Isaiah 26:20,21, Amos 5:13, Ecclesiastes 9:12, and I Thessalonians 5:3.

The soldiers in Europe will volunteer to be in the army of Antichrist when they see him bring down fire from heaven. This is described in Revelation 13:13, and in II Thessalonians 2:9-12. When this happens, the Pope and the Vatican will tell the people in Europe that only the Antichrist would have this power, and then in Revelation 17:12-18 the ten Common Market leaders will give their military strength to him, and the Unified European Army, or the army of the Antichrist will loot the city of Rome. Then they will burn the city, and the Antichrist will destroy it with nuclear missiles. The nuclear attack is described in Revelation 18:1-4, Revelation 18:8, and Revelation 18:19.

Millions of people will flock to receive the swastika when the Antichrist has the power to bring down fire from heaven in Revelation 13:13. He will receive this power so the people who do this will be condemned to the Lake of Fire. When these events occur, you should know that World War III has begun.

The people in the European nations listed here will be included in the famine of the Antichrist. The nations in the Middle East, South Africa, Japan, Northeast China, and Korea will be occupied by the army of the Antichrist during World War III. My evacuation plan for them is:

NATION	LANGUAGE	DESTINATION
Albania	Albanian	Peru
Austria	German	Zimbabwe
Belgium	Dutch	Suriname
Bulgaria	Bulgarian	Australia
Denmark	Danish	Greenland
Egypt	Arabic	Sudan
England	English	Canada, United States
Finland	Finnish	Newfoundland
France	French	French Guiana, Quebec
Germany	German	Gabon
Greece	Greek	Australia
Hungary	Magyar	Australia
Iran	Persian	Afghanistan, Sudan
Iraq	Arabic	Algeria
Ireland	Irish	Australia
Israel	Hebrew	United States
Italy	Italian	Argentina
Japan	Japanese	Madagascar
Jordan	Arabic	Libya
Korea	Korean	South China
Kuwait	Arabic	Somalia
Lebanon	Arabic	Libya
Luxembourg	French	Quebec
NE China	Chinese	South China
Netherlands	Dutch	Suriname
Norway	Norwegian	Labrador
Oman	Arabic	Somalia
Poland	Polish	Brazil
Portugal	Portuguese	Brazil

Romania	Romanian	Brazil
Saudi Arabia	Arabic	Algeria
Scotland	Scottish	United States
South Africa	English	Tanzania, Zambia
Spain	Spanish	Mexico, Venezuela
Sweden	Swedish	Labrador
Switzerland	French	Newfoundland
Syria	Arabic	Libya
Turkey	Turkish	Mauritania
Soviet Union	Russian	Angola, Chad, Niger, Mali
UAE	Arabic	Somalia
Yemen	Arabic	Sudan
Yugoslavia	Croatian	Australia
Czechoslovakia	Czech	Chile
Liechtenstein	German	Morocco

The people in these nations who don't want to starve to death, and lose their souls to the Antichrist have to move to their new host nation. If you stay in Europe, your soul will be condemned to burn in the fires of the sun forever.

According to the numbers of people moving from each nation in Europe and from other nations, the number of travel trailers needed in each new host nation will be:

FROM	DESTINATION	NUMBER
Albania	Peru	825,000
Austria	Zimbabwe	2 million
Belgium	Suriname	2.5 million
Bulgaria	Australia	2.3 million
Denmark	Greenland	1.5 million
Egypt	Sudan	16.5 million
England	Canada, United States	15 million
Finland	Newfoundland	1.3 million
France	French Guiana, Quebec	15 million
Germany	Gabon	21 million
Greece	Australia	2.8 million
Hungary	Australia	2.5 million
Iran	Afghanistan, Sudan	17.3 million
Iraq	Algeria	6 million
Ireland	Australia	1 million
Israel	United States	1.4 million

Italy	Argentina	15 million
Japan	Madagascar	32 million
Jordan	Libya	1.2 million
Korea	South China	18 million
Kuwait	Somalia	500,000
Lebanon	Libya	1 million
Luxembourg	Quebec	110,000
NE China	South China	30 million
Netherlands	Suriname	4 million
Norway	Labrador	1.2 million
Oman	Somalia	600,000
Poland	Brazil	10 million
Portugal	Brazil	2.5 million
Romania	Brazil	5.5 million
Saudi Arabia	Algeria	5.3 million
Scotland	United States	1.5 million
South Africa	Tanzania, Zambia	11 million
Spain	Mexico, Venezuela	10 million
Sweden	Labrador	2.5 million
Switzerland	Newfoundland	2 million
Syria	Libya	4.3 million
Turkey	Mauritania	16.3 million
Soviet Union	Angola, Chad, Niger, Mali	73 million
UAE	Somalia	600,000
Yemen	Sudan	3.8 million
Yugoslavia	Australia	3 million
Czechoslovakia	Chile	2.6 million
Liechtenstein	Morocco	8,000

Since the total number is over 365 million, the travel trailer manufacturers will probably run out of some of the components for them. These are: Rubber tires, plastic siding, pressed wood, steel beams, hot water heaters, propane tanks, etc. If there is a shortage of these items later on, you should contact the United Nations Organization.

On the next pages I will describe the army of the Antichrist, the reason why limited tactical nuclear weapons will have to be used against them by the Pentagon, (If the US military fights against them in Europe), and the reason why this will cause a global nuclear war.

In Revelation 9:16 the army of the Antichrist is described as having 200 million soldiers. The army will reach that number by the end of World War III. This is verified in Daniel 11:40-43. In Revelation 16:12 the army of the

Antichrist will go across the Euphrates River to occupy the land of Israel, and to take the world oil supply.

I watched a video film on TV one day, which said that the Euphrates River has a dam across it, and when the dam is closed, the river dries up. Then I looked at a map of Syria, and I found that the Tabka Dam just east of Aleppo, Syria is probably the one. This is described in Revelation 16:12. The angel described in this verse found a way to close the dam, so the water in the Euphrates River would dry up. You see, the army of the Antichrist has to move down to the Middle East, so the words of God in the Bible will be fulfilled. Therefore the water in the river has to dry up, in order for the tanks in that army to cross over it.

In Revelation 9:13-20 the four angels from the Garden of Eden will cause the army to fight against itself, and kill one third of its own soldiers, or 66.6 million men. This is verified in Ezekiel 38:21. In Ezekiel 38:22 the plague of hail and fire from Revelation 8:7 will kill 100 million more of the soldiers in the army. This is verified in Ezekiel 39:2, where one sixth of the army will remain, after the tank battle and the plague of hail and fire.

Then in Revelation 16:16, and in Revelation 19:19-21 the remnant of the army will be killed by the Lord Jesus Christ, when he returns to the earth at the end of World War III. Therefore, you can see that the biblical plan for the war does not include the Pentagon or the US military at all. In Daniel 7:24,25, and in Revelation 13:7 the Antichrist will make war with the armies of the Christian nations of Europe, and he will win the war. In Revelation 13:5 the army of the Antichrist will spend 42 months conquering all of the nations in Europe. If the Pentagon tries to interfere in the war in Europe, this is what will happen:

The US military bases in Europe will have to be defended against 100 million soldiers from Russia, and from Eastern Europe after they join the army of the Antichrist; which will be the Unified European Army. To fight against an army this large, the Pentagon will have to use their limited tactical nuclear weapons. The killing caused by these weapons will be so horrible, that the Antichrist will use total nuclear retaliation against America. (The 100 million soldiers will have to be killed to ensure a US military victory, and using limited tactical nuclear weapons in Europe in a battle this large will kill about 200 million civilians). This will cause total nuclear retaliation by the Antichrist for certain.

To prove that the army of the Antichrist will start out at 100 million soldiers, and then increase to 200 million by the end of World War III, I will use Bible Scripture. In Revelation 13:2 the army will include all of the soldiers in the Russian army because the bear is the symbol for Russia, and the feet of the beast will be, "as the feet of a bear," because an army walks on its feet. In Daniel 7:5 the three ribs in the mouth of the bear represent the 666 in Revelation 13:18, which is the start of World War III by the bear, or the Russian army. In Revelation 6:4 the great sword in the hand of the Antichrist is the Russian army starting World War III. The phrase, "to take peace from the earth," means to start World War III.

In Daniel 7:7 the beast devoured and brake in pieces, and stamped the residue of cities and nations with the feet of it, or with its army. This is also written in Daniel 7:19.Therefore the army will be more than adequate to take Western Europe. This is verified in Daniel 7:25, and in Revelation 13:7, where the Antichrist will make war with the saints, and will overcome them. These are the saints in Europe. This is also written in Daniel 7:21. In Daniel 7:5 the phrase, " Arise, devour much flesh", means to take all of Europe. Since the saints represent the churches in Europe, when they are overcome, all of Europe will be lost.

In Daniel 7:25, and in Revelation 13:5 the army of the Antichrist will dominate Europe for 42 months, or three and one half years. Again, you can see that the Pentagon is not included in the biblical plan for World War III in Europe. This means that they must close the US military bases in Europe now, and go back to defend America during World War III.

In Daniel 8:24 the phrase, "his power shall be mighty, but not by his own power," means that the soldiers from Russia and the Eastern Bloc nations in Europe will comprise the 100 million soldiers in the army of the Antichrist. In other words the army will not consist of German soldiers exclusively. This is proof that the Russian army, with 60 million soldiers, will join the Antichrist.

To be logical about this, only about 20% of the total population in Russia and in Eastern Europe could join this army. This means that 60 million Russian troops, and 40 million Eastern European troops will be eligible; and at $600 dollars a month, this many men will join it. This will make an army of 100 million soldiers.

There will be 40 million soldiers from Western Europe who will join the army of the Antichrist. This is written in Revelation 17:12,13. The last 60 million troops in the army will come from Turkey, Syria, Lebanon, Iraq, Iran, and Egypt in the Middle East. This is written in Daniel 11:30,31. The phrase, "And arms shall stand on his part," means that the armies of the terrorist nations in the Middle East will join the army of the Antichrist.

This could also be why the army will be convinced to fight against itself in Revelation 9:15-20: About 60 million of the soldiers will be Arabic, which is a different race than the soldiers from Europe. This could cause problems over the rights to the oil.

278

The most important verse about this army from Daniel is written in Daniel 11:22. If you picture the Antichrist standing in Berlin, Germany at the dividing line, facing Western Europe, then look at this phrase: "And with the arms of a flood shall they be overflown from before him." The arms of a flood means the 100 million soldiers, coming from Russia and Eastern Europe. The phrase, "shall they be overflown from before him," means the people of Western Europe, will be overrun by the army. Then the phrase, "and shall be broken," refers to Daniel 7:7, where the beast devoured cities, and broke them in pieces with its army. This means that Western Europe will be lost to the Antichrist. The next phrase, "Yea, also the prince of the covenant," means that the Vatican will be overrun by the army. Now because the ten Common Market kings will give their military strength to the Antichrist, and will then destroy Rome with their armies in Revelation 17:12-18, this means they will unify with the Russian army, instead of fighting against them. This is verified in Daniel 11:22, where the takeover of Western Europe happens at the same time the Vatican is overrun and the city of Rome is destroyed.

The word, "overflow" is also used in Daniel 11:40, where the army will be 200 million strong. In the first year it will have 100 million soldiers, which is the number of men needed to overrun Western Europe so easily. Also the phrase, "And with the arms of a flood shall they be overflown from before him," tells you that the army will come from Eastern Europe, and will overrun Western Europe. This is one of the few verses that indicate the Eastern European soldiers will join the Russian army to form the army of the Antichrist. He could do this under the pretense of forming a Unified European Amy, which would fool everybody.

The Common Market will have a unified common currency, and a unified Banking system, as well as a unified method of conducting trade with other nations. Therefore the Antichrist will say that they should have a unified army. This process is described in Revelation 17:12-18. In Revelation 17:12,13 the ten Common Market leaders will have one mind, which means unification. They will give their power, which means economic power, and their strength, which means military strength to the beast, or to the Antichrist. (In Revelation 20:10 it is clear that the beast is the kingdom of the Antichrist). They will do this because he will be the leader of the Common Market; and they will do it to unify their economic power, which is the objective of the Common Market to begin with. The one subtle difference in Revelation 17:13 is that the Antichrist will call for a Unified European Army. He will have to do this before he declares his famine, and then the troops will actually enforce it for him even in their own nations. This explains how he will get control of all the troops in Europe. You see, if the armies in Western

Europe believe that they are a part of the Unified European Army, then they will join the Russian army when they get to Western Europe, instead of fighting against them.

The army is also described in Joel 2:1-11. In Joel 2:2 the army is described as, "a great people and a strong; there hath not been ever the like, neither shall be any more after it, even to the years of many generations." This phrase indicates unification, and it also describes the size of the army. It will be 50 times larger than any other army in the history of the world. In Joel 2:3 the phrase, "and nothing shall escape them," is a reference to I Thessalonians 5:3, to the phrase, "and they shall not escape." This means the people in Europe. The Pentagon must move from Europe now, and then the people who live in Europe must evacuate. Remember, you will burn in the fires of the sun forever, if you stay in Europe. In Joel 2:5 the phrase, "like the noise of chariots on the tops of mountains," is a description of the tanks in the Russian army. You can hear the noise from the tanks best when they are on the tops of mountains. These tanks are also described in Revelation 9:17-19.

In Joel 2:6 the faces of the people in Western Europe will show pain and depression, when they see the 100 million soldiers in the army. In Joel 2:7, "they shall climb the wall like men of war." This means the Berlin Wall. This is a figure of speech. Taking this wall down made it possible for the Antichrist to start World War III, and now his men will climb the wall like men of war, on their way to Western Europe. This verse verifies the fact that the Berlin Wall and the dividing line in Germany is the wound in Revelation 13:3, and Revelation 13:14. If you have ever seen the Russian army marching through Red Square in Moscow, with their tanks and troops, then you will agree that this verse gives a perfect description of them:

Joel 2:5: "as a strong people set in battle array."

In Joel 2:7 the phrase, "and they shall march every one on his ways, and they shall not break their ranks," signifies the Russian army being joined by the Eastern European armies, as they march westward. This explains the phrase, "Neither shall one thrust another," in Joel 2:8. In other words, the armies will not fight against each other. They will walk in their own path, and, " When they fall upon the sword, they shall not be wounded." The sword is a symbol for battle; therefore battles will not affect the army of the Antichrist. This is logical because there will be 100 million troops in the army. These two phrases in Joel 2:8 prove that the soldiers in Western Europe will not fight against the Russian army, and the only logical explanation for this is unification.

Nothing will stop this army according to Joel 2:8, including the neutron bombs used by the Pentagon. (If used however, these will cause a global nuclear war). When the verse says, "When they fall upon the sword, they shall not be wounded," that is exactly what it means. The army of the Antichrist cannot be defeated in battle, and they cannot be destroyed by any group of soldiers on earth. One of the spiritual principles of World War III is that only Christ can destroy the army of the Antichrist. This is what the American people must make the Pentagon understand: World War III will be a war between Christ and his army in heaven, and the Antichrist and his army on earth. This is written in Revelation 19:11-21, Revelation 9:16-21, and Revelation 16:12-16. No one else can be allowed to interfere. The army of the Antichrist cannot be defeated in battle until the Lord Jesus Christ destroys it at Armageddon. Here again the biblical plan for World War III in Europe does not include the Pentagon.

In Joel 2:10, "The earth shall quake before them." This phrase indicates an army of 100 million soldiers, and then 40 million troops will be added to the army in Western Europe. In Joel 2:11 is the statement that the army belongs to the Lord, which is correct. It will be used to punish Israel because they crucified Christ. This is written in Matthew 23:37-39, Matthew 21:42-46, Daniel 11:31, Daniel 8:13,14, Matthew 24:15 and in Luke 21:20-24. This is verified by Proverbs 16:4. It is actually Luke 21:20-22 which verifies Joel 2:11. The phrase, "the days of vengeance," means revenge for the crucifixion of Christ.

In Joel 2:12-14 is a commandment from the Lord for all people on earth to repent and accept Christ to avoid destruction by the army of the Antichrist. In Joel 2:15,16 the reference to Zion, and the bride and bridegroom, signify the rapture of the church in Revelation 19:7-9, and Revelation 21:9-11. In II Thessalonians 2:2-9 the day of Christ will not come until after the Antichrist and his army appear in Europe and start World War III. Again, in II Thessalonians 2:8 it is Christ who will destroy the Antichrist and his army. No one else should even try to do this, including the Pentagon. There are spiritual principles that should not be interfered with in this war, which is why I'm writing this chapter.

In Revelation 17:12,13 the ten kings are the political leaders of the ten Common Market nations, and they will give their economic power and their military strength to the Antichrist. Then there will be a Unified European Army. The thing that causes this is written in Revelation 17:16-18. The ten kings will hate the whore, which is the city of Rome. They shall make her desolate and naked, and shall eat her flesh, and burn her with fire. The phrase, "shall eat her flesh," is a reference to Daniel 7:5, to the command, "Arise, devour much flesh." This command is given to the bear, which is the Russian army. To devour much flesh means to conquer Europe. Rome will be totally destroyed as an example for the other nations, so they will not fight against the Antichrist.

The word conquer is used in Revelation 6:2, where the Antichrist will take Europe peacefully in his first year. In order to do this he will have to use the idea of unification into the Common Market. This means he will claim all of the armies of Russia, Eastern, and Western Europe without even fighting. Revelation 6:2 proves that he will call for a Unified European Army because he will conquer peacefully. You can see he will not start World War III until his second year, and this is written in Revelation 6:4. Therefore in Revelation 6:2 he will conquer peacefully by using the idea of unification. The people in Europe won't even know that anything unusual has happened, and this is why the leopard is used for camouflage in Revelation 13:2. The Unified European Army is the camouflage that the Antichrist will use to take the entire continent of Europe. You can see in Revelation 13:2 that the camouflage of the leopard comes first, then the bear which is the Russian army, and then the lion which means to devour all of Europe. Therefore unification will occur in the first year, and this is how the Russian army will be incorporated into Western Europe. When this happens, the combined armies will devour all of Europe like a lion.

What this means for the Pentagon is that the political leaders in Western Europe will forsake NATO, and their armies will join the Antichrist and the Warsaw Pact nations. This will be done under the pretense of making a Unified European Army. Therefore the US military soldiers will be killed by the people they are trying to protect, while they are retreating from the Russian army, because the armies in Western Europe will join the Antichrist. This is stated plainly in Revelation 17:13. I cannot overstate the importance of this because it will cause the deaths of 25 million American soldiers. This is written in Revelation 17:12-18. The NATO armies in Western Europe will join the Warsaw Pact, and they will form a Unified European Army. This army will be controlled by the Antichrist.

The Pentagon must be aware of this coming strategic disaster in Europe. They should also realize that the citizens in Europe would protest over the nuclear weapons. This will cause a public relations disaster for the President and the Pentagon. It can be avoided by working with the United Nations, and by having the United Nations Organization announce to the TV news, that the Pentagon will remove their neutron bombs.

The only way to avoid the loss of 25 million American soldiers will be to close all of the US military bases in Europe immediately, dismantle all of the neutron bombs and other nuclear weapons which are in Europe, and then bring them and the American troops home to the USA. By doing this the Pentagon will avoid a global nuclear war against the Antichrist. The President should give the order to close the US military bases in Europe no later than 2008 to be absolutely safe. He must state his intent to remove the nuclear weapons from Europe, before the public anger mounts against the US military. If he doesn't do this, the US soldiers in Europe will have to fight civilians to protect their own military bases; and believe me, this will cause a public relations disaster.

Now I will explain why you must follow Bible principles to prevent nuclear war. First of all, nuclear war is 100% dependent on the act of retaliation to happen. This is why the atomic bomb was dropped on Japan in 1945 to retaliate for the attack on Pearl Harbor in 1941. Without retaliation nuclear war cannot become a reality. This is the reason for the theology of non-retaliation in Matthew 5:39-48.

This idea is written in every verse individually to stress the importance of this theology because it is the only way to prevent nuclear war. You may have thought these ideas were unusual before, but now you know the real reason for this theology.

In Matthew 5:43-45 Jesus said to, "Love your enemies, bless them that curse you, do good to them that hate you, and pray for them which despitefully use you, and persecute you."

This may sound unusual, until you realize that non-retaliation is the only way to prevent nuclear war. In other words, your nation must use these principles in their relations with other nations, and they must remain neutral during times of war. Therefore when you are perfect as in Matthew 5:48, even as your Father which is in heaven is perfect, you will be able to prevent nuclear war by using non-retaliation as a military principle. Then you will realize that it is the will of God to prevent nuclear war. This is verified in Matthew 24:22, where Christ will return to earth early to stop the nuclear war at the end of World War III to save the human race.

Now that you know you must use non-retaliation to avoid nuclear war, you must eliminate everything that would cause retaliation. For America this means closing all US military bases in Europe, Japan, Korea, and England. The bases on US islands and territories can be left open, with minimum numbers of personnel, all of whom go to church every week. Then if they are killed, their souls will be saved by Christ, and the only thing lost will be some land. Then the US military will not have to retaliate.

I've just realized that having everyone go to church is also an important part of the theology of non-retaliation. This is very important for the US military and for US citizens as well. You will have won the victory if you are killed, as long as *you* are going to church. This idea will be important for non-retaliation; because there is no reason to seek revenge, if the souls of everyone killed in an attack have been saved by Christ. Therefore the US Government and all other governments in the world should convince their people to go to church throughout World War III.

If 25,000 people were killed in the attack on Pearl Harbor, then the atomic bomb retaliation in 1945 was intended to get even for their deaths, as well as to end World War II with Japan. If these people in Pearl Harbor were all going to church every week, then their souls would have been saved by Christ.

You win the victory over Satan by going to church, and you win the victory by non-retaliation. This is why Christ explained the theology in Matthew 5:39-48.

It will also be important for national morale during World War III to have everyone go to church. If there is a chemical warfare attack in Florida, or a car bomb explosion in New York, it will be encouraging to know that everyone killed was going to church every week, and that their souls were saved by Christ. This will be our bright light, our hope in Christ to help us overcome the depression described in Matthew 24:12. It will be an important part of our national direction to have everyone go to church every week. This is how to win World War III.

The next step for the US military is to build ABM defense systems, (Anti-ballistic missile defense), on the East, West, and Gulf Coasts of the USA. To do this the US Government must eliminate the 1972 ABM Treaty. The US Government must also do everything possible to eliminate all nuclear weapons in the USA, Russia, China, England, France, and India. When you eliminate all of the nuclear missiles in the world, there will not be any weapons left to start a nuclear war. This is very important, since the Antichrist will appear in Europe within just six years, and he will be the most evil person to ever live on the earth.

The Pentagon should study the armor of God, which is described in Ephesians 6:10-18 because World War III will be a spiritual war. It will happen for reasons that only the Bible can explain. This is written in Ephesians 6:12. To survive World War III and to win a victory, the Pentagon will have to use the principles for spiritual warfare described in Ephesians 6:10-18. The phrase, "the evil day," in Ephesians 6:13 means World War III. Therefore the phrase, "that ye may be able to withstand in the evil day," means to survive World War III. There are also warnings about this written in Ecclesiastes 9:12, Proverbs 1:27-33, and in Luke 23:31. This means that the Bible says to remain neutral during World War III. To survive World War III you must first avoid nuclear war. Now I will describe the armor of God:

1. Ephesians 6:14: "having your loins girt about with truth."

This means to speak the truth about nuclear war, and to avoid using lies and fear as tactics to get public support. This is important advice for the Pentagon: Stick to the truth of the gospel of Christ to avoid nuclear war. If you use lies, you wander into the domain where Satan rules. This is written in John 8:44. The USA must remain neutral during World War III.

2. Ephesians 6:14: "and having on the breastplate of righteousness."

This is a symbol of defense, and righteousness means to help the people in America prepare for World War III the right way, which is to use the Church Committee Plan.

3. Ephesians 6:15: "And your feet shod with the preparation of the gospel of peace."

This also means to remain neutral during World War III. It means to work toward evangelism too, which publication of this book will do.

4. Ephesians 6:16: "Above all, taking the shield of faith, wherewith ye shall be able to quench all the fiery darts of the wicked."

The shield of faith includes the idea of non-retaliation, while ABM defense will help to stop incoming nuclear missiles. To quench the fiery darts of the wicked sounds a lot like destroying incoming missiles. Therefore ABM defense will be very important toward stopping nuclear war because it will eliminate the need for retaliation. Christ will save us when we have faith in him, and when the Pentagon works on national defense in America.

5. Ephesians 6:17: "And take the helmet of salvation."

This means to allow the mind of Christ to save America. This also means that a change is necessary in the principles used by the Pentagon for warfare, which is why I'm explaining the principles recommended in the Bible. The Antichrist will use the mind of Satan and his devils to fight in World War III. The Pentagon must use the mind of Christ to survive and to win.

6. Ephesians 6:17: "And the sword of the Spirit, which is the word of God."

This is the sharp two-edged sword in Revelation 1:16, Revelation 19:15, and in Revelation 19:21. This sword proceeds out of the mouth of Christ because he speaks the word of God. This is written in John 8:28, and in John 12:49. In Revelation 19:21 Christ will use the two-edged sword to destroy the army of the Antichrist. In Genesis 1:1-31 the word of God created the universe, and in Revelation 19:21 the word of God will destroy the army of the Antichrist. This is verified by II Thessalonians 2:8, where the sword is called the, "Spirit of his mouth." The Pentagon must realize that Christ has already won World War III for them. They must help America to survive the war to win the victory.

7. Ephesians 6:18: "Praying always with all prayer and supplication in the Spirit, and watching thereunto with all perseverance and supplication for all saints."

The Church Committee Group and the church ministers in the USA will help pray for America, and for the US Government during World War III. An important part of these prayers should be for the Pentagon, that they will recognize and honor the power of Christ, and that they will not interfere in his divine plan for the destruction of the army of the Antichrist. The most important part of the spiritual principles of World War III for the Pentagon and the US military will be:

To really believe that Christ will destroy the Antichrist and his army, in exactly the same way it is written in the Bible. I will describe this later in this chapter. As long as the Pentagon believes that Christ will win World War III, then they will do what this book and the Bible tells them to do to survive. This is known as walking in the light.

Ephesians 5:8: "For ye were sometimes darkness, but now are ye light in the Lord: walk as children of light."

This is important because the Pentagon has used lies and fear to get public support for their funding, which are elements of the power of darkness. To overcome this they must use the truth of the gospel of Christ, and walk in the light. This is how you win the victory over Satan during World War III.

Once the army of the Antichrist is assembled in Europe in its 100 million-soldier strength, then half of the job of convincing the Pentagon that Christ will win World War III will be over. When you see the army come together like the Bible says it will, then you must believe that the army will be destroyed the way the Bible says it will. It will be the responsibility of the President to be sure that the Pentagon officers and personnel really believe that Christ can destroy this army, since God was able to create it, and you must believe that God was able to create it, when you see the army in Europe right in front of your eyes.

It will also be the responsibility of the people in America to be sure that the Pentagon believes that Christ will win World War III. Then the US military can prepare national defense for the USA.

Proverbs 30:5: "Every word of God is pure: he is a shield unto them that put their trust in him."

This is a reference to the shield of faith in Ephesians 6:16. When you have faith in God, he will protect your nation. It is very important that the nations have faith in God and in Christ throughout World War III. Then their national direction will be correct. This can be defined as: What the people in America think the Pentagon and the US military should do in relation to the Antichrist and his army.

If the people want the Pentagon to fight, then there will be a nuclear war. If the people want the Pentagon to remain neutral, then America will survive, and Christ will win World War III for us.

It will be my responsibility to convince the people and the Pentagon to remain neutral, no matter what happens during World War III, and no matter how angry they get about the atrocities in Europe. The public reaction to Europe is described in Matthew 24:8, and in Matthew 24:12.

The phrase, "The valley of the shadow of death," in Psalm 23:4, means World War III. We will fear no evil because Christ is with us. The phrase, "Thy rod and thy staff they comfort me," means that we are comforted because Christ will destroy the Antichrist and his army. This is verified in Revelation 2:26,27, and in Revelation 19:15. The rod and the staff are used to rule the nations. In Revelation 19:21 Christ will destroy the army with the sword, which proceeds from his mouth. Therefore the rod and the staff of Christ will comfort us.

An example of wrong national direction would happen, if I tried to convince the Pentagon to remain neutral in World War III, while the people in America want the US military to fight valiantly against the army of the Antichrist. This is why the people must first have faith in Christ, then believe what the Bible says about World War III, and convince the Pentagon to stay out of the war. Then the national direction will be correct.

Now I will explain more of the verses that describe the army of the Antichrist. It is possible that the Antichrist will start a unified army of the Common Market, or a Unified European Army, before the Russian army takes Western Europe. This would explain why the ten kings in Revelation 17:12-18 will give their military strength to Germany and the Antichrist.

The Vatican is more concerned with the suffering of the victims, than with the strategy of the persecutors. The Pentagon is paid to analyze military strategy, and hopefully they won't be involved in Europe. This could actually be why the US military is not included in the book of Revelation, while the city of Rome is.

The Bible verses which describe the army of the Antichrist are Revelation 9:16, which puts the number of soldiers at 200 million. In Micah 5:8 the Gentiles are the soldiers in the army, as in Revelation 11:2, and Luke 21:24. In Ezekiel 38:2 the land of Magog is Russia. Then in Ezekiel 38:2,3 Gog is described as the chief prince of Meshech and Tubal. This means he is the leader of the army, or the Antichrist. You should notice that the word Gog is included in the word Magog. Therefore you know that the Antichrist will be associated with Russia in some way. The earliest prophecy about the army of the Antichrist is written in Deuteronomy 28:49-57. So you can see this was predicted 3,400 years ago. The tribes in Ezekiel 38:2,3 and in Ezekiel 38:6 are named after the sons of Noah in Genesis 10:1-3. In Genesis 10:5 these descendants are called Gentiles, as in Revelation 11:2, Micah 5:8, and in Luke 21:24.

In Isaiah 22:1-14 is a description of Jerusalem under siege, which is also written in Luke 19:43,44. In Isaiah 5:26-30 the arrows of the army will be sharp, and their wheels will be like a whirlwind. In Jeremiah 5:15-18 they are described as a mighty nation, and an ancient nation. In Jeremiah 6:22-26 they will come from the north country; a great nation shall be raised from the sides of the earth, set in array as men of war. This sounds like the Russian army, set in array as they march through Red Square in Moscow. The description in Jeremiah 6:22 is a reference to Daniel 7:5, where the bear, or Russia, is raised up on one side, with three ribs in its mouth. This represents the 666, or World War III. In Revelation 6:4 the Russian army is the great sword in the hand of the Antichrist, and he will use it to start World War III.

In Joel 2:10 the earth shall quake before them, when the army marches. In Ezekiel 38:5 the nations in Persia, Ethiopia, and Libya will join the army of the Antichrist, after it goes south to the Middle East. These are the terrorist nations in Daniel 11:30, which the Antichrist will convince to help him take the oil from Saudi Arabia, Oman, Yemen, and Kuwait.

In Ezekiel 38:15 the army will come from the north, a mighty army. In Ezekiel 38:8 this will happen in the latter years. This is also written in Ezekiel 38:16. The destruction done by the army in the Middle East is described in Ezekiel 38:9-17. The destruction in Europe done by the army is described in Joel 2:1-11, and in Revelation 6:4-8. In Ezekiel 38:17 and in Amos 3:6-11 the Lord God gives you a warning about this army through his servants the prophets. You should listen to the warning.

The army of the Antichrist will be in the Middle East in varying strength during 7 years of World War III; and then the 200 million soldiers will be there at the end of the war. The nations which will be occupied by the army of the Antichrist in the Middle East will be: In Daniel 11:23-28 Saudi Arabia, Oman, Yemen, and Kuwait will be occupied. Then in Daniel 11:30-32 Egypt, Iraq, Syria, and Lebanon will allow the army to surround Israel, which means that it will occupy their nations. In Daniel 11:40 the army, "shall enter into the countries, and shall overflow and pass over." This phrase indicates the 200 million soldiers in Revelation 9:16 in the end of World War III. This is verified by the phrase, "And at the time of the end," in Daniel 11:40. In Daniel 11:41,42 Jordan, which is described as Edom, Moab, and Ammon in Daniel 11:41, will not be occupied, but Egypt will be. In Daniel 11:43 Libya and Ethiopia will be partially occupied by the army.

In Ezekiel 38:5 Persia, Ethiopia, and Libya will have soldiers who will join the army of the Antichrist. This will probably happen continually throughout World War III; and the land of Persia includes Iraq, Iran, Syria, and Lebanon. During the Old Testament times, the land of Persia stretched from a line between Eastern Europe and North Africa on the west to India on the east; and from Russia on the north to the Gulf of Oman on the south. It was a very large kingdom. Therefore when Ezekiel 38:5 says that the soldiers

288

from Persia will join the army of the Antichrist, this means approximately 60 million soldiers from Iraq, Iran, Syria, Lebanon, and possibly Turkey. Then the entire Middle East will be occupied in varying strength from the third to the tenth year of the war.

The actual destruction of the army of the Antichrist will happen in several ways. They will be attacked by the ships of Chittim, or the Italian Navy. This is written in Daniel 11:30, and this attack could consist of Cruise missiles or Battleship bombardments. This will cause the Antichrist to consult with the terrorist nations in the Middle East, which surround Israel, and to use chemical warfare against Jerusalem. This is why he will recruit 60 million soldiers from the Middle East to join his army. When you think about this, it is very intelligent strategy. If he uses chemical warfare without recruiting the soldiers from the terrorist nations first, then they might fight against him.

The chemical warfare attack against Jerusalem is described in Daniel 8:11-14, Daniel 11:30,31, Matthew 24:15, and in Mark 13:14. It is called the abomination of desolation because the city will be left desolate after the attack. This is described by Christ in Matthew 23:37,38. When this happens, the two prophets from Revelation 11:3-7 will appear in Jerusalem to fight against the army of the Antichrist. In Revelation 11:5 they will kill the soldiers of the Antichrist with fire that proceeds out of their mouths. This fire will be able to go 400 yards from the two prophets, and will kill thousands of soldiers. This is written in Isaiah 30:27, Isaiah 30:30, Isaiah 30:33, and in Isaiah 31:8,9. The reason for this is written in Jeremiah 5:11-17.

In Revelation 11:3 the two prophets will be in Jerusalem for three and one half years. In Isaiah 9:5-7 they will fight the army with burning and fuel of fire, just before the Second Coming of Christ.

In Isaiah 17:12-14 the destruction of the army is prophesied. The nations will rush to Israel, and God shall rebuke them, and they shall flee far off. This refers to the nations that have soldiers that will join the army of the Antichrist. The soldiers will flee from the two prophets, or they will be burned alive. This is also written in Isaiah 33:8-13. In Ezekiel 38:16, Ezekiel 38:23, Ezekiel 39:7, Ezekiel 39:13, Ezekiel 39:20-22, and in Ezekiel 39:28,29 all of these things will happen to glorify the Lord God.

In Micah 7:16,17 the people will hide in holes in the ground, and they will be afraid of the Lord. The reason for this is written in Revelation 6:12-17, where the soldiers will hide in caves during an earthquake. This is also written in Isaiah 2:9,10, Isaiah 2:19-21, and Isaiah 29:6. These events are described in order in Ezekiel 38:19-23. First is the shaking, which means earthquakes. This is why the earthquakes will be in divers places in Matthew 24:7, Mark 13:8, and in Luke 21:11. In Ezekiel 38:19,20 the whole earth will shake at the coming of the Lord. Some of the soldiers in the army of the Antichrist will be killed in these earthquakes.

In Ezekiel 38:21 every soldier in the army will use his sword against his brother. This is described in Revelation 9:15-21, where the tanks in the army of the Antichrist will be used to kill the soldiers in the same army. In Revelation 9:15 the four angels from the Garden of Eden will convince the soldiers to kill each other. The Iraqi army will probably start a battle over rights to the oil in Saudi Arabia. In Daniel 11:40 the king of the south, or the king of Saudi Arabia, will fight a war against the army of the Antichrist. This will probably be when the army begins fighting against itself over rights to the oil. Then 66.7 million soldiers will die in this battle.

The plague of hail and fire in Revelation 8:7 will be used against the army of the Antichrist, and it was used in Exodus 9:24 against Egypt.

In Ezekiel 38:22 the pestilence and blood is a reference to the plague of hail, and fire mingled with blood in Revelation 8:7. The description of great hailstones in Revelation 16:21 matches the description in Ezekiel 38:22. Every hailstone will be equal to the weight of a talent, which is 75 pounds. This will mean serious destruction for the army, especially with fire coming down with the hail. In Ezekiel 39:1,2 is this phrase, "And I will turn thee back, and leave but the sixth part of thee."

This means that while 66.7 million soldiers will kill each other in battle, then 100 million more will die in the hailstorm, with hail and fire falling from the sky. This will leave 33.3 million soldiers, which is one sixth of the original 200 million.

In Isaiah 66:14-16 the Lord will come with fire to render his anger with fury. This will be the plague of hail and fire in Revelation 8:7. In Nahum 1:9-11 the army of the Antichrist will burn as stubble fully dry. This is also written in Isaiah 29:5,6, where the chaff that passes away is the army that will burn up, and the storm and tempest is the hail and fire in Revelation 8:7.

The final method of destruction for the army of the Antichrist will happen at the battle of Armageddon. This is written in Revelation 16:12-17, and you should notice that the destruction will be immediate.

When Christ returns to earth in Revelation 19:11-16, the army of the Antichrist will be at Armageddon in Revelation 16:16, and in Revelation 19:17-19; and then Christ will destroy them with the two-edged sword which proceeds from his mouth in Revelation 19:20,21, Revelation 19:15, Revelation 1:16, and in II Thessalonians 2:8. It is called the day of the wrath of the Lamb in Revelation 6:16,17.

By definition, the Antichrist is the enemy of Christ. The word "anti" means against or opposed to. Therefore it is the responsibility of Christ to destroy the Antichrist. This is one of the spiritual principles of World War III, and it is why the battle of Armageddon will happen on the day of the Lord. Jesus Christ is the Lord, and it will be his day to destroy the forces of evil at Armageddon. It is called the day of the Lord in Isaiah 13:6, which will come as a destruction from the Almighty. In Amos 5:18-20 the day of the Lord will be darkness to the land of Israel because of the army of the Antichrist that will be there. This is verified in Joel 2:11, Zechariah 14:1, Obadiah 1:15, and in Zephaniah 1:14-18. In Zephaniah 2:1-3 it is called the day of the Lord's anger. In Joel 3:14 the day of the Lord will be near, when the army is gathered in the valley of decision, which is the valley of the son of Hinnom in Israel.

In Zephaniah 1:7,8 there will be a sacrifice prepared on the day of the Lord, which will be the army of the Antichrist. This is described in Revelation 19:17-21, and in Ezekiel 39:17-20. In Zephaniah 1:8 the phrase, "I will punish the princes, and the king's children, and all such as are clothed with strange apparel," is a reference to the parable of the wedding feast in Matthew 22:11-13. In these verses the man who did not have on a wedding garment was cast out into outer darkness. This is the meaning of the phrase, "strange apparel," in Zephaniah 1:8. The Antichrist and his army didn't choose to go to the Marriage Supper of the Lamb in Revelation 19:7-9, so they will be the main course in the feast of the fowls in Revelation 19:17-21.

THE VALLEY OF THE SON OF HINNOM

It took 16 years of very serious Bible study for me to understand the events surrounding the army of the Antichrist during World War III. There are two places where the army will be destroyed by the Lord God Almighty, and by the Lord Jesus Christ. The first one is in the valley of the Son of Hinnom; and it took me 15 years to even find this place on a map of Israel. Here are the reasons for the occupation of Israel by the army of the Antichrist.

In II Chronicles 33:6 Manasseh caused the children of Israel to be sacrificed in the fire in the valley of the Son of Hinnom. It will be the place where the army of the Antichrist gathers, which is the punishment to Israel for the sins of Manasseh and the people. It is called the valley of slaughter in Jeremiah 7:32, and in Jeremiah 19:6. In Isaiah 30:25 it is called the day of great slaughter. I think the description in Revelation 14:20 also refers to the valley of slaughter because of the blood which will be five feet deep there, after the tank battle in Revelation 9:13-19.

The phrase, "without the city," in Revelation 14:20 means that it will happen just outside of Jerusalem; and this is where the valley of the Son of

Hinnom is. This is also described in Ezekiel 38:21, where the army will fight against their own soldiers.

In Joel 3:2, and in Joel 3:12 it is called the valley of Jehoshaphat. In Isaiah 22:1-14 it is called the valley of vision, and the sins of Israel are described. Of all the verses that describe it, here is the key verse:

Joel 3:14: " Multitudes, multitudes in the valley of decision: for the day of the Lord is near in the valley of decision." The multitudes described here means the army of the Antichrist, and the phrase, "for the day of the Lord is near in the valley of decision," means that the battle of Armageddon is about to happen, after the tank battle in the valley of the Son of Hinnom. Of course this means there will be two places where the army will be destroyed:

1. The valley of the Son of Hinnom, which is just south of Jerusalem
2. Armageddon at Megiddo, which is 10 miles southwest of Nazareth

The reason for the names, the valley of decision, the valley of vision, the valley of Jehoshaphat, and the valley of slaughter is to emphasize the importance of the place where 166.7 million troops in the army of the Antichrist will be killed. This is described in Ezekiel 38:21, and Revelation 9:13-19, where one third of the army will be killed; and this means that 66.7 million of them will die in the tank battle. Then in Ezekiel 38:22, and in Isaiah 30:30 the Lord God Almighty will send the plague of hail and fire from Revelation 8:7, and it will kill 100 million soldiers in the army of the Antichrist. This can be verified in Ezekiel 39:2, where only one sixth of the army will be left after the events in the valley of the Son of Hinnom; and these events are described in the previous verses, in Ezekiel 38:21-23. This means that only 33.3 million troops will be left to fight at Armageddon.

In Nahum 1:9,10 the plague of hail and fire will burn the army as stubble fully dry. In Nahum 1:11 the phrase, "a wicked counselor," means the Antichrist. In Nahum 1:13 the Lord will break his yoke from off of Israel. In Nahum 1:14 the Lord will make a grave for his army. Of the 200 million soldiers, 166.7 million will be killed in the valley of the Son of Hinnom, and 33.3 million will be killed at Armageddon.

ARMAGEDDON

In Revelation 16:14 Armageddon is called the battle of that great day of God Almighty. Christ is the Word of God, and he will destroy the army of the Antichrist at Armageddon. In Zephaniah 1:18 it is called the day of the Lord's wrath; and in Revelation 6:16,17 it is called the day of wrath of the Lamb because Christ is the Lamb of God. This is verified in John 1:29, and in John 1:35-37. In Ezekiel 39:8 is the phrase, "It is done." This exact statement is also written in Revelation 16:17, and it refers to the battle of Armageddon.

In Micah 4:11,12, Zephaniah 3:8, and in Isaiah 13:4 many nations will gather against Israel. This is a reference to all of the armies from Russia, Eastern Europe, Western Europe, and the Middle East that will join the army of the Antichrist. In *Halley's Bible Handbook* on page 206 is the quote: "More blood has been shed at Megiddo hill than at any other spot on earth, it is said".[387] Halley says that Megiddo is ten miles southwest of Nazareth, and that the battle of Armageddon will happen there.

In Ezekiel 39:3-5 the Lord will smite the bow out of the left hand of the Antichrist, and cause his arrows to fall out of his right hand. This could be a reference to the bow described in Revelation 6:2; and it means that Christ will destroy the army of the Antichrist while it is standing at Armageddon, and he will destroy them from the sky. This is described in Revelation 19:21, where the remnant is the remaining soldiers in the army. In Ezekiel 39:4 the army will fall upon the mountains of Israel, with all of its bands. Then the ravenous birds will eat their dead bodies in Ezekiel 39:4, Ezekiel 39:17, and in Revelation 19:17-21.

No other army has to be at Armageddon to fight against the army of the Antichrist. In Revelation 19:11-16 the armies in heaven will follow Christ upon white horses, and then in Revelation 19:21 he will destroy the army of the Antichrist with his own power, which is infinite. This is the meaning of Revelation 1:8, where Christ has the power of Almighty God. The word, "Almighty" means infinite power. This is also written in Revelation 16:14, where Armageddon is called the battle of that great day of God Almighty.

In Revelation 16:14 the spirits of devils will gather their armies, which comprise the forces of evil to fight at Armageddon. In Revelation 16:16 the Lord God will gather the forces of evil at Armageddon, so Christ can destroy them. Therefore no one has to be there to fight against the army of the Antichrist. If you believe that you have to be there, then you have been fooled by the devils, which will gather their armies. In I John 4:6 devils are called the spirits of error because they can cause people to make wrong decisions. I'm telling you this, so you won't make a wrong decision about Armageddon. You don't have to be there.

In Ezekiel 39:9-16 the people of Israel will burn the weapons, shields, and bucklers, and it will take seven years to get rid of them all. The reason for the seven years is to cut up the iron and steel tanks, trucks, and vehicles of the army. This explains the difference in time, where it will only take seven months to bury the bodies in Ezekiel 39:12, and in Ezekiel 39:14. You see it will take much longer to get rid of the tanks and vehicles than the dead bodies. Also in Ezekiel 39:11 the place is called the valley of Hamongog. This is also written in Ezekiel 39:15.

You can see that the Pentagon doesn't need to use their neutron bombs to destroy the Russian tanks, when they move to take Western Europe because the tanks will be dismantled and sold for scrap iron after the battle of Armageddon in Israel. This is written in Ezekiel 39:9. There is no mention of tanks, vehicles, missiles, jet aircraft, televisions, or any other modern inventions in the Old Testament in the Bible. The reason is that the people who lived 2,500 years ago would have known about them before their time, which could have upset history. This is one reason for the old style of language used in the King James Bible. Modern language would have upset history.

Even though the King James Bible doesn't directly mention any modern inventions, it still describes World War III in perfect detail. The tanks in Revelation 9:15-21, and the missiles in Psalm 7:13 are described by using symbolism, instead of using modern descriptions. This way no one could decipher the meanings of these verses, until the seals were removed from the book in Revelation 5:1-14, and Revelation 6:1-17. The removal of the seals means to reveal the meaning of the symbolism, which is why it is called the book of Revelation.

The important thing to remember here is that the Pentagon and the US military are not included in the biblical plan for World War III in Europe. The US Army is not mentioned anywhere in the book of Revelation, or in Daniel, Matthew 24, II Thessalonians 2, Mark 13, or Luke 21. It will be a losing strategy to use the neutron bombs in Europe to destroy the Russian tanks because then they won't be available to kill the 66.7 million soldiers in Revelation 9:15-21. In Ezekiel 38:21 the Lord will call for a sword against the army of the Antichrist, and every sword will be against his brother. This refers to Revelation 9:18, where the fire, smoke, and brimstone from the tanks will kill one third of the soldiers, which is 66.7 million. In Revelation 9:16 the original number of soldiers is 200 million.

Therefore the Pentagon must not try to stop these tanks, or to kill the soldiers in the tanks by using neutron bombs. If they destroy these tanks, then they will just create 66.7 million more soldiers to fight against. If the Pentagon interferes in the destruction of the army of the Antichrist, then that army will not be destroyed. Using the neutron bombs will also cause a global nuclear war.

This means that the people in the USA must convince the Pentagon to close the US military bases in Europe, and England. Then the US troops and the neutron bombs must be removed from Europe.

There is a motive for the soldiers in the Unified European Army to double-cross their own people in Eastern and Western Europe. The Antichrist will give them the land, hotels, restaurants, houses, and everything else. They will have to accept the swastika, and then enforce the famine of the Antichrist to receive money or property. The $600 dollars per month will be a great deal for the Russian and the East European soldiers. Then after the army is gathered together, with 60 million Russian troops, 40 million Eastern European troops and some Western European troops, it will be the pride of Europe. All of the people will brag about their army, and this is written in Revelation 13:4, and Joel 2:2. Then the Antichrist will declare his famine after 100 million troops are assembled into the Unified European Army. This is the meaning of Joel 2:3, where the land will be as the Garden of Eden before them, and after them a desolate wilderness. Joel 2:6 describes the reaction of the people to this. The phrase, "all faces shall gather blackness," means depression. This is also described in Matthew 24:8, where the famine of the Antichrist is called the beginning of sorrows.

The dividing of gain is described in Daniel 11:24, Daniel 11:39, and in Daniel 11:43. This will be the motive for the troops to cause World War III. The Antichrist will offer the land, hotels, restaurants, money, houses, wine, and everything in Europe to the soldiers if they will accept the swastika and declare the famine in Europe for him. This will have to be done after the army is united, or they will rebel at the idea, which will cause divisions in the army. The people in Europe don't like the swastika, so unification will have to come first. Then the Antichrist will divide the spoils and riches among his soldiers, after they accept the mark of the beast in Revelation 13:16,17, Revelation 16:2, and Revelation 19:20. This will be a swastika placed on the right hand or on the forehead. The soldiers who accept the mark willingly will get it placed on their right hand. The people who resist, and then give up later in the famine, will get the mark on their foreheads.

This motive of dividing the spoils and riches explains the unification in Revelation 17:12-18 to destroy Rome, the famine across all of Europe in Revelation 13:16,17, and the 200 million soldiers in Revelation 9:16. You see there is an unusual set of events described here. The Western European armies will unite with the Antichrist to help him destroy Rome, instead of fighting against the Russian army. There are two incentives that the Antichrist could use to cause this. First he will call for a Unified European Army, paid by the Common Market. This explains the funding for the army. Earlier in this book I said that he would pay the Russian army with money from the Common Market. This will still be true, but the soldiers will be part of the Unified European Army. Then no one will even be suspicious about the buildup of troops in Western Europe. This is when he will declare the famine.

He will offer to give all of Europe to his soldiers, if they will accept the mark of the beast. This explains the lust and greed in Revelation 17:16. It is also the meaning of the phrase, "pleasure in unrighteousness," in II Thessalonians 2:12. This means to enjoy lust and greed. The people in Europe will be fooled because they will think the Antichrist is a hero, after he unites the Common Market. This is how he is pictured in Revelation 6:2. They will applaud him like they did with Hitler in World War II, and they will be proud of his army until it destroys everything they own. This is when the Antichrist will go from the hero in Revelation 6:2 to the man of sin in II Thessalonians 2:3.

The dividing up of gain explains how the army will grow to 200 million soldiers, in spite of the war in Europe and the famine. If the soldiers in Western Europe fight against the Antichrist, then those 40 million soldiers will be killed, along with 5 million soldiers in his army. If this happened, then the army wouldn't get to the 200 million soldiers in Revelation 9:16. Therefore the unification in Revelation 17:12-18 must take place before the takeover of Europe. This will be done with the idea of a Unified European Army, paid by the Common Market.

Now ask yourself this question: How can this army be 50 times larger than any army in history? Here is the answer: The soldiers who join it will divide up the entire Continent of Europe, and then the Middle East later. This is why the 200 million soldiers are described in Revelation 9:16. It is also why the armies in Western Europe will double-cross their own people. This is why his army will destroy Rome, Italy in Revelation 17:16-18. The destruction of Rome verifies Revelation 13:7, Daniel 7:21, and Daniel 7:25, where the Antichrist will make war with the saints and overcome them. When the Vatican complains about the dividing up of Europe, and the famine of the Antichrist, the unified armies of Europe will help the Antichrist destroy Rome. It is possible that the Vatican will complain about the unification of the army, instead of the famine. This is how it is written in Revelation 17:12-18. The army unifies, and then destroys Rome. Why? The Vatican will probably complain about the size of the army. You can see in Revelation 17:12-18 that the armies of the ten Common Market nations will join the side of evil because in Revelation 17:13 they will give their power and strength to the beast, which is the same beast in Revelation 13:1, that is the kingdom of the Antichrist.

The question now is, can the Pentagon sit through all of the tragedies in Europe during World War III without fighting? These include:

The military takeover of Europe by the Russian army, the nuclear attack on Rome, the famine of the Antichrist, the mark of the beast, the takeover of the world oil supply, and the nuclear war at the end of it. The number of deaths here could be 3 billion. To save these souls for Christ the people must go to church every week, and they must be killed for their faith.

I will say no, the Pentagon will not be able to restrain their actions. When you know that the Pentagon won't stay out of World War III, you must find a safety device to keep them out. This is the Church Committee Plan.

Question: Why do generals always want to fight in wars? Answer: That is their job. Question: What if the people don't want them to do this job? Answer:

They must have a way to stop them, or they will have to look at charts, graphs, and diagrams like they did in the Desert Storm War in Kuwait. The Pentagon tries to get public support for their military campaigns, yet they really act independently of the people. They have been known to out-maneuver the President. For this reason, it is of the utmost importance to close the US military bases in Europe, and the ones in England now, and remove the nuclear weapons and troops.

Generals have a 40-year career, and they are not elected officials. They receive glory from their military victories, and sometimes they don't listen to the people. The only example I could find on removal of a general is when President Harry Truman fired General Douglas MacArthur on April 11, 1951. There was then a Senate investigation, and General MacArthur resigned. Thus the procedure is removal by the President, and then investigation by the Senate. The people of America must be aware of this, and if necessary they can ask the President for the removal of military officers.

Generals compete with each other for glory, and because of this you must know how to get rid of a renegade officer, especially if he orders an attack against the Antichrist. The enlisted personnel in the US military should know that it could cause a nuclear war if they attack the army of the Antichrist. However, any safety device in the US military to keep America out of World War III will not be 100% reliable because it is the job of generals to fight in wars.

What will be almost 100% effective will be to close all of the US military bases in Europe. Then the US Senate can pass a law to give offensive military power to the Church Committee, which will make my device for prevention of nuclear war 100% effective. The Senate should also give the power to declare war, and the power to launch nuclear missiles to the Church Committee. This plan will be 100% effective if the Church Committee Group reports any unauthorized activity to the American people. Then if the Pentagon or the US military sends a battle group of ships to England when they are blockaded by the Antichrist, the Church Committee Group can report this to the American people in the TV news and the press. Then the people can demand that the President call back the battle group of ships, before they start a nuclear war. This book will give ample warning to the people in England. Then if necessary the US President can remove the officer who ordered the ships to go to England. The Senate can investigate the incident also.

This is the only way to give power to the Church Committee Group, so they will have authority over the government. This power cannot come from the government; it should come from the people. The Church Committee Group will provide food, housing, fallout shelters, water tanks, and gas masks for the people, so the people should support them.

The people cannot leave these decisions up to the Pentagon because military generals cover for each other in times of trouble. The same is true for the hawks in the Senate, and the nuclear weapons industry. This makes it difficult to get at the truth, and this alone could destroy America in a nuclear war. That is right, not telling the truth can cause a nuclear war.

I think the Pentagon wants to stop the Russian army in Europe because they think that Russia would eventually attack America. So the Pentagon wants to stop them in Europe, before they can do this. The problem here is that fighting the Russian army in Europe will cause the Antichrist to attack America with total nuclear retaliation. If the Pentagon leaves them alone, the USA won't be involved in World War III at all. Being the policeman for the world is dead because the Antichrist will have 200 million soldiers. The NATO nations will join the Warsaw Pact, which means that the Pentagon will have no reason to be in Europe.

Therefore the Pentagon should look at the situation this way: If the Antichrist were going to fight against America, he would have to spend $2 trillion dollars to update the Russian military, and then $1 trillion dollars to export their weapons and troops to fight against America. There is at least $5 trillion dollars in the Middle East, not counting the world oil supply itself. This is a swing of $8 trillion dollars if the Antichrist goes south with his army as it is written in the Bible.

I've said four or five times that the Pentagon and the US military are not included in the biblical plan for World War III in Europe. If they include themselves and interfere, then 10 million American soldiers could be vaporized, so the biblical plan will remain the same. It is like the time machine idea of going back to the past, where if you change history, the future will be upset. This is very dangerous, and I will describe it this way: If the Pentagon interferes with the wrath of God, then what will they suffer? They will suffer the wrath of God, and the US troops could be vaporized, so the biblical plan will remain the same. There could also be a judgment against America for this. Now this is not written anywhere in the book of Revelation, Daniel, Matthew 24, or in II Thessalonians 2; but this is what would have to happen for the plan for World War III in Europe to be the same as it is written in the Bible.

The Pentagon will have to be very careful not to leave any US military personnel anywhere on the whole continent of Europe, or there will be a nuclear war against the Antichrist. This is what the American people must be aware of; and this includes England, Scotland, and Ireland because it would be too easy to fire missiles from the safety of England.

THE SINS OF ISRAEL

The army of the Antichrist will be created to come against the land of Israel to punish it for the sins written in the Old Testament, and in the New Testament when they crucified Christ. This is written in several verses, and I will explain some of them for the benefit of the Pentagon, so they will know why the US military cannot interfere with the army of the Antichrist.

In Jeremiah 5:23-31 the people of Israel were rebellious, and their sins caused wickedness. In Micah 1:5 this is repeated, and in Micah 1:7 the idols will be destroyed. In Micah 1:6 the land of Samaria will be destroyed. In Micah 2:3 the evil time is World War III, and in Micah 2:4,5 the Antichrist will divide up the land in Israel. This is verified in Daniel 11:39. In Zephaniah 1:14-18 the day of the Lord will be a day of wrath, distress, desolation, darkness, and gloominess. In Zephaniah 1:17 this will happen because Israel sinned against the Lord. In Amos 5:18-23 the day of the Lord will be darkness and not light to the land of Israel.

In Isaiah 2:6-18 the people of Israel worshipped idols, which were the work of their own hands. This is also written in Isaiah 31:6,7. In Ezekiel 39:22-29 there is an explanation of the punishment for Israel. In Ezekiel 39:24 the uncleanness means idolatry, and the transgressions mean sins. In Ezekiel 39: 26-29 the people of Israel will receive the blessing of Zion, after they have borne their shame for their trespasses.

In Jeremiah 7:30-34 the people of Israel sacrificed their sons and their daughters in the fire. This is verified in II Chronicles 33:6, and in Jeremiah 19:4-8; and because of it the people will be killed, and then Jerusalem will be laid desolate by the army of the Antichrist, which is also written in Jeremiah 7:34, Jeremiah 5:15-17, Luke 19:43,44, Revelation 11:2, and in Luke 21:22-24. In Isaiah 29:1-4 the people will speak out of the dust because the city will be laid even with the ground. This is verified in Luke 19:43,44. The siege against Jerusalem is described in Isaiah 22:1-14.

In Isaiah 13:1-8 the army of the Antichrist will punish Israel. In Isaiah 26:21 the Lord will punish the inhabitants of the earth for their iniquity. This means during World War III. This is repeated in Isaiah 13:9-11. In Joel 2:11 the army of the Antichrist belongs to the Lord because he will use it to punish Israel for their sins. The army will be sent there specifically to come against the land of Israel in the latter days. This is written in Ezekiel 38:8-17. In Ezekiel 38:17 the prophets have prophesied about this, and in Ezekiel 38:18-23 the Lord will destroy the army of the Antichrist. The order of events in the process of destruction of the army is described here in these verses. World War III itself is rather complicated, but it is described in detail in the Bible.

In Zephaniah 3:5-8 the Lord will be in Zion, but at the present the unjust still commit sin. In Zephaniah 3:6 there is a description of what the cities of Europe will look like, after the army of the Antichrist has destroyed them. This is a good reason to evacuate all of the merchandise from Europe. In Zephaniah 3:7 the people should receive instruction, but they are still corrupt. Then in Zephaniah 3:8 the Lord will rise up to the prey to destroy the Antichrist and his army, after they have destroyed Israel. In Jeremiah 5:11-18 one of the sins was mockery toward the prophets and to the Lord, and this is why the two prophets will be in Israel. In Jeremiah 5:17 the Warsaw ghetto tactic will be used against Jerusalem. This is also described in Luke 19:43.

There are instructions for the Christian people, the Jews who convert to Christianity, and for the Pentagon in Isaiah 26:20,21. We are told to hide during World War III, until the indignation is over. This means to stay out of the war because in Isaiah 26:21 the Lord will punish the army of the Antichrist. In Amos 5:13 we are told to keep silent during World War III. In Revelation 13:10 anyone who fights in World War III will be destroyed with the sword. In Ephesians 6:13 we are told to take the armor of God, so that we may be able to withstand in the evil day, which means to survive World War III. In Psalm 23:4 are instructions to let the Lord Jesus Christ rule the nations during World War III. This is verified in Revelation 2:26,27, Revelation 19:15, and in Revelation 19:19-21. In Joel 2:12-14 we are instructed to pray, and to use fasting, weeping, and mourning; for this may cause the Lord to have mercy upon us. In Joel 2:15-20 the priests and the ministers of the Lord are instructed to weep, and to pray for the deliverance of the people. Then in Joel 2:20 the army of the Antichrist will be destroyed.

The army of the Antichrist is supposed to punish Europe because the people there will worship the Antichrist, like they did with Hitler in World War II. This is written in II Thessalonians 2:9-12. And the army is supposed to punish Israel because of past sins, and because they crucified Christ. This is written in Matthew 23:37-39. Therefore the Pentagon must not interfere because these things are pre-ordained to happen.

FIRE IN ENGLAND AND JAPAN

In Ezekiel 38:1-4 the land of Magog is Russia, and Gog is the Antichrist. Then in Ezekiel 39:6 is this statement:

Ezekiel 39:6: "And I will send a fire on Magog, and among them that dwell carelessly in the isles: and they shall know that I am the Lord."

The phrase, "and among them that dwell carelessly in the isles," means all of the islands surrounding Europe. This will include England, Scotland, Ireland, Japan, Corsica, Sardinia, Sicily, and Crete.

This is very important news because it means that the plague of hail and fire from Revelation 8:7, and Ezekiel 38:22 will also happen in these islands, as well as in the entire continent of Europe. This verifies my evacuation plan for Europe, and for the surrounding islands.

You see, when all of Europe surrenders to the Antichrist, the resulting kingdom will be called Magog, as it is in Ezekiel 39:6. Then the word, "fire," in this verse means the plague of hail and fire from Ezekiel 38:22, and Revelation 8:7. It is a shortened expression because it follows the same explanation in Ezekiel 38:22.

The people who dwell carelessly in the isles will dwell carelessly because they will watch the famine of the Antichrist in Europe, and they will see the mark of the beast, which will be the swastika, forced upon everyone who lives there. The people on the surrounding islands will be taking a very real chance that the swastika will also be forced on them. Then this is the meaning of the phrase, "and among them that dwell carelessly in the isles."

For this reason, all of the people in England, Scotland, Ireland, Japan, Corsica, Sardinia, Sicily, and Crete must evacuate, and they should move to the new host nation for them on the Evacuate Europe List. Earlier in this book I said that England and Japan would probably be blockaded by the Antichrist. Now I know that the situation will be worse than I thought because these islands will also get the plague of hail and fire from Ezekiel 38:22, and Revelation 8:7. This plague will happen at the end of World War III. The reason why this plague will happen is that the Lord God wants these people to move, so they will not be condemned to the Lake of Fire by the Antichrist. The extra four islands can move to Argentina with Italy. These are Corsica, Sardinia, Sicily, and Crete.

PRAYER

I will write about prayer, since it will be very important to us in the future. In Matthew 6:9-13 Jesus told us to use the Lord's Prayer. The reason for one set prayer is that some people are in danger because they believe they can talk to the Lord God like they do with people. When they are upset or angry, they speak blasphemy by criticizing the Lord God. In Matthew 12:31,32 you will be condemned to the Lake of Fire if you speak one word against the Holy Ghost, or against God. This is why Jesus told us to use the Lord's Prayer. He also protects us from blasphemy by saying to criticize him instead of God. This is written in Matthew 12:32.

St. Paul always said that giving thanks to God is important in prayer. This is written in Colossians 1:3, Colossians 3:17, Colossians 4:2, Romans 1:8, I Corinthians 1:4, I Corinthians 15:57, Philippians 4:6, I Thessalonians 1:2, II Thessalonians 1:3, II Timothy 1:3, and in Philemon 1:4. This is true because thanksgiving is the opposite of complaining. Since complaining will condemn you to the Lake of Fire because it is blasphemy, you should make it a point to thank the Lord Jesus Christ as often as possible because he died on the cross to save you. Therefore it is best to use the Lord's Prayer, and to give thanks to Christ.

I Thessalonians 5:18: "In every thing give thanks: for this is the will of God in Christ Jesus concerning you." It is the will of God for you to give thanks because it is the opposite of complaining. For an example of what will happen when you complain, look at Hebrews 3:8-19.

In Ephesians 1:16, and in Philippians 1:3,4 St. Paul always gave thanks for the faithful Christians, when he said his prayers to God, in the name of Jesus Christ. David said thanks to God in Psalm 18:49, Psalm 26:7, Psalm 30:12, Psalm 35:18, and in Psalm 69:30. He also said praise to God continually, and he blessed the Lord always. In fact the Psalms of David will give us a good example to follow in prayer during World War III. Here are the key verses:

Psalm 37:18,19: "The Lord knoweth the days of the upright: and their inheritance shall be for ever.

They shall not be ashamed in the evil time: and in the days of famine they shall be satisfied."

The phrase, "the evil time" is World War III. If we give thanks and praise to God through our Lord Jesus Christ, we will have food throughout the war.

You should notice that St. Paul prayed in his Epistles much like David did in the Psalms. This is known as praying in the Spirit, which is described in Revelation 4:8. It is possible to pray for the gift of praise to the Lord Jesus Christ, and this will help you to pray in the Spirit of God. In Isaiah 41:25 I have received the gift of the Holy Spirit, and I pray to the Lord Jesus Christ continually every day.

Christ told us to say the Lord's Prayer in Matthew 6:9-13, and to say it together. When the people say this prayer together, they should also go to church together, and they should work together to prepare for World War III.

302

Therefore the Lord's Prayer is written the way it is, in order to bring families together in the church. This is what John the Baptist was supposed to do in the prophecy of Malachi 4:5,6; but the people did not obey the prophecy.

Malachi 4:5,6: "Behold, I will send you Elijah the prophet before the coming of the great and dreadful day of the Lord:

And he shall turn the heart of the fathers to the children, and the heart of the children to their fathers, lest I come and smite the earth with a curse."

The curse described here is AIDS, and this is verified in Revelation 2:20-23. If the people of the world had returned to the family values described in these verses from 25 AD to 1970 AD, and abstained from fornication and adultery, then there would not have been a need for the plague of AIDS.

Therefore you can see that John the Baptist, who was Elijah, was supposed to bring family values back to the hearts of the people of the world. This is the meaning of Malachi 4:5,6. Since I am sent to tell you about the Second Coming of Christ, it is also my duty to bring family values back to the hearts of the people, so they will go to church and worship Christ: Then they will be saved. This is why the Lord's Prayer is written the way it is. The phrase, "Our Father which art in heaven," indicates that we are supposed to say the prayer together to our Creator, the Almighty Father of our Lord Jesus Christ. Then we should also go to church together, and prepare for World War III together.

You may have noticed that watching sports like football, soccer, baseball, basketball, and others is the pastime for almost all nations. This will have to change, as the world begins to prepare for World War III. You see, people concentrate on sports during peacetime; but they concentrate on food storage, travel trailers for housing, fallout shelters, and gas masks going into a war. All nations not in Europe or the Middle East must remain neutral, and they must begin preparing for World War III now.

TRIBULATION

I have heard many Christian Ministers say that the rapture of church will happen before the tribulation described in Matthew 24:6-12, and Matthew 24:15-21 in the Bible. Part of their reason for saying this is, in my opinion, to convince more people to join their church so they can avoid the great tribulation period. It is more important to learn what the Bible says about this subject, however, than to try to build up false hopes in the people who are trying to decide what to do about joining the church.

To understand this you must realize that the tribulation itself will be caused by World War III, and the war is described in Revelation 6:3-8,

Revelation 12:17, and Revelation 13:1-18. You must also understand where the idea of a pre-tribulation rapture came from. I have heard statements about this several times, and then one day a Christian Minister mentioned Revelation 3:10 on a television program. The phrase that he emphasized was this:

"Because thou hast kept the word of my patience, I also will keep thee from the hour of temptation, which shall come upon all the world."

The Minister assumed correctly that, "the hour of temptation" is a reference to World War III, and the famine of the Antichrist. What he guessed wrong about is the method used to avoid it. Look at this verse about the city of Rome:

Revelation 18:4: "And I heard another voice from heaven, saying, Come out of her, my people, that ye be not partakers of her sins, that ye receive not of her plagues."

These are instructions from Christ in heaven telling the Christian people to leave Rome, Italy; and to leave the continent of Europe before World War III begins. This is what Christ meant in Revelation 3:10, when he said to the church that he, "will keep thee from the hour of temptation" or World War III in Europe. Therefore you can see that the method used to avoid the hour of temptation is for the Christian people to move out of Europe, rather than a pre-tribulation rapture.

The hour of temptation really refers to the famine of the Antichrist described in Revelation 6:5-8, and in Revelation 13:16,17; and it means that the army of the Antichrist will fence off all of the major cities in Europe, then starve the people in them, and will give food to only those who will agree to receive the mark of the beast, which will be the swastika. In other words, they will use temptation against the people trapped in the cities in Europe to condemn them to the Lake of Fire. This is written in Revelation 14:11.

Then the real truth about the rapture of the church and the tribulation period can be found here:

II Thessalonians 2:1-4: "Now we beseech you, brethren by the coming of our Lord Jesus Christ, and by our gathering together unto him,

That ye be not soon shaken in mind, or be troubled, neither by spirit, nor by word, nor by letter as from us, as that the day of Christ is at hand.

Let no man deceive you by any means: for that day shall not come, except there come a falling away first, and that man of sin be revealed, the son of perdition;

Who opposeth and exalteth himself above all that is called God, or that is worshipped; so that he as God sitteth in the temple of God, shewing himself that he is God."

In verse 3 here the day of Christ, or the day of his return to the earth and the rapture of the church, will not come until after the appearance of the Antichrist and World War III. The son of perdition described here is the Antichrist. This means that there will not be a pre-tribulation rapture.

And then the verses that state this plainly are:

Revelation 6:9-11: "And when he had opened the fifth seal, I saw under the altar the souls of them that were slain for the word of God, and for the testimony which they held:

And they cried with a loud voice, saying, How long, O Lord, holy and true, dost thou not judge and avenge our blood on them that dwell on the earth?

And white robes were given unto every one of them; and it was said unto them, that they should rest yet for a little season, until their fellow servants also and their brethren, that should be killed as they were, should be fulfilled."

The Lord God Almighty expects the faithful Christians to be killed for their belief in Christ, and for their testimony in Christ, rather than having them avoid the tribulation of World War III. And you should realize that church attendance will increase much more dramatically as a result of World War III, than it will because of the idea of a pre-tribulation rapture.

Since the United States will not be able to protect any other nations during World War III because any military action involving US troops will lead to a nuclear war against the Antichrist, the nations of the world will have to follow specific instructions in order to save their people. And it is extremely important to realize this, knowing that their people will be in danger of burning in the fires of the sun forever, if their leaders fail to follow these instructions. Here is the first phase:

Every person in every nation of the world excluding those in Europe and in the Middle East must convert to Christianity now. This means that every man, woman, and child must begin going to Christian Churches (Catholic or Protestant) as soon as my books on World War III are published. They must ask to be baptized in Christian Churches; and they must receive communion bread and communion wine every week if possible. This is known as the body of Christ with the bread, and the blood of Christ with the wine. You must receive these in Christian Churches to be saved.

Here is the second phase of the instructions: Every adult in every free nation of the world must be given a rifle and ammunition to use to defend their nation if they are attacked or invaded by the army of the Antichrist. If possible every adult who is eligible to do so should join the military in their nation and fight to defend it. And every adult must fight to the death while defending their families and their nations, but they should not be involved in offensive military action during the war.

Here is the theology involved in this strategy. First every man, woman, and child in every free nation of the world excluding those in Europe and in the Middle East will be saved by Christ if they are going to Christian Churches every week. Second, every adult who is killed, while fighting to defend their nation will be saved by Christ, instead of being forced to worship the Antichrist. This is verified in Matthew 16:24-26.

There will be no room for fear by anyone who is involved in this. The strategy will have to be adopted by every nation of the world. Even the people who will be stranded or left in Europe can be saved by converting to Christianity, and by fighting to the death against the army of the Antichrist. And the objective is to be killed for your faith in Christ.

RELATIVE DATES DURING WORLD WAR III

I have found in writing books about World War III that the best way to inform people about the events in the war is to write lists of the relative dates in it. Even though I don't know exactly when the war will begin, I do know about the events that will happen in it. You may agree later that these could be the most important pages in the book. The first list describes the national projects that should be completed by all nations, except those in Europe and the Middle East, in varying degrees before World War III begins. The second list describes the events that will happen during the war itself. And these lists are to be used to help the people prepare for the war.

National Projects:

1. Close all US military bases in England, Europe, Japan, Korea, and in the Middle East
2. Drill more natural gas wells
3. Build more natural gas pipelines
4. Build 50,000 natural gas refill stations
5. Build natural gas refill stations on US military bases in America
6. Build an anti-ballistic missile defense on US Navy ships and submarines
7. Elect the Church Committee Group, and begin training in Congress
8. Increase farmland
9. Pay farm subsidies for greenhouses
10. Increase travel trailer manufacturing
11. Set up the National Emergency Vote

12. Issue a federal order to convert to natural gas fuel
13. Begin the conference on SAFTA (South America Free Trade Agreement)
14. Train US Army personnel to convert all US military vehicles and weapons systems to natural gas fuel in America
15. Begin manufacturing chemical and biological agent test kits
16. Increase the manufacture of gas masks
17. Increase the manufacture of Geiger counters, and welder's goggles
18. Set up a Martial Law Plan, and tell the people how it will work
19. Issue a federal order to increase the Christian ministry

Relative Dates During World War III

The numbers in the left column tell you the year in which the events will occur, in relation to World War III.

Year: Events during the war

-2:   The Antichrist appears in Germany
-1:   The Antichrist unites the Common Market in Europe
-1:   The Antichrist brings down fire from heaven: Revelation 13:13
-1:   Millions of people cheer the Antichrist: II Thessalonians 2:8-12
-1:   A major US troop buildup at this time could cause a nuclear war
0:      The Antichrist makes a deal with the Russian army
1:      The army of the Antichrist is deployed in Western Europe: Daniel 11:21,22, Revelation 17:12,13, Revelation 17:16-18
1:      The Antichrist uses nuclear missiles to destroy Rome, Italy: Revelation 18:1-8, Revelation 18:10, Revelation 18:19
1:      The famine of the Antichrist begins in Europe: Revelation 6:5-8, Revelation 13:16,17
2:      The Antichrist shuts down all world trade with Europe
2:      The World War III Stock Market crash occurs
3:      The Antichrist blockades England, Scotland, and Ireland
3:      The Antichrist goes to Israel, and to the oil nations in the Middle East
3:      The Antichrist uses his army to take the world oil supply in the Middle East: Daniel 11:23-25
3:      There will be 100 million homeless and starving Americans; or millions of people will be homeless and starving in your nation
4:      The Antichrist begins building a Naval base in South Africa
4:      The Antichrist makes a deal with Japan
5:      The Antichrist sends soldiers to Northeast China and to Korea
6:      The ships of Chittim (Italy) grieve the Antichrist: Daniel 11:30

6:      The Antichrist makes a deal with the terrorist nations surrounding Israel: Daniel 11:30

6:      Begin building freezer warehouses and water tanks in your nation

7:      The Antichrist uses chemical warfare against Jerusalem: Daniel 11:31

7:      The two prophets appear in Jerusalem: Revelation 11:3-6

8:      The Antichrist sends his army to fight in Northeast China and Korea

9:      The tank battle in Israel kills 66.6 million soldiers in the army of the Antichrist: Revelation 9:13-18

9½: Issue a Federal order to slaughter livestock before the major nuclear war, and the nuclear winter: Revelation 8:10-12

10:    The plague of hail and fire kills 100 million soldiers in the army of the Antichrist: Ezekiel 38:22, Revelation 8:7

10:    The big nuclear war between the Antichrist and China: This is described in Revelation 8:10-12, and Matthew 24:20-22

11:    The Second Coming of Christ: Revelation 19:11-16

11:    The battle of Armageddon: Revelation 16:13-16

11:    The Rapture of the Church: I Thessalonians 4:16-18

11:    The nuclear war plague: Zechariah 14:12-15

11:    The holy city of Zion comes down in Jerusalem: Revelation 21:9-22

EPILOGUE

I already know what the Pentagon will do to try and discredit me, and my work because they have done the same thing to the nuclear winter scientists. When you read the Nuclear Winter chapter in my book titled, *World War III: Nuclear War*, you will probably agree that the subject matter is very complicated.

With this in mind, try to picture yourself coming home from work. You come in the front door, and then walk over to the refrigerator to get a can of beer; and then you get a cigarette, and go over to your recliner. You get the remote control to the television, turn it on, and then sit down. There is a TV News program about the research done by the nuclear winter scientists, and some of the complicated statistics are read on TV by one of them. You have a difficult time trying to understand it all, and you really don't want to think about something as terrible as nuclear winter to start with.

Then about a week later you come home, and you sit down to read the newspaper. You find an article about nuclear winter, and as you read it, you find that other scientists say that the nuclear winter theory is not valid, and the name itself should be changed to nuclear autumn. You also find that these people are saying that the nuclear winter scientists were using propaganda to scare the people. At this point you think back about the very complicated explanations of the nuclear winter theory, and you let out a sigh of relief because you don't have to study the horrible details about it anymore.

Now try to imagine coming home from work, going over to the refrigerator and getting a beer, and then walking over to the recliner to sit down and watch TV. You find a TV News program where the people are having a discussion about the complicated theology in the books written by a man named Gary Wilson. Then a week later you come home and read the newspaper, and you find an article about the books written by Gary Wilson. It says the theology is very complicated, and that no one can be sure of the interpretations of these verses; and since Gary Wilson admits in his books that he has been plagued by devils for years, he should be considered to be a demoniac, and a religious fanatic.

Then you sit back in your recliner, turn the TV on, and then drink your beer and let out a sigh of relief because you don't have to try and understand all of the complicated theology anymore. About two weeks later you see a TV News program, in which Gary Wilson explains these verses:

Matthew 11:16-19: "But whereunto shall I liken this generation? It is like unto children sitting in the markets, and calling unto their fellows,

And saying, we have piped unto you, and ye have not danced; we have mourned unto you, and ye have not lamented.

For John came neither eating nor drinking, and they say, He hath a devil.

The Son of man came eating and drinking, and they say, Behold a man gluttonous and a winebibber, a friend of publicans and sinners. But wisdom is justified of her children."

It says here that the enemies of Christ said that John the Baptist was a demoniac; and that he was a gluttonous man and a winebibber. You can therefore see that these accusations have been used before against some very important people. You should notice this phrase in Matthew 11:19, where Jesus gave a description of John the Baptist and himself, in relation to their work for the kingdom of God:

"But wisdom is justified of her children."

At this point I must warn the American people that the Pentagon is able to use their massive economic power, and their power in the TV News, the magazines, and the newspapers in the USA to start a national movement, which tries to discredit my work. And it will be they who cause all of the attacks against me in the media. In fact the Pentagon will have to attack the Bible itself to defend their position, but the ways in which they do it will not be obvious because they will have other people do it for them. You never see the Joint Chiefs of Staff in the TV news throwing slanderous remarks at someone else because they know that it would not look dignified; and they never want to appear to be undignified because it would change their image in the minds of the American people. If this were to happen, then they could lose some of their financing.

Looking back at the 1980s, you can see that the nuclear winter scientists were being accused by thousands of other scientists, of using propaganda to hype their cause; and it seemed like they almost had to scream because of the hundreds of unfavorable magazine and newspaper articles which were written about their studies. But the Pentagon still appeared to be dignified because they were not directly involved in the argument. This is how they win against their opponents. They use the dirtiest, and most underhanded tactics to

WORLD WAR III: NUCLEAR WAR

destroy their enemies, while they themselves are not even involved in the fight.

The terrible thing about it this time is that the Pentagon will condemn millions of people to the Lake of Fire by trying to convince the people not to read my books. In Revelation 20:14, Psalm 19:4, Psalm 21:9, and Matthew 25:41 the Lake of Fire is the sun. If the Pentagon works to condemn people to the Lake of Fire then they will go there too. They will burn in the fires of the sun forever because they wanted to argue to keep their annual budget intact.

The human race has waited for 1900 years to have the mysteries in the Bible solved, and when the books are published, the Pentagon will indirectly try to convince you not to read them. When this happens just try to continue reading at your own pace; and never let anyone condemn you to the Lake of Fire.

I watched a TV video about war recently, and I learned that from the examples of World War I and World War II that the people of the world now know that war is the industrialized slaughter of men, generally speaking. If that is the case, then why are we being bombarded by all of the documentaries that glorify war on our TV sets?

As you can see, I have written four books about World War III, and I know that it will begin by the year 2012. In Revelation 9:16 the army of the Antichrist will have 200 million soldiers at the end of World War III. This means that the Pentagon will have to save all of the US military forces to protect America at the end of the war, which also means that the USA cannot afford to become involved in the ground war in Europe during the first year of World War III. If the Pentagon tries to fight in the war anyway, then the US military will lose 25 million troops in the first year in Western Europe.

In order to prevent this, the US President may have to use his executive powers as the Commander-in-Chief of the US military to force the Pentagon to withdraw all US Armed forces personnel back into America. He has the power to order them to do this, and if they refuse, then he has the power to fire the generals and the admirals who refused to follow his orders. He can also fire the US military officers who refuse to keep America neutral during World War III; and I believe that he can do this without the consent of the war hawks that work on the Armed Services Committees, and the Appropriations Committees in the House of Representatives and the Senate.

AFTERWORD

S omeone asked me in 2003 if there will be a happy ending at the end of
World War III, and I said that the only way there could be, from the
viewpoint of all of the people on earth, would be to have everyone
accept Christ and go to Christian churches at the beginning of the war. Then
all of the people on earth would receive eternal life with Christ in heaven
after World War III is over, except for those people in Europe who will
follow the Antichrist.

This is why the 21 plagues in the book of Revelation are described for
mankind before World War III even begins. They are there to serve as a
warning of the wrath of God, which is coming upon the earth so the people
will separate themselves from the evil of Satan and his devils before the 21
plagues and World War III occur. The plagues described in chapter 8 in the
book of Revelation will cause disaster in third parts to warn the people about
the wrath of God coming upon Satan and the third part of the angels in
heaven, which followed him when he was cast out to the earth. This is
described in Revelation 12:4, and Revelation 12:7-9. Where it says, "And his
tail drew the third part of the stars of heaven," in Revelation 12:4, it means
that one third of the angels followed Satan when he was cast out of heaven.
In Revelation 1:20 the symbol for the angel is the star, and therefore the third
part of the stars means the third part of the angels of heaven. This means that
God himself is telling you here that you must begin going to Christian
churches now to be saved.

When you read about the rapture of the church in I Thessalonians 4:16-18,
and the holy city of Zion described in Revelation 21:9-27, you should know
that these things represent and are part of the happy ending at the end of
World War III, but to take part in them you have to accept Christ now.
Everyone in the world will have to receive the communion bread and the
communion wine in Christian churches during World War III to be saved by

Christ if they are killed during the war. The happy ending will occur when everyone saved by Christ receives immortality in heaven.

BIBLIOGRAPHY

1. *A View to a Kill*: Movie, United Artists, © 1985
2. Angier, Natalie; Article, *Time*: Magazine, P. 56-57, Los Angeles: Time, Inc., © 12-24-1984
3. Aronson, Shlomo; *The Politics and Strategy of Nuclear Weapons in the Middle East*, Albany: State University of New York Press, © 1992
4. Article I, Section 8, United States Constitution; World Book Encyclopedia, Vol. 4, Chicago: World Book, Inc., © 2002
5. Begley, Sharon; Barry, John; Article, *Newsweek*: Magazine, P. 65, New York: Newsweek, Inc., © 3-31-1986
6. *Broken Arrow*: Movie, Twentieth Century Fox, © 1996
7. Caldicott, Dr. Helen, *Missile Envy*, New York: William Morrow and Company, Inc., © 1984
8. Clinton, William J., President; Budget of the United States Government, Fiscal Year 1997-Supplement, Washington DC: United States Government Printing Office, © 1996
9. Congress A to Z, Washington DC: Congressional Quarterly, Inc., © 2003
10. Congressional Quarterly's Guide to Congress, Washington DC: Congressional Quarterly, Inc., © 2000
11. Congressional Research Service, The Congressional Standing Committee System, Report 92-707 GOV, Jurisdiction: Committee on Armed Services, Washington DC: Library of Congress, © 1992
12. Declaration of Independence; World Book Encyclopedia, Vol. 5, Chicago: World Book, Inc., © 2002
13. Ehrlich, Paul; Harte, John; Harwell, Mark; Raven, Peter H.; Sagan, Carl; et al.; Article, *Science*: Magazine, P. 1293-1299, Washington DC: The American Association for the Advancement of Science, © 12-23-1983
14. Encyclopedia Americana, Danbury, Connecticut: Grolier, Vol. 20, © 1993
15. Encyclopedia Britannica, London: Encyclopedia Britannica, Inc., Vol. 11, © 1997
16. Fisher, Arthur; Article, *Popular Science*: Magazine, P. 8-12, New York: Popular Science, Inc., © 7-1985
17. Fisher, David; *Fire and Ice*, New York: Harper and Row, © 1990

18. Fitzgerald, A. Ernest; *The Pentagonists*, Boston: Houghton Mifflin Company, © 1989

19. Gabriel, Richard A.; *Military Incompetence*, New York: Hill and Wang Publishers, © 1985

20. *Goldeneye*: Movie, United Artists, © 1995

21. Greenberg, Joel, Editor; Article, *Science News*: Magazine, P. 397, Washington DC: Science Service, Inc., © 12-22-1984

22. Greenberg, Joel, Editor; Article, *Science News*: Magazine, P. 249, Washington DC: Science Service, Inc., © 4-19-1986

23. Greene, Owen; *Nuclear Winter*, New York: Cambridge Polity Press, © 1985

24. Grinspoon, Lester; The Long Darkness, New Haven, Connecticut: Yale University Press, © 1986

25. Halley, Dr. Henry; *Halley's Bible Handbook*, Grand Rapids: Zondervan, © 1959

26. Harwell, Mark; *Nuclear Winter*, New York: Springer-Verlag Publishers, © 1984

27. Hauck, Rex; Fire from the Sky: Video, Turner Original Productions, © 1997

28. The Holy Bible, Authorized King James Version, London, England

29. International Herald Tribune, October 21, 1981, Neuilly Cedex, France, © 1981

30. Kegley, Charles W.; Wittkopf, Eugene R.; *The Nuclear Reader*, New York: St. Martin's Press, © 1985

31. Keesing's Research Report, Disarmament Negotiations and Treaties, New York: Scribner Publishers, © 1972

32. Lewis, John W.; Litai, Xue; *China Builds the Bomb*, Stanford, California: Stanford University Press, © 1988

33. Lincoln, Abraham; The Gettysburg Address, World Book Encyclopedia, Vol. 8, Chicago: World Book, Inc., © 2002

34. Luttwak, Edward N.; *The Pentagon and the Art of War*, New York: Simon and Schuster, © 1984

35. McCarthy, Pat; 2003 Election Manual, Tacoma, Washington: Pierce County Auditor, © 2003

36. McNamara, Robert S.; *Blundering Into Disaster*, New York: Pantheon Books, © 1986

37. Neal, Tommy; *Lawmaking and the Legislative Process*, Phoenix, Arizona: Oryx Press, © 1996

38. New Standard Encyclopedia, Chicago: Ferguson Publishers, Vol. 6, © 1991

39. Overbye, Dennis; Article, *Discover*: Magazine, P. 24-32, New York: Time, Inc., © 1-1985

40. Piel, Jonathan, Editor; Article, *Scientific American*: Magazine, P. 60-62, New York: Scientific American, Inc., © 2-1985

41. Powers, Thomas; Article, The *Atlantic Monthly*: Magazine, P. 53-64, Boston: The Atlantic Monthly Company, © 11-1984

42. Preamble, United States Constitution; World Book Encyclopedia, Vol. 4, Chicago: World Book, Inc., © 2002

43. Raloff, Janet; Article, *Science News*: Magazine, P. 314-317, Washington DC: Science Service, Inc., © 11-12-1983

44. Raloff, Janet; Article, *Science News*: Magazine, P. 171-174, Washington DC: Science Service, Inc., © 9-14-1985

45. Sagan, Carl; Turco, Richard P.; *A Path Where No Man Thought*, New York: Random House, © 1990

46. Sagan, Scott D.; Waltz, Kenneth N.; *The Spread of Nuclear Weapons: A Debate*, New York: W. W. Norton, © 1995

47. Singer, Fred; Article, *Newsweek*: Magazine, P. 12, New York: Newsweek, Inc., © 9-14-1987

48. Sorensen, Theodore C.; *Kennedy*, New York: Harper and Row, © 1965

49. Suddaby, Adam; *The Nuclear War Game*, London: Longman Publishing Group, © 1983

50. Szumski, Bonnie, Editor; *Nuclear War: Opposing Viewpoints*, St. Paul, Minnesota: Greenhaven Press, © 1985

51. Thompson, Starley; Schneider, Stephen; Article, *Foreign Affairs*: Magazine, P. 981-1005, New York: The Council on Foreign Relations, © Summer 1986

52. Turco, Richard; Toon, Brian; Ackerman, Tom; Pollack, James; Sagan, Carl; TTAPS Study Report, Article, *Science*: Magazine, P. 1283-1292, Vol. 222, Washington DC: The American Association for the Advancement of Science, © 12-23-1983

53. Turco, Richard; Toon, Brian; Ackerman, Tom; Pollack, James; Sagan, Carl; Article, *Scientific American*: Magazine, P. 33-43, New York: Scientific American, Inc., © 8-1984

54. Turco, Richard; Toon, Brian; Ackerman, Tom; Pollack, James; Sagan, Carl; Article, *Science*: Magazine, P. 166-174, Washington DC: The American Association for the Advancement of Science, © 1-12-1990

55. United Nations SCOPE Study Report 28, Volumes I and II, Scientific Committee on Problems of the Environment, International Council of Scientific Unions, New York: The United Nations Organization, © 1985

56. United States Congress; The Effects of Nuclear War, Washington DC: Office of Technology Assessment, © 1979

57. Vogel, Shawna; Article, *Discover*: Magazine, P. 26, New York: Time, Inc., © 11-1989

58. Weiner, Tim; *Blank Check*, New York: Warner Books, © 1990

59. Weisbecker, Allan C.; *In Search of Captain Zero*, New York: Penguin Putnam, Inc., © 2001

60. Wekesser, Carol; *America's Defense: Opposing Viewpoints*, San Diego: Greenhaven Press, © 1991

61. The World Almanac and Book of Facts 1998, Mahwah, New Jersey: K-111 Reference Corporation, © 1997, Congressional Budget Office

62. The World Almanac and Book of Facts 2004, New York: World Almanac Education Group, Inc. © 2004, Congressional Budget Office.

63. World Book Encyclopedia, Chicago: World Book, Inc., Vol. 3, © 1960

64. World Book Encyclopedia, Chicago: World Book, Inc., Vol. 14, © 1997

65. World Book Encyclopedia, Chicago: World Book, Inc,. Vol. 18, © 1997

INDEX

ENDNOTES

[1] Halley's Bible Handbook, P. 763, Dr. Henry Halley, © 1959, Zondervan

[2] Ibid., P. 62, 68, 69

[3] Ibid., P. 69

[4] New Standard Encyclopedia, P. E-247, Vol. 6, © 1991, Ferguson Publishers

[5] *Blundering Into Disaster*, rear book cover, Robert S. McNamara, © 1986, Pantheon Books

[6] Ibid., P. 85

[7] *The Nuclear Reader*, Preface, Charles Kegley, Eugene R. Wittkopf, © 1985, St. Martin's Press

[8] *The Spread of Nuclear Weapons: A Debate*, P. 78, 79, Scott D. Sagan, Kenneth N. Waltz, © 1995, W. W. Norton

[9] Ibid., P. 79

[10] Ibid.

[11] *Nuclear War: Opposing Viewpoints*, P. 20, Bonnie Szumski, Editor, © 1985, Greenhaven Press

[12] Ibid., P. 172

[13] *The Nuclear Reader*, P. 312, Charles Kegley, Eugene R. Wittkopf, © 1985, St. Martin's Press

[14] The Gettysburg Address, Abraham Lincoln, World Book Encyclopedia, P. 177, Vol. 8, © 2002, World Book, Inc

[15] Preamble, United States Constitution, World Book Encyclopedia, P. 1004, Vol. 4, © 2002, World Book, Inc

[16] Article I, Section 8, United States Constitution, World Book Encyclopedia, P. 1007, Vol. 4, © 2002, World Book, Inc

[17] Declaration of Independence, World Book Encyclopedia, P. 78, Vol. 5, © 2002, World Book, Inc

[18] *Disarmament Negotiations and Treaties*, P. 32, Keesing's Research Report, © 1972, Scribner Publishers

[19] Ibid.

[20] *Blundering Into Disaster*, P. 34, Robert S. McNamara, © 1986, Pantheon Books

[21] *Missile Envy*, P. 194, Dr. Helen Caldicott, © 1984, William Morrow and Company, Inc

[22] *A View to a Kill*: Movie, © 1985, United Artists

[23] *Goldeneye*: Movie, © 1995, United Artists

[24] *Broken Arrow*: Movie, © 1996, Twentieth Century Fox

[25] *Blundering Into Disaster*, P. 157, Robert S. McNamara, © 1986, Pantheon Books

[26] *International Herald Tribune*, October 21, 1981, © 1981

[27] *Missile Envy*, P. 34, Dr. Helen Caldicott, © 1984, William Morrow and Company, Inc

[28] Ibid., P. 118

[29] Ibid.

[30] Ibid., P. 183

[31] Ibid., P. 88

[32] Ibid., P. 89

[33] Ibid., P. 173

[34] *Blundering Into Disaster*, P. 157, Robert S. McNamara, © 1986, Pantheon Books

[35] *Missile Envy*, P. 37, Dr. Helen Caldicott, © 1984, William Morrow and Company, Inc

[36] Ibid., P. 42,43

[37] Ibid., P. 47

[38] Ibid., P. 38

[39] Ibid., P. 84

[40] Ibid., P. 117

[41] Ibid., P. 84

[42] Ibid., P. 90

[43] Ibid., P. 91

[44] Ibid., P. 104

[45] Ibid., P. 101

[46] Ibid., P. 108

[47] Ibid., P. 109

[48] Ibid., P. 114

[49] Ibid., P. 118

[50] Ibid., P. 114

[51] Ibid., P. 127

[52] Ibid., P. 130

[53] Ibid., P. 138
[54] Ibid.
[55] Ibid.
[56] Ibid., P. 209
[57] Ibid., P. 209, 210
[58] Ibid., P. 140
[59] Ibid.
[60] Ibid., P. 155
[61] Ibid., P. 162
[62] Ibid.
[63] Ibid.
[64] Ibid., P. 184
[65] Ibid., P. 174
[66] Ibid., P. 183
[67] Ibid., P. 192
[68] Ibid., P. 143, 176, 181, 182,183,191,192
[69] Ibid., P. 195
[70] Ibid., P. 196
[71] Ibid., P. 198
[72] Ibid., P. 200
[73] Ibid., P. 201
[74] Ibid., P. 204
[75] Ibid., P. 206
[76] Ibid.
[77] Ibid., P. 212
[78] Ibid., P. 213
[79] Ibid., P. 216
[80] Ibid., P. 222
[81] Ibid., P. 223
[82] Ibid., P. 241
[83] Ibid.
[84] Ibid., P. 336
[85] Ibid., P. 326
[86] Ibid., P. 331
[87] *Blundering Into Disaster*, P. 5, Robert S. McNamara, © 1986, Pantheon Books
[88] Ibid., P. 13
[89] Ibid., p. 14
[90] Ibid., P. 21

[91] Ibid., P. 28

[92] Ibid., P. 33

[93] Ibid., P. 34

[94] Ibid., P. 35

[95] Ibid., P. 36

[96] Ibid., P. 44

[97] Ibid., P. 175

[98] *Missile Envy*, P. 263-286, Dr. Helen Caldicott, © 1984, William Morrow and Company, Inc

[99] Ibid., P. 174

[100] Ibid., P. 33

[101] Ibid., P. 34

[102] Ibid., P. 35

[103] Ibid.

[104] Ibid., P. 37

[105] Ibid., P. 88, 89, 212

[106] World Book Encyclopedia, P. 759, Vol. 3, © 1960, World Book, Inc

[107] *Missile Envy*, P. 223, Dr. Helen Caldicott, © 1984, William Morrow and Company, Inc

[108] Ibid., P. 248

[109] World Book Encyclopedia, P. 602, Vol. 14, © 1997, World Book, Inc

[110] *Missile Envy*, P. 172-178, 180-224, 236-262, Dr. Helen Caldicott, © 1984, William Morrow and Company, Inc

[111] Ibid., P. 144

[112] Ibid., P. 148

[113] Ibid., P. 86, 87

[114] Ibid., P. 87

[115] Ibid., P. 196

[116] Ibid., P. 194-195

[117] *In Search of Captain Zero*, front book flap, Allan C. Weisbecker, © 2001, Penguin Putnam, Inc

[118] Ibid., P. 168-169

[119] Ibid., P. last page in the book

[120] *The Pentagonists*, Table of Contents, A. Ernest Fitzgerald, © 1989, Houghton Mifflin Company

[121] Ibid., rear book cover

[122] The World Almanac and Book of Facts 1998, P. 109, © 1997, K-111 Reference Corporation

[123] World Book Encyclopedia, P. 602, Vol. 14, © 1997, World Book, Inc

[124] *Fire and Ice*, P. 131, David Fisher, © 1990, Harper and Row

[125] TTAPS Study Report, Richard Turco; Brian Toon; Tom Ackerman; James Pollack; Carl Sagan; Article, *Science*: Magazine, P. 1283-1292, Vol. 222, © 12-23-1983, The American Association for the Advancement of Science

[126] *Fire from the Sky*: Video, Rex Hauck, © 1997, Turner Original Productions

[127] Ibid.

[128] *Fire and Ice*, P. 129, David Fisher, © 1990, Harper and Row

[129] Ibid.

[130] Ibid., P. 130

[131] Ibid., P. 131

[132] Ibid.

[133] Ibid., P. 132

[134] Ibid., P. 133

[135] United Nations SCOPE Study Report 28, Vol. I and II, Scientific Committee on Problems of the Environment, © 1985, The United Nations Organization

[136] *Fire and Ice*, P. 136, David Fisher, © 1990, Harper and Row

[137] *Foreign Affairs*: Magazine, P. 981-1005, Starley Thompson, Stephen Schneider, © June 1986, The Council on Foreign Relations

[138] *The Long Darkness*, p. 92, Lester Grinspoon, © 1986, Yale University Press

[139] Ibid., P. 65

[140] Ibid., P. 96

[141] Ibid., P. 106

[142] *Fire and Ice*, P. 126, David Fisher, © 1990, Harper and Row

[143] *The Long Darkness*, P. 109-110, Lester Grinspoon, © 1986, Yale University

[144] *Blundering Into Disaster*, P. 95-96, Robert S. McNamara, © 1986, Pantheon Books

[145] *The Long Darkness*, P. 120, Lester Grinspoon, © 1986, Yale University

[146] Ibid., P. 111

[147] *Foreign Affairs*: Magazine, P. 984, Starley Thompson, Stephen Schneider, © June 1986, The Council on Foreign Relations

[148] *Science News*: Magazine, P. 317, Janet Raloff, © 11-12-1983, Science Service, Inc

[149] *Discover*: Magazine, P. 26, Shawna Vogel, © 11-1989, Time, Inc.

[150] *Newsweek*: Magazine, P. 65, Sharon Begley, John Barry, © 3-31-1986, Newsweek, Inc

[151] *Foreign Affairs*: Magazine, P. 986-987, Starley Thompson, Stephen Schneider, © June 1986, The Council on Foreign Relations

[152] Ibid.

[153] Ibid., P. 1002-1003

[154] Ibid., P. 1003

[155] Ibid.

[156] Ibid., P. 983

[157] *Time*: Magazine, P. 56, Natalie Angier, © 12-24-1984, Time, Inc

[158] *The Atlantic Monthly*: Magazine, P. 64, Thomas Powers, © 11-1984, The Atlantic Monthly Company

[159] Ibid., P. 59

[160] *Nuclear Winter*, P. 3-6, Owen Greene, © 1985, Cambridge: Polity Press

[161] *Scientific American*: Magazine, P. 60, Jonathan Piel, Editor, © 2-1985, Scientific American, Inc

[162] *Science News*: Magazine, P. 171, Janet Raloff, © 9-14-1985, Science Service, Inc

[163] *Science*: Magazine, P. 1293, Paul Ehrlich, John Harte, Mark Harwell, Peter Raven, Carl Sagan, et al., © 12-23-1983, The American Association for the Advancement of Science

[164] Ibid., P. 1298

[165] *Scientific American*: Magazine, P. 33, Richard Turco, Brian Toon, Tom Ackerman, James Pollack, Carl Sagan, © 8-1984, Scientific American, Inc

[166] Ibid., P. 38

[167] Ibid., P. 39

[168] *Fire and Ice*, P. 33, David Fisher, © 1990, Harper and Row

[169] *Science*: Magazine, P. 166, Richard Turco, Brian Toon, Tom Ackerman, James Pollack, Carl Sagan, © 1-12-1990, The American Association for the Advancement of Science

[170] Ibid.

[171] *Science*: Magazine, P. 1293, Paul Ehrlich, John Harte, Mark Harwell, Peter Raven, Carl Sagan, et al., © 12-23-1983, The American Association for the Advancement of Science

[172] *Scientific American*: Magazine, P. 33, Richard Turco, Brian Toon, Tom Ackerman, James Pollack, Carl Sagan, © 8-1984, Scientific American, Inc

[173] *Science*: Magazine, P. 166, Richard Turco, Brian Toon, Tom Ackerman, James Pollack, Carl Sagan, © 1-12-1990, The American Association for the Advancement of Science

[174] *Foreign Affairs*: Magazine, P. 981, Starley Thompson, Stephen Schneider, © 6-1986, The Council on Foreign Relations

[175] Budget of the United States Government, Fiscal Year 1997- Supplement, P. 48-49, President William J. Clinton, © 1996, US Government Printing Office

[176] *Science News*: Magazine, P. 249, Joel Greenberg, Editor, © 4-19-1986, Science Service, Inc

[177] Ibid.

[178] *Discover*: Magazine, P. 26, Dennis Overbye, © 1-1985, Time, Inc

[179] *Science News*: Magazine, P. 314, Janet Raloff, © 11-12-1983, Science Service, Inc

[180] Ibid.

[181] Ibid., P. 316

[182] Ibid.

[183] *Blundering Into Disaster*, P. 41, Robert S. McNamara, © 1986, Pantheon Books

[184] *Time*: Magazine, P. 57, Natalie Angier, © 12-24-1984, Time, Inc

[185] *The Atlantic Monthly*: Magazine, P. 54, Thomas Powers, © 11- 1984, The Atlantic Monthly Company

[186] Ibid., P. 58

[187] *Nuclear Winter*, P. 65, Mark Harwell, © 1984, Springer-Verlag Publishers

[188] Ibid., P. viii, Foreword

[189] *Fire and Ice*, P. 126, David Fisher, © 1990, Harper and Row

[190] Ibid., P. 127

[191] *A Path Where No Man Thought*, P. 24, Carl Sagan, Richard P. Turco, © 1990, Random House

[192] Ibid., P. 201

[193] Ibid., P. 41

[194] Ibid., P. 65

[195] *Nuclear Winter*, P. 54, Owen Greene, © 1985, Cambridge: Polity Press

[196] Ibid., P. 55

[197] Ibid., P. 58

[198] *Fire and Ice*, P. 122, David Fisher, © 1990, Harper and Row

[199] *A Path Where No Man Thought*, P. 37, Carl Sagan, Richard P. Turco, © 1990, Random House

[200] *Nuclear Winter*, P. 84, Owen Greene, © 1985, Cambridge: Polity Press

[201] *Nuclear Winter*, P. 66, Mark Harwell, © 1984, Springer-Verlag Publishers

[202] *Fire and Ice*, P. 126, David Fisher, © 1990, Harper and Row

[203] *Nuclear Winter*, P. 89, Owen Greene, © 1985, Cambridge: Polity Press

[204] Ibid., P. 32

[205] Ibid., P. 33

[206] *Nuclear Winter*, P. x, Foreword, Mark Harwell, © 1984, Springer-Verlag Publishers

[207] Ibid., P. 13

[208] *A Path Where No Man Thought*, P. 197, Carl Sagan, Richard P. Turco, © 1990, Random House

[209] Ibid., P. 202

[210] Ibid., P. 270

[211] Ibid., P. 330

[212] Ibid., P. 203

[213] Ibid., P. 350

[214] Ibid.

[215] Ibid., P. 123

[216] Ibid., P. 346

[217] Ibid., P. 123

[218] Ibid., P. 203

[219] Ibid., P. 194

[220] Ibid., P. 347

[221] Ibid., P. 119

[222] *Nuclear Winter*, P. 28, Mark Harwell, © 1984, Springer-Verlag Publishers

[223] Encyclopedia Americana, P. 519, Vol. 20, © 1993, Grolier

[224] World Book Encyclopedia, P. 976-980, Vol. 18, © 1997, World Book, Inc

[225] Encyclopedia Americana, P. 520, Vol. 20, © 1993, Grolier

[226] *Nuclear Winter*, P. 44, Owen Greene, © 1985, Cambridge: Polity Press

[227] *Nuclear Winter*, P. 44, Mark Harwell, © 1984, Springer-Verlag Publishers

[228] *Fire and Ice*, P. 7, David Fisher, © 1990, Harper and Row

[229] *Nuclear Winter*, P. 44, Mark Harwell, © 1984, Springer-Verlag Publishers

[230] *A Path Where No Man Thought*, P. 48, Carl Sagan, Richard P. Turco, © 1990, Random House

[231] Ibid.

[232] Ibid., P. 49

[233] Ibid., P. 52

[234] Ibid., P. 53

[235] Ibid., P. 57

[236] *Fire and Ice*, P. 7, David Fisher, © 1990, Harper and Row

[237] *Nuclear Winter*, P. 184, Owen Greene, © 1985, Cambridge: Polity Press

[238] *Nuclear Winter*, P. 53, Mark Harwell, © 1984, Springer-Verlag Publishers

[239] *A Path Where No Man Thought*, P. 38, Carl Sagan, Richard P. Turco, © 1990, Random House

[240] Ibid.

[241] *Nuclear Winter*, P. 104, Mark Harwell, © 1984, Springer-Verlag Publishers

[242] Ibid.

[243] Ibid., P. 122

[244] Ibid

[245] Ibid., P. 124

[246] Ibid., P. 123

[247] Ibid., P. 122-123

[248] Ibid., P. 124

[249] Ibid., P. 126

[250] Ibid.

[251] Ibid., P. 127

[252] *Nuclear Winter*, P. 139, Owen Greene, © 1985, Cambridge: Polity Press

[253] *A Path Where No Man Thought*, P. 76, Carl Sagan, Richard P. Turco, © 1990, Random House

[254] *Nuclear Winter*, Owen Greene, © 1985, Cambridge: Polity Press

[255] *Nuclear Winter*, P. 156-160, Mark Harwell, © 1984, Springer-Verlag Publishers

[256] Ibid., P. 161

[257] *Nuclear Winter*, P. 65-66, Owen Greene, © 1985, Cambridge: Polity Press

[258] Ibid., P. 14

[259] Budget of the United States Government, Fiscal Year 1997- Supplement, P. 48-49, President William J. Clinton, © 1996, US Government Printing Office

[260] Ibid., P. 49

[261] Ibid., P. 48-49

[262] Ibid., P. 49

[263] *The Nuclear War Game*, P. 74, Adam Suddaby, © 1983, Longman Publishing Group

[264] Budget of the United States Government, Fiscal Year 1997- Supplement, P. 49, President William J. Clinton, © 1996, US Government Printing Office

[265] The Effects of Nuclear War, P. 3, United States Congress, © 1979, Office of Technology Assessment

[266] Ibid., P. 4

[267] Ibid.

[268] Ibid.

[269] Ibid., P. 5

[270] Ibid., P. 8

[271] Ibid., P. 9

[272] Ibid., P. 94

[273] Ibid.

[274] *Nuclear Winter*, P. 153, Owen Greene, © 1985, Cambridge: Polity Press

[275] Ibid., P. 164

[276] *The Long Darkness*, P. 104, Lester Grinspoon, © 1986, Yale University

[277] Ibid.

[278] Ibid., P. 118

[279] Ibid., P. 119

[280] Ibid.

[281] Ibid., P. 120

[282] Ibid., P. 107

[283] Ibid.

[284] *A Path Where No Man Thought*, P. 204, Carl Sagan, Richard P. Turco, © 1990, Random House

[285] Ibid., P. 146

[286] *The Spread of Nuclear Weapons: A Debate*, P. 2, Kenneth N. Waltz, Scott D. Sagan, © 1995, W. W. Norton

[287] Ibid.

[288] Ibid., P. 3

[289] Ibid.

[290] Ibid., P. 21

[291] Ibid., P. 11

[292] Ibid.

[293] Ibid.

[294] Ibid.

[295] Ibid.

[296] Ibid., P.16

[297] *Nuclear War: Opposing Viewpoints*, P. 166, Bonnie Szumski, Editor, © 1985, Greenhaven Press

[298] Ibid.

[299] *Blundering Into Disaster*, P. 79-80, Robert S. McNamara, © 1986, Pantheon Books

[300] *The Spread of Nuclear Weapons: A Debate*, P. 3, Kenneth N. Waltz, Scott D. Sagan, © 1995, W. W. Norton

[301] Ibid., P. 29

[302] *The Politics and Strategy of Nuclear Weapons in the Middle East*, Shlomo Aronson, © 1992, State University of New York Press

[303] *Missile Envy*, P. 216, Dr. Helen Caldicott, © 1984, William Morrow and Company, Inc

[304] Ibid.

[305] Ibid., P. 206

[306] Ibid.

[307] Ibid., P. 217

[308] Ibid., P. 216

[309] Ibid.

[310] *Military Incompetence*, front book flap, Richard A. Gabriel, © 1985, Hill and Wang Publishers

[311] Ibid.

[312] *Blundering Into Disaster*, P. 79-80, Robert S. McNamara, © 1986, Pantheon Books

[313] *Kennedy*, P. 603, Theodore C. Sorensen, © 1965, Harper and Row

[314] Ibid., P. 604

[315] Ibid., P. 603

[316] *Missile Envy*, P. 131, Dr. Helen Caldicott, © 1984, William Morrow and Company, Inc

[317] *America's Defense: Opposing Viewpoints*, P. 24, Carol Wekesser, © 1991, Greenhaven Press

[318] Ibid., P. 25

[319] Budget of the United States Government, Fiscal Year 1997- Supplement, P. 48-49, President William J. Clinton, © 1996, US Government Printing Office

[320] Ibid., P. 49

[321] *Blank Check*, front book flap, Tim Weiner, © 1990, Warner Books

[322] *Military Incompetence*, front book flap, Richard A. Gabriel, © 1985, Hill and Wang Publishers

[323] *Blundering Into Disaster*, P. 41, Robert S. McNamara, © 1986, Pantheon Books

[324] *Missile Envy*, P. 195, Dr. Helen Caldicott, © 1984, William Morrow and Company, Inc

[325] Ibid.

[326] *Blundering Into Disaster*, P. 34, Robert S. McNamara, © 1986, Pantheon Books

[327] *America's Defense: Opposing Viewpoints*, P. 26, Carol Wekesser, © 1991, Greenhaven Press

[328] *The Pentagon and the Art of War*, front book flap, Edward N. Luttwak, © 1984, Simon and Schuster

[329] The World Almanac and Book of Facts 1998, P. 107, © 1997, K-111 Reference Corporation

[330] *America's Defense: Opposing Viewpoints*, P. 25, Carol Wekesser, © 1991, Greenhaven Press

[331] *The Spread of Nuclear Weapons: A Debate*, P. 67, Kenneth N. Waltz, Scott D. Sagan, © 1995, W. W. Norton

[332] *Missile Envy*, P. 75, Dr. Helen Caldicott, © 1984, William Morrow and Company, Inc

[333] *The Spread of Nuclear Weapons: A Debate*, P. 16, Kenneth N. Waltz, Scott D. Sagan, © 1995, W. W. Norton

[334] Ibid., P. 17

[335] Ibid., P. 33

[336] Ibid., P. 44

[337] Ibid., P. 21

[338] Ibid., P. 47

[339] Ibid., P. 42

[340] Encyclopedia Britannica, P. 619, Vol. 11, © 1997, Encyclopedia Britannica, Inc

[341] Ibid.

[342] *Lawmaking and the Legislative Process*, P. 28, Tommy Neal, © 1996, Oryx Press

[343] Ibid.

[344] Ibid.

[345] Ibid., P. 29

[346] The Congressional Standing Committee System, Report 92-707 GOV: Jurisdiction: Committee on Armed Services, Congressional Research Service, © 1992, Library of Congress

[347] Ibid.

[348] Ibid.

[349] Ibid.

[350] Ibid.

[351] Ibid.

[352] *Lawmaking and the Legislative Process*, P. 32, Tommy Neal, © 1996, Oryx Press

[353] Ibid., P. 34

[354] Ibid.

[355] Ibid., P. 36-37

[356] Ibid., P. 39

[357] Ibid., P. 42-43

[358] Ibid., P. 45

[359] Ibid.

[360] Ibid.

[361] *Congress A to Z*, P. 18, © 2003, Congressional Quarterly, Inc

[362] Ibid., P. 27

[363] Ibid., P. 18

[364] Ibid., P. 19

[365] Ibid., P. 20

[366] Ibid., P. 23

[367] Ibid., P. 25

[368] Ibid., P. 192

[369] *Congressional Quarterly's Guide to Congress*, P. 540, © 2000, Congressional Quarterly, Inc

[370] Ibid., P. 539

[371] Ibid., P. 535

[372] Ibid., P. 581

[373] Ibid.

[374] Ibid.

[375] *The World Almanac and Book of Facts 2004*, P. 118-119, © 2004, World Almanac Education Group, Inc

[376] *Blundering Into Disaster*, Robert S. McNamara, © 1986, Pantheon Books

[377] 2003 Election Manual, P. 28, Pat McCarthy, © 2003, Pierce County Auditor

[378] Ibid., P. 24

[379] Ibid., P. 41

[380] Ibid., P. 23

[381] Ibid., P. 24

[382] Ibid., P. 26

[383] Ibid., P. 27

[384] Ibid., P. 28

[385] Ibid., P. 41

[386] *Missile Envy*, P. 89, Dr. Helen Caldicott, © 1984, William Morrow and Company, Inc

[387] Halley's Bible Handbook, P. 206, Dr. Henry Halley, © 1959, Zondervan

Printed in the United Kingdom by
Lightning Source UK Ltd., Milton Keynes
139290UK00002B/66/A